Radical Critiques of the Law

An AMINTAPHIL *Volume*

Radical Critiques of the Law

Edited by
Stephen M. Griffin
Robert C. L. Moffat

University Press of Kansas

© 1997 by the University Press of Kansas
All rights reserved

Published by the University Press of Kansas (Lawrence, Kansas 66049), which was
organized by the Kansas Board of Regents and is operated and funded by Emporia
State University, Fort Hays State University, Kansas State University, Pittsburg State
University, the University of Kansas, and Wichita State University

Library of Congress Cataloging-in-Publication Data

Radical critiques of the law / edited by Stephen M. Griffin, Robert
    C. L. Moffat.
        p.   cm.
    "An AMINTAPHIL volume."
    Papers from a conference held by the American Section of the
International Association for Philosophy of Law and Social
Philosophy, Allentown, Pa., Oct. 1992.
    Includes index.
    ISBN 0-7006-0845-1 (alk. paper).—ISBN 0-7006-0846-X (pbk. :
alk. paper)
    1. Critical legal studies—Congresses. 2. Feminist jurisprudence-
Congresses.   3. Punishment—Philosophy—Congresses. I. Griffin,
Stephen M., 1957–   . II. Moffat, Robert C. L. III. International
Association for Philosophy of Law and Social Philosophy. American
Section.
K225.R33   1997
340′.1—dc21   97-11001

British Library Cataloguing in Publication Data is available.

Printed in the United States of America

10 9 8 7 6 5 4 3 2 1

The paper used in this publication meets the minimum requirements of the American
National Standard for Permanence of Paper for Printed Library Materials Z39.48-
1984.

To my parents,

Carl and Velma Moffat

R.C.L.M.

To Starlynn and Christina Griffin

S.M.G.

CONTENTS

PREFACE

The chapters in this volume stem from the conference Radical Critiques of the Law held by AMINTAPHIL, the American Section of the International Association for Philosophy of Law and Social Philosophy, at Muhlenburg College, Allentown, Pennsylvania, in October 1992. Many thanks are due to Professor Christine T. Sistare for an excellent job of hosting the conference. She received important assistance from her colleagues: Professor Ralph Lindgren at Lehigh College and Professor Roberta Kevelson at Penn State–Berks in Reading.

The content of this volume is dictated in part by the somewhat unique structure of AMINTAPHIL conferences. Papers are not presented formally but are read in advance, as are comments on the principal papers. The conference then discusses the various topics and arguments raised by the papers, rather than consuming time with lengthy presentations. Some of the chapters in this volume have comments and others do not, simply because that was the way the exchange among AMINTAPHIL scholars evolved. In addition, the chapters in Part 3 all began as commentaries on various principal papers. This volume, then, reflects the unique purpose and structure of AMINTAPHIL itself.

We thank the School of Law at Tulane University for providing the facilities necessary in preparing the essays for submission. The assistance of Charlene Washington was especially valuable. Professor Griffin would like to record his thanks to the contributors to the volume for their cooperation in the lengthy process that led to publication and to Professor Moffat for keeping the volume focused and on track. Finally, Professor Moffat wishes to record the great debt of gratitude that all participants in this project owe to Professor Griffin for taking on primary responsibility for selecting the papers to be included in the volume, for submitting the product to publishers for consideration, and for converting the computer disks to the standard format necessary for submission to the publisher. Without his major efforts, this volume would not have seen print.

EDITORS' INTRODUCTION

The past two decades have seen an outpouring of work in legal theory that is self-consciously critical of aspects of American law and the institutions of the liberal state.[1] This book is a largely philosophic response to this work in that most of the contributors are philosophers or political scientists rather than legal scholars. The conference from which this book originated was much concerned with whether the critiques advanced in the recent legal theory were critical enough to be called truly radical critiques of the law. This inquiry then produced attention to the question of what a radical critique of American law should look like, a question considered in several contributions to the volume, most notably in the chapters in Part 3.

The first two chapters in Part 1, Richard Nunan's "Critical Legal Parricide" and Lawrence B. Solum's "Indeterminacy and Equity," are the chapters most directly concerned with the movement in legal theory known as Critical Legal Studies (CLS). Nunan examines in detail the similarities and differences between Legal Realism and Critical Legal Studies and criticizes the standard CLS account of the failings of Legal Realism. Nunan argues, contrary to the standard CLS account, that Legal Realists such as Jerome Frank and Karl Llewellyn did in fact understand the role of political ideology in adjudication and did not reject the moral evaluation of legal institutions out of a supposed commitment to ethical relativism. Thus Legal Realism has more in common with CLS than CLS scholars usually acknowledge. At the same time, Nunan argues that there are some significant differences between Legal Realism and CLS. CLS scholars do not believe, as did the Legal Realists, that social science studies will be sufficient to generate significant reform of legal institutions and they accept a different form of ethical relativism, one that is similar to Jean-Paul Sartre's existentialist philosophy.

Solum explores the debate (to which he has been a notable contributor) over the claim, made by some of the scholars associated with CLS, that

1

the law is indeterminate. Solum's premise is that the Aristotelian idea of equity can illuminate the indeterminacy debate. He first carefully sets out stronger and weaker versions of the indeterminacy thesis, drawing distinctions between the kinds of indeterminacy at issue in the debate. In particular, Solum distinguishes between ex ante and ex post versions of the indeterminacy thesis. He then summarizes Aristotle's idea of equity and analyzes the relationship between indeterminacy and equity, developing an argument that the practice of equity illustrates an important sense in which the law does not determine the outcome of particular cases. The practice of equity thus confirms the validity of the ex ante indeterminacy thesis, but unlike CLS scholars who have advanced the indeterminacy thesis, Solum believes that this does not undermine the rule of law.

The other two chapters and comment in Part 1 examine radical legal theories outside the United States. Norman Fischer's "Jürgen Habermas's Recent Philosophy of Law and the Optimum Point between Abstract Universalism and Communitarianism" reviews Habermas's recent work on law and ethics in which Habermas presents a way of synthesizing abstract universalism with communitarianism's emphasis on concrete social relations. Fischer shows how Habermas arrives at his position, through an account of Hegel's critique of Kant's ethics and of Lawrence Kohlberg's attempt to accommodate communitarianism in Kohlberg's universalist moral theory. Fischer then shows the impact of Habermas's blend of abstract universalism and communitarianism on his concrete legal ethics.

Larry May's chapter, "Legal Advocacy, Cooperation, and Dispute Resolution," poses the question of whether legal advocacy must be adversarial. May argues that the adversarial legal model is often unnecessarily coercive and insufficiently attentive to what is best for the client or for the shared values in a community. He examines the thought of a prominent early Soviet legal theorist, E. B. Pashukanis in order to explore a legal theory that focuses on the cooperative aspects of dispute resolution. May then considers some criticisms of Pashukanis made by Hans Kelsen and concludes that the cooperative approach is most appropriate where there is some reason to think that the parties have shared values. Finally, May uses the example of divorce mediation to illustrate how cooperative dispute resolution could work in practice.

Douglas Lind's comment, "From Radical Critique to Alternative Dispute Resolution," extensively criticizes May's chapter. He argues that May never makes clear what exactly a cooperative approach to dispute resolu-

tion involves and that legal tools like negotiation, while appearing cooperative, are actually part of the adversarial process. In addition, Lind con-
tests May's assertion that a cooperative approach works best where the
parties share values. Using the example of environmental litigation and
regulation, Lind argues that a cooperative approach may in fact be most
appropriate where the parties are divided over key values, and he describes
his favored form of alternative dispute resolution, a process of mediation
leading to agreement.

The chapters in Part 2 are directed at the concerns raised by feminist
political and legal theory. In particular, they explore the idea of sex difference and the "dilemma of difference" as expressed in the work of Martha
Minow. Although the chapters discuss many other political theorists, such
as Michael Sandel, Iris Marion Young, Will Kymlicka, and Catherine
MacKinnon, the problems raised by Minow are central to both the principal chapters and the commentaries. Indeed, the issues raised by Minow are
considered throughout this book, not only in Part 2 but in Parts 3 and 4.

Emily Gill's chapter, "Autonomy and the Encumbered Self," first
reviews some contemporary theorists of difference who have argued that
the standard liberal ideals of universality and impartiality are illusions. Gill
employs Sandel's distinction between voluntarist and cognitive modes of
human agency to explore the impact on autonomy of these theories of difference and some ways in which the affirmation of particularity may contribute to autonomy in the area of sex difference. Gill argues that both
liberals and communitarians can appreciate the value of autonomy from
their own perspectives. She concludes: "Liberals can admit the role of particularity in the constitution of the self without relinquishing their emphasis on individual choice, just as proponents of community can value the
cultural structure or context of choice without insisting upon a particular
cultural character."

In their responses, Natalie Dandekar and Suzanne Jacobitti raise various questions that bear on Gill's ability to transcend the differences between the liberal and communitarian approaches to autonomy. Jacobitti,
in particular, provides a detailed account of the difficulties that attend Gill's
attempt to mediate these differences. She further develops Gill's account
of the self by relating it to the account offered by Hannah Arendt.

Patricia Smith's chapter, "Feminist Legal Critics: The Reluctant Radicals," begins by noting that feminist legal criticism originated not as a radical critique of the law but as a liberal argument for the universal application

of traditional standards against discrimination. In recent decades, however, women have discovered that there are serious limitations to this liberal approach, which has led many feminists to a more radical evaluation of law. Specifically, feminists have seriously challenged traditional ways of thinking about discrimination. Smith illustrates these points by setting out how feminists gradually realized the limits of equal-protection-clause litigation in combating sex discrimination. Smith then moves to examine how feminist thought developed in the direction of advocating radical reform in light of the failure of the liberal approach.

Smith contends that the focus of future feminist legal criticism should be directed at two continuing problems. The first problem is how to keep discrimination that used to be overt from continuing in covert forms through unfounded stereotypes. The second problem is how to get those in power to understand that the norms they see as natural are in fact contingent, and that many of them disadvantage women unfairly. Smith concludes that both problems can be addressed by recognizing the contradiction between universal liberal categories and patriarchal practices. The continuing legacy of a patriarchal order is in fact contrary to liberalism, but its overthrow will require not simply the vigorous application of liberal principles but "the eventual transformation of our most fundamental institutions."

Diana Tietjens Meyers's "Law and Social Exclusion" explores Martha Minow's important treatment of the problem of social exclusion. Meyers is sympathetic to Minow's basic approach but takes issue with several of her major claims. Specifically, Meyers argues that some forms of difference are not best understood as social constructions resting on illegitimate uses of power and that some social consequences of difference should not be neutralized. In addition, what Minow calls "social relations analysis" includes two approaches to moral and legal reflection: impartial reason and empathic thought. Some forms of the problem of social exclusion are best approached through impartial reason; others, through empathic thought. Introducing empathic thought into legal reasoning does not sever the problem of social exclusion from the discourse of rights, for many rights are best understood as founded on both impartial reason and empathic thought.

In their comments, Carol Gould and Bruce Landesman raise several points with respect to both Smith and Meyers. Although Gould endorses many of the points made in their chapters, she finds it surprising that the feminist critique of the law has been limited to the contexts of equal protection and the criminal law. Gould would also like to see Meyers fill out the argument on how empathic thought can justify rights. It is evident from Meyers's argument that the rights so justified are not intended to be applicable only to the particular person who is the object of empathy. But if the rights derived from empathy are universal in some sense, then the argument appears to have the form of the traditional justification for rights founded on impartial reason.

Landesman also agrees with Smith's analysis but finds it puzzling that Smith regards it as a challenge to traditional liberal thought on problems of discrimination. Like a number of the philosophers in this volume (including those represented in Part 3), Landesman argues that those professing "radical" feminist ideas in fact accept key elements of liberalism. If this is the case, however, what is the real difference between liberal and radical critiques of the law? With respect to Meyers, while agreeing with many of her points on Minow's work, Landesman thinks that she has improperly identified impartial reason with bureaucratic reason in arguing that empathic thought can cure some of the problems caused by impartial reason. Landesman argues that impartial reason, properly construed, can address the difficulties posed by differences between persons.

The chapters in Part 3 originated as comments to some of the principal papers presented at the 1992 AMINTAPHIL conference. They are set out separately because they best represent one pervasive theme of the conference: that critical legal scholars and feminist theorists have not yet earned the label "radical" because they do not truly put fundamental aspects of liberalism into question.

In "Are Feminist and Critical Legal Theory Radical?" Richard T. De George challenges feminist and critical theories to demonstrate that they are in fact radical. Taking Karl Marx as his paradigm example of a truly radical approach, he shows that feminist and critical theories typically take only the first of the three steps necessary to a genuinely radical approach. That first step is identifying the problems that are the target of the critique. De George believes that feminist and critical approaches generally focus on this "consciousness-raising" step. However, once the problems have been identified, the next step in a radical approach requires proposing an alternative structure that not only eliminates the problems identified in the first step but also produces new positive gains to replace the old problems. Occasionally, De George believes, some of the theories make tentative sorties in the direction of step two but even then remain at best quite fuzzy, even about what the alternative structure of society might be. And, he believes, they tend to disappear completely when it comes to attempting to show how the alternative structure would eliminate the problems they target, let alone demonstrating what the positive gains of the new structure would be.

The third step De George identifies is a more practical one. It requires a plan of revolution to move from the present situation to the alternative structure that will replace it. As De George points out, Marx did not address his program to the existing establishment. Instead, he sought to organize the proletariat to overthrow the prevailing order, a power structure that would become completely irrelevant once the revolution had prevailed. The point of revolutionary change is that piecemeal change is no help at all because step-by-step reform fails to address the deep problems at their root or radical level. Those problems cry out for the drastic alteration of social structure that only revolution can provide.

However, De George asserts that feminist and critical theorists are completely silent regarding this third step. That silence, of course, is no reason to reject their claims; it simply questions the justification for classifying their theories as radical. But De George's point is not one of the correct terminology. His object is to question why feminists and critical theorists claim that their theories are radical. If their theories are not, in fact, radical, then there is no reason for them to attack liberalism, as though liberals were the cause of the problems they identify in step one. If their program is not actually revolutionary, their attack on the existing structure of society is inappropriate because their real wish is to effect change within that structure. If the real objective of feminists and others is consciousness-raising and persuasion, De George points out that there is no reason to attack liberals, many of whom share the same goals and ideals.

Similar themes are expounded in Wade Robison's "Liberalism and Radical Critiques of the Law." He begins with an analysis of Daniel Defoe's *Roxana*, as an example of an eighteenth-century feminist critique of the discriminatory nature of the marriage contract. From this analysis, Robison derives two propositions. The first is that compelling arguments against discriminatory law can be mounted within the framework of existing legal theory. The second is that real change within the existing social order is seldom effectuated without real power, even though good theoretical contract arguments may be offered for change. Hence, liberals are just as able as radicals to criticize biased, unfair, or discriminatory laws. Indeed, he can see no reason that such arguments against discrimination should be termed radical. In fact, "everything within a legal system is open to question on liberal principles." If the process for mounting an attack is provided for within the legal and political system, then that attack cannot appropriately be termed radical.

But the counterpoint is that even though arguments against bias are not really radical, nonetheless real change requires empowerment. Accordingly, theoretical arguments are only a small part of the process of effecting change. However, it must be noted that Robison's view of the limited scope of legal change derives from a legal positivist view of the legal system that considerably restricts the range of arguments available to courts. That view is founded on the assumption that the social contract limits courts to the terms of the Constitution. However, we should not overlook the sometimes extensive use that courts have made in constitutional adjudication of terms they found to be implied in the Constitution or even in the context of particular provisions. Even so, that qualification does not detract from Robison's assertion that the so-called radical critiques are not of principles of liberalism but of justifications offered to buttress particular positions in contract theory.

The doubts that such purported criticisms of liberalism are actually radical are shared by Joseph Ellin in his "Liberalism, Radicalism, Muddlism." He considers the belief that there are major differences between standard liberal positions and feminist criticisms to be a muddle, founded on smaller muddles regarding more specific issues. Ellin's position is different from that of De George and Robison in one highly notable respect. Whereas they generally agree with the substance of feminist criticisms of existing law, Ellin enters his disagreement on a number of those substantive issues, most particularly some of the proposed revisions of the law of rape.

Ellin first takes up the issue of bias and perspectivism, which he considers the prime muddle. In its essence, he echoes Ronald Dworkin's devastating critique of the Critical Legal Studies movement. If CLS urges us to be skeptical of positions of the liberal establishment because any position is merely a matter of perspective, then we should by the same token be equally skeptical of the CLS claim that skepticism is the right answer. Similarly, Ellin argues that perspectivism is necessarily self-contradictory. If all views are biases, then nothing can be judged a bias because there is no objective standard left according to which a bias could be detected. However, if the point of the critique is only the more modest objection to bias in our rules and their applications, then the self-styled radicals are simply embracing a well-established fundamental liberal principle.

More specifically on the issue of discrimination, Ellin examines the principles that have been developed by our courts in the application of the constitutional principle requiring equal protection of the laws. He argues that those principles should be adequate to deal with most asserted problems of bias or discrimination. Those principles do fall short, he concedes, of prohibiting the denial of practices that disadvantage only some women, such as maternity leaves. To prohibit such results might require an additional principle of exclusive burdening, and he believes that liberals could adopt such a principle. But because of quite a number of anomalous possible applications, Ellin is doubtful that adoption of such a principle would be wise.

Ellin then takes up the problem of "Minow's Dilemma," that is, that preferences designed to help females overcome past discriminatory treatment also stigmatize them for needing additional help to compete. Family leave policies might be one such advantage to women, Ellin suggests, and expresses doubt as to the feasibility of such policies on a widespread basis. However, his assumption that such policies primarily benefit females, even when such policies are facially neutral, may be belied by the changing pattern of family life, which is leading a growing number of men to seek leave in order to participate in the early childhood development of their children. Finally, he launches an attack on some of the recent modifications of rape law that have made it easier to obtain rape convictions. His opposition is based on the importance of civil liberty and on the interest of women in not having men subjected to haphazard prosecutions for rape. However, he assumes that even the proponents of the more drastic expansions of exposure to rape conviction share his belief that consensual sexual contact between men and women is desirable. It may be less clear than he thinks that his assumption is widely shared among that particular group of advocates.

That suspicion is likely to become stronger after reading Joan McGregor's "Feminism, Women, and the Criminal Law." McGregor's chapter is the first of several in Part 4 that focus on current issues of legal reform. She surveys the critiques of the law of rape that a number of feminists have offered. Readers must surely be appalled to read what McGregor relates in the first half of her chapter: how the law of rape has historically taken a male orientation. That perspective is reflected in traditional requirements, such as resistance by the victim and rigorous standards of proof of force and nonconsent. In this portion of her chapter, McGregor is reporting principally the essentialist critique of Catherine MacKinnon. MacKinnon concludes that rape law is deliberately designed to enslave women and force them to be the objects of male sexual desires. MacKinnon's solution is incontestably radical: instead of focusing on the state of mind of the rapist, examine the meaning of the event to the woman. From an objective (male) view, we should switch to a subjective view, which is to be judged from the standpoint of the female victim. As McGregor observes, MacKinnon's solution would apparently favor making rape a crime of strict liability.

There can be no question that MacKinnon disagrees vigorously with Ellin's assumption, that it is in the interests of both men and women that consenting adult partners should be able to consummate their mutual desires without fear of interference from the law. McGregor notes that Susan Estrich has somewhat more moderately opted for a negligence standard in rape, but she also correctly observes that criminal law theorists have vigorously criticized criminal liability founded on mere negligence.

McGregor next addresses "Minow's Dilemma" in regard to the conflict between equality and difference. She comments that if law is framed to protect females who play the passive role, then that may seem satisfactory in the short run to protect those who appear helpless. However, the long-run cost is that the law is being used to encourage women to sell themselves short by following the stereotypical female gender role. One example of the equality approach is the modern gender-neutral sexual battery statute. After learning of the horrors recounted in her first section, the reader is likely to sigh in relief upon learning that more than half the states had adopted such a statute by 1980. That relief may be short-lived, however, for McGregor raises the difference problem: if the law takes a gender-neutral stance, it must necessarily ignore the question of whether women react the same as men. Moreover, the difference approach assumes that rape (no matter how gender-neutral in definition) is an injury that is inflicted on women by men. Of course, those feminists who assume that "men rape, not women," ignore the problem raised by Robison of male victims of sexual assault. They also make essentialist assumptions about female sexuality that run counter to the cautions of family planning workers or what we know of behavior in women's prisons. In other words, the difference position assumes a stereotypical view of female sexuality that is highly traditional and, as McGregor points out, casts women in the helpless-victim role.

The preceding dilemma between equality and difference is deepened in McGregor's examination of the problem of sex and sexuality. If statutory rape laws protect only underage females, then they represent assumptions that females cannot handle sexual autonomy and that males can. However, in states that now have gender-neutral statutory sexual battery laws, young women receive no greater protection than young men, thereby running afoul of the need to respect difference. But as McGregor points out, variation in sexual expression requires that individuals be free to explore those parameters.

In her final section, McGregor suggests new directions whereby the law of rape might be improved. She favors an approach in which the crime would turn on the absence of consent with gradations for levels of seriousness founded on the aggravated nature of the crime. Her proposals are straightforward and seem designed to appeal to common sense. As she points out, her reform proposals are not dependent in any way on adopting the stereotypes propounded by feminist essentialists. Yet she seems torn. She would like to use the law to protect those who are least capable of defending themselves, thus indulging the essentialist stereotype to that extent. The problem is that there is no effective legal mechanism to determine whether a particular female is genuinely timid (and thereby warrants the enhanced legal protection McGregor favors) or is merely feigning weakness in order to take undue advantage (thus harming the image of women taking on greater autonomy). The point is important not only to the evenhanded administration of justice but also to the value of autonomy that McGregor very much wishes to protect and enhance. Regrettably, the dilemma persists. Despite McGregor's best efforts, she too has not divined a way to extend enhanced protection to the weakest while applying that same rule of law to advance the autonomy of all those seeking liberation from suffocating essentialist stereotypes. Nonetheless, it is a worthy dilemma, and McGregor helps us clarify our understanding of our ambivalence.

James Doyle feels no ambivalence in offering "A Radical Critique of Criminal Punishment." Doyle takes aim at what he takes to be the conventional view of punishment as based on an "ethics of obligation." Philosophically, the view derives from the traditional deontological approaches we identify with Kant and Rawls, among others. Typically, it sees the individual as autonomous, so that the legal community depends upon a formal contractual promise to justify the limits upon autonomy that the law imposes. In this idealized community, individuals deal with one another as independent moral agents who, as free willing persons, offer relevant ethical justifications for the actions they take. If irrationality rears its ugly head in the setting of such pristine reason, punishment is obviously not simply in order but absolutely required.

Doyle urges serious consideration of Martha Minow's critique of this "rights analysis" because it excludes notions of community. Instead, Doyle proposes that we adopt her radical alternative: an "ethics of social relations." Such an approach requires a recognition that rights grow out of individuals' social relations with one another and within the community. Although Doyle does not put the contrast in terms of legal philosophy, what he calls for is a shift from the traditional approach rooted in the power orientation of legal positivism to one of sociological jurisprudence, which sees the obligations enforced by law as growing out of the reciprocity created in human interaction. This point is made more clear by his reliance on the work of Annette Baier, who makes the point that we individuals are social creations, an observation that has its roots in symbolic interactionism, an approach thought to be sociological but formulated by the pragmatic philosopher George Herbert Meade.

Interesting corollaries of the "social relations" approach include the observation that in a society in which legitimacy is vibrant, punishment becomes of peripheral importance as a source of social control. At the same time, weak authority requires tremendous reliance on coercive force, which in turn weakens authority even more. Moreover, the more punishment is relied on as a source of authority, the less it tends to be effective in controlling crime. The mammoth difficulties that the Soviet Union had in deterring the stealing of state property would be an example. Such failures of punishment rest on an assumption that punishment is employed (as in the Soviet example) by a coercive state warring against its citizens. Doyle urges alternatives to punishment such as therapeutic and social services approaches. We must maintain caution on that front, however, for, as George Orwell pointed out, coercive therapeutic treatment may be far worse than plain, old punishment. Nonetheless, the social relations approach does have the merit of reminding us that law should enforce the obligations that arise from our human interactions. When it does so, it will generate legitimacy, and only that legitimacy, arising from the community, can justify law in the eyes of the community, including the occasional necessity to employ sanctions when the law has failed. Doyle's radical critique reminds us that the law should be a positive instrument to reinforce the bonds of community generated by social relations. When a government feels it must rely on punishment, Doyle's critique tells us that the law has failed to fulfill its central mission.

A number of similar themes are sounded in Randall Curren's "Punishment and Inclusion: The Presuppositions of Corrective Justice in Aristotle and What They Imply." As his title indicates, however, his interest is in the correct interpretation of Aristotle's views on justice. As he points out, that is a topic that has attracted considerable contemporary interest from philosophers, particularly as applied to the law of torts. Curren believes that Aristotle's conception of corrective justice is at least equally applicable to criminal law. Indeed, he thinks it possible to found a radical critique on Aristotle, where *radical* is understood as revealing deficiencies that threaten the legitimacy of a fundamental social institution.

Curren bases his reading of Aristotle in part on the fact that Aristotle was highly familiar with Plato and normally expressed his disagreements quite clearly. However, he apparently accepted Plato's argument in *The Laws* that if punishment is to be justified, there must be a rule of law. Only then can the law have a claim to legitimacy. But in Plato's scheme, proper education is necessary to assure conformity with reason and law. That condition must be met in order to claim that the law rests on genuine consent. Curren offers evidence that Aristotle shared Plato's view on this subject and believes on that basis that Aristotle saw valid corrective justice as assuming a form of distributive justice that permits the development of the individual as a rational, willing being. Such a person can comprehend the reasons for the law and is therefore capable of giving the consent required to make law legitimate. By extension, a society that does not meet those standards cannot justify punishment of transgressors if they are not blameworthy because of their ignorance. Even in cases in which punishment cannot be justified, though, Curren would still permit society to incapacitate on the basis of a self-defense justification.

Curren's position may not sound terribly radical until we consider the requirements that society would have to meet in order to be justified in blaming wrongdoers. Significant change would be required not only in education but also in family and welfare law. In fact, intervention would be required to assure that every child received adequate care and socialization. When we stop to think of the thoroughgoing intervention in what passes as family life that would be necessary to meet that standard, we can begin to appreciate how truly radical the proposal is. Indeed, the system of communal child rearing proposed in Plato's *Republic* may be the sort of scheme required to meet such standards.

That these requirements would be truly radical is confirmed by Curren's comparison of his critique with the Marxist view. Although he finds that they share basic principles, he concludes that his Aristotelian critique is more demanding than the Marxist one and would be more radical in its demands for intervention in the socialization of future citizens. Curren speaks of these as very substantial social investments, which indeed they would be. His focus seems to be on the financial sacrifices society would have to make to adopt such practices. Surely more significant would be the radical intervention in the lives of many families and single parents that would be required to meet his standards. Curren is persuasive that the changes he proposes are necessary in order to justify punishment. Indeed, it seems likely that those changes may be essential to the survival of a viable society. One of Curren's fundamental Aristotelian points is the necessity of education as a foundation of consent. More daunting would be the education necessary to win acceptance of such radical changes in our child-rearing practices.

Thomas Simon takes on quite a different set of problems in "Jurisprudential Indeterminacy: The Case of Hate Speech Regulation." He examines three current, but very different, radical legal theories, each of which, perhaps surprisingly, purports to favor regulation of hate speech. From his analysis, he concludes that Law and Economics, Communitarianism, and Critical Race Theory each suffer from what the advocates of Critical Legal Studies call indeterminacy. Indeed, Simon finds that each of their efforts to justify regulating hate speech displays substantial indeterminacies. Law and Economics takes a quantitative approach, producing an equation that is supposed to allow us to determine whether speech should be protected. The problem, however, is that values must be assigned to the variables in the free speech equation in order to determine under what circumstances interference with speech might be warranted. The fatal indeterminacy stems from the fact that the judgments of value of speech turn out to be highly indeterminate. On the Law and Economics formula, crude hate speech should be of much lower value than sophisticated hate speech. Simon argues, however, that such an assumption is highly tenuous. In fact, crude speech may open up possibilities of dialogue, and sophisticated speech may be much more devastating in impact. In addition, the harmfulness of speech does not necessarily depend on either its hateful intent or on how clear it is that a particular group is the target of the speech.

Communitarians also defend hate speech regulation but on different grounds. They see each person's moral identity founded in his or her group affiliations. Because group identity defines the individual, racial identity poses a central problem as Simon sees it. Members of a racial group that is the target of abusive speech should not be made to take on the victim role.

The source of the hate speech should instead be scrutinized for its lack of humanity. But communitarian regulation of hate speech depends on race as a central constituent of the self. However, as Simon points out, hate speech incidents may sometimes occasion an individual's discovery of a previously unrealized ethnic identity. Moreover, communitarians also face indeterminacy in their inability to distinguish between groups that deserve protection and groups that might be considered less worthy. In other words, what is to prevent any group from claiming victim status? Yet that is certainly not the conclusion that the communitarians favor.

Finally, even Critical Race Theory suffers from the dreaded fate of indeterminacy. Its proponents are not bashful in identifying race as a focal point of victim status. Yet the victim perspective means that in order to avoid paternalism, only the victims could be regulators. But who decides who qualifies as a victim? If many groups claim victim status as groups seem increasingly inclined to do, critical race theory provides no basis for excluding them from protection nor from the claim of harm. In addition, such regulations can be used, as they often are, to limit the range of speech of racial minorities. Simon concludes that a focus on hate speech can easily prove to be a diversion from the much deeper problems of institutional racism.

David Adams also addresses hate speech regulation in "First Amendment Liberalism and Hate Speech: After *R.A.V. v. St. Paul*." He undertakes a comprehensive analysis of the liberal position and the radical theories offered by critical race theorists and feminists, as well as their responses to each other. The radicals take two positions: one favoring vigorous and comprehensive regulation of hate speech, and one offering a more moderate proposal of weak or minimal regulation of hate speech. Adams concludes that strong regulation cannot be justified under any reading of the First Amendment. Liberal detractors doubt that weak regulation is worth the trouble, but Adams disagrees. He believes that although it is true that weak regulation could not possibly rid campuses of racism and sexism, that such limited regulation can still serve a useful purpose. Moreover, even though liberals tend to say otherwise, he contends that a narrowly tailored weak regulation could be consistent with the limits set forth by the Court in *R.A.V. v. St. Paul*. That is so because that case should not be read to exclude regulation of what he calls targeted vilification.

Adams also denies the liberal argument that such restrictions on speech unfairly penalize only one side in the debate. He holds that it would be impossible for a civil rights advocate to convey racial tolerance in conjunction with nasty insults directed at the person who is perceived to be a racist. Indeed, Adams contends that slurs and epithets are not used by women and racial minorities but only, apparently, by bigoted white males. Of course, liberals who disagree with his conclusion no doubt see hate speech as a more widespread phenomenon. Even though Adams sees the need for us to listen to the narratives of women and racial minorities, he does not mention a similar need to listen to disfavored minorities such as rednecks, who may see themselves as even more excluded.

Adams concludes from his analysis of *R.A.V.* and *Chaplinsky* that vicious slurs could be constitutionally proscribed as analogous to "fighting words." He argues in addition that such injuries are recognized by the courts in cases of intentional infliction of emotional distress. Finally, he argues that such regulation is desirable because of the injury that speech of that kind can produce. Moreover, he does not see how such "assaultive epithets" can be banished from the classroom without university regulations prohibiting targeted vilification. Perhaps because his proposal is so narrow, he does not raise the problems that have beset more ambitious speech regulations. For example, he does not address whether such regulations may produce backlash behavior, particularly if the rules are perceived as being applied selectively. Nor does he consider whether the powerful ostracism of the social climate on the university campus may be a more effective sanction. Quite possibly, he hopes that his proposed weak regulation would work in tandem with the informal social sanctions, so that the two would reinforce each other.

This survey of the search for radical critiques yields an ironic conclusion. As De George, Robison, and Ellin show, the claim to radicalism is highly problematic. Few, if any, of the radical critiques offered by the feminists, as described by Gill, Smith, Meyers, and McGregor, could not equally well be offered within the confines of a liberal critique. Moreover, as Nunan, Solum, and Simon show, the claim of Critical Legal Studies and other purported critical approaches to be unmasking fatal indeterminacies in the liberal legal order is subject to a variety of difficulties. So should we then conclude that radical critiques of the law are illusory or even not possible? That would be much too hasty a judgment.

The analyses presented here of radical critiques include alternative critiques that embody considerably greater promise of being truly radical. Fischer's exposition of Habermas's synthesis of abstract universalism and concrete social relations offers a sample of what direction radical thought might take. May explores the approach of Eugene Pashukanis, who propounded the only truly Marxian theory of law. As De George reminds us, Marx may be taken as the paradigm of a radical critique. But, interestingly, the most radical critiques offered here are those of Doyle and Curren. What is the foundation of their radicalism?

In Doyle's case, it is the ethics of social relations (a symbolic interactionist sociological jurisprudence) proposed by the moderate feminist Martha Minow. If, however, it is surprising to find real radicalism lurking in the shadows of such seemingly innocuous sociological jurisprudence, consider Curren. His proposal would require fundamental alteration of child rearing and education. That must surely be the most radical proposal in this entire collection of essays. Does it deepen our understanding of the nature of truly radical approaches to discover that the foundation of Curren's proposal is Aristotle?

We should note that the common thread pulling together the approaches of Doyle and Curren is a focus on the social dimension of society and law. That same theme characterizes the approaches of Marx, Pashukanis, and Habermas. Such approaches find too limiting the individualism of liberal theories such as utilitarianism and legal positivism. As this fundamental contrast becomes better understood in the academic community, perhaps we can anticipate a greater outpouring of truly radical critiques of the law.

Note

1. A number of anthologies provide useful introductions to the leading ideas in Critical Legal Studies, feminist legal theory, and Critical Race Theory. For Critical Legal Studies, see Peter Fitzpatrick and Alan Hunt, eds., *Critical Legal Studies* (New York: Basil Blackwell, 1987); Allan C. Hutchinson, ed., *Critical Legal Studies* (Totowa, N.J.: Rowman & Littlefield, 1989); David Kairys, ed., *The Politics of Law: A Progressive Critique* (New York: Pantheon, 1990). For a historical account of the development of Critical Legal Studies, see Neil Duxbury, *Patterns of American Jurisprudence* (New York: Oxford University Press, 1995), 421–509.

For feminist legal theory, see Katharine T. Bartlett and Rosanne Kennedy, eds., *Feminist Legal Theory: Readings in Law and Gender* (Boulder, Colo.: Westview Press, 1991); Leslie Friedman Goldstein, ed., *Feminist Jurisprudence: The Difference Debate* (Lanham, Md.: Rowman & Littlefield, 1992); Patricia Smith, ed., *Feminist Jurisprudence* (New

York: Oxford University Press, 1993); D. Kelly Weisberg, ed., *Feminist Legal Theory: Foundations* (Philadelphia: Temple University Press, 1993).

For critical race theory, see Kimberle Crenshaw, Neil Gotanda, Gary Peller, and Kendall Thomas, eds., *Critical Race Theory: The Key Writings That Formed the Movement* (New York: New Press, 1995); Richard Delgado, ed., *Critical Race Theory: The Cutting Edge* (Philadelphia: Temple University Press, 1995); Mari J. Matsuda, Charles R. Lawrence III, Richard Delgado, Kimberle Williams Crenshaw, *Words That Wound: Critical Race Theory, Assaultive Speech, and the First Amendment* (Boulder, Colo.: Westview Press, 1993).

Part I

Critical Legal Studies and
Critical Legal Theory

Chapter 1

Critical Legal Parricide, or: What's So Bad About Warmed-Over Legal Realism?

Richard Nunan

Early on in the development of the Critical Legal Studies movement participants undertook to trace their intellectual ancestry to the Legal Realist tradition that flourished and "died" between the two world wars.[1] A few years ago G. Edward White characterized this "self-conscious identification of Realism as a progenitor of . . . the CLS movement" as a "grasp at legitimacy."[2] White suggested that apart from the substantial conceptual affinities between the two movements, Legal Realism may appeal to CLS advocates because the history of Realism's reception in the community of legal scholars and practitioners provides CLS scholars with a modest defense in the face of increasingly vitriolic attacks from their mainstream colleagues; the same kind of vituperation had been directed at the Realists back in the 1930s, yet many Realist insights eventually triumphed over that hostility and came to permeate legal consciousness. So too, the story goes, will CLS elaborations of Realist insights eventually prevail over the current witch hunt.[3]

In a later paper, however, White points out that the link with Legal Realism is a problematic one for CLS scholars: "My main concern is . . . to ask why, if Realism is widely perceived as something that ran itself into the sand as a coherent intellectual force in American legal thought, the Critical Legal Studies movement, which seeks intellectual prominence, if certainly not respectability, would claim Realism as an influence."[4] Legal Realism did not really succeed in transcending the voices of its critics. Unlike CLS scholarship, which has been steeped in controversy from its inception, the most aggressive attacks on Legal Realism came late in its career, and, mainstream absorption of Realist doctrines notwithstanding, the tradition did not survive those attacks as a cohesive movement. Consequently, if CLS theorists want to claim Legal Realism as their intellectual heritage, they must also be fairly confident that their own program is sufficiently distinct from Realism to make it impervious to the attacks that ultimately scuttled Realism. Intellectual movements are even more anxious to carve out their own ecological niche in the environment of ideas than they are to recognize their ancestors. In this regard CLS is no different from other movements. Incestuous citation practices within CLS have produced a more or less standardized mythology about the rise and fall of Legal Realism, complete with edifying comparisons to the broader scope, more clear-sighted vision, and tougher moral fiber of CLS scholarship.[5]

I want to suggest that CLS does indeed offer a distinctive approach to legal theory, but the real distinction has often been lost in the rhetoric used to distance CLS from Legal Realism. If we get clearer on the substantive differences between the two movements, it will be easier to evaluate anti-Realist attacks on Critical Legal Studies.

I

Legal Realism was an amalgam of two conflicting research programs. One dimension of Realism was the desire to expose the indeterminacy of received precedent, statutes, and constitutional provisions. None of these, the Realists argued, could really provide settled answers to legal disputes. If that were the case, litigation would never make it to the courtroom.[6] On the other hand, Realists were also legal reformers who wanted to replace the arbitrary and dictatorial practices of oracular judges with a more rational approach to implementation of laws. This they proposed to achieve by relying on objective social science research to determine the practical outcome of rival interpretations of particular laws, and then choosing the interpretation that yielded the most desirable outcome.

The oracular theory of judging dominant in nineteenth-century jurisprudence held that judges simply *discovered* the proper meaning of preexisting law as applied to particular cases. Realists, moved by the idea that the substance of the law is simply that which officials appointed to implement the law actually choose to do about disputes,[7] set out to demonstrate that the oracular theory of judging was nothing more than a fraud perpetrated on the American public. They did this by means of case analysis revealing the inconsistency of judicial decisions over time; the incoherence of the arguments underlying those decisions; the chronic ambiguity of the language in which legal concepts were expressed; and the effects of the psychological predilections of individual judges. In short, judges effectively made up (and re-created) the law as they went along.

Thus far, nothing about this picture of Legal Realism is inaccurate. But the CLS version of Realism's history goes on to attribute a kind of tragic flaw that distinguishes the Realists from Critical Legal scholars. On this account, the Realists didn't have the courage of their convictions. They were quite successful in debunking mechanistic jurisprudence, the myth that judicial decisions were deductive consequences of an established body of law, gleaned by dispassionate professionals trained in the rigors of legal reasoning. Yet the Realists either failed to recognize the broader implications of their critique of mechanical jurisprudence and oracular judging or were appalled by those implications and chose to reject them. In particular, together with their successors in the Legal Process School and the Law and Society movement, the Legal Realists failed to acknowledge the extent to which political ideology influences both judicial adjudication and legislative decisions.[8]

The failure to recognize the influence of political ideology was really a failure of nerve. If turn-of-the-century law was, in reality, a systematic attempt to ratify and enforce convictions then prevalent about, say, the inviolability of property rights, the subservience of women in society, the virtues of capitalism, the vices of Negroes, and so on, and if this pattern can be generalized, then law is not the product of objective standards of justice or fairness. In that case, why should legal constraints have any moral claim upon us? According to the CLS history of Realism, the Realists were ultimately hesitant about acknowledging the influence of political ideology because they did not want to confront this corrosive question.

It is at least true that Legal Realists did not want to destroy the authority of the law; they merely wanted to reform it. But on the CLS account of the Realists, their heavy reliance on sociological studies of the law in action served a dual purpose in this regard. First, it enabled them to avoid acknowledging the pervasive influence of ideology by providing a source of local and idiosyncratic explanations for inconsistency and indeterminacy in judicial adjudication. Jerome Frank's psychological analysis of the vagaries of individual judges is the most-well-known example of this kind of strategy.[9] Second, the Realists shared in the positivist faith in the objectivity of empirical studies prevalent in the 1920s and 1930s. They were confident that sociological studies of law in action would enable them to discern how law could be reformed in pursuit of good social policy, meaning the social and political ambitions of the New Deal. In other words, our legal institutions could after all be held accountable to, and be reshaped to express, our moral ideals. We simply needed to sort out the real consequences of existing legal practices:

> Positing a tangible, determinate world of facts . . . whose operation could be seen at work upon, behind, or beneath the illusory world of legal doctrine, the Realists pointed to what seemed to be a foundation for the reconstruction of legal science: the observation of "reality." . . . Empirical methods would . . . unearth the *real* objective forces that determine law's response to social needs, reveal the *real* functional necessities of social life, specify the *real* indwelling norms that were shaped by these objective forces and functions, and equip reformers with the tools to perfect bodies of rules and systems of governance.[10]

In short, the Realists' efforts to undermine the judiciary's claim to apolitical objectivity were not especially troubling to them so long as they were also convinced that reliance on sociological and behavioral studies of the activities of the participants in legal institutions would reinstitute an objective basis for evaluating the law. For CLS scholars, however, the reliability that Realists attributed to sociological studies was really just a form of self-deception:

> Faced with the fundamental indeterminacy of the law, the apparent impossibility of objective legal reasoning, and the (probable) awareness that such ideas could undermine the power and the prestige of the legal academy, the profession, and its institutions, many Realists retreated into the safe harbor of legal objectivity. Rather than focus on the contingent and inherently political nature of legal representations of the social world, Realists sought to stabilize the uncertainty they had exposed with a new source for legal representations—an empirically knowable "reality." . . . Thus Realism was Janus-faced—at the same time a critical practice and a legitimating ideology.[11]

If this analysis of the Realists' position is correct, CLS sympathizers tell us, then it becomes apparent that the Realists did not fully appreciate the revolution that epistemology has undergone in this century.[12] They were willing to question the fact/value distinction as applied to the "science" of legal reasoning exercised by judges, suggesting that judges were dressing personal prejudice, political ideology, economic interests, and a battery of other value judgments in the objective-sounding garb of "relevant" precedent, statutory analysis, and a dispassionate assessment of the facts of the case. Yet the Realists were not prepared to extend the same skepticism to the social sciences. They had embraced the logical positivists' conviction that studies based on empirical observation could supply the objectivity and true knowledge that had escaped the late-nineteenth-century formalists who indulged in abstract metaphysical speculations concerning the "real" meaning of legal concepts.[13]

Perhaps the Realists suspected that empirical social science research was a pretty thin reed on which to base the rehabilitation of objectivity in law.[14] At any rate, however firmly convinced some Realists might have been about the power of the social sciences, the self-deception could not withstand the pressures associated with the rise of Nazism and other forms of fascism in Europe during the mid-1930s. In the context of a proto-McCarthyite atmosphere in the legal community, critics confronted the Realists with the implications of the debunking aspects of their scholarship. Faced with the need for a conceptual apparatus that would justify attacks against totalitarian legal institutions and provide an adequate foundation for defending liberal ideals, mainstream legal theorists and Catholic Natural Law advocates berated the Legal Realists for fomenting ethical relativism and undermining the hypothesis that legal institutions could and should implement objectively valid principles of justice.[15] As pressure to conform intensified, most Realists eventually felt compelled to recant their heresies and profess that they had always subscribed to some form of Natural Law theory.[16] At least, that is how the story is supposed to go.

This "Critical Legal history" concludes with the claim that CLS scholars differ from the Realists primarily because they have embarked on the enterprise of debunking the myth of determinate law with their eyes open to the consequences of their actions. They are not afraid to acknowledge the relativistic implications of critical analysis, and they recognize the full extent to which ideology informs the interpretation and application of legal doctrines. This is because CLS scholars, unlike the Realists, are not liberals, wedded to the belief that the law has an autonomous core not subject to the indeterminacy that Realists associated with oracular judging.[17] Where Realism called for empirical studies to reveal the legitimate purposes of the law, purposes otherwise buried in judicial fiat and rationalization, CLS holds instead that all law is politics by another name. The purposes of the law are nothing more or less than the purposes that the social elite "find" in the law through manipulation of legislative process and judicial adjudication, usually to serve the interests of that elite.

II

To recapitulate, CLS acknowledges an intellectual debt to the Realists because they were the first to recognize the full extent of the indeterminacy of the law. But CLS also repudiates Legal Realism because the Realists could not or would not comprehend the ideological underpinnings of judicial adjudication, and could not or would not confront the ethical relativism inherent in their own views. In the final analysis, CLS scholars think Realists had a failure of nerve. I will argue that none of these charges can be sustained.

In light of the judicial history of the first third of this century, particularly as it concerns the Supreme Court, the accusation that Realists failed to appreciate the influence of ideology is truly astonishing. Oliver Wendell Holmes's famous dissent in *Lochner v. New York,* wherein he accused the majority of using the Fourteenth Amendment to enact Herbert Spencer's social Darwinism and a libertarian economic ideology that "a large part of the country does not entertain,"[18] was one of the initial sources of inspiration for Realist scholarship. But where Holmes merely chided his colleagues for allowing ideology to influence their judgment, suggesting that they should defer to legislative decisions about the wisdom of wage-and-hour reform measures, the Realists became convinced that ideological input was an inevitable facet of judicial adjudication. The unflagging libertarian vigilance of William Howard Taft and the *four horsemen,*[19] who routinely overturned economic reform legislation up until the mid-1930s,[20] provided the Realists with a constant reminder of the role that ideology was capable of playing in judicial adjudication, even at the level of the Supreme Court.

It is true that the Realists expended a lot of paper and ink discussing influences other than political and economic ideology, but that does not mean they lost sight of the relevance of ideology. Jerome Frank is usually offered as the paradigmatic case of a Realist who attempted to supplant ideological analyses of judicial outcomes with sociological or psychological determinants. But Frank himself acknowledged the importance of ideological considerations. He argued, however, that the bulk of the work on the role of ideology had already been done: "It is to the economic determinists and to the members of the school of 'sociological jurisprudence' that we owe much of the recognition of the influence of the economic and political background of judges upon decisions. For this much thanks. But their work has perhaps been done too well."[21] Consequently, Frank chose instead to pursue psychological investigations of judicial motives, in hopes of explaining the causal stimuli that inspired the political and economic predilections of the judiciary in the first place:

> But are not those categories—political, economic and moral biases too gross, too crude, too wide? What are the hidden factors in the inferences and opinions of ordinary men? The answer surely is that these factors are multitudinous and complicated, depending often on peculiarly individual traits of the persons whose inferences and opinions are to be explained. These uniquely individual factors often are more important causes of judgments than anything which could be described as political, economic or moral biases.[22]

In short, Frank's work was misconstrued by his critics because he focused on the initial premise rather than on the middle term in the syllogism, which explains judicial decisions in terms of personal idiosyncrasies by means of ideological perspective. The critics thought Frank had simply dismissed the view that ideology had a mediating influence.[23]

In fairness to his critics, it is worth noting that Frank did have a habit of getting carried away by his own rhetoric, and this did not help his cause. Karl Llewellyn clearly had Frank in mind when he made the following remarks:

> Much of the controversy turns on cross-purposing of this sort: X alleges that the psychology of judges needs study, and tries some study along behavioristic lines. Y reads that X is trying to *substitute* behavioristic psychology for rules and principles, to deny free will to judges, and to urge as law whatever judges take it into their heads to do. I.e., much cross-purposing turns on reading an X's insistence that something or other goes into or is part of Jurisprudence—is a spoke—as being an allegation that the something is the exclusive *all* of Jurisprudence: wheel and hub. This is an inevitable accompaniment of exploratory writing. The explorer commonly over-stresses, in language and in flavor, the value or significance of the particular thing he is after.[24]

Llewellyn, of course, is himself subject to the same temptation. He generated a lot of heat with his famous assertion: "*What these officials* [judges, sheriffs, prosecutors, et al.] *do about disputes is, to my mind, the law itself.*"[25] The implication seemed to be that judges literally make up the law as they go along; there are no serious constraints on judicial fiat. Worse, if that is all there is to the law, then nothing remains to be said about the rightness of the law. What officials do will count as law in some legitimate sense even if some of us are appalled at what they do in that official capacity.

If this particular analysis were accurate, then Llewellyn at least, the scholar who coined the term *Legal Realism*,[26] would subscribe not merely to ethical relativism concerning the moral status of rules of law but to a thoroughgoing nihilism: the rules have no moral value at all. In other words, contrary to the CLS history of Legal Realism, some Realists may prove to be even more radical in their views about the relationship between law and morality than I am prepared to argue here. In reality, however, I believe this analysis is no more accurate about Llewellyn or the Realists than it is about CLS scholars today.

To begin with, Llewellyn was addressing himself to first-year law students, who, in the course of their training, were certainly going to be exposed to a very instrumental perspective on the law. They were going to learn how to manipulate judges and juries for the sake of their clients. From that perspective, the law is indeed whatever judges and juries decide to do to one's client. In his capacity as adviser to such students, Llewellyn was simply echoing Oliver Wendell Holmes's account of the bad man's view of the law, under which the law is identified exclusively with its material consequences for those on the receiving end.[27] But Llewellyn also wanted to affirm another aspect of Holmes's view (expressed in the same paper): that the law could be the embodiment of the purposes adopted by a particular society at a particular moment in its history. Whether the law *did* adequately express the common morality of *our* society circa 1930 was a question that could be answered only by examining the content of the law, *as implemented by officials*. Hence the importance of that focus.

In "A Realistic Jurisprudence—The Next Step," the paper in which Llewellyn first outlined the tenets of Legal Realism, it is already quite clear that he thought Realists scrutinized the behavior of officials in order to ensure that the law conformed to currently prevailing views about the common moral purposes of society. There Llewellyn acknowledged that Realists were primarily interested in investigating the actual actions of the courts and the effects of their behavior—"real rules" as distinct from the "paper rules" that can be found in the statute books.[28] He asked rhetorically whether this focus was a form of backsliding, a case of regarding the law as nothing more than the set of remedies that legal institutions are in the habit of enforcing, uninformed by any concept of substantive moral rights as justifications for the existence of such remedies:

> A reversion, do you say, to the crude and outmoded thinking of rules in terms of remedies only, to confining legal thinking to the vagaries of tradition-bound pro-

cedure? Not quite. It is a reversion to the realism of that primitive point of view. But a sophisticated reversion to a sophisticated realism. Gone is the ancient assumption that law is because law is; there has come since, and remains, the inquiry into the purpose of what the courts are doing, the criticism in terms of searching out purposes and criticizing means.[29]

In other words, the ultimate goal of Realist investigations into what officials actually do is law reform rather than the validation of nihilist theses about the moral substance of the law. Realists wanted to make sure that our legal institutions do in fact conform to the normative ideal that Holmes envisioned for the law: that it should implement the moral consensus characteristic of today's society. To do this, legal scholars have to appraise the current reality of legal institutions and the current vision of social purposes in order to determine what gaps exist between the two, so that repairs might be undertaken.[30]

There still remains the question whether the Realists think the ideals against which legal institutions might be evaluated are absolute or are relative to a particular society at a particular time, as Holmes suggested. To resolve this issue, we need only to look once again at the historical context in which the Realist tradition matured. At the turn of the century, the Progressive political movement emerged as a reaction against the uncompromising economic libertarianism of late-nineteenth-century law, with its concomitant contribution to human misery among the poor and the working class. The Progressives conceived of society on an evolutionary model, and assumed that human beings had the capacity to promote increasingly humane and beneficial policies in the course of this social evolution. Although laissez-faire capitalism might have been appropriate for the young and growing economy of the nineteenth century, Progressives thought it was time to regroup and make provisions for the potential victims of unregulated capitalism. Holmes's remarks and the Sociological Jurisprudence of theorists like Roscoe Pound, Benjamin Cardozo, John Dickinson, and the early Felix Frankfurter emerged in turn as a reaction against what Progressives perceived as willfully obstructionist behavior on the part of appellate courts generally and the Supreme Court in particular with respect to economic reform legislation.

The subsequent work of the Legal Realists was similarly motivated, with the important difference that their views about ideals of justice matured in the 1920s and 1930s, after experiencing two disastrous calamities engineered by human beings: World War I and the stock market crash of 1929. As G. Edward White has explained,[31] these events were significant because they discredited the optimism implicit in the views of the early Progressives and the Sociological Jurisprudes who exhibited uncritical faith in the possibility of effective social planning in pursuit of liberal ideals.[32] The events of World War I made it tragically clear that a particular set of moral ideals did not necessarily remain constant or become more firmly entrenched in society. The stock market crash and ensuing depression reaffirmed that lesson for anyone who did not learn it the first time.

From these experiences the Realists concluded that no consensus about moral issues was assured: "[If law is] a means: *whose* means, to *whose* end? Discussions of law tend lightly to assume 'a society' and to assume the antecedent discovery of social objectives. . . . Where is the unity, the single coherent group?"[33] Even if some kind of consensus is available, there is no reason to conclude that it constitutes an improvement over the previous consensus. It is simply *our* consensus, the one to which we happen to be committed. As Llewellyn put it, the concept of a moral right is really nothing more than what is customary in our legal institutions:

> The idealists (and they, by the way, are orthodox and powerful, and have in this matter controlled the legal thinking of the past) see primary rights—my right, e.g., that you perform your agreement with me—almost as things. Almost, these primary rights are real. They are the *substance* of that insubstantial thing, the law. The idealists therefore have no great difficulty in thinking of you as having a perfectly good right which—simply because your only witness dies—is unenforceable. It is only the secondary thing, the remedy, which has failed. The right remains, to comfort you.
>
> The cynic, on the other hand, says: a right is best measured by effects in life. Absence of remedy is absence of right. Defect of remedy is defect of right. A right is as big, precisely, as what the courts will do. . . . I hold with the cynics.[34]

It is clear from this passage that Llewellyn regards rights as social constructs, relative to a particular time and a particular set of legal institutions. It is also easy to see how Llewellyn could be misinterpreted as a nihilist rather than a cultural and temporal ethical relativist. If rights are not *things* that enjoy an existence independent of whatever formulation they receive through our legal institutions, then how can laws express moral obligations or moral values? An alternative interpretation is available however, one more sympathetic to Llewellyn's real perspective. *Legal* rights are indeed only social constructs, but they are subject to comparison with another set of social constructs: the prevailing moral intuitions of a particular society at a particular time. All rights are social constructs, but some of them are culturally autonomous from legal rights, permitting normative evaluation of the latter:

> [Realists] suspect, with law moving slowly and the life around them moving fast, that some law may have gotten out of joint with life. This is a question in the first instance of fact: what does law *do,* to people, or for people? In the second instance, it is a question of ends: what *ought* law do to people, or for them? But there is no reaching a judgment as to whether any specific part of present law does what it ought, until you can first answer what it is doing now.[35]

Note that Llewellyn is asserting here not only that moral considerations are relevant to an evaluation of the law but also that there are two open questions to be addressed. In addition to the one about whether judge-made law is suited to its intended purposes, there is also a question about the purposes themselves. Should we endorse them, in light of our continually evolving social circumstances? The latter question suggests not that value judgments are irrelevant to an analysis of the law but that they are relative to time, place, and circumstances.

III

Thus far, we have examined the charges that Realists failed to grasp the extent of the influence of political ideology on judicial adjudication and that they would not confront the ethical relativism inherent in their own views. Both charges seem to be groundless. What, then, about the third charge, that CLS scholars think Realists had a failure of nerve?

As evidence for this view, G. Edward White has cited Llewellyn's 1940 article "On Reading and Using the Newer Jurisprudence," and Frank's preface to the 1949 edition of *Law and the Modern Mind.*[36] I presume the relevant passage in Llewellyn is the following:

> To Pound, the heart and core of jurisprudence is what the heart and core of jurisprudence ought to be to any scholar: to wit, right guidance to the judge—or to the legislator—or to the administrator. And I for one am ready to do open penance for any part I may have played[37] in giving occasion for the feeling that modern jurisprudes or any of them has ever lost sight of this. They seem to me to be singularly affected, one and all, with zeal for justice, and with zeal for improving the *legal* techniques for doing the law's business.[38]

These remarks need not be construed as a repudiation of Llewellyn's earlier views, however. He never proposed that legal institutions were not
intended to pursue moral purposes. He simply acknowledged that as implemented in the courtroom, laws did not always pursue those purposes effectively. As he had repeatedly asserted earlier,[39] the Realists were chiefly
interested in law reform, and to that end they certainly had goals in mind
as the potential end product of that reform movement. But none of that
precludes Realists from recognizing the purposes themselves as a product of
social decision making, subject to future revision.

> In Frank's case, I presume White had the following passage in mind: as some Roman
> Catholics have read into [Law and the Modern Mind] an implied criticism of the
> Scholastic (Thomistic) version of Natural Law, I want now to say this: I do not
> understand how any decent man today can refuse to adopt, as the basis of modern
> civilization, the fundamental principles of Natural Law, relative to human conduct,
> as stated by Thomas Aquinas.[40]

Here again the evidence for recanted heresy is weak. Frank does say he
believes in some general principles traditionally associated with Natural
Law doctrine, but he presents that belief as a conscious *choice* rather than
a *discovery*. He thinks that those who want to construct a "modern civilization," who value the features characteristic of such a society, will surely
choose likewise. Here too the implication is that the Realists embraced,
and continued to embrace, a form of cultural ethical relativism. The goal
was to develop a clear vision of the kind of society one would like to shape
by means of legal institutions, and then see what could be done about it in
the trenches, so to speak.

The same kind of attitude can be seen at work in the behavior of
William O. Douglas during his four decades on the Supreme Court. An
unrepentant Realist if ever there was one, Douglas repeatedly adopted the
practice of asking himself which decision in a case would best further the
larger purposes that he thought legal institutions ought to foster. Judicial
adjudication, for Douglas, was simply a matter of searching for a legal rationale for a predetermined right decision. The right decision was revealed not
by a review of precedent and statutory or constitutional language but by cast-
ing an eye toward the kind of society in which we should want to live:

> At bottom, *Skinner* and *Griswold* rested on two rhetorical questions that Douglas
> put in the course of his doctrinal analysis. The question in *Griswold* was stated
> explicitly: "Would we allow the police to search the sacred precincts of marital bed-

rooms for telltale signs of the use of contraceptives?" The question in *Skinner* had been posed implicitly when Douglas juxtaposed the hypothetical chicken thief and the habitual embezzler of chickens others had entrusted him. "Should we allow the state of Oklahoma to sterilize the thief but not the embezzler?" was the question. In both cases the answer was an immediate and obvious no. In those questions and the answers they elicited lay the essence of the cases: *Skinner* involved a patently unfair legislative classification and *Griswold* involved a patently intrusive legislative edict. Douglas sensed that both cases were "easy" cases in that sense: he knew that the result he reached was "right." The only difficulties were analytical, created by awkward doctrinal barriers.[41]

Confident that his own intuitions about the character of a desirable society were also embraced by most of his fellow citizens, Douglas was not afraid to base adjudication on political ideology. Good Realist that he was, he was convinced that his colleagues on the bench were surely doing the same, consciously or unconsciously.

IV

If the Critical Legal history of the divergences between the Legal Realism and CLS is flawed, we need to ask whether, after all, there is any difference between the two movements. For if there is not, if the Realists understood the influence that ideology has on adjudication, recognized the relativistic implications of their views, and embraced both of these in their scholarship, why then are we experiencing today the revival of an intellectual movement that was, if not dead and buried, at least co-opted by mainstream legal thought?

It seems to me that insofar as generalizations about these two rather heterogeneous groups are possible, there still remain two significant differences between the Realists and the Critical Legal scholars. First, the CLS movement does not share the Realists' optimism concerning the potential value of social science studies of legal institutions. Second, the kind of ethical relativism embraced by most Critical Legal scholars is different from, and philosophically more coherent than, the relativism characteristic of the Realists.

Concerning the first issue, the CLS reaction against Realist reliance on social science, that reaction was fueled by an intermediary: the Law and Society movement. One way to characterize the Law and Society movement is to think of it as a variant on the positive research program of the Realists, the legal reform program that was supposed to emerge from social science studies. The Law and Society movement departed from the Realist enterprise, however, to the extent that it abandoned the Realists' negative research program, the analysis of the scope of indeterminacy in the law.

After the concept of objective rule of law was symbolically reaffirmed when legal institutions were employed in the condemnation of the Nazis at Nuremberg, and once it appeared that the threat of totalitarianism might be held in check by the Cold War, the Law and Society movement revived the Realist conviction that the methods of the social sciences provided a better prospect for a genuine legal science than any rehabilitated form of legal reasoning. In fact Law and Society scholars proposed an even more ambitious program for social science research than did the Legal Realists. The Realists believed that social science might provide an analysis of the currently prevailing social norms that our society would like implemented in our legal institutions, together with an analysis of the gaps that existed between those consensual norms and the law as it was actually practiced.[42] But in the Law and Society movement the social sciences could also be relied upon to reveal the common features of human nature and therefore the conditions of human flourishing. On this view, instrumental studies of the gap between actual law and ideal purposes reveal the extent to which our legal institutions promote or detract from human flourishing. This approach offered an objective grounding for legal doctrine that the Realists no longer imagined possible:

> Society was perceived as an object, like the solar system, with invariant relationships and determinate regularities. In this context, social science could be imagined as a neutral technique to grasp the regularities that govern the operation of this object. . . . Most post-Realist scholars sought some substitute for the normative authority of the lost doctrinal tradition. . . . If society were a system obeying objective laws, and if positive science could identify those laws and unearth the social policies that were consistent with them, then policy formation would once again be grounded on a neutral and objective basis.[43]

This rehabilitation of social scientific studies of the law has run into trouble from a different quarter, however. During the interval between the demise of Realism and the emergence of the Law and Society movement, a considerable amount of philosophical work attacking traditional epistemology had emerged. Not only had the picture theory of knowledge[44] been called into question by the American Pragmatists and the Logical Positivists, but the Positivists' substitute[45] had been undermined in turn by collapsing the distinction between observation statements and theoretical statements, and that between facts and values.[46]

Critical Legal Studies, by its own account, was the first school of legal theory to really grasp the significance of the new epistemology.[47] Where the Law and Society movement was saddled with the antiquated epistemology of the logical positivists, CLS scholars recognized that the social sciences could not yield the kind of objectivism legal theorists still sought: "Many critics have questioned the positivist account of objectivity in social knowledge. . . . An alternative view, which I shall call 'discursivity' . . . starts with the recognition that social knowledge does not mirror an objective reality that is somehow 'out there,' but is instead part of the process through which social relations are formed and reformed . . . the very concepts we use to describe and explain society contribute to the constitution of social relations."[48] If social science accounts of social relations have this discursive effect, then from the CLS perspective the empirically oriented studies generated by the Law and Society movement, and the Legal Realists before them, were just inadvertent smokescreens for the creation of new ideology disguised as an objective parsing of social structures and social relations. In the case of the Law and Society movement, Trubek argued that the net effect of this pseudo-objectivity was usually the perpetuation of old ideology.[49]

The second difference between CLS and Legal Realism, the variation in the kind of relativism endorsed by the two movements is, in part, the basis for the first difference, but is I think far less widely recognized. Apart from the phenomenon of discursivity, Critical Legal scholars are compelled to reject Realist and post-Realist optimism about the objective validity of social science research because CLS does not recognize the existence of one of the principal subjects of that research. Instrumental gap studies about the divergence between legal ideals and law as practiced have some validity, but social science studies directed at revealing the proper goals of the legal reform movement are a chimera. From the CLS perspective, it doesn't matter whether the goals are conceived as the product of a shared vision that a particular society is trying, at a particular time, to articulate through its social institutions (the Realist view) or whether the goals devolve from an analysis of society as an object exhibiting invariant relationships and determinate regularities (the Law and Society view). Critical Legal scholars simply don't believe that social goals, conceived in either of these ways, actually exist, so there is no fact of the matter to be unearthed about the content of social goals by social science or by any other means.

What then do CLS advocates believe? This is a bit tricky because, as I noted earlier, CLS scholars are not a heterogeneous bunch. But to the extent that there is a common thread to their research, I would characterize them as existentialist jurisprudes. More specifically, I think a comparison between CLS scholarship and Jean-Paul Sartre's brand of atheistic existentialism is quite instructive. Consider Sartre's summary of value theory:

> Aetheistic existentialism . . . states that if God does not exist, there is at least one being in whom existence precedes essence, a being who exists before he can be defined by any concept, and that this being is man. . . . What is meant here by saying that existence precedes essence? It means first of all, man exists, turns up, appears on the scene, and only afterwards defines himself. . . . Thus, there is no human nature, since there is no God to conceive it. . . .
>
> Man is nothing else but what he makes of himself. Such is the first principle of existentialism. It is also called subjectivity, the name we are labeled with when charges are brought against us. . . . But if existence really does precede essence, man is responsible for what he is. Thus, existentialism's first move is to make every man aware of what he is and to make the full responsibility of his existence rest on him. And when we say that a man is responsible for himself, we do not only mean that he is responsible for his own individuality, but that he is responsible for all men. . . . In creating the man that we want to be, there is not a single one of our acts which does not at the same time create an image of man as we think he ought to be. To choose to be this or that is to affirm at the same time the value of what we choose.[50]

As far as I know, the parallels between CLS and Sartre's brand of existentialism have gone unnoticed, but they are quite dramatic. Critical scholars regard the Law and Society enterprise as misguided precisely because they do not subscribe to the view that there is an objective human essence to be explored, whether at the level of the individual or in our role as social animals. It is because CLS scholars believe that we are individually responsible for the value judgments we embrace that they are unsympathetic to the Realist conviction that jurisprudence ought to engage itself in the business of reforming legal institutions so that they conform to a currently prevailing orthodoxy about the purposes the law ought to serve. To use Sartre's language, the practice of appealing to a purported consensus about the purposes that legal institutions should foster is to engage in false consciousness, to hide behind a kind of determinism about values.[51]

Although it is true that Legal Realists, unlike some Law and Society scholars, do not conceive their commitment to a particular set of social values as being determined by analysis of some objective human essence and its implications for human flourishing, their commitment to social values is nonetheless contingent, not determined. Prevailing public sentiment is the source of the Realists' catalogue of social values, and that sentiment is already determined independently of the Realists' efforts to reveal it. It is the public will that legislatures should enact economic reform measures to reverse the social consequences of the economic libertarianism of nineteenth-century jurisprudence. The Realist is simply rendering the content and implications of that public will more explicit. For the CLS scholar, however, revelation of such a consensus, if indeed it exists at all, is not reason enough to endorse it. The Realist is simply refusing to acknowledge responsibility for advocating the values that he or she has attributed to a public consensus.[52] As far as the CLS scholar is concerned, the burden is on the Realist to explain why these values are worthy of pursuit. To embrace them simply because they are perceived to be widely shared is no justification at all.

To summarize, where the Legal Realist advocates a brand of cultural ethical relativism, with respect to a society's legal culture at least, the CLS scholar embraces subjective ethical relativism. Once the implications of existing legal practices are fully recognized, each must decide whether the practices are morally acceptable, or what alternative value system to advocate.

It is because CLS scholars believe that each individual has to come to grips with his or her own value judgments that, in their doctrinal analysis, they are concerned not with what the law *is* but with what it *does* in society. Instead of worrying about the actual content of legal doctrine, "critical scholars seek to expose the assumptions that underlie judicial and scholarly resolution of such issues, to question the presuppositions about law and society of those whose intellectual product is being analyzed, and to examine the subtle effects these products have in shaping legal and social consciousness."[53] Critical Legal Studies is conceived by its proponents as a component of transformative politics: by exposing the worldviews embedded in modern legal consciousness, CLS hopes to conduct a kind of mass psychotherapy whereby the flaws in that consciousness will be revealed to its adherents, so that they might subsequently be disposed to reform legal consciousness in progressive ways: "social actors, like psychoanalytic patients, can be freed of the constraints of delusions once the nature of the delusions is identified."[54] Once this has been achieved, individual members of the audience for CLS scholarship will be better disposed to make their own judgments about what constitutes progressive reform of our legal institutions. If their intuitions on this subject do not then conform to those of the CLS "psychoanalysts," however, nothing more remains to be said to them, for they have simply expressed a divergent value system in creating their vision of what humans ought to be. The best that Critical scholarship can hope for from the transformative enterprise is the emergence of some rough consensus in values, at least sufficient to inform a legal reform movement. But even that is not guaranteed, given the subjectivity of value judgments.

Upon examination, then, the real basis for distinguishing Critical Legal Studies from the Realist movement is the kind of value relativism embraced in each tradition. Apart from the programmatic sketch of that difference set forth above, the business of enumerating evidence for this interpretation of the CLS enterprise is beyond the scope of this chapter. But I think a proper recognition of the subjective ethical relativism inherent in most CLS scholarship will contribute significantly to clarifying much confusion about the thrust of that scholarship.[55]

Notes

1. The connection was first made by David Trubek in "Complexity and Contradiction in the Legal Order: Balbus and the Challenge of Critical Social Thought About Law," *Law and Society Review* 11 (1977): 540–45. It has subsequently surfaced in a variety of other places, e.g., "Note, 'Round and 'Round the Bramble Bush: From Legal Realism to Critical Legal Scholarship," *Harvard Law Review* 96 (1982): 1669; John Henry Schlegel, "Notes Towards an Intimate, Opinionated, and Affectionate History of the Conference on Critical Legal Studies," *Stanford Law Review* 36 (1984): 391; Mark Kelman, *A Guide to Critical Legal Studies* (Cambridge: Harvard University Press, 1987), 10–13, 45–48.

2. G. Edward White, "The Inevitability of Critical Legal Studies," *Stanford Law Review* 36 (1984): 650.

3. Ibid., 650–51.

4. G. Edward White, "From Realism to Critical Legal Studies: A Truncated Intellectual History," *Southwestern Law Journal* 40 (1986): 820. Even in White, "The Inevitability of Critical Legal Studies," the main thrust is to explain why the appeal to realism is a strategic error for CLS, which adopts at least the rhetoric of revolution rather than reform of existing legal institutions. From the CLS perspective, to be absorbed into mainstream jurisprudence is to be co-opted, neutralized, and even trivialized. If that was the fate of Legal Realism, CLS advocates should want no part of it.

5. For a few of the available examples of this folklore at work, see "Note, 'Round and 'Round the Bramble Bush"; Kelman, *Guide to Critical Legal Studies;* David Trubek, "Here the Action Is: Critical Legal Studies and Empiricism," *Stanford Law Review* 36 (1984): 593–598; Mark Tushnet, "Critical Legal Studies and Constitutional Law: An Essay in Deconstruction," *Stanford Law Review* 36 (1984): 623; Joan C. Williams, "Critical Legal Studies: The Death of Transcendence and the Rise of the New Langdells," *New York University Law Review* 62 (1987): 442–44; Elizabeth Mensch, "The History of Mainstream Legal Thought," in *The Politics of Law,* ed. David Kairys, rev. ed. (New York: Pantheon, 1990), 14, 21–33.

6. Cf. Karl Llewellyn, "Some Realism about Realism: Responding to Dean Pound," *Harvard Law Review* 44 (1931): 1239.

7. Karl Llewellyn, *The Bramble Bush* (New York: Oceana, 1951), 3.

8. See, e.g., "Note, 'Round and 'Round the Bramble Bush," 1676; Mensch, "The History of Mainstream Thought," 24–33.

9. Jerome Frank, *Law and the Modern Mind* (New York: Brentano's, 1930). Joan Williams argues that Frank thought reliance on a psychological analysis of the behavior of judges meant we could dispense with any appeal to legal doctrine to explain the outcome of cases. See Williams, "Critical Legal Studies," 443–44.

10. David M. Trubek and John Esser, "'Critical Empiricism' in American Legal Studies: Paradox, Program, or Pandora's Box?" *Law and Social Inquiry* 14 (1989): 9. See also Gary Peller, "The Metaphysics of American Law," *California Law Review* 73 (1985): 1159; White, "From Realism to Critical Legal Studies," 823.

11. See David M. Trubek, "Back to the Future: The Short, Happy Life of the Law and Society movement," *Florida State University Law Review* 18 (1990): 18–19.

12. See Williams, "Critical Legal Studies"; White, "The Inevitability of Critical Legal Studies," 667.

13. Felix Cohen, "Transcendental Nonsense and the Functional Approach," *Columbia Law Review* 35 (1935): 809.

14. See White, "From Realism to Critical Legal Studies," 823–24. As early as 1931 Roscoe Pound was questioning the heavy burden of responsibility that Realists had placed on the social sciences. See Pound, "The Call for a Realist Jurisprudence," *Harvard Law Review* 44 (1931): 702–4, where he charges Realists with a desire to set up "a science of law analogous to mathematical physics" and proceeds to question the feasibility of that project.

15. See, e.g., Pound, "The Call for a Realistic Jurisprudence"; Mortimer Adler, "Legal Certainty," *Columbia Law Review* 31 (1931): 91; Brendan Brown, "Natural Law and the Law-Making Function in American Jurisprudence," *Notre Dame Lawyer* 15 (1939): 9; Lon Fuller, *The Law in Quest of Itself* (Chicago: Foundation Press, 1940).

16. See G. Edward White, "From Sociological Jurisprudence to Realism: Jurisprudence and Social Change in Early Twentieth-Century America," *Virginia Law Review* 58 (1972): 1026; Edward Purcell, *The Crisis of Democratic Theory: Scientific Naturalism*

and the Problem of Value (Kentucky, Mass.: Lexington Books, 1973), John Henry Schlegel, "American Legal Realism and Empirical Social Science: From the Yale Experience," *Buffalo Law Review* 28 (1979): 459; Mensch, "The History of Mainstream Legal Thought," 24.

17. See Tushnet, "Critical Legal Studies and Constitutional Law," 625–27; Williams, "Critical Legal Studies," 485–88; Allan C. Hutchinson and Patrick J. Monahan, "Law, Politics, and the Critical Legal Scholars: The Unfolding Drama of American Legal Thought," *Stanford Law Review* 36 (1984): 204–5, 216–17.

18. *Lochner v. New York*, 198 U.S. 45 (1905), 75.

19. Willis van Devanter (appointed to the Supreme Court in 1910); James C. McReynolds (1914); George Sutherland (1922); and Pierce Butler (1922). Edward Sanford, appointed in 1923, also shared the same judicial philosophy.

20. The continuing influence of Stephen Field's judicial philosophy concerning property and contract law ensured similar decisions for the period between *Lochner* and the arrival of the last of the four horsemen. For a good discussion of this period, see G. Edward White, *The American Judicial Tradition*, expanded ed. (New York: Oxford University Press, 1988): 84–108, 178–99.

21. Frank, *Law and the Modern Mind*, 105. The writings of Robert Hale and Morris Cohen on the ways in which the concepts of property and contract were used in judicial adjudication provide good examples of this kind of work. Indeed, it is virtually indistinguishable from the kind of deconstructive analysis done by CLS scholars today. See Hale, "Coercion and Distribution in a Supposedly Non-Coercive State," *Political Science Quarterly* 38 (1923): 470; Hale, "Value and Vested Rights," *Columbia Law Review* 27 (1927): 523; Cohen, "Property as Sovereignty," *Cornell Law Quarterly* 13 (1927): 8; Cohen, "The Basis of Contract," *Harvard Law Review* 46 (1933): 553.

22. Frank, *Law and the Modern Mind*, 105–6.

23. In one area of judicial activity however, Frank did think that personal idiosyncrasies had a direct influence on judicial behavior, without the intervention of ideology. This was at the level of interpretation of the facts of a case, as distinct from the evaluation of rules and precedent. Ibid., 106. See also Frank's discussion of the distinction between rule skeptim and fact skepticism in the preface to *Law and the Modern Mind* (New York: Coward-McCann, 1949), viii–xvii.

24. Karl Llewellyn, "On Reading and Using the New Jurisprudence," *Columbia Law Review* 40 (1940): 605.

25. Llewellyn, *The Bramble Bush*, 3; italics Llewellyn's.

26. Karl Llewellyn, "A Realistic Jurisprudence—The Next Step," *Columbia Law Review* 30 (1930): 431.

27. Karl Llewellyn, "The Path of the Law," *Harvard Law Review* 10 (1897): 457.

28. See Llewellyn, "A Realistic Jurisprudence," 447–53, for Llewellyn's explanation of the difference between paper rules and real rules.

29. Ibid., 448–49.

30. I make no effort here to indicate either the proper rule, or the proper action on any legal subject. I do, however, argue . . . that as soon as one turns from the *formulation* of ideals to their *realization*, the approach here indicated is vital to his making headway It is only in terms of a sound descriptive science of the law . . . that ideals move beyond the stage of dreams." Ibid., 463–64. See also H. E. Yntema, "The Rational Basis of Legal Science," *Columbia Law Review* 31 (1931): 935: "The scientific movement in law in this country is obscured by its empirical devices, if there be not seen beneath them the quest of science to ascertain justice."

Frank provides yet another example of this kind of reasoning in the preface to the 1949 edition of *Law and the Modern Mind* (xxvi–xxvii):

> I was surprised at the comments of some critics that in this book I encouraged "anti-rationalism" and "antiidealism; devoted myself solely to what happens in the courts. . . . The truth is that, like most of the "constructive skeptics," I was motivated by an eager—perhaps too eager—desire to reform our judicial system, to inject, as far as feasible, more reason and more justice into its daily workings. To accomplish such reform, however, one needs to look at, not away from, the nonrational and nonidealistic elements at play now in court-house government. . . . There can be no greater hindrance to the growth of rationality than the illusion that one is rational when one is the dupe of illusions.

31. This discussion of the difference between Realism and Sociological Jurisprudence is inspired by White's "From Sociological Jurisprudence to Realism."

32. Ibid., 1007–8. Later (1024) White adds: "Sociological jurisprudence could just as easily have been termed progressive jurisprudence. Its philosophical premises—the inevitability of change, ultimate confidence in the ability of governmental mechanisms to respond to change, a desire to maintain certain values in the face of change . . . and a faith that moral and ethical 'rights' could be perceived and distinguished from 'wrongs'—were those of progressivism at large."

33. Llewellyn, "A Realistic Jurisprudence, 461.

34. Llewellyn, *The Bramble Bush*, 94. See also Joseph Bingham, "The Nature of Legal Rights and Duties," *Michigan Law Review* 12 (1912): 2, for a much earlier expression of this view: "The term *right* or the term *wrong* is but an asserted label which cannot be appreciated accurately except in the light of purposes which inspired and the mental processes which produced the application . . . [There is] no external measure of the correctness or incorrectness of a particular assertion of moral rectitude or delinquency." Compare also Benjamin Cardozo, *The Paradoxes of Legal Science* (New York: Columbia University Press, 1928), in which he abandons the assumption that continuous progress is the natural outcome of social evolution and concedes that although it is appropriate for judicial decisions to express current moral values, that set of values may be distinct from those accepted by the previous generation or the next one.

35. Llewellyn, "Some Realism about Realism," 1223.

36. White, "From Sociological Jurisprudence to Realism," 1026, n. 142.

37. Here Llewellyn cites the infamous passage from *The Bramble Bush*, 3. (See note 26, above, and accompanying text.)

38. Llewellyn, "On Reading and Using the New Jurisprudence," 603.

39. See notes 30 and 31, above, and accompanying text.

40. Frank, *Law and the Modern Mind*, xvii.

41. White, *The American Judicial Tradition*, 407.

42. Compare notes 10, 32, 33, 34, above, and accompanying text.

43. Trubek, "Back to the Future," 34–35.

44. According to the picture theory, knowledge consists of an accurate representation (usually verbal) of an external reality, and depends on careful definition of the abstract essences embodied in the set of objects and events that populate that reality.

45. Objects are no longer to be conceived as abstract essences; they are simply logical constructs composed from a collection of experiences or observations that we discern as being interrelated in some way. Electrons, for example, ought not be thought of as particular kind of entities existing independently of our cognition, the features of which we are attempting to discover. As far as our objectively valid knowledge claims go, electrons are really nothing more than a compendium of observable consequences of experimental procedures that we undertake and then lump together in a particular way to construct a theory of electrons. (See, e.g., A. J. Ayer, *Language, Truth, and Logic*, 2d ed. [New York: Dover, 1946].)

46. The work of Ludwig Wittgenstein and Willard van Orman Quine in the forties and fifties was particularly influential in this regard. It was further developed in the subfield of philosophy of science in the sixties by Norwood Russell Hanson, Thomas Kuhn, Paul Feyerabend, and others.

47. See Williams, "Critical Legal Studies," for a detailed account of the nature of the new epistemology and its influence on CLS.

48. Trubek, "Back to the Future," 34–35.

49. Trubek reasoned that the empirical studies conducted by Law and Society scholars tended to reinforce the ideological preconceptions that they were designed to expose. Although the avowed purpose of such studies was to demonstrate that law in action served the interests of powerful elites rather than the implementation of liberal ideals of justice, the success of these studies tended to reinforce the conviction that there was an inescapable necessity about this arrangement, i.e., that we should resign ourselves to the status quo. See Trubek, "Where the Action Is," 567. See also White, "From Realism to Critical Legal Studies," 834–35.

50. Jean-Paul Sartre, *Existentialism and Human Emotions* (New York: Philosophical Library, 1957), 15–17.

51. Ibid., 44–46.

52. "If you seek advice from a priest, for example, you have chosen this priest; you already knew, more or less, just about what advice he was going to give you. In other words, choosing your advisor is involving yourself." Ibid., 27.

53. Trubek, "Where the Action Is", 588–89.

54. Ibid., 610. Note also the parallel with the existentialist reliance on psychoanalysis. (See Sartre, *Existentialism and Human Emotions*, 68–83.) For a more detailed discussion of the transformative politics aspect of CLS, see my "Hegemony and Gender Law: Is Critical Legal Studies Empirical?" forthcoming.

55. A nice example of the extant confusion is illustrated by the reception of Joseph Singer's "The Player and the Cards: Nihilism and Legal Theory," *Yale Law Journal* 94 (1984): 1. Compare John Stick, "Can Nihilism Be Pragmatic?" *Harvard Law Review* 100 (1986): 332; Williams, "Critical Legal Studies"; Steve Fuller, "Playing Without a Full Deck: Scientific Realism and the Cognitive Limits of Legal Theory," *Yale Law Journal* 97 (1988): 549. For a discussion of the way in which the existentialist interpretation of CLS helps to illuminate this particular debate, see my "Critical Legal Studies, Nihilism, and Existentialist Jurisprudence," in progress.

Chapter 2

Indeterminacy and Equity

Lawrence B. Solum

This chapter investigates the relationship between two ideas about law: indeterminacy and equity. The first idea, legal indeterminacy, is the notion that legal outcomes, for example, judicial decisions, are not constrained by the legal rules, for example, constitutions, statutes, and case law. The second idea, equity, refers to the practice of departing from the rules in order to do justice in a particular case. The premise of this chapter is that exploring the idea of equity will illuminate the indeterminacy debate. In legal systems that incorporate the practice of equity, legal indeterminacy will hold in the following sense: for any legal rule, there is at least one possible case in which application of the rule would require one result, but equity would require a different result. This version of indeterminacy does not, however, undermine the liberal claim that contemporary legal systems in the North Atlantic democracies should and (for the most part) do adhere to the ideal of the rule of law. When equity is done by a judge who possesses the judicial virtues, departure from the rules is not the exercise of arbitrary discretion. Rather, a judge with judicial integrity is motivated to ensure that her departure from the letter of the rules accords with their spirit. Thus, our examination of the practice of equity leads to the conclusion that the way in which the law may be indeterminate is not necessarily inconsistent with the values associated with the rule of law.

My investigation of this thesis begins in the first section with a brief exploration of the debate over legal indeterminacy. My next step, in the second section, is to summarize Aristotle's account of the idea of equity. In the third section I analyze the relationship between the two ideas, developing the thesis that attention to the practice of equity illustrates an important sense in which the law does not determine the outcome of particular cases.

The Indeterminacy Thesis

Call the claim that the law (broadly defined to include the various sources of legal rules, such as cases, rules of procedure and evidence, regulations, statutes, constitutional provisions, and other legal materials) does not determine legal outcomes "the indeterminacy thesis." Claims about indeterminacy have been advanced by some (but only some) of the scholars associated with the Critical Legal Studies movement (CLS).[1] Liberal critics of CLS have argued that critical claims about indeterminacy are incorrect and even confused; critical legal scholars have replied by defending their claims about indeterminacy and by arguing that liberals have misunderstood the indeterminacy thesis. This debate has been called "the key issue in legal scholarship today,"[2] and it has also been referred to as "ultimately vacuous."[3] Given this disparity, the following observation by Drucilla Cornell is hardly surprising: "Perhaps no phrase has been more misunderstood by legal scholars than the 'indeterminacy thesis' developed by the Conference of Critical Legal Studies."[4] The debate over this thesis has a tangled history. The aim of this section is to clarify some of its aspects by identifying several distinct claims that might be made about the indeterminacy of law.

What Does Indeterminacy Mean?

Care about what is meant by indeterminacy is especially important because advocates and analysts of the thesis charge that it is badly misunderstood by its critics.[5] One approach to this charge of misunderstanding would be to attempt to identify the canonical version of the indeterminacy thesis and limit analysis to that version. Such an enterprise seems doomed to fail because there are almost as many different ideas about what the indeterminacy thesis really means as there are critical scholars who have addressed the topic. A better approach is to identify clearly the distinct versions of the indeterminacy thesis and then to consider each version on its own merits.

Before we begin to untangle the strands of the indeterminacy debate, we ought to put the debate in context by recalling the point of the indeterminacy thesis. Contemporary versions of the thesis are part of a radical critique of liberal legal theory. The overall thrust of the critique might be summarized by the slogan "Law is politics." The contrasting liberal claim is expressed by the ideal of the rule of law. The rule of law is a complex notion,[6] but if the indeterminacy thesis is true, then legal justice will fall short of the ideal of the rule of law in at least three ways: judges will rule by arbitrary decision because radically indeterminate law cannot constrain judicial decision; the laws will not be public, in the sense that the indeterminate law that is publicized could not be the real basis for judicial decision; and there will be no basis for concluding that like cases are treated alike because the very idea of legal regularity is empty if law is radically indeterminate.

A Brief Review of the Indeterminacy Debate

The following discussion summarizes several moves made in the indeterminacy debate, with the aim of identifying different versions of the indeterminacy thesis. Exposition begins with the strongest or most radical version of the thesis. An objection to this version is considered, followed by a variety of defenses and modifications of the thesis. At the outset, let me disclaim any pretense of providing a full and fair exposition of the debate; my selective review highlights themes that will serve the purpose of this chapter—an examination of the relationship between equity and indeterminacy.

The Strong Thesis or Radical Indeterminacy. Our investigation of the indeterminacy debate begins with the formulation of the strongest (the most ambitious) claim about the indeterminacy of law. As a preliminary formulation, we might say that "the strong indeterminacy thesis" is the claim that in every possible case, any possible outcome is legally correct. In other words, the strong indeterminacy thesis is the claim that the law is radically indeterminate. In a prior article, I distinguished between this "strong" version of the indeterminacy thesis with what I called "weak" versions of the thesis—versions that make a qualified or relatively modest claim about indeterminacy.[7] This section investigates the strong thesis; weak versions are considered below.

Our preliminary and somewhat informal statement of the strong indeterminacy thesis can be made more precise by analyzing its constituent elements. A case is a legal event in which a court or other legal body processes a legal unit (identified by pleadings or other legal actions) that includes a set of facts about actions and events. The final outcome of a case is the end product of the processing of facts and law by the court. Typically, in Anglo-American courts, the final outcome of a case includes three elements: the decision (a verdict for one or more parties); the order (a criminal sentence or civil relief); and the opinion (a formal statement of the reasons for a decision). Reformulated in accord with this analysis, the strong thesis makes the following claim:

> In any set of facts about actions and events that could be processed as a legal case, any possible decision, order, or opinion will be legally correct.

To falsify the strong indeterminacy thesis, then, one would need to establish that there is at least one possible case in which at least one possible outcome is legally incorrect. Of course, this refutation would disprove the strong indeterminacy thesis only in the sense stipulated here; it would not establish that the law is always, usually, or even frequently determinate.[8]

The Argument from Easy Cases. One way to establish that there is at least one possible case in which at least one outcome is legally incorrect could be called "the argument from easy cases."[9] In its simplest form, the argument from easy cases points to a hypothetical case in which only one outcome seems consistent with the norms of legal correctness.[10] The following paragraph attempts to formulate one such easy case.

Consider the following case, consisting of facts, a legal rule, and a legal event. First, postulate the following set of events and actions: I (the author) visited Point Magu State Beach in Ventura County, California, between the hours of 12:30 P.M. and 4:00 P.M. on Sunday, February 14, 1996. Second, consider the following legal rule: Section 2 of the Sherman Antitrust Act states, "Every person who shall monopolize or attempt to monopolize, or combine or conspire with any other person or persons, to monopolize any part of the trade or commerce among the several States, or with foreign nations, shall be deemed guilty of a felony."[11] Third, consider the following claim about a possible case: my visit to the beach on the date and time specified would not constitute a violation of Section 2 of the Sherman Act. Of course, fully to convince you of this, I would need to tell you more about what went on at the beach on that day. The details will include my looking at the ocean, speaking with friends about politics, reading a book, and so forth. Children flew kites; a friend grilled chicken and hot dogs. You might want to know whether I discussed any business dealings at the beach. I did not. But no matter how many questions you asked, no matter how hard you tried, you would not be able to make out a legally valid case that the Sherman Act was violated. If a prosecution were filed against me, the only correct result would be a verdict of innocence. Of course, it is possible that things would go wrong in some way. Perjury might be committed; the judge assigned to the case might be deranged. Our system of justice is hardly foolproof, but that does not entail the further conclusion that any result is legally correct.

Predictability Distinguished from Legal Correctness. The upshot of my example of an easy case is this: there is at least one possible case in which at least one possible outcome is legally incorrect. Therefore, the strong indeterminacy thesis (as I have defined it) is false. Notice my argument is not that the outcome of an antitrust prosecution based on the facts I outline is predictable.[12] Rather, my claim is that only one outcome would be legally correct.[13] If the law is correctly applied and the witnesses testify truthfully, the prosecution should fail.

A further piece of clarification is in order at this point. What is meant by "legally correct" in this context? The question is important because the indeterminacy thesis is itself a challenge to the notion that there is such a thing a legal correctness, and it might be contended that by smuggling in an undefined standard of legal correctness, my argument begs the question and assumes what I set out to demonstrate. For the purposes of the argument so far, I mean the phrase "legally correct" to refer to the understandings of competent[14] legal practitioners, that is, of judges, lawyers, other participants in the legal system—those who take up what H. L. A. Hart calls the "internal point of view."[15] My claim is that with respect to easy cases, there will be a strong consensus on what constitutes the legally correct outcome in easy cases among those who take up the internal point of view. Notice then, that I am not making the claim that those who do not take up the internal point of view will agree about easy cases, nor am I claiming that those who do take up the internal point of view will reach a strong consensus about more difficult cases.

But Is My Example Really a Case? At this point, one might object that there is an illicit move in my argument. I have set up a hypothetical case in which I am prosecuted for violating Section 2 of the Sherman Act based on an actual trip to the beach. Is this legitimate? Could such a legal event really be called a case? This section pursues the argument that lies behind these questions. Anthony D'Amato has raised similar concerns with respect to another alleged easy case:

> "If a homeowner eats ice cream in the privacy of her home, it will not give rise to any legal action." But there is no dispute here! No one is claiming that the home-owner has injured anyone else by eating ice cream, and hence there is no occasion to cite a legal rule that she may have violated. . . .
>
> Nonetheless, given temporary license to be gruesome, the [advocate of the inde-terminacy thesis] can supply such a case: the homeowner's child is starving (and indeed starves to death) while the homeowner eats ice cream. In this case, the homeowner's action (or inaction) gives rise to a criminal case; the state will (or at least should) bring charges of criminal manslaughter.[16]

D'Amato makes two points in his attempt to refute this example of the argument from easy cases. First, the ice cream example is not a case because no legal event has occurred. Second, one can add facts to the hypothetical situation so that the legal outcome would be changed.

The first charge is a fair one, although one can alter the example to add a legal event, such as the charge of manslaughter that D'Amato himself adds in the second paragraph of the quoted passage. The trip-to-the-beach example introduced above does provide such a legal event—a Sherman Act prosecution.

D'Amato might respond that the addition of the hypothetical prosecu-tions is not sufficient to transform a simple trip to the beach into a case. Just as no prosecutor would have any reason to prosecute the innocent homeowner (the one who didn't have a starving baby) for manslaughter, no one in the Antitrust Division of the Justice Department would see my expedition to Point Magu as a case. In normal circumstances, of course, this is absolutely right. Our perception of the beach trip or the ice cream case is filtered by our understanding of what constitutes a legally redressable wrong, and we do not see such a wrong in these easy cases.

The question is, "What shall we make of the fact the law shapes our perception of what constitutes a case?" This fact does not show that the law is radically indeterminate. Rather, the phenomenon that D'Amato identi-fies is powerful evidence that the strong indeterminacy thesis, as I have defined it, is untrue. The fact that the law shapes our perception of what counts as a case is very persuasive evidence for the proposition that the law does in some way determine outcomes.

The second point—that the hypothetical can be changed so as to change the legally correct outcome—is not responsive to the argument from easy cases. Let us stipulate for the sake of argument that it is always be possible to add facts to an easy case such that the addition of the new facts will change the legally correct outcome of the case. This does not demonstrate that there are no easy cases. Quite the contrary, the fact that the advocate of the strong indeterminacy thesis needed to add facts to the easy case in order to change the legally correct outcome shows that as originally stated, the easy case was not indeterminate.[17] Putting the point a bit differently, we might say that the new facts or the changed facts tend to confirm rather than topple the judgment about the old facts.[18] If the strong indeterminacy thesis were true, then a reasonable legal argument should be available on the facts as originally stated in the hypothetical. The additional facts should not be necessary. That facts must be added to transform the easy case into a hard one demonstrates that the law does constrain the set of legally correct outcomes.

Weak Versions of the Indeterminacy Thesis. This chapter certainly will not settle the matter,[19] but let us assume that the strong indeterminacy thesis is not viable. One might still defend the notion that the law is indeterminate by advancing what I call a "weak" version of the thesis. For example, it might be conceded that there are some cases that are determinate, but that all important legal cases are indeterminate: this might be called the "important-case indeterminacy thesis." Or it might be conceded that the law sometimes does determinate the outcome of cases, but that this could be otherwise—in other words, that indeterminacy is always a possibility. Because this weak version of the thesis uses the modal ideas of necessity and possibility, we might call it "the modally weakened indeterminacy thesis."

In addition, one might qualify the indeterminacy thesis by introducing a distinction between "indeterminacy" and "underdeterminacy" of law. Thus far, I have accepted the implicit assumption that indeterminacy and determinacy are exhaustive categories, that is, that the decision of a case either is determined by the law or is indeterminate. This assumption is not correct. A legal dispute may be constrained by the law but not determined by it.

Roughly, a case is underdetermined by the law if the outcome (including the formal mandate and the content of the opinion) can vary within limits that are defined by the legal materials.[20] This approximation can be made more precise by considering the relationship between two sets of outcomes of a given case. The first set consists of all imaginable results—all the imaginable variations in the mandate (affirmance, reversal, remand, etc.) and in the reasoning of the opinion. The second set consists of the outcomes that can be squared with the law—the set or legally acceptable outcomes. The distinctions between indeterminacy, underdeterminacy, and determinacy of the law with respect to a given case may be marked with the following definitions.

> The law is *determinate* with respect to a given case if and only if the set of results that can be squared with the legal materials contains one and only one member.
>
> The law is *underdeterminate* with respect to a given case if and only if the set of results that can be squared with the legal materials is a non-identical subset of the set of all imaginable results.
>
> The law is *indeterminate* with respect to a given case if the set of results that can be squared with the legal materials is identical with the set of all imaginable results.

The notion of a "hard case" can now be explicated with reference to the category of underdetermination. A case is a "hard case" if the outcome is underdetermined by the law in a way such that the appellate judge must choose among legally acceptable outcomes in a way that changes who will be perceived as the "winner" and who the "loser."

The point is that the outcome of a case need not be completely indeterminate in order for it to be a hard case; a case in which the results are underdetermined by the law will be "hard" if the legally acceptable variation makes the difference between loss or victory for the litigants.[21] Thus, a weak version of the indeterminacy thesis might be the following: most (or almost all) cases that are actually litigated are hard cases. Let us call this "the actually-litigated-indeterminacy thesis." This claim about indeterminacy is not refuted by the argument from hypothetical easy cases. Confirmation of the actually-litigated-indeterminacy thesis would require empirical investigation. There is, however, an important question about the critical force of this version of the thesis: if potential litigants choose not to settle in part on the basis of indeterminacy, does the actually-litigated-indeterminacy thesis have any critical bite? I will not answer this question in this chapter, but I will observe that some of the rule-of-law values will be served by a system that settles disputes on the basis of law, even if that settlement occurs outside the judicial process.

Epistemic and Metaphysical Indeterminacy. One more point needs to be made about the content of the indeterminacy thesis: is it the indeterminacy of the law itself or of our knowledge about the law that is at issue? Ken Kress calls the claim that the law itself is indeterminate "metaphysical indeterminacy" and the claim that it is our knowledge of the law that is indeterminate "epistemic indeterminacy." As Kress explains the distinction:

> Metaphysical indeterminacy speaks to whether *there is* law; epistemic indeterminacy, to whether the law *can be known.* We might say that question of abortion in a particular jurisdiction is metaphysically (or ontologically) determinate (at some particular time) if there is a right answer to question whether a woman has a right to an abortion in that jurisdiction. It might nevertheless be epistemically indeterminate whether women have that right, because the right answer is not demonstrable, or because there is no method for determining the right answer, or because there is great controversy among lawyers or other persons about what that right answer is.[22]

A legal question can be epistemically indeterminate without being metaphysically indeterminate, but not vice versa. With this final point from the contemporary debate in view, let us turn our attention to another distinction that has not heretofore been fully articulated.

Indeterminacy from What Point of View

So far, my discussion has assumed that the indeterminacy thesis is a claim about the outcomes of particular cases from an ex-post perspective. The ex-post perspective could be defined as the perspective of someone looking back at the outcome of the case, after the facts and the law have been processed by the legal system. The nature of the ex-post perspective can be elaborated by considering in more detail the ways in which the legal system processes facts and law.

Courts process facts in a variety of ways. At trial, evidence is introduced in formal proceedings bound by the rules of evidence. Judges, attorneys, and court reporters participate in the production of a formal record. The finder of fact (a judge or jury) may make formal finding of facts in the form of a written opinion or answers to special interrogatories. After the trial stage, the facts may be limited to this formal record. At earlier stages, facts are introduced by way of formal pleadings in connection with a motion for judgment on the pleadings; declarations, depositions, and other material can be brought before a court considering a motion for summary judgment.

Courts also process law using a variety of mechanisms. Briefs and oral arguments bring particular constitutional provisions, statutes, regulations, rules, and precedents to the attention of the judge or judges. Judges and their law clerks engage in legal research. In addition to this process of law finding, courts also receive various inputs regarding the interpretation of the law. Such input may come in the form of argument by the parties, analysis by a law clerk, or the creative legal thinking of a judge or group of judges.

Thus, the claim that there is ex-post indeterminacy of outcomes is the claim that the law does not determine decisions, orders, and opinions in particular cases in which (a) the facts are already fixed through formal legal proceedings and (b) the law has already been processed to the extent that the relevant legal materials have been identified. The claim could be put a bit differently as follows: any possible outcome of a case that has progressed to the stage in which conditions (a) and (b) have been met, can be made legally correct by input in the form of interpretations of fact or by legal argument and analysis or by a combination of these.[23]

The ex-post perspective is distinguished from an ex-ante perspective, looking at the case before it has been processed at a point in time where the facts have yet to be determined and the relevant law is yet to be identified.[24] What is the meaning of the claim that law is indeterminate from the ex-ante perspective? Consider two possibilities.

First, the claim that law is indeterminate from the ex-ante perspective might be given the following interpretation: before facts are found and law identified in a particular case, the outcome of that case is epistemologically indeterminate—any outcome is consistent with what is known about the case. Even this claim may not be true if construed in the most ambitious way possible. Even without knowing anything at all about a possible case arising under American law, I may know that some outcomes are legally incorrect, at least so long as we are limiting the set of possible cases to those that might arise in the future of the actual world, given that the laws of physics do not change. For example, in no possible case would the legally correct outcome be an injunction requiring that the Joseph Stalin who led the Soviet Union during the Second World War be president of the United States. We might

modify the ex-ante indeterminacy claims as follows: before one knows anything about the facts and law (including the identity of the legal system and
the possible world in which the case occurs) in a particular case, the outcome of that case is epistemologically indeterminate. This claim is true, but
it is absolutely trivial. If one knows nothing about a possible state of affairs,
one knows nothing about what the law requires in that state of affairs.

Consider a second interpretation of ex-ante indeterminacy. The claim
that the law is indeterminate from an ex-ante perspective might be stated
as follows: there is no formulation of the set of legal rules such that the satisfaction of the conditions specified by a given rule is sufficient to determine the outcome of all cases that satisfy those conditions. This
formulation is somewhat abstract. It can be clarified in two ways. The first
clarification, a rough approximation of the idea, is this: for any legal rule,
there will be an exceptional case, in which the rule would lead to one outcome, but the legally correct outcome is quite different. The second clarification, a more formal elaboration of the second interpretation of the
ex-ante thesis, can be expressed by use of two definitions:

> *The Full Specification of a Legal Rule.* For any legal rule R in a legal sys-
> tem S, the full specification of the rule will consist of a set of descriptions
>
> 1. C, which includes the condition descriptions $c_1, c_2, \ldots c_n$ that spec-
>   ify the event types that trigger the application of the rule,
> 2. E, which includes the exception descriptions $e_1, e_2, \ldots e_n$ that spec-
>   ify the event types that constitute exceptions to the rule, and
> 3. O, which specify the outcomes $o_1, o_2, \ldots o_n$ that are the event types
>   the subsequent occurrence of which are required by the rule.[25]

> *The Ex-Ante Indeterminacy Thesis.* For every legal rule R of legal system
> S, there is a possible case P, such that P satisfies the conditions of C and
> does not satisfy any exception in E, but in which the set O specified by
> R in these conditions is not the legally correct outcome.

This is the version of the indeterminacy thesis that will be the subject of
the remainder of this essay.

Equity

The term "equity" has acquired a number of meanings in contemporary
legal discourse. Legal historians use "equity" to describe the law adminis-

tered by the Court of Chancery in England and other common law countries. Some economists use the same term to refer to the idea of distributive justice. Our word "equity" is from the Middle English "equite," which
in turn is from Old French; the next step back is to the Latin word
"aequitas,"[26] which was the Roman rendering of the Greek *epieikeia*.[27] The
classic sense of this term was fixed by Aristotle; it refers to a quality of character, which we might translate as fair-mindedness. The classical idea of
equity refers to a practice as well as a virtue. Doing equity is doing what is
fair in the particular case, when the written rule (whether prescribed by
statute, regulation, or decisional law) would lead to an unfair result. Equity
is premised on the observation that written rules will inevitably lead to
unfair results in some cases because of the inherent generality of rules and
the infinite variety of particular human circumstances.

The classical notion of equity as departure from the rules is rooted in
Aristotle, and the best exposition is Aristotle's statement of the problem of
equity and justice in chapter 10 of book 5, *Nicomachean Ethics*:

> What causes the difficulty is the fact that equity is just, but not what is legally just:
> it is a rectification of legal justice. The explanation of this is that all law is uni-
> versal, and there are some things about which it is not possible to pronounce
> rightly in general terms; therefore in cases where it is necessary to make a general
> pronouncement, but impossible to do so rightly, the law takes account of the
> majority of cases, though not unaware that in this way errors are made. And the
> law is none the less right; because the error lies not in the law nor in the legisla-
> tor but in the nature of the case; for the raw material of human behavior is essen-
> tially of this kind.[28]

As is frequently the case with Aristotle, the text is ambiguous. Nonetheless, one Aristotelian view is that the practice of equity has at least two fundamental and interconnected characteristics, which I shall call *rule
transcendence* and *particularism*.[29]

By the claim that equity is a rule-transcendent practice, I mean that
equity takes into account the spirit of the legal rules but goes beyond their
letter. This rather mysterious formulation can be given a straightforward and
familiar gloss. Any general rule may be overinclusive or underinclusive with
respect to the goal the rule is meant to achieve.[30] Tentatively, we might
hypothesize that in many cases, this lack of perfect fit between purpose and
rule does *not* justify a departure from the rule. In these cases, the best course
of action for an adjudicator is to accept the cost of less than perfect justice

in order to achieve publicity, regularity, and predictability—some of the values associated with the idea of the rule of law. In other cases, however, application of the rule might lead to serious injustice in the particular case; moreover, in some such cases a departure from the rule may not pose a serious threat to the rule of law values. Let us hypothesize a category of cases in which the best result involves a departure from the rule in the particular case; this category represents the domain of the legal practice of equity.

Elaborating on Aristotle's formulation, we might say that equity corrects the law's generality by filling gaps in the law, by adjusting conflicts and tensions among legal provisions, and by making exceptions in cases in which the rule leads to unanticipated and unjust results. Along with Aristotle, we can observe that an equitable departure from the rules can relate to the intentions of legislators[31] in two distinct ways. In some cases, doing equity requires the judge to realize the intention of the legislator. In other cases, it may require the judge to correct a defect in the law that the legislator did not or could not have anticipated—for example, in cases in which circumstances have changed or previously unknown facts have come to light.

The second characteristic of equity was particularism. Equity tailors the law to the requirements of the particular case. The Aristotelian idea of equity as a response to the particular case is rooted in a conception of practical reason. To be even more specific, the practice of equity requires a decision maker who has the moral vision to see the conflict between law and justice, and the practical judgment to frame an appropriate response; in Aristotle's terms, such a person is a *phronimos,* one who possesses the intellectual virtue of *phronesis* or practical wisdom.

Understanding equity as a particularized practice allows us to distinguish it from other practices that involve a departure from legal rules. For example, equity is not identical to the resolution of conflicts between law and morality in favor of the latter. Judges might nullify a statute that legalized the practice of human slavery on the ground that slavery is always morally wrong. This is not an example of the practice of equity, because such a decision would not involve a departure from the rule on the basis of the facts of the *particular* case. Rather, the decision would be based on a general moral principle—that statutes establishing the institution of slavery are so wicked that they may never be enforced. The key difference is between the notion that the rule should be disregarded because it is the wrong rule and the notion that the rule should not be followed even though it may be the best available rule.

Indeterminacy as Equity

The thesis of the chapter can now be restated: in a legal system that allows the practice of equity, the ex-ante indeterminacy thesis is true. My defense of this thesis has two parts: an elaboration of what would constitute a legal system allowing the practice of equity; and an argument that the ex-ante indeterminacy thesis holds in any system that allows the practice of equity.

The first task is to elaborate on the idea that the practice of equity can be incorporated into a legal system. What does a legal system have to do in order to allow the practice of equity? The answer to this question is that there are many different practices that would count as implementations of the practice of equity. Consider three possibilities. First, a legal system might grant ordinary judges the power to do equity. Each judge would have the authority to depart from the legal rules when fairness and the circumstances of the individual case required that result. Second, a special tribunal might be given the authority to override the decisions of ordinary legal tribunals. This notion may describe the self-understanding of the chancellors during an early period in the history of English equity.[32] Third, practices of rule interpretation might incorporate the idea of equity into the theories of statutory and constitutional interpretation that guide rule application. References to purposive or equitable interpretation of statutes may reflect this third method of institutionalizing the practice of equity.

The second task is to argue that the ex-ante indeterminacy thesis holds in any system that does allow the practice of equity. Recall that the ex-ante indeterminacy thesis is the contention that for any legal rule, there is a possible case, such that there is one correct outcome if only the rule and its exceptions are considered as grounds for decision, but the legally correct outcome is not that outcome. More formally, we put it: "For every legal rule R of legal system S, there is a possible case P, such that P satisfies the conditions of C [the triggering conditions of the rule] and does not satisfy any exception in E, but in which the set O [of outcomes] specified by R in these conditions is not the legally correct outcome."

How can one show that the ex-ante indeterminacy thesis holds in systems that allow the practice of equity? There is a difficulty here. Consider two strategies for producing an argument that the thesis holds. The first strategy would rely on an a priori or theoretical argument. This strategy seems likely to fail, given the Aristotelian account of equity as particularistic. The reasons for equitable departures from the rules are rooted in particular cases and not in some general feature of legal cases that can be identified a priori or deduced from a theory of law.[33]

The second strategy for showing that the ex-ante indeterminacy thesis holds would be a practical argument. One would take examples of legal rules and show that there are possible cases in which the result required by the rule would not be the equitable result. One would then argue that such examples offer a good reason to take the ex-ante thesis as established for practical purposes.

Consider the following examples. The general rule is that the president must be thirty-five years of age, but the particular circumstances are that a deadly plague has killed almost all Americans over that age. The general rule is that no vehicle shall be driven in the park, but the particular circumstance is that an ambulance entered the park in order to save a heart-attack victim. The general rule is that no one shall sleep in the railroad station, but the particular circumstance is that a passenger dozed off late at night while waiting for a connection. One can imagine that the offering of such examples might go on for quite some time.

Of course, this second strategy also has a problem: it does not prove that the ex-ante indeterminacy thesis is true—it only offers confirming evidence. No matter how many such examples are offered, the ex-ante indeterminacy thesis may still be disproved by offering an example of a single rule for which there is no such equitable exception.[34] Assume that by offering many examples of ex-ante indeterminacy of particular rules, the advocate of the ex-ante thesis has succeeded in shifting the burden of persuasion to the opponents of the thesis.

The burden is now on the opponents of ex-ante indeterminacy to produce a rule without exceptions, a "perfectly equitable rule," so to speak. The problem of argument by example shifts with the burden of proof. No matter how many examples of an allegedly perfectly equitable rule are given, each example can be refuted by producing even a single case in which the equitable outcome is different from that selected by the rule. Even the failure to produce such an exceptional case may simply reflect a lack of imagination on the part of those involved in the debate rather than nonexistence of the case.

Suppose that the following pattern emerges from the debate. Advocates of the ex-ante thesis produce many examples of legal rules for which there is at least one case in which the equitable outcome differs from the outcome selected by the rule. Although opponents of the thesis come up with many rules that seem plausible candidates of the perfectly equitable rule, advocates of the ex-ante indeterminacy thesis manage to come up with clever counterexamples in almost every case. What would we make of the pattern of argument that gives rise to this impasse?

This last question gains some urgency because the hypothesized pattern of argument arguably characterizes the existing debate over indeterminacy. The pattern is not yet in focus for two reasons: first, because the advocates of the indeterminacy thesis frequently fail to specify with precision what they mean by the indeterminacy thesis, and second, because the critics of the thesis usually have the strong ex-post indeterminacy thesis as their target. Nonetheless we have already seen something close to the hypothetical pattern of argument in the case of the underaged president.[35] Adding facts to a case (e.g., adding the plague) to make it indeterminate is an illegitimate move if one is attempting to demonstrate that the strong ex-post indeterminacy thesis is true, but the same move is legitimate if made in support of the ex-ante indeterminacy thesis.

So what do we make of the indeterminacy debate, if we understand the debate as having implicitly addressed the truth of the ex-ante indeterminacy thesis? First, if one can usually or almost always produce examples in which equitable outcomes differ from the outcomes sanctioned by a given legal rule, then a weak (but not trivial) version of the ex-ante thesis has been confirmed: "For most legal rules R of our legal system S, there is a possible case P, such that P satisfies the conditions of C and does not satisfy any exception in E, but in which the set O specified by R in these conditions is not the legally correct outcome." Second, until a knockdown example of a perfectly equitable rule is produced, the evidence for the strong version of the ex-ante thesis seems sufficiently convincing for acceptance of the thesis as a working hypothesis. We might say that we have practical confirmation of the strong ex-ante indeterminacy thesis. Third, given that the ex-ante hypothesis is a hypothesis of practical reason, practical confirmation is all that we should expect. This is not the sort of matter where deductively valid arguments will provide a resolution that will convince all with apodictic certainty. In sum, I have identified a plausible strategy for arguing that the ex-ante thesis holds in any system that allows the practice of equity. The strategy depends on the discussion of many specific cases—something that I have not yet done—but it does seem at least plausible, if not likely, that the necessary work could be done to produce the confirming examples.

Advancing the debate to this point leaves a critical question unanswered: does the practical confirmation of the ex-ante indeterminacy thesis undermine the liberal claim that contemporary legal systems in the North Atlantic democracies should and do (to some substantial degree) adhere to the ideal of the rule of law? An answer to that question requires the answers to two prior questions. First, do modern legal systems allow the practice of equity? Second, does the practice of equity undermine the rule of law?

The question as to whether equity is practiced in particular contemporary legal systems requires a complex empirical investigation that is outside the scope of this chapter. In the case of the current legal system of the United States, however, there are some obvious starting points for the inquiry. Among these starting points are the following: (1) the survival of the equitable powers of the judges of courts of general jurisdiction, (2) the role of informed discretion in a variety of legal contexts, (3) the use of case-by-case balancing tests, (4) the principle that statutes should be construed so as to avoid an absurd or manifestly unjust result, and (5) the use of arguments of principle and policy in the decision-making process of American judges. A variety of legal phenomena seem, on the surface at least, to point toward the existence of legal practices that incorporate the practice of equity.

As to the second question, whether the practice of equity undermines the rule of law, I have argued on another occasion that the answer is no.[36] A good case can be made for the claim that the values of the rule of law are served best by a system that allows departure from the letter of the law in order to serve its spirit. Again, a full development of the argument is outside the scope of this chapter, in part because the argument relies on what I have called a "virtue-centered theory of judging"—the full explication of which cannot be accomplished in this chapter. The core notion of that theory is that legally correct decisions are those that would be made by a virtuous judge, that is, by a judge possessing the judicial virtues, including judicial intelligence and wisdom as well as judicial courage, good temper, and justice. Given this very bald statement of the theory, three brief points can be made in support of the proposition that the practice of equity is not necessarily incompatible with the rule of law.

First, when equity is done by a virtuous judge, departure from the rules is not the exercise of arbitrary discretion. One of the characteristics of a good judge is the possession of the virtue of judicial integrity, and an adjudicator with this virtue cares about the coherence of the law and is motivated to insure that her departure from the letter of the rules accords with their spirit. The purposes and values immanent in the law itself still hold sway, despite the departure from the letter of the law. As Judith Shklar put a related point, "In Aristotle's account the single most important condition for the Rule of Law is the character one must impute to those who make lawful judgments. Justice is the constant disposition to act fairly and lawfully."[37]

The second argument for reconciliation of the rule of law with the practice of equity is that the notion of moral and legal vision that grounds the practice of equity is also necessary to understanding the application of legal rules. Rule application can take place only after a judge comprehends the facts of the case. Moral and legal vision is required in order to reveal that a case is governed by a rule. For this reason, both the application of legal rules and the practice of equity require the virtue of judicial wisdom or *phronesis*. We all know that it is possible to produce arbitrary and unpredictable results by strictly adhering to the letter of the law. Perhaps the most familiar example of this phenomenon is the practice of labor unions disrupting a work environment by working to the book, adhering strictly to the letter but not the spirit of the rules. This takes us back to Aristotle's discussion of the basis for equity: no general rule can be framed with sufficient precision to yield the expected outcome in all particular cases. In some cases, the practice of equity will make outcomes conform to expectations and hence make the law more rather than less predictable.

The third argument for the reconciliation of law and equity is that the recognition of equity as a distinct practice may serve to increase the regularity and predictability of rule application in the legal system as a whole. Without a publicly acknowledged practice of equity, the pressure to do justice in particular cases may be relieved by loosening the constraints that legal rules place upon judicial decision in general. "Equity will out," we might say to summarize a point first made by Roscoe Pound.[38] Undergirding this argument is the assumption that the degree to which a system of rules constrains the actual decisions made by adjudicators is a matter of social practice: a system can be tightly rule bound or loosely rule guided. If equitable departure from legal rules is an accepted and acknowledged (but limited) exception within a general practice in which legal rules determine outcomes, then judges can tolerate the constraint of binding rules. Without this safety valve, judges will have good reason to engage in interpretive practices that give them considerable freedom of choice in every case and not just the exceptional one. Assuming that the pressure felt by judges to do justice in the cases that come before them is substantial (as I think it is), then the open practice of equity in a limited class of cases is likely to increase the adherence of the system as a whole to the requirements of the rule of law.

In sum, a version of the indeterminacy thesis holds in legal systems that incorporate the practice of equity. This version of the indeterminacy thesis is not the familiar claim that in any case, any outcome can be squared with the law. Rather, it is the claim that for any legal rule, there can always be cases in which application of the rule would require one result, but equity (and hence in systems that allow equity, the legal system as a whole) requires a different result. The truth of this version of the indeterminacy thesis in a given legal system might be thought incompatible with the proposition that the requirements of the rule of law are met in that system, but this incompatibility is contingent on the particular practices of judging that occur in a given legal system. The practice of equity by virtuous judges may reinforce rather than undermine the values that are served by the requirements of the rule of law.

Notes

1. For contributions to the indeterminacy debate, see works cited below and the following: Andrew Altman, *Critical Legal Studies: A Liberal Critique* (Princeton: Princeton University Press, 1990); Brian Bix, *Law, Language, and Legal Determinacy* (Oxford: Clarendon Press, 1993); Kent Greenawalt, *Law and Objectivity* (Oxford: Oxford University Press, 1992); Jürgen Habermas, *Between Facts and Norms,* trans. William Rehg (Cambridge: MIT Press, 1996), 194–237; Scott Altman, "Beyond Candor," *Michigan Law Review* 89 (1990): 296–351; Kent Greenawalt, "How Law Can Be Determinate," *UCLA Law Review* 38 (1990): 1–86; John Hasnas, "Back to the Future: From Critical Legal Studies Forward to Legal Realism, or How Not to Miss the Point of the Indeterminacy Argument," *Duke Law Journal* 45 (1995): 84–132; Allan C. Hutchinson, "Democracy and Determinacy: An Essay on Legal Interpretation," *University of Miami Law Review* 43 (1989): 541–76; Ken Kress, "A Preface to Epistemological Indeterminacy," *Northwestern University Law Review* 85 (1990): 134–47; Ken Kress, "Legal Indeterminacy," *California Law Review* 77 (1989): 283–337; David Leonard, "On 'Right' and 'Wrong' Answers: A Reply to Professor Hayden," *Journal of Legal Education* 40 (1990): 477–83; Lawrence B. Solum, "On the Indeterminacy Crisis: Critiquing Critical Dogma," *University of Chicago Law Review* 54 (1987): 462–503; George C. Thomas, "Legal Skepticism and the Gravitational Effect of Law," *Rutgers Law Review* 43 (1991): 965–1012; Christian Zapf and Eben Moglen, "Linguistic Indeterminacy and the Rule

of Law: On The Perils of Misunderstanding Wittgenstein," *Georgetown Law Journal* 84 (1996): 485–520.

Anthony D'Amato has made a number of contributions to the indeterminacy debate: "Harmful Speech and the Culture of Indeterminacy," *William and Mary Law Review* 32 (1991): 329–51; "Pragmatic Indeterminacy," *Northwestern University Law Review* 85 (1990): 148–89; "Aspects of Deconstruction: Refuting Indeterminacy with One Bold Thought," *Northwestern University Law Review* 85 (1990): 113–18; "Aspects of Deconstruction: The 'Easy Case' of the Under-Aged President," *Northwestern University Law Review* 84 (1989): 250–56; "Can Any Legal Theory Constrain Any Judicial Decision?" *University of Miami Law Review* 43 (1989): 513–39. Kenney Hegland has engaged in a lively debate with D'Amato. See Hegland, "Goodbye to Deconstruction," *Southern California Law Review* 54 (1985): 1203–21; "Goodbye to 2525," *Northwestern University Law Review* 85 (1990): 128–33; "Indeterminacy: I Hardly Knew Thee," *Arizona Law Review* 33 (1991): 509–27.

Indeterminacy has also become a theme in articles discussing a variety of specific jurisprudential issues and doctrinal topics. See, *e.g.*, Douglas M. Branson, "Indeterminacy: The Final Ingredient in an Interest Group Analysis of Corporate Law," *Vanderbilt Law Review* 43 (1990): 85–123; Paul Butler, "Racially Based Jury Nullification: Black Power in the Criminal Justice System," *Yale Law Journal* 105 (1995): 677–725; Daniel A. Farber and Suzanna Sherry, "Legal Storytelling and Constitutional Law: The Medium and the Message," in *Law's Stories: Narrative and Rhetoric in the Law*, ed. Peter Brooks and Paul Gewirtz (New Haven: Yale University Press, 1996); David Frisch, "Buyer's Remedies and Warranty Disclaimers: The Case for Mistake and the Indeterminacy of U.C.C. Section 1–103," *Arkansas Law Review* 43 (1990): 291–343; William B. Gwyn, "The Indeterminacy of the Separation of Powers in the Age of the Framers," *George Washington Law Review* 57 (1989): 474–505; Robert A. Hillman, "The Crisis in Modern Contract Theory," *Texas Law Review* 67 (1988): 103–36; John A. Miller, "Indeterminacy, Complexity, and Fairness: Justifying Rule Simplification in the Law of Taxation," *Washington Law Review* 68 (1993): 1–78; Mark Tushnet, "Constitutional Interpretation and Judicial Selection: A View from the Federalist Papers," *Southern California Law Review* 61 (1988): 1669–99; Steven L. Winter, "Indeterminacy and Incommensurability in Constitutional Law," *California Law Review* 78 (1990): 1441–541.

2. D'Amato, "Pragmatic Indeterminacy," 148 (citing Steven Winter, "Bull Durham and the Uses of Theory," *Stanford Law Review* 42 [1990]: 639–93).

3. Dennis Patterson, "Conscience and the Constitution," *Columbia Law Review* 93 (1993): 270–307, at 278 (reviewing Phillip Bobbitt, *Constitutional Interpretation* [Oxford: Blackwell, 1991]).

4. Drucilla L. Cornell, "Institutionalization of Meaning, Recollective Imagination and the Potential for Transformative Legal Interpretation," *University of Pennsylvania Law Review* 136 (1988): 1135–229, at 1196.

5. See David Millon, "Objectivity and Democracy," *New York University Law Review* 67 (1992): 1–66, at 35 n. 93 ("Misunderstanding of the CLS indeterminacy argument has resulted in several misguided critical ripostes"); Joseph William Singer, "The Reliance Interest in Property," *Stanford Law Review* 40 (1988): 611–751, at 624 n. 40 ("It is perhaps inevitable that the indeterminacy thesis is misunderstood"); Guyora Binder, "Beyond Criticism," *University of Chicago Law Review* 55 (1988): 888–915, at 892 ("The motivation of critical legal scholars in presenting the indeterminacy thesis is easily misunderstood because, like the doctrinal rules it attacks, the indeterminacy thesis is itself indeterminate"). See also Jay M. Feinman, "The Significance of Contract Theory," *University of Cincinnati Law Review* 58 (1990): 1283–318, at 1312; Richard Michael Fischl, "Some Realism about Critical Legal Studies," *University of Miami Law Review* 41 (1987): 505–32, at 528; Robert W. Gordon, "Critical Legal Histories," *Stanford Law Review* 36 (1984): 57–125, at 125; Charles M. Yablon, "Law and Metaphysics," *Yale Law Journal* 96 (1987): 613–36, at 634 (reviewing Saul Kripke, *Wittgenstein on Rules and Private Language* [Cambridge: Harvard University Press, 1982]).

6. See Lon Fuller, *The Morality of Law* (New Haven: Yale University Press, 1977), 33–94; John Rawls, *A Theory of Justice* (Cambridge: Harvard University Press, 1971), 235–43; Geoffrey de Q. Walker, *The Rule of Law* (Melbourne: Melbourne University Press, 1988), 1–48; Joseph Raz, "The Rule of Law and Its Virtue," *The Authority of Law: Essays on Law and Morality* (Oxford: Oxford University Press, 1979), 210–29.

7. Solum, "On the Indeterminacy Crisis," 488–95.

8. I will offer an argument for the external negation and not the internal negation of the indeterminacy thesis. I will show that "it is not the case that the law does not determine the outcome of all cases" but not that "it is the case that the law does determine the outcome of all cases." For discussion of the importance of this distinction, see Jon Elster, *Political Psychology* (Cambridge: Cambridge University Press, 1993), 73–78.

9. Frederick Schauer, "Easy Cases," *Southern California Law Review* 58 (1985): 399–440.

10. Of course, refutation of the strong indeterminacy thesis does not require the production of a case in which only one outcome is legally correct. All that is required is the identification of a case in which at least one possible outcome is legally incorrect.

11. 15 U.S.C. sec. 2 (1994); 26 Stat. 209 (1890).

12. It does seem highly likely that no such prosecution will ever be brought; if one were brought, it would also seem highly likely that it would fail. We can, however, imagine circumstances in which it would be predictable that the legally incorrect outcome would result. Imagine that both the prosecutor and the judge are fanatic devotees of CLS who conspire to ensure that I am convicted in order to prove the indeterminacy thesis is true.

13. It might turn out that the legally correct result is not predictable. For example, if the judge assigned to the case is known as an erratic adjudicator who frequently arrives at legally incorrect outcomes, then it might be the case that the outcome determined

as correct by the law is not the predicted outcome. More realistically, we might predict a legally incorrect outcome if we knew that the judge assigned to the case were erratic or biased in some way.

14. By referring to "competent" legal practitioners, I mean to exclude nonstandard cases, including practitioners who are suffering from mental illness or delusion.

15. See H. L. A. Hart, *The Concept of Law* (Oxford: Clarendon Press, 1961), 86, 77–150. See also Ronald Dworkin, *Law's Empire*, (Cambridge: Harvard University Press, 1988), 13–14; Frederick Schauer, "Fuller's Internal Point of View," *Law and Philosophy* 13 (1994): 285–312, at 286; Robert Justin Lipkin, "Indeterminacy, Justification and Truth in Constitutional Theory," *Fordham Law Review* 60 (1992): 595–643, at 637–39.

16. D'Amato, "The 'Easy Case' of the Under-Aged President," 256 (discussing example from Solum, "On the Indeterminacy Crisis," 472).

17. See Solum, "On the Indeterminacy Crisis," 472.

18. I owe this way of expressing the idea to Roger Shiner.

19. Various other defenses of the strong thesis are explored in Solum, "On the Inderterminacy Crisis," 476–88.

20. These distinctions are discussed in greater detail, ibid., 472–74.

21. See ibid., 473–74.

22. See Kress, "A Preface to Epistemological Indeterminacy," 138–39.

23. Notice that there may be several ex-post perspectives within a single case. Thus, after the pleadings are complete, there may be an ex-post perspective on a motion for judgment on the pleadings but an ex-ante perspective on summary judgment, trial, and appeal.

24. This version of the thesis is related to the Duncan Kennedy's important and influential work on the phenomenology of judging, "Freedom and Constraint in Adjudication: A Critical Phenomenology," *Journal of Legal Education* 36 (1986): 518–62. A shorter version of the article has been anthologized: "Toward A Critical Phenomenology of Judging," in *The Rule of Law: Ideal or Ideology*, ed. Allan C. Hutchinson and Patrick J. Monahan (Toronto: Carswell, 1987).

25. Each of the sets, C (condition descriptions): E (exception descriptions): and O (obligation descriptions), can be structured in a variety of complex ways. For example, each set of descriptions may include disjunctive and conjunctive relationships, such as $(c_1 \wedge c_2) \vee (c_3 \wedge c_4)$: $(o_1 \wedge o_2)$, where "$\wedge$" represents conjunction and "$\vee$" represents disjunction. This symbolizes the situation in which the triggering conditions of the rule are satisfied if either events of type one and type two are present or if events of type three and four are present or if any three of these event types are present; the rule requires outcomes o_1 and o_2.

26. *The American Heritage Dictionary of the English Language*, 3d ed. (Boston: Houghton Mifflin, 1992): 622.

27. J. M. Kelly, *A Short History of Western Legal Theory* (Oxford: Clarendon Press, 1992), 52.

28. Aristotle, *The Ethics of Aristotle: The Nicomachean Ethics*, trans. J. A. K. Thomson, rev. Hugh Tredennick (Harmondsworth, Middlesex: Penguin, 1976), 1137ᵇ9–1137ᵇ24. Citations are to the pagination of I. Bekker's standard edition of the Greek text of Aristotle.

29. The account in this chapter is an attempt to improve upon that offered in Lawrence B. Solum, "Equity and the Rule of Law," in *Nomos XXXVI: The Rule of Law*, ed. Ian Shapiro, (New York: New York University Press, 1994): 120–47. For an excellent and important account of Aristotle's view of equity, see Roger A. Shiner, "Aristotle's Theory of Equity," *Loyola of Los Angeles Law Review* 27 (1994): 1245–64.

30. Frederick Schauer, *Playing by the Rules: A Philosophical Examination of Rule-Based Decision-Making in Law and Life* (Oxford: Clarendon Press, 1991), 31–34.

31. I mean "legislator" to refer to rule makers broadly. Common law judges who make (or discover) new rules of common law are legislators in the sense intended here.

32. The locus classicus of this view is Christopher Saint Germain, *Doctor and Student*, 17th ed., ed. William Muchall (London: T. Whieldon, 1787), 45. Another edition is Christopher Saint Germain, *Doctor and Student*, ed. T. F. T. Plucknett and J. L. Barton (London: Selden Society, 1974), 95.

33. Roger Shiner suggests that one might be able to discern whether a given legal system employed the practice of equity from its general features, without looking at particular cases. One simply needs to know whether the system is rule-based and whether the system is committed to follow the rules, even when a rule is substantially overinclusive or underinclusive.

34. Recall the formulation of the ex-ante indeterminacy thesis: "For every legal rule R of legal system S, there is a possible case P, such that P satisfies the conditions of C and does not satisfy any exception in E, but in which the set O specified by R in these conditions is not the legally correct outcome." Thus, if there is any Rule R for which it could be shown that there is no possible case P satisfying the conditions of C and not satisfying any exception E where O is not the legally correct outcome, then the ex-ante thesis would be false. Of course, this showing will be difficult, because what must be demonstrated is the nonexistence of any possible case P. I owe thanks to Roger Shiner for clarification of this point.

35. The literature surrounding this case is reviewed in D'Amato, "The 'Easy Case' of the Under-Aged President."

36. Solum, "Equity and the Rule of Law."

37. Judith Shklar, "Political Theory and the Rule of Law," in *The Rule of Law: Ideal or Ideology*, ed. Allan C. Hutchinson and Patrick J. Monahan (Toronto: Carswell, 1987), 3.

38. Roscoe Pound, "The Decadence of Equity," *Columbia Law Review* 5 (1905): 20–35, at 23–24.

Chapter 3

Jürgen Habermas's Recent Philosophy of Law, and the Optimum Point Between Abstract Universalism and Communitarianism

Norman Fischer

In Jürgen Habermas's recent work on law and ethics, he presents a way of synthesizing abstract universalism with communitarian emphasis on concrete social relations. My first task is to show how Habermas arrives at his position through his nuanced account of both Hegel's critique of Kant's ethics and Lawrence Kohlberg's attempt to accommodate communitarianism in his universalist moral theory. My second task is to show the impact of Habermas's blend of abstract universalism and communitarianism on his concrete legal ethics.[1]

I

Habermas has gone directly to the source of much of the controversy over abstract universalism and communitarianism, namely, the debate over Kantian *Moralität* and Hegelian *Sittlichkeit*. Whereas *Moralität* is composed of abstract and universal moral principles, rationally grounded, *Sittlichkeit* is composed of social practices that are used by their practitioners as ethical principles. The former is favored by what might be called the ideal liberal legal tradition; the latter, by radical communitarian legal critics. Note that on this definition the two concepts are not per se incompatible. Some or all of the abstract universal principles of *Moralität* may be social practices. Some or all of the social practices of *Sittlichkeit* may be abstract universal principles, rationally grounded. From Hegel to recent communitarian critiques of Kant and ideal liberalism, however, a problem with Kantian *Moralität* and ideal liberal principles has always been their excessive thinness, as opposed to a thick communitarian ethic. This seems to be more than the

67

contingent critique that there is not enough overlap between the two realms. Rather, some communitarians assume that rationally grounded universal principles must remain thin because an abstract quality makes them inimical to life and social practice. Liberal theorists have countered that communitarians, in their desire to embed moral principles, must increasingly care less about their universality and rationality.[2]

However, in the debate over a thin ideal liberal *Moralität* versus a thick communitarian *Sittlichkeit*, Habermas has recently tried to claim both attributes for his ethical and legal theory. Habermas is certainly aware of the high degree of abstractness and thinness of his ethical principles, a result of the centrality of formality and procedurality in attaining both rational universalism and the impartial moral point of view from which universal principles are derived. However, he thinks that an impartial moral point of view can be embedded in a thick *Sittlichkeit*, or set of social practices, which is not defined so procedurally and formally.[3] Habermas's enterprise involves showing that the impartial moral point of view is more dependent on structures giving solidarity than is usually thought. Solidarity is not impartiality or equality or liberty. It is sui generis. It is the quality in social life as a whole which allows, fosters, and facilitates action with others. It goes back to the Hegelian and Marxist emphasis on the capacity of embedded practices to inhibit egoism. Formal moral and legal principles, along with the moral point of view from which they are generated, are embedded in solidarity-producing social practices. These contain thicker communitarian elements influencing law from outside, elements from which they would be more distanced in other forms of ideal liberalism.

Habermas's mix of liberalism and communitarianism, however, runs into problems when applied concretely to law. The first is that in order for it to work, the *Moralität* of law and the *Sittlichkeit* of law have to be specified in a detailed way. The second problem is the lack of substance in Habermas's account of the moral and legal principles to which the moral point of view gives rise. A solution to the first problem is simply to be more precise about the boundaries of *Moralität* and *Sittlichkeit* in law. A solution to the second problem, however, involves critiquing Habermas's refusal to expand in fact his thin notion of formality and procedurality to include more substantive principles of rights, particularly equality rights, as derivable in some sense from the moral point of view. Indeed, these two approaches must work together in order for Habermas's enterprise to succeed, for the concrete blending of *Moralität* and *Sittlichkeit* that Habermas envisages can occur only if he simultaneously recognizes that some of his accounts of the universal aspect of moral and legal principles are so impossibly thin that they defeat his very reason for emphasizing the impartial moral point of view in the first place. At the same the communitarian social relations, the *Sittlichkeit*, in which abstract ideal liberal moral and legal principles are embedded, must be specified in enough detail that the influence of society on abstract legal principles becomes demonstrated.

Habermas clarifies his idea of the integration of *Moralität* into *Sittlichkeit* in his most recent work on Kohlberg's moral theory. Kohlberg himself, in one of his last essays, had become dissatisfied with the abstractness that he had given in his earlier work to the universal principles and impartial moral point of view as they operated in his famous sixth stage of moral development, what he called "the stage of universal ethical principles." When this stage is attained, "particular laws or social agreements are usually valid because they rest on such principles. . . . The reason for doing right is that, as a rational person, one has seen the validity of principles and has become committed to them."[4] Habermas, in his response, said that he could agree with this dissatisfaction and that his aim was to integrate the impartial moral point of view, as it operated in the individual when he or she attains the sixth stage, into the context of morality as supplied by the continual engagement in society as a whole of people in action oriented to understanding.[5] In technical Habermasian terms, this means that a discourse theory of ethics, which can be defined in part as commitment to the impartial moral point of view and the universal principles generated from it, is integrated into a context provided by society for helping it flourish. For Habermas, discourse ethics and the moral point of view are very abstract. "The principle of discourse ethics— that only those norms may claim validity that could find acceptance by all those concerned as participants in a practical discourse . . . is a procedure that explains the moral point of view." However, "discourses are a reflective form of understanding-oriented action that, so to speak, sit on top of the latter."[6] The societal context of (1) action oriented to understanding, or, in technical Habermasian terms, communicative action, is the ocean on which the individual engages in the moral point of view of (2) discourse ethics.

Habermas's discourse ethics is not just characterized by (a) the moral point of view, and (b) the universal principles derived from it. It is also characterized by the attainment of (a) and (b) through democratic participation. The societal context of communicative action is the *Sittlichkeit* in which the *Moralität* of discourse ethics, both as moral point of view and universal principles, and as democratic participation, is embedded. The solidarity that this *Sittlichkeit* produces must and can aid both impartiality and democratic participation.[7] Habermas's belief that we can anchor democratic participation and the moral point of view on such a rich *Sittlichkeit* forms the background to his refusal to follow Kohlberg's revision of his sixth stage.

Habermas's revision of Kohlberg has perhaps been facilitated by the fact that Kohlberg as well, under pressure from communitarian critique of the abstractness of the sixth stage, spelled out more clearly the social background of his account of the moral point of view in the sixth stage. Kohlberg suggested that the sixth stage, the stage of moral autonomy and justice, the stage that both Habermas and Kohlberg had always seen as classically representing the impartial moral point of view and the rationally grounded universal principles of ideal liberalism, must now include a specific emotion of benevolence—a more concrete identification with others and their welfare—as distinct from the more procedural formality of justice.[8]

Although Habermas opposed this solution, he makes it clear that the kind of thinking it represents is partly appropriate and partly inappropriate. It is appropriate, in that he thinks that the sixth stage should be amplified with a more explicit account of how the moral point of view is sustained. However, instead of giving more content to the impartial moral point of view, as Kohlberg does, Habermas is more inclined, in the face of communitarian critiques, to give it less content than ever. He reaffirms and strengthens the idea that the moral point of view must be not only impartial but also formal and procedural; only then can universality be grounded. However, for Habermas this formal and procedural impartial moral point of view has to be anchored in social institutions that allow the individual to attain the moral standpoint. These social institutions, insofar as they create the possibility of a moral point of view, give what Habermas calls solidarity, which is what he likes about communitarian ethics.

But this solidarity is not directly in the formal, procedural moral point of view or the sixth stage. Solidarity is, rather, the precondition for the formal moral point of view and for the sixth stage. The solidarity enters in that no individual can engage in discourses revealing and preserving formal, procedural justice if there is not even any hope of living in a society that provides a context for such discourses. Note that Habermas's formulation is not inconsistent with his claim that formal, procedural discourse ethics does not depend on the discourse's being accepted.[9] It is not the specific traditions, so loved by communitarians, but the general structures of society on which discourse ethics depends. Nevertheless, these general structures are anchored in concrete societies, so Habermas does not entirely escape communitarian particularism here.[10]

Habermas's account can be seen as a deepening of his idea that a context of communicative action provides the thick background for discourse ethics. Communicative action provides solidarity and *Sittlichkeit*. Discourse ethics provides procedural justice and *Moralität*. It contains a thin moral point of view and a correspondingly thin democratic participation. In contrast, for Kohlberg, benevolence—what he likes about communitarian ethics—is actually in the moral point of view and the sixth stage itself. Hence, at the very last stage of their collaboration, Habermas and Kohlberg moved in different directions.

I must emphasize that the outcome of Habermas's most recent discussion of Kohlberg is not only to stress the value of a thin *Moralität* but also to anchor it in a thicker *Sittlichkeit*. Habermas does not, in general, follow some ideal liberals and make *Moralität* thicker by deriving more substantive principles from the moral point of view itself. This approach to thickening the moral point of view and Habermas's ultimately ambivalent attitude toward it are clarified by his account of John Rawls's early theory of justice. It is not the elaborate philosophical nature of Rawls's theory that he objects to, for Habermas thinks such elaboration is appropriate for the sixth stage, but the specific direction that it takes. He thinks that Rawls's theory is substantive in a way that belies the formal, procedural nature of the sixth stage. Habermas believes, for example, that Rawls's principles of justice cannot be derived in any sense from the nature of the impartial moral point of view but, rather, depend on the context of the society that may or may not uphold them.[11] Habermas's criticism, it should be noted, is not from the standpoint of particularistic communitarianism but from the universalism of the highly abstract version of the moral point of view and democratic participating that he finds in his version of the sixth stage.

Habermas's criticism of Rawls is closely related to his criticism of Kohlberg's new benevolence theory as well. Basically, Habermas seems to think that Kohlberg's addition of benevolence disturbs the procedural and formal nature of the moral point of view, and the autonomy gained by these features. Early Rawlsian substance differs radically from late Kohlbergian substance. The former continues abstract universality and derives concrete principles of justice from it; the latter supplements impartial justice with a notion of benevolence. In contrast to both, Habermas claims that discourse ethics can interpret the sixth stage in two ways: first, as a procedural theory of justice along completely formal lines, committing oneself to an impartial moral point of view and to the democratic participation necessary to attain it; and, second, as an abstract moral standpoint that depends on solidarity arising out of *Sittlichkeit*, seen as the continued participation of the moral individual in communicative action generally. This is the method of thickening the sixth stage that Habermas opposes to both early Rawls and late Kohlberg. The essence of his criticism is that they thicken ideal liberal abstraction in the wrong way.

But are these criticisms of Kohlberg and of Rawls really consistent with each other? Habermas's concrete philosophy of law suggests that they are not, for the simple reason that in order to add solidarity as the *sittlich* context of *Moralität*, more substantive equality and liberty rights must be derivable from the moral point of view than would be consistent with Habermas's criticism of Rawls's *Theory of Justice*. Solidarity, seen in the context of law, will simply not help strengthen the impartial moral point of view if specific fundamentals of liberty and equality are not built firmly into the law as *Moralität* in the first place. This latter position would be a way of overcoming thinness within the heart of *Moralität* itself.[12] Yet in his revision of Kohlberg, Habermas sticks exclusively to his fundamental direction of overcoming the thinness of his ideal liberal theory, namely, of integrating a thin *Moralität* into a richer *Sittlichkeit*. He assumes that this is a better way of thickening ideal liberal principles than either Kohlberg's acceptance of empathic benevolence or Rawls's acceptance of an impartial moral point of view that entails substantive claims of liberty and equality. But Habermas himself is at other times drawn closer to this more Rawlsian strategy. Finally, his concrete philosophy of law suggests that he can accomplish his fundamental task of adding solidarity to the moral point of view only by undertaking, as did early Rawls, an endorsement of specific liberty and/or equality rights on the basis of the abstract moral point of view. At the same time he is drawn to state more clearly exactly what the *Sittlichkeit* is in which *Moralität* is embedded. Habermas thus applies the results of his search for an optimum point between liberalism and communitarianism to concrete legal ethics.

II

Habermas's concrete philosophy of law, developed between 1976 and 1991, sheds light on the metaethical issues raised in his account of *Moralität, Sitt-*

lichkeit, and the sixth stage of moral development. Habermas is forced, as he applies his thin procedural, formal/thick solidarity-producing model, to give legal examples that expand the range of both the thick *Sittlichkeit* aspect of law and the thin *Moralität* aspect. Indeed, his recent metaethics leads logically to the result that the theory of law becomes increasingly important, and the psychology of moral development, viewed in abstraction from law and other social institutions, becomes less important. The centrality of law is built into Habermas's moral system for a variety of reasons.

First, the very procedural, formal analysis of impartiality that Habermas adopts suggests strongly the search for a general and neutral procedure for achieving justice, the kind of search that some theorists have found at the heart of at least liberal accounts of law. Particularly important here is the idea that discourse ethics is characterized as having a form separate from other types of principle of human action.[13] Here Habermas takes a clear position in the debate between radical communitarians and ideal liberals in regard to law. It is the idea that there is such a neutral principle, above the fray of competing interests, that unites in their opposition communitarians who simply critique law as any type of centerpiece of social morality and those who critique its ideal liberal version.[14] Neither would allow a morality, even one that does not label itself clearly as a legally oriented one but that can nevertheless be seen to be one using these criteria, to escape the name of law or ideal liberal law. Hence, radical legal communitarians and Habermas might agree that ideal liberal law is a *telos* toward which his moral theory is heading.

Second, when Habermas's moral reconstruction of Marx and classical sociology is pressed to reveal examples, the clearest often are legal in nature. His aim is always to show that the autonomous, posttraditional personality that has attained Kohlberg's sixth stage of moral development ultimately needs the possibility of expressing himself or herself through an institution such as law, which at least potentially could capture the rationally grounded universal aims of such an individual, free from the constraints of money and power.[15] Habermas never said that the existing systems of law of Western societies accomplished this, but he never claimed either, and indeed always doubted, that it was their stated commitment to universalism that prevented them from accomplishing this. Universal law was and is seen as a potential instrument for attaining the moral society. It must be remembered that Kohlberg's sixth moral stage, even before he revised it, hovered uneasily, perhaps, between being an account of the psychology of moral development and an account of the context of that development, a context Habermas as early as 1976 in his moral reconstruction of Marxism had seen to lie in law.[16]

These two ideas, of morality tending toward the status of law and of law providing the context of morality, might seem in conflict. However, that is not the case if the law toward which morality tends and the law that provides its context are seen as two different aspects of law, law (1) and law (2). In that case both aspects would be present in Habermas's recent legal ethics, for the idea of morality tending toward law aids in defining law (1) as *Moralität*; and the idea of law (2) providing the social context for a morality that itself is like law (1) in that both incorporate the moral point of view aids in defining law (2) as *Sittlichkeit*. This distinction between law (1) and law (2), even though Habermas does not explicitly make it, provides a charitable reading of his recent philosophy of law as it arises out of his long quest to unite the ideal liberal and the communitarian aspects of ethics. How does Habermas use his formal, procedural discourse ethics to show that law (1) is a *Moralität* embedded in law (2) as *Sittlichkeit*? Both of these elements must be relevant for Habermas's account of law, and they are relevant because both are helpful in understanding Habermas's critique of legal positivism.

The fundamental assumption throughout Habermas's Tanner lectures on law and morality is that legal positivism has been overthrown, and the arguments of the ideal liberals such as Ronald Dworkin, who have claimed against legal positivism that legitimate law must have an element of justified morality in it, have been won. Rather than going over the arguments that have been used by thinkers like Dworkin to establish this, Habermas selects certain ones that shed particular light on his moral aims. Habermas accepts the general line of antipositivist thought, that is, that law and morality must be fused, arguing that insofar as the internal moral dimension of law is demonstrated against positivism, the concept of discourse ethics can be substituted for the concept of the general and autonomous moral rules entailed by any antipositivist account of law that shows how legal commands can be legitimate. Hence, we can now talk about a discourse theory of law, which represents Habermas's acceptance, in his own terms, of the fusion of law and morality that the critique of legal positivism necessitates.[17]

But how exactly is morality to be incorporated into the law? For, in Habermasian terms, this morality that judges law must be seen as always a potential *Moralität*, limited by and yet able to transcend the *Sittlichkeit* on which it rests. The problem is that if Habermas's legal theory is really going to incorporate his discourse ethics and his theory of the sixth moral stage, then it must incorporate his metaethical integration of liberal and communitarian themes and show the connection between the *Moralität* and the *Sittlichkeit* of law, between law (1), as it embodies the procedural and formal sixth moral stage, and law (2), as it embodies the solidarity-generating social relations in which the sixth stage is embedded. But we already know the fundamental problems that Habermas faces in this analysis. First, by not filling in more completely what the context of solidarity is, and second, by excluding so much substance from the impartial core of justice and the sixth stage, Habermas is in danger of leaving his nonpositivistic theory of law in a very thin void. We saw in section I that from his general metaethical perspective Habermas has two ways of emerging from this void. The first is to expand his account of the *sittlich* origins of law in solidarity-producing social relations. The second is to expand his account of the substance of law and rights within discourse ethics and *Moralität*.

Habermas does present a potential solution to the first problem of filling in the content of solidarity and *Sittlichkeit*. That solution is along the lines that even as people elaborate the stringent formal procedures of law, insofar as law is seen to represent the moral point of view and the democratic participation necessary to achieve it, they also reproduce the social relations that support these formal procedures and democratic participation, thus reproducing solidarity. What exactly, however, is the *Sittlichkeit* on which this discourse theory of ethics is based? *Sittlichkeit* is characterized in terms of the social relations and institutions that form the background in communicative action for discourse ethics. These social relations give rise to solidarity. Solidarity, it must be remembered, is neither benevolence nor the substantive liberty and equality rights that some ideal liberals might derive from the impartial moral point of view itself. It is sui generis. It is the quality in social life as a whole that allows, fosters, and facilitates action with others and inhibits egoism. But what is the legal meaning of the relation between these solidarity-producing social relations and the impartial moral point of view, between law (2) and law (1)?

The legal principles of law (1) themselves become the clearest model of discourse ethics. A certain wavering can be detected in Habermas's account on the question of whether the discourse theory of law might or might not be a more complete theory of ethics than discourse ethics as such. Nevertheless, Habermas seems to lean toward the affirmative. The idea that abstract law is the *telos* of abstract discourse ethics would clarify Habermas's attempt to embed a thin discourse ethics as *Moralität* into law (2), that is, social-relations-producing solidarity, which forms the *Sittlichkeit* context for discourse ethics abstraction and for law (1). For Habermas emphasizes that because the formal procedure is not spelled out as well in morality per se, as opposed to posttraditional law (law 1), there is a kind of incompleteness in morality.[18] This admission is extremely significant because it suggests that law (1) more readily represents discourse ethics as a social ethics than does nonlegal morality. But is this consistent with the claim that Habermas has been making since his moral reconstruction of Marxism in 1976, that law provides the context of morality? Only if we distinguish between law (1) and law (2) can we show how law, as law (2), provides the context for morality, as law (1).

Habermas goes on to argue that one reason for morality's present weakness is the relative uncoupling of posttraditional *Moralität* from *Sittlichkeit*. This seems to suggest that law (2) supplies the *Sittlichkeit*, and law (1) the *Moralität*, that an increasingly formal morality no longer has the resources to supply without law.[19] It would almost be as though the formalization of law (1) and morality move in two fundamentally different directions. The formalization of law (1) leads to the creation of a new *Sittlichkeit*. The formalization of morality leads to lack of *Sittlichkeit*, and thus to the greater need for law (1) and law (2) to back up morality, as well as for other social relations to back up morality. Law (1), law as *Moralität*, backs up morality because it formalizes it more. Law (2), law as *Sittlichkeit*, backs up both morality and law (1) by providing institutional forms of solidarity. The latter range from economic solidarity to other forms of group identity in society.

This formulation sheds light on the relation between communitarianism and ideal liberalism. With this account Habermas emerges as the ideal liberal legal theorist that he essentially always has been, but still in dialogue with those who emphasize the social relations and contexts of law, ranging from those—call them satisfied communitarians—who emphasize that such social relations and contexts are a consistent ocean in which formal legal procedures are embedded, to those—call them dissatisfied communitarians—who emphasize that they are an inconsistent ocean. Furthermore, the whole move fits in well with his revision of Kohlberg. Solidarity, that is, the individual's participation in the range of institutions that depend upon communicative action, is reinforced, just as the moment of formal procedural morality is reinforced. Thus Habermas's philosophy of law is thickened by bringing in solidarity-producing *sittlich* relations. But can this solution work when law (1), law as *Moralität*, remains so thin itself?

Could Habermas thicken his philosophy of law by expanding *Moralität* as well as *Sittlichkeit*, and by showing that some substantive rights are derivable from the impartial moral point of view, from law (1), unless it is made so impossibly thin that such derivations are ruled out from the start? Habermas had seemed to rule out this possibility by his critique of the thickness of Rawls's early theory of justice. Nevertheless, in his critique of positivism Habermas argues that even though the abstract and general form of law may serve the function of power, it also can serve the function of a more general autonomous morality that demands some commitment to equality.[20] Thus, once Habermas actually begins on his program of developing some sort of legal content from the impartial moral point of view, he does speak in terms of substantive rights. Hence, there is a question concerning the extent to which Habermas wavers between defining the *Moralität* aspect of law purely formally, and following other ideal liberals in deriving substantive liberty and equality rights from the moral point of view.

Indeed, it is quite obvious from this example that the internal discussion of positivism draws Habermas in the direction of making his formal theory less thin, the more he talks about the substantive morality of rights. Dworkin's own critique of positivism is based very much on the necessity of fusing morality and legality in talking about substantive constitutional rights. Habermas seems committed to such a view too, when he says that human rights represent the moral substance of our legal theory.[21] From this moral interpretation of law, Habermas draws the conclusion that since law in modern society is, at least in principle, postconventional, that is, oriented toward Kohlberg's sixth stage of morality, therefore, it can be justified as legitimate only in light of general moral principles related to rights.[22] The implication is that what I have called law (1) is not entirely formal and procedural.

Habermas's consideration of the use of abstract principles in concrete situations sheds light on this issue as well. For Habermas, an example of the application of principles is the progressive displaying of the true meaning of human rights.[23] This seems, again, to come very close to Dworkin, who also has argued that the meaning of rights can be progressively displayed. However, it must be remembered that for Dworkin, substantive principles of liberty and equality are derived from his concept of justified law.[24] But according to the way Habermas often characterizes his thin theory of formal, procedural justice, such substantive principles must be put outside the core notion of justice and law (1), and into contingent social practices.

This signals a general problem with Habermas's attempt at a conciliatory argument here. He cannot give to the communitarian in ethics the idea that the application of the principle becomes more important than the principle. Indeed, a problem of compatibility seems to be raised here for combining (a) Habermas's notion that the meaning of fundamental rights is gradually revealed, and (b) his notion that formal, procedural justice (law 1) must exclude more substance than is usually excluded by modern ideal liberalism. Is it the philosopher's job only to lay out the universal and abstract principles behind human rights, without being committed to any single specific human right? Should not the philosopher also look at contested unfoldings of human rights in specific situations? Wouldn't that lead to a more substantive theory of rights incorporated into the impartial core of morality, into law (1)?

Habermas could and should agree with this criticism. It is the a priori elements in his version of the moral point of view that are an obstacle to acceptance of at least some substantive rights into the core of justice, of law (1). For the notion of a purely procedural rationality, as the core of justice, seems to rest upon a particularly strong a priorism, which makes it unsuitable for a theory of developing rights. Yet the problem is that Habermas oscillates between the idea that the abstract core of justice is in a first stage, in which the a priori language and negotiating skills of human beings as moral beings as such are expressed, and that the core of justice is in a second stage, that is, the achievement of wills coming to moral agreement through democratic participation. If the core of justice is in the first stage, and if the second stage is just contingently derived from that first stage, then the third stage, that is, the stage when democratically participating individuals actually talk about, say, the substance of rights and justice, can be seen as a nonphilosophical addition, as Habermas claims to see it. But, in contrast, if the core of justice is in the second stage, then at least some of the substantive details of rights must be part of, or at least derivable from, the moral point of view as elaborated and expressed in the second stage. Then, the third stage cannot be just a nonphilosophical addition, as Habermas says the rights derived from Rawls's two concrete principles of justice are.

But the core of justice cannot be entirely in the first stage because the first stage does not yet incorporate the more communitarian, dialogical, social psychology of the sort that Kohlberg and Habermas themselves finally developed in the 1980s. To put all the emphasis on the first stage is simply inconsistent with the theory that the social relations that people follow in communicative action provide the necessary context for even formal, procedural morality; for these social relations must be seen as historical and specific. Indeed, Habermas himself started off his moral theory of law in his 1976 moral reconstruction of Marxism by showing that the social relations emphasized by Marxists were connected with the rationality of modern Western law, which is also historical and specific, and certainly not simply a priori in the sense that the first stage is.[25] As Kohlberg and Habermas have both sought, in their recent writings, to make good on the promise of a genuine social analogue to the more individual perspective of original Kohlbergian psychology, it does seem natural that a philosophy of substantive law and substantive rights is called for. Such substantive rights could function as a prototype of *Moralität* (law 1) and also, in a broader sense, depend on social relations and *Sittlichkeit* (law 2), laying out the social context for morality.

This is exactly the kind of solution that Habermas needs in order to achieve in legal ethics the optimum point that he wants between ideal liberalism and communitarianism. He could then blend strong fundamental rights with a strong account of solidarity coming from society as a whole. As we have seen, Habermas's opposition to Kohlberg's solution to linking liberalism and communitarianism is that the benevolence theory does not clearly provide a social context for law. For Habermas's account to be adequately grounded in social ethics, it needs solidarity, but, I would add, it also needs strong fundamental rights. At least some of these rights must be generated by law (1) and discourse ethics. But in order to generate fundamental rights, law (1) must operate at neither a first stage, laying out a too formal a priori theory of morality, nor a third stage, laying out too contingent a theory of morality. The first stage would be pure a priori thinking without development; the third stage would be pure participation in development, without inherent limits. In contrast to both these possibilities, there is no intrinsic reason that Habermas could not follow out the logic of his search for an optimum point between communitarianism and ideal liberalism, and see the abstractions and rights of law (1) coming from a second stage, of wills entering into dialogue about fundamental rights. Such dialogue about fundamental rights could easily be linked with currents of solidarity arising out of the whole of society. Hence, Habermas would have a legal ethics incorporating law (1), an abstract moral point of view contributing to a properly limited but not impossibly thin theory of fundamental substantive rights, and law (2), a thicker *sittlich* context, which provides the solidarity necessary to achieve law (1).[26]

Notes

1. This chapter concentrates on Habermas's work from 1983 through 1991, with some references to work done between 1976 and 1983. To retain the character of the paper presented at the 1992 AMINTAPHIL conference and to concentrate on a unified body of work, I have confined to footnotes all references to later work, particularly Habermas's *Faktizität und Geltung: Beiträge zur Diskurstheorie des Rechts und des Demokratischen Rechtsstaats* (Frankfurt: Suhrkamp, 1992); English translation, *Between Facts and Norms: Contributions to a Discourse Theory of Law and Democracy* (Cambridge: MIT Press, 1996).

2. Of the vast literature on this topic, both in regard to modern communitarians and liberals and to the Kant-Hegel debate, I would cite Benjamin Barber, *The Conquest of Politics* (Princeton: Princeton University Press. 1988), 3–21, for the communitarians, and Ronald Dworkin, *Taking Rights Seriously* (Cambridge: Harvard University Press, 1978), 147, for the liberals. Letting Kant and Hegel speak for themselves I would choose Immanuel Kant, *Critique of Practical Reason* (Indianapolis: Library of Liberal Arts, 1956), 49, and G. W. F. Hegel, *Hegel's Philosophy of Right* (Oxford: Oxford University Press, 1967), 33.

3. See Habermas, "Morality and Ethical Life: Does Hegel's Critique of Kant Apply to Discourse Ethics?" *Moral Consciousness and Communicative Action* (Cambridge: MIT Press, 1990), 207; "Was Macht ein Lebensform Rational?" In *Erläuterungen zur Diskursethik* (Frankfurt: Suhrkamp, 1991), 36–40. Habermas's recent decision to opt for a linking of *Moralität* and *Sittlichkeit* depends for its details on the development of his own moral theory, particularly in its psychological and legal aspects. It can be, and is in this chapter, looked at independently of the historical question of whether there are any Hegelian texts that make *Moralität* and *Sittlichkeit* appear compatible. However, it should be noted that Habermas has recently cited as evidence for the existence of weaker versions of the commitment to embedded *Sittlichkeit* in Hegel the following quotation from one of the recent publications of student notes taken from various lectures on which *Hegel's Philosophy of Right* was ultimately based: "What is rational *becomes* real, and what is real *becomes* rational." (Hegel, *Philosophie des Rechts: Die Vorlesung von 1819/20, in einer Nachschrift* [Frankfurt: Suhrkamp, 1983], 5, cited in Habermas, *The Philosophical Discourse of Modernity* [Cambridge: MIT Press, 1987], 41.) Habermas's comment that this reveals a weaker "institutionalism" than the claim in *Hegel's Philosophy of Right* that the real *is* the rational, could justify counterposing a Hegel for whom *Moralität* and *Sittlichkeit* are compatible to one for whom they are not. See Hegel, *Philosophy of Right*, 10.

4. Lawrence Kohlberg, Dwight R. Boyd, and Charles Levine, "The Return of Stage 6: Its Principle and Moral Point of View," in *The Moral Domain*, ed. Thomas Wren (Cambridge: MIT Press, 1990), 153–58; Lawrence Kohlberg, *Essays on Moral Development*, vol. 1, *The Philosophy of Moral Development* (San Francisco: Harper & Row, 1981), 412.

5. Habermas, "Justice and Solidarity: On the Discussion Concerning Stage 6," in *The Moral Domain*, ed. Thomas Wren (Cambridge: MIT Press, 1990), 244–49.

6. Ibid., 235, 245.

7. Habermas, "Lawrence Kohlberg und der Neoaristotelismus," in *Erläuterungen zur Diskursethik* (Frankfurt: Suhrkamp, 1991), 96–97. Prior to Habermas's *Faktizität und Geltung*, which makes democratic participation central, Habermas's clearest statement on the role of democratic participation in discourse ethics is "Ist der Herzschlag der Revolution zum Stillstand gekommen: Volkssouveränität als Verfahren," in *Die Ideen von 1789 in der Deutschen Rezeption*, ed. Forum für Philosophie (Frankfurt: Suhrkamp, 1989), now reprinted in *Faktizität und Geltung*.

8. Kohlberg et al., "The Return of Stage Six," 153–58.

9. Habermas, *Moral Consciousness and Communicative Action*, 61.

10. Habermas, "Justice and Solidarity," 246–47.

11. Habermas, *Moral Consciousness and Communicative Action*, 66. See John Rawls, *A Theory of Justice* (Cambridge: Harvard University Press, 1971), 60–64.

12. For the opposite approach, see Roberto Unger, *The Critical Legal Studies Movement* (Cambridge: Harvard University Press, 1986), 5–14.

13. Habermas, "Justice and Solidarity," 225.

14. For an example of the former, see Barber, *The Conquest of Politics*, 120–51; for an example of the latter, see Unger, *The Critical Legal Studies Movement*, 13–14.

15. Habermas, *The Theory of Communicative Action* (Boston: Beacon Press, 1984): 249–52.

16. Habermas, "Überlegungen zum Evolutionaren Stellenwert des Modernen Rechts," in *Zur Rekonstruktion des Historischen Materialismus* (Frankfurt: Suhrkamp, 1976), 264–65.

17. Habermas, "Law and Morality," in *The Tanner Lectures on Human Values*, ed. Sterling M. McMurrin, vol. 8 (Salt Lake City: University of Utah Press, 1988), 245, 275. For Dworkin's critique of positivism, see *Taking Rights Seriously*, 14–80.

18. Habermas, "Law and Morality," 244.

19. Ibid., 244–45.

20. Ibid., 227.

21. Dworkin, *Taking Rights Seriously*, 184–206; Habermas, *Moral Consciousness and Communicative Action*, 205.

22. Habermas, *Moral Consciousness and Communicative Action*, 205; "Law and Morality," 245; "Was Macht ein Lebensform Rational?" 42–45.

23. Habermas, "Was Macht ein Lebensform Rational?" 42–43.

24. Dworkin, *Taking Rights Seriously*, 150–83.

25. Habermas, "Überlegungen zum Evolutionären Stellenwert des Modernen Rechts," 264–65.

26. For an assessment of Habermas's philosophy of law up to 1992, see Robert Shelly, "Habermas and the Normative Foundations of a Radical Politics," *Thesis Eleven* 35 (1993): 62–83. For the Frankfurt school Marxist background, see William E. Scheuerman, *Between the Norm and the Exception: The Frankfurt School and the Rule of Law* (Cambridge: MIT Press, 1994). For Habermas's further development of the theme of law's relation to the abstract moral point of view and solidarity in society, see *Factizität und Geltung*, particularly chaps. 1 and 2. The reader should note that Habermas's distinction, in chapters three and four of that book, between Law 1 and Law 2, has analogies with, but is not the same as, my distinction between law (1) and law (2) to facilitate reconstruction of his work between 1983 and 1991.

Legal Advocacy, Cooperation,
and Dispute Resolution

Larry May

Does legal advocacy have to be adversarial? The standard law texts, including texts in legal ethics, assume that the adversarial role and the advocacy role are virtually the same.[1] Legal advocates are said to have the duty to be zealous and aggressive in promoting the interests of their clients over the interests of others. Lurking here is the assumption that advocacy is a zero-sum game. But advocacy merely means that one argues for and promotes the cause of another. In many instances, it may be more effective to be conciliatory or cooperative rather than adversarial. Lawyers have known this for quite a long time, as is seen in the tremendously effective and common practice of plea bargaining. Yet, the model of law in the Anglo-American tradition continues to be portrayed as one in which advocacy and the adversarial role are synonymous, and the socialization of lawyers rarely stresses nonadversarial advocacy.

The adversarial legal model is often unnecessarily coercive and insufficiently attentive to what is best for the client or for the shared values in a community. In this chapter I wish to give serious consideration to alternative models of advocacy and dispute resolution. I will begin by discussing a prominent early Soviet legal theorist, E. B. Pashukanis, who advocated a nonadversarial approach to law. I next examine some criticisms of Pashukanis offered by Hans Kelsen in an attempt to discern the limits of nonadversarial approaches to advocacy and dispute resolution. Then, I will provide some additional argumentation from the standpoint of contemporary critical theory against the exclusive reliance on the adversarial model. Finally,

---

Chapter 4 originally appeared in *The Socially Responsive Self* (Chicago: University of Chicago Press, 1996)

I will explore a model of empathic advocacy based on a consideration of divorce mediation cases.

Contemporary American law has increasingly been taken up with disputes to be settled through rules already recognized as regulating conduct within governmental or organizational structures. Owen Fiss has argued that "courts exist to give meaning to our public values, not to resolve disputes. Constitutional adjudication is the most vivid manifestation of this function, but it also seems true of most civil and criminal law."[2] Fiss believes that public resource allocation, rather than private dispute resolution, will be a dominant strain of law in the near future. If Fiss is right, professional lawyers will have to become as concerned about facilitating pluralistic dialogue as they previously have been concerned about pitting one person's interest against that of another. And this change will also mean that lawyers will have to emphasize cooperative interaction rather than adversarial interaction in certain cases. Law schools will have to change the way lawyers are socialized so as to reflect these changes in the lawyer's role.

A Model of Nonadversarial Advocacy

The early Soviet legal theorist E. B. Pashukanis tried to make practical sense of the Marxist contention that both the state and law would wither away in postcapitalist societies. Pashukanis took as his point of departure Friedrich Engels's contention that in communist society there would be a replacement of the "rule of law" by the "administration of things."[3] A system of technical rules was to provide a noncoercive way to allocate disputed resources and services in order to achieve ends already accepted by the members of a society. A system of law had traditionally been conceived as providing a coercive way to settle conflicts among essentially private parties who could not otherwise agree about either the means or ends of proper conduct. For Pashukanis, the Marxist concept of law first and foremost demanded a decline in the threat of state coercion as a means of regulating social relationships.

Pashukanis proposed a theory of law that stressed the cooperative rather than the adversarial dimension of "dispute" resolution. In this regard he relied on an analogy to the rules embodied in a standard train timetable. The timetable tells prospective train passengers when and where they need to arrive in order to be admitted into a passenger train headed toward a particular destination.[4] Just as in the case of the rules regulating wills, the timetable "rules" are noncoercive, for the only penalty that follows upon nonconformity to the "rules" (for instance, by arriving five minutes late) is that the train crew will not wait for you. But this "penalty" need be conceived as a penalty only if you wanted to catch that train. Train timetables are rules for cooperation. If someone wants to catch a train to a particular destination on a particular day, then that person is told what is required of her. These "rules" facilitate the accomplishment of common goals. H. L. A. Hart points out that a large part of contemporary practices governed by law are, at least in part, of this sort rather than of the sort for which individuals are in dispute or disagreement about goals.[5]

With the change in economic relations that were supposed to occur under communism, the conflicts of interest that made traditional law indispensable for maintaining social order in precommunist societies were to have diminished. In its place there was to arise a greater unity of interests that would usher in the two major changes in law in postcapitalist society: state coercion would be less and less needed; and legal rules would not concern adversarial adjudications among private isolated subjects.

> The form of law—with its aspect of a subjective investiture with rights—is born in a society, which consists of isolated possessors of private, egoistic interests. When the entire economic life is built upon the principle of accord of independent wills, then—as if reflected in a mirror—every sort of social function takes on a legal character—that is to say, it becomes more than a social function; it becomes also the right of the person who is carrying out the function. . . . A characteristic feature of bourgeoise society is specifically the fact that general interests are segregated from—and are opposed to-private interests—but in this antithesis they themselves involuntarily take on the form of private interests—that is to say, the form of law.[6]

Yet these general interests will not always be best characterized as merely private interests to be weighed against other private interests, with each given roughly equal weight. Only because of the fact that legal socialization causes lawyers to conceive of disputes in terms of conflicts of private interests must this juxtaposition be maintained. Only because it is assumed that discord is essential to human relationships is it necessary to conceive of justice as requiring adversarial adjudications.

But is it not utopian to posit harmony of interests and unity of purpose, given what we see around us today? I will try to render this position more plausible but not without being critical of some of Pashukanis's contentions. Consider another of Pashukanis's examples, the "rules" that doctors give patients to follow.[7] These rules apply to a group of persons, patients, who share with their doctors a common interest in the promotion of health. Patients are not seen as isolated organisms with unrelated medical problems. One does not start from the premise that each sick person, in pursuing his or her health interests, will be in an adversarial relationship to his or her doctor or to each other sick person. Rather, these interests do not necessarily compete with each other; it is through cooperation in the sharing of medical records and research that the common goal of health can be achieved.

In the example of the rules of train regulation, the two main elements of law are both missing. The egoistic subjective element that is, for Pashukanis, the hallmark of law is replaced by a normative element that is rooted in cooperation. The objective coercive element, which makes the rules reasonably inflexible and extends their application to all cases of a similar sort regardless of the results that will be achieved by this inflexibility, is replaced by a conditional formulation: if you want x you must do y (but where it is not dictated that you must want x, or that you will be penalized for not doing y). The only potentially coercive element here, as we saw, occurs in the following scenario. If you want to catch the train but arrive five minutes late, the train crew will not wait for you, thereby "penalizing" you for failing to conform to the rule. But this penalty is again merely conditional, it affects you only if you wanted that which was governed by the technical rule. This is clearly a type of social constraint rather than the kind of explicit display of political coercion that occurs when one is threatened with imprisonment for violating a law. (Pashukanis chooses to characterize the difference as that between state power and social constraint.) Indeed, if this is coercion at all, it is coercion to do that which a person already considers to be what is best for herself or himself. Although this position has rather dangerous implications, as we will see from Kelsen's criticisms, it is clearly different from the model of adversarial law.[8]

Problems with Nonadversarial Advocacy

Administrative law, according to a nonadversarial model of law, may be conceived as a set of rules concerned with the allocation of resources, services, and positions within a social structure characterized by the fact that the members of this structure accept the general goals and purposes of that organization, although they disagree about certain specifics. Think of unemployment compensation proceedings. In such proceedings there need not be an antagonistic relationship between employer and former employee; indeed, both parties may wish to cooperate to obtain the agreed-upon compensation from the state fund into which the employer has been dutifully paying. Some legal theorists such as Fiss have contended that it will be best to regard each of the parties as representing an entire class or group of individuals, all similarly situated. And the state does not need to be conceived as an adversary either, especially if there is a compensation "table" that has already been decided upon as a matter of public policy. Emphasizing such cases will set the stage for a cooperative approach to law.

Some family law courts in a number of societies operate on a cooperative model in that the judge tries to get all of the parties to reach agreement about what is in the best interest of the whole family. But in reaching these agreements, often a judge will have to impose a settlement on the parties that none of the parties favored. Alice Ehr-Soon Tay has extensively criticized these family courts as what she calls "new forms of star chamber" proceedings. She asserts that they become a "scandalous law unto themselves" "because they are exposed neither to public scrutiny nor to the full rigor of proper judicial appeal."[9] Those who are least powerful, such as children, are not given adequate protection against judges who often have no interest in protecting the children's rights. This is a standard criticism of communistic or communitarian views, and it is a criticism I take quite seriously. Procedural due process should be an important concept in a cooperative as well as in an adversarial model of law, for without it abuses of power are too likely to occur even where there are many values shared by a community.

Tay's criticism can best be applied to Pashukanis concerning another of his examples, the rules of the military.[10] Pashukanis contended that the members of a company of soldiers are not in adversarial relations with one another or with their sergeant. Indeed, the soldiers cooperate with one another and with the sergeant by following rules to achieve a common, mutually accepted goal. Yet, it must be admitted, abuses that arise in these military relations have been notoriously difficult to end precisely because the soldiers have little procedural recourse if they disagree with what the sergeant has ordered them to do. Especially in settings where force is likely to occur, a nonadversarial model should not be left unrestrained by an absence of procedural due process. To the extent that a nonadversarial model of law fails to take such factors into account, this view is vulnerable to obvious counterarguments.

Hans Kelsen points us toward another major objection to views like those of Pashukanis's. Kelsen claimed that Pashukanis had failed to show why the "technical rules" that will regulate communist society are not themselves properly legal rules. By downplaying the fact that technical rules must also often be coercive, Pashukanis failed to show that the supposed "unity of purpose" underpinning technical rules actually exists.

> The assumption that there exists a "unity of purpose" in any case whatever where constraint is exercised by one individual against another, is an obvious fiction. The very fact that one individual must be forced to comply with the will of another shows clearly that the purpose of the one, and that means his immediate purpose, is not the purpose of the other, and it is the immediate purpose which alone comes into consideration when "unity" is in question. Otherwise, there would be unity where there exists the greatest antagonism.[11]

The mere fact that there might be agreement about the long-term end is not sufficient to establish the kind of unity of purpose that would distinguish technical from legal rules. According to Kelsen, law is essentially bound up with the settlement of disputes about means, and rather immediate means at that. To show that technical rules are significantly different from legal rules, Pashukanis, or a contemporary defender of nonadversarial approaches to law, would have to show that even the immediate means are not in dispute. Otherwise, we will again be faced with a situation where one party employs socially sanctioned coercion to compel another to follow his or her will, the paradigm of the adversarial model of advocacy.

In Pashukanis's example of the doctor–patient relationship, says Kelsen, the doctor is merely forcing the patient to do what is clearly in that patient's interest. Since the patient, according to this early-twentieth-century understanding of things, does not often comprehend what is good for him or her, the doctor must exercise force to bring about the purpose that the patient wants. The doctor–patient relationship is noncoercive only if the patient agrees to undergo each and every application to his or her own case of a rule of medicine that the doctor mandates. This is quite unlikely, says Kelsen, and it is even more unlikely when dealing with criminal matters instead of medical matters.

Kelsen's main point is that coercion will be smuggled into the system of technical rules whether Pashukanis wants it or not. This coercion is at the very least necessary to cause people to act according to the general set of technical rules rather than in an anarchic fashion to the detriment of others within society. The social coercion in medicine or the military is still coercion, and merely differs from state coercion in that it is not officially legitimated by the society at large. Even administrative agency proceedings are ultimately backed by the coercive power of the state, for if they were not, why would anyone trust that the agreed distribution of resources or services will indeed be provided. If there is literally no state power above the administrative agency, and similarly no level of legal appeal above the administrative ruling, then the administrative agency would be sovereign unto itself. And as Tay argued, when these agencies approach the point of sovereignty, those who must rely on these agencies are placed in an increasingly vulnerable predicament.

Cooperation and Participation

There are two distinct issues at stake in the preceding discussion. First, we have been discussing whether law as practiced should conform to the adversarial model of advocacy and dispute resolution or to a nonadversarial model of administration through "technical rules." Second, we have also been discussing whether law must, at some deeper, motivational level, be coercive or whether a system of rules can operate effectively without coercion. Law can be understood to be cooperative at each of these levels, that is, at the level of how people, especially through their lawyers, resolve their conflicts or at the level of what motivates people ultimately to resolve their disputes nonviolently. I am inclined to agree with Kelsen about the second level, namely, I think that even in the most-close-knit community there will be disagreements about how best to pursue commonly accepted goals. And such disagreements will require some sort of coercion as at least a background threat to bring people to the bargaining table. But I am also inclined to agree (at least partially) with Pashukanis about the first level, that is, I do not believe that all legal advocacy is best conceptualized according to an adversarial model.

According to the adversarial model of advocacy, lawyers are supposed to act as if the interests of two parties cannot be reconciled by appeal to shared values, and hence one client's interests are always best served when they are pitted against the interests of the other client, ignoring what they agree upon. Adversarial advocacy comes to resemble trial by ordeal: the least worst alternative will win the day so as to guard against the most worst. Lawyers and their clients are often trapped, unable to embrace alternatives that often would be best for all concerned. The larger community's interest in justice, which lawyers are supposed to uphold, is not necessarily best served when lawyers provide the most diligent adversarial representation of a client's case.

I propose that we limit the adversarial aspect of dispute resolution to those areas of law where there is a demonstrable inability to resolve disputes by appeals to shared values. But in those areas of law where there is a history of success in obtaining out-of-court settlements, we should not insist that lawyers operate as adversaries. Indeed, it may be better, given that lawyers have been socialized to be combative, not to have lawyers present at all and to rely instead on mediators who have been socialized to seek consensus.[12] In any event, for those areas of law where there is no history of irreconcilable differences between parties, a more cooperative approach to dispute resolution should be embraced, while still allowing for some adversarial protection of procedural due process.

I should say a bit about which types of dispute in law seem most conducive to the cooperative approach. Family law is currently one of the least adversarial branches of American law, but many critics have claimed that this has led to many problems especially for women. Because of the emphasis on cooperation in many family law courts, battered wives, for instance, are pressured to settle for conflict resolutions that provide less than adequate protection of their rights.[13] It is my view that certain aspects of real estate law may be better suited to a cooperative model than family law. It appears that more cooperative negotiating goes on in this domain, and in many cases the parties are already on more of an equal footing than is true in most family law cases. Indeed, in many states it is common for real estate brokers and mortgage company agents rather than lawyers to represent buyer and seller at closing.[14] In general, civil law is easier to conceptualize as cooperative than is criminal law, although there are some legal scholars who are exploring nonadversarial models in criminal matters.[15]

Critical theorists such as Jürgen Habermas have articulated a model of social interaction, called "communicative action," that places a premium on participatory modes of discourse that are noncoercive and that facilitate reaching consensus about shared values.[16] They have been highly critical of the intrusion of coercive state structures into all aspects of social life. I am very sympathetic to critical theory on these issues. Critical theory, itself a descendent of Marxism and left-Hegelianism, has provided an alternative between traditional liberal and communist models of politics and law. I wish to draw on critical theory's insights in arguing for a model of advocacy that includes elements from the cooperative and adversarial models.

Habermas has consistently stressed that a cooperative or consensus approach to shared values is not a call for forced compromise.[17] The worries expressed by Alice Ehr-Soon Tay concerning the "star-chamber" atmosphere in some family courts is really a worry about the kind of forced compromises that are also anathema to those of us who favor a cooperative and consensus-oriented approach to certain areas of law.[18] Law must operate to offset the consolidation of power in the hands of the powerful, not to enhance the ability of the powerful to force their wills upon the powerless in the uncritical rush to achieve compromise.

Throughout this chapter I have been motivated by a desire to find a model of advocacy that does not conceptualize social interaction as a battlefield between irreconcilable interests. What I have been exploring is a model of advocacy that is "more appropriate to these [various] contexts of interaction,"[19] that is, a model that is sensitive to context and that does not mandate that in all contexts people see themselves as adversaries, although where there will still be a place for some adversarial advocacy. This is a piece of the larger struggle that Habermas described as the struggle against the "colonization of the lifeworld," the tendency of state processes of legalization to take over customary forms of organization.[20] The adversarial model of advocacy is held in such high esteem that it has been much harder for alternative forms of advocacy to get their day in court.

There is a stronger criticism of the adversarial method of advocacy and dispute resolution that is inspired by critical theory. When the adversarial method colonizes the political domain, it may jeopardize the participatory system of democracy. A participatory system of government depends on a certain degree of solidarity and communal sympathy among the citizenry. The adversarial model of advocacy and dispute resolution, when extended into the political domain, breaks down solidarity and community. As the Founding Fathers were well aware, the greatest threat to democracy is factionalism, and factionalism is often inspired by a group acting as if its interests were always at odds with a competing interest group. The adversarial model calls for people to think of their own interests in just this way, as irreconcilably pitted against the interests of another party. This model, which stresses conflict rather than cooperation, drives a wedge between parties who are, in most instances, more alike than different. This situation disrupts solidarity and community and makes participatory democracy all the more difficult.

I should say once more that I am aware that minorities within some societies should continue to have a basis from which they can challenge an oppressive majority. In certain situations, an adversarial response to that majority may be the best way to protect minority rights. It would be contrary to my own liberationist goals to deny this possibility.[21] Rather, what I am claiming is that when each interest group sees itself as irreconcilably at odds with each other one, a position our society seems to be approaching, community breaks down. What we need is a sensitivity to context that will allow for a more reasonable appraisal of whether a particular group should feel driven to regard other groups as adversaries. I have suggested that contextual and historical considerations will often provide a reasonable basis for making such determinations. What I find suspect, though, is the colonization of social life by legal adversarialism, which makes us insensitive to these matters of context and history.

Empathy, Sensitivity, and Advocacy

In the remainder of this chapter I use the example of divorce mediation to explain how the role of advocate should change in certain situations in which two parties have at least some interests and values in common. The problem with adversarial advocacy in divorce cases is well known. As Charles Wolfram puts it: "Mediation has received particular attention recently in divorce. For some time, observers have complained that the presence of adversary lawyers in a divorce can exacerbate rather than solve problems, principally because some lawyers, habituated to the milieu of litigation, act as provocateurs rather than conciliators."[22] In divorce mediation, a mediator sees himself or herself as a facilitator and an advocate for a couple rather than for a single individual. In this sense there is advocacy (advocacy for the couple) without individual representation. The best way to aid the couple in reaching an amicable and reasonable solution to custody and property problems is for the mediator to keep both sides talking in a productive way toward the goal of reaching consensus. To do this, it is absolutely required that the mediator not take sides or feel that the interests of either or both people must be zealously pursued.[23]

While discussing virtue, Aristotle says that it is very difficult to hit the mean (where true virtue lies) rather than one or the other extreme. Divorce mediation is involved in just such an attempt to find the reasonable mean between the initially often extreme positions of two people who have decided to get a divorce. In attempting to hit the mean, mediators come to see two related facts. First, resolution of a problem is made easier if someone, normally the mediator, already has a solution in mind. And second, resolution is easier to achieve when one of the parties is willing to be the first to compromise. In both cases, problems of autonomy arise because, knowing these facts, a mediator is likely to put pressure on one or the other party to compromise rather than to hold his or her ground.

It might initially seem that divorce mediation is better than the adversarial model in terms of autonomy. After all, the mediator is only helping the couple to facilitate the details of a solution they have already reached. But what often takes place is that two lawyers doing battle for the two parties are replaced by a lawyer/mediator who acts more like a judge than a facilitator. In such a situation there may be even less autonomy for the parties in mediation than there was under the adversarial model, where it is assumed that both parties have distinct interests and have no reason to want to agree to a settlement that is not completely acceptable to themselves. To avoid these various problems, in addition to procedural safeguards a high premium needs to be placed on instilling empathy and sensitivity in mediators.[24]

In many divorce cases, two individuals are struggling to extricate themselves from a legal relationship with an equitable property and custody settlement. But in some cases, they are also struggling to retain a less formal relationship, even in the face of strong emotions of anger, regret, frustration, and even retribution. This is especially true when young children are also involved. It would be important, in most divorce cases, for the parents to retain enough of a relationship so that the day-to-day parenting decisions could be negotiated amicably. As Wolfson and many others have pointed out, lawyers often exacerbate the strongly negative feelings two divorcing individuals feel.

A socially responsive lawyer would worry that the zealous, aggressive, and single-minded promotion of the rights of parties to a divorce could make things worse for them as well as for the society at large. But given standard legal socialization, it is not clear that lawyers have much choice. If they try to be nonadversarial, they discover that very little that they learned in law school provides them with resources to be good counselors. This is why it is important for legal socialization to be changed so that lawyers are trained to be empathic to the uniquely situated persons who are their clients, and to be sensitive to the feelings of these parties as well as to the history and context of their present predicament. Some have suggested that this would best be done if lawyers were trained to be therapists.[25] Although I find this suggestion potentially problematic, there is some merit to the spirit of this suggestion.

Lawyers need to develop some of the same skills as therapists if they are to deal with their increasingly important roles as counselor, mediator, conciliator, and bargainer, which often require cooperation more than competition among people. The reason that the skills of the therapist are valuable is that the focus is on understanding the client's interests in his or her own terms. Here, facilitating a person's interests, especially when his or her interests are somewhat dependent on the fulfillment of the interests of others, will be harmed by an overly zealous and aggressive adversarial approach. Of course, as I suggested previously, there are certainly other cases where the adversarial approach is warranted.

Indeed, there have been a number of problems with divorce mediation, at least some of which are traceable to the complete lack of adversarialism in these proceedings. The lack of procedures aimed at protecting the rights of the individuals in the divorce case often means that the structure works to the advantage of the most powerful and sophisticated of the parties. Given current circumstances in the United States, this means that the woman's rights are not nearly as well protected as those of the man in divorce mediation cases. In addition, when mediators try to correct for this potential imbalance, paternalism on the part of the mediator occasionally surfaces as the mediator tries to do what he or she thinks is best for the woman, even though it may be against the woman's explicitly stated wishes at the moment.

It is important to recognize the possible pitfalls of nonadversarial arrangements. As I said earlier, some types of cases, especially where it is quite likely that differences of interest and power would make it likely that a party would be systematically disadvantaged, are best handled through adversarial advocacy. But the pitfalls of nonadversarial advocacy can be minimized in certain types of cases, especially where there is significant agreement about common goals, making it true that nonadversarial advocacy is best for this type of case. What we need is a new model of legal socialization that stresses both roles, adversarial as well as cooperative advocacy, based on which kind of case is involved.

The debate about adversarial advocacy parallels the debate between liberals and communitarians about the role of mediating institutions in the democratic political process. In that debate, it seems to me that the truth lies somewhere in between liberalism and communitarianism. And it similarly seems to me that we do not have to choose between adversarial and nonadversarial advocacy. Rather, the best society may be one in which lawyers are trained to perform both forms of advocacy. Liberalism, with its traditional championing of adversarial advocacy, and communitarianism, with its championing of cooperative advocacy, can coexist, as is beginning to be true in actual legal practice in the United States. Here, plea bargaining, labor negotiation, and divorce mediation occur in the same system with highly adversarial litigation.

Conclusion

Throughout this chapter I explored the problems and advantages of an adversarial as well as a nonadversarial approach to advocacy and dispute resolution. I have argued that a nonadversarial approach makes more sense than an adversarial one when there is a history of agreement about matters of shared value. But also this claim is modified in full recognition that there remain many areas of contemporary life that are not marked by consensus about goals. And I have been critical of some proponents of nonadversarial advocacy for failing to recognize that even when there is consensus, procedural due process needs to be safeguarded. In addition, I pointed out that an uncritical reliance on the adversarial model, especially when that is extended into other areas of social and political life, runs contrary to the spirit of participatory democracy. This last point, which clearly could be the subject of a chapter in its own right, should—it is hoped—break the stranglehold of the adversarial model, especially in the socialization of lawyers, which has made life so hard for those who favor alternative forms of advocacy and of dispute resolution, especially concerning social groups.[26] As our society begins to see the value of nonadversarial legal advocacy, we may also see ways of increasing the sense of community in our pluralistic society.[27]

Notes

1. See Charles Wolfram, *Modern Legal Ethics* (St. Paul, Minn.: West, 1986), 593.

2. Owen Fiss, "Foreword: The Forms of Justice, The Supreme Court 1978 Term," *Harvard Law Review* 93 (November 1979): 29.

3. E. B. Pashukanis, "The General Theory of Law and Marxism" (1924), trans. H. W. Babb, reprinted in *Soviet Legal Philosophy*, ed. H. W. Babb and John N. Hazard, (Cambridge: Harvard University Press, 1951).

4. Pashukanis, "The General Theory of Law and Marxism," 137.

5. H. L. A. Hart, *The Concept of Law* (Oxford: Clarendon Press, 1961), esp. chaps. 3 and 4.

6. Pashukanis, "The General Theory of Law and Marxism," 155–56.

7. I do not necessarily agree with Pashukanis that doctors impose rules on their patients; I am here merely reporting what he says.

8. Charles Wolfram rightly points out that the adversarial model of law did not literally evolve from such dispute-resolution models as trial by combat. See his discussion of this point in *Modern Legal Ethics*, 567.

9. Alice Ehr-Soon Tay, "The Law, the Citizen, and the State," in *Law and Society: The Crisis in Legal Ideas*, ed. Eugene Kamenka, Robert Brown, and Alice Ehr-Soon Tay (New York: St. Martin's Press, 1978), 8.

10. Pashukanis's two other major examples, discussed earlier, are railway timetables and medical orders.

11. Hans Kelsen, "Pashukanis's Theory of Law," *The Communist Theory of Law* (New York: Praeger, 1955), 104.

12. For an interesting discussion of the German "inquisitorial" system, which places much more emphasis on the role of judge-mediators than on lawyer-adversaries, see David Luban, *Lawyers and Justice* (Princeton: Princeton University Press, 1988), 93–103.

13. For a good discussion of the difficulties facing battered women in American legal contexts see Deborah Rhode, *Gender and Justice* (Cambridge: Harvard University Press, 1989), 237–44. Also see Dories Klein, "The Dark Side of Marriage: Battered Wives and the Domination of Women," in *Judge, Lawyer, Victim, Thief*, ed. Nicole Hahn Rafter and Elizabeth A. Stanko (Boston: Northeastern University Press, 1982).

14. See my "Conflict of Interest," in *Professional Ethics and Social Responsibility*, ed. Daniel Wueste (Lanham, Md.: Rowman & Littlefield, 1994), 67–82, where I address at some length the roles and conflicts in real estate settlements.

15. See Kit Kinports, "Evidence Engendered," *University of Illinois Law Review*, no. 2 (1991).

16. For the most accessible work on this topic, see Jürgen Habermas, *Moral Consciousness and Communicative Action* (Cambridge: MIT Press, 1990).

17. Jürgen Habermas, "Law and Morality," in *The Tanner Lectures on Human Values*, vol. 8, ed. Sterling M. McMurrin (Salt Lake City: University of Utah Press, 1988), esp. 231. For a revealing discussion of this issue in the context of analytical jurisprudence, see David Ingram, "Dworkin, Habermas and the CLS Movement on Moral Criticism in Law," *Philosophy and Social Criticism*, 1992, esp. 255–56.

18. Thomas McCarthy has argued that Habermas and others have misunderstood the importance of nonargumentative forms of compromise. See his "Practical Discourse: On the Relation of Morality to Politics," *Ideals and Illusions: On Reconstruction and Deconstruction in Contemporary Critical Theory* (Cambridge: MIT Press, 1991), esp. 198.

19. Kenneth Baynes, *The Normative Grounds of Social Criticism* (Albany: SUNY Press, 1992), 166.

20. See Jürgen Habermas, *The Theory of Communicative Action*, vol. 2 (Boston: Beacon Press, 1987).

21. See the final chapter of my *Sharing Responsibility* (Chicago: University of Chicago Press, 1992), where I defend a view that I have labeled "liberationist communitarianism" and I am specifically concerned to show how communitarian social theory can have a place for procedural rights.

22. Wolfram, *Modern Legal Ethics*, 730.

23. Douglas Lind suggests in his commentary on this chapter that I have misunderstood the nature of mediation. He contends that the mediator is involved in adjudication, not advocacy, and that if the mediator is an advocate at all, he or she is an advocate for the process of mediation. This is a curious construal of what actually occurs in the practice of mediation. In my experience, divorce mediators tell both parties that they are advocates for the parties collectively. Lawyers have great difficulty understanding their roles if they cannot identify for whom they are the advocate. This was the main issue discussed at a panel on divorce mediation that I was asked to participate in more than a decade ago. Lind also suggests that I have confused adjudication and advocacy. Again, in my experience this is also true of most practicing lawyers, who feel that as long as they are good advocates, they will also contribute best to an adjudication of the issue that separates the parties. So, while I find Lind's distinction highly suggestive theoretically, I do not find it helpful in understanding legal practice. Lind should be read as providing the textbook construal of how divorce mediation is supposed to work. But what is ideally true is not always actually true. This is especially apparent when Lind ignores the fact that women, who are far more likely to compromise first, generally do worse in divorce mediated settlements than do men, who are far more likely to be resistant to any form of compromise. Although I have generally embraced divorce mediation as an interesting alternative form of adjudication and advocacy, I, unlike Lind, remain highly skeptical of its ability to overcome traditional patterns of socialization of men and women, as well as traditional patterns of socialization of lawyers.

24. I am grateful to Ralph Lindgren for first making me aware of the practical importance of empathy in mediation.

25. See Michael Joseph Rosanova, "Divorce-Related Mediation," *Perspectives on the Professions* (newsletter of the Center for the Study of Ethics in the Professions, Illinois Institute of Technology) 2, nos. 3/4 (September/December 1982): 2–6.

26. See Larry May and Marie Failinger, "Litigating Against Poverty: Legal Services and Group Representation," *Ohio State Law Journal* 45, no. 1 (1984): 1–56. I discuss the question of justice for groups in the final chapter of my book *The Morality of Groups* (Notre Dame: University of Notre Dame Press, 1987).

27. This chapter is part of *The Socially Responsive Self* (Chicago: University of Chicago Press, 1996). This project was funded by a grant from the National Science Foundation's Program in Ethics and Value Studies.

Comment

From Radical Legal Critique
to Alternative Dispute Resolution

Douglas Lind

Larry May's chapter raises a pair of fundamental questions for contemporary American legal practice: Does legal advocacy have to be adversarial? Should dispute resolution in this country continue to follow the traditional adversarial model of litigation in the courts? May answers both questions in the negative, arguing that the adversarial model is unworkable for large classes of cases where, by emphasizing individual interests and factional points of view, it breaks down community and threatens democracy. In its stead, May recommends what he calls a "cooperative approach to law"—a normative approach "rooted in cooperation," where nonadversarial interaction supplants the adversarial system in matters involving parties who, in substantial part, live by "shared values."

Although May identifies a case that sorely needs making, he fails, for several reasons, to make it. First, instead of articulating and defending straightforwardly a particular cooperative, nonadversarial model of law, May shifts somewhat confusingly between several distinct considerations. He suggests noble objectives: a model of law that is "sensitive to context" and emphasizes "a cooperative or consensus approach to shared values," one that does not pit parties against each other as if on a battlefield. Yet it is unclear how he envisions the implementation of these objectives in practice. He canvasses a broad range of alternatives, taking into consideration questions of legal administration, modes of advocacy, and alternative methods of dispute resolution. Early in the paper he places heavy reliance on the Marxist legal philosopher E. B. Pashukanis, endorsing the latter's cooperative model of legal "administration through 'technical rules.'" Yet no sooner does he entice us with the suggestion that adjudication could be replaced by a nonadversarial (indeed, non-conflict-oriented) system of administrative law than he drops Pashukanis in favor of Habermas, upon whom he relies for the proposition that lawyers should become more cooperative and less adversarial in representing their clients' interests. Finally, he turns to the practice of divorce mediation, suggesting apparently that that method of dispute resolution provides an apt model for advocacy. By the chapter's end it is entirely unclear what model or forms of nonadversarial law May recommends.

Second, this lack of clarity is heightened by the fact that May does not address independently the two very separate prongs of his inquiry. In calling into question the adversarial model, May proposes giving "serious consideration to alternative models of advocacy and dispute resolution." He does not seem to appreciate, however, that advocacy and dispute resolution are not the same. "Advocacy" in law is one aspect of the representation of clients by lawyers;[1] "dispute resolution" refers generally to a variety of methods for handling conflicts among persons or parties. In the adversarial system, the dominant method of dispute resolution is adjudication, and advocacy certainly does take on a competitive cast. Yet critics of the adversarial system must be very clear on whether the problems they cite lie with adjudication per se or arise from the behavior and techniques of advocacy used by lawyers working within the system. May does not provide that clarity, for he uses the terms "advocacy" and "dispute resolution" interchangeably, leaving open to question whether his concerns go principally to the conduct of lawyers or to adjudication as a method of dispute resolution.

Third, to the extent May is concerned primarily with advocacy, he provides very little insight into how he envisions it becoming less adversarial. He suggests that legal education should stress "cooperative advocacy," by which he apparently means techniques of advocacy such as plea bargaining, settlement, and labor negotiation. Yet what he overlooks is that negotiating a plea bargain or civil settlement falls squarely within the adversarial model of advocacy.[2] Skilled lawyers recognize, certainly far better than we academics, that often they can best (with the greatest "zeal") protect a client's interests through negotiation and settlement. That is, any lawyer adept at the craft of trial advocacy understands, like a general or a quarterback, that there are times when to do other than retreat or punt would be foolhardy. It is all part of the adversarial process.

Fourth, turning to dispute resolution, although May uses a number of illustrative examples, they do little to clarify his vision of a cooperative, nonadversarial model of law. He relies in part on examples drawn from Pashukanis such as train schedules and doctor-patient relations. These nonconflict examples say little about how to reform (or replace) adjudication as the dominant method of dispute resolution. May's suggestion that real estate law provides the best example of an area of law already infused with cooperation likewise fails to show what he has in mind for a cooperative, nonadversarial method of dispute resolution, for, as he acknowledges, most real estate transactions already proceed smoothly and result in no legal conflicts.

Finally, and most important, May stresses that cooperative dispute resolution is most needed for handling conflicts arising between parties who live by "shared values." He predicates this claim on the woeful inadequacy of the adversarial system to resolve disputes between parties who share a set of common values or goals. He writes:

> I propose that we limit the adversarial aspect of dispute resolution to those areas of law where there is a demonstrable inability to resolve disputes by appeals to shared values. . . . For those areas of law where there is no history of irreconcilable differences between parties, a more cooperative approach to dispute resolution should be embraced. . . .
>
> I have argued that a nonadversarial approach makes more sense than an adversarial one when there is a history of agreement about matters of shared value.

To the contrary, I want to suggest that it is precisely those areas of law *least* characterized by "shared values" that stand most in need of alternative dispute resolution. Environmental law is perhaps the clearest example. No area of law has grown more in the past two decades than environmental law, and no area of law has amassed a worse litigation record. Although Congress and state legislatures have enacted hundreds of environmental statutes, many with citizen-suit provisions allowing environmentally minded parties to use the courts to forestall environmental despoliation, the overall litigation cost to society from environmental lawsuits has been enormous compared to the rather negligible environmental benefits.

Statutes such as the National Environmental Policy Act of 1969 (NEPA)[3] and the Comprehensive Environmental Response, Compensation, and Liability Act of 1980 (CERCLA)[4] have resulted in scores of lawsuits, yet very few development projects challenged under NEPA have actually been canceled. Very little remediation has occurred at hazardous waste sites as a result of private-party response actions under CERCLA. Federal environmental litigation boasts, more than anything else, a record of consummate delay. More often than not, litigation reaps little environmental improvement; none of the parties leave satisfied; and even the party who prevails finds victory to be quite hollow, given the huge expenditure of time and money.

A lack of shared values explains the dismal record of environmental law. Environmental litigation is so unsatisfactory because the parties very often hold divergent, even conflicting, value structures. Although every environmental controversy involves particular parties (those possessing the legal status of "standing"), environmental disputes in a very real sense raise issues going far beyond the specific interests of the parties or the technical legal positions advanced by their lawyers in the adversarial context. These disputes involve normative issues grounded in different and often conflicting value structures, such as the inviolability of property rights versus the value of wilderness, endangered species, or wetlands. When these disparate value structures become hardened, they can lead to factional strife and systemic social conflict within communities. Today the West is rife with such conflict arising from disagreements over the use of federal lands and the protection of endangered species. The traditional adjudicatory process is particularly ill equipped to handle such matters because it encourages the parties, who already hold divergent and often conflicting values and goals, to become even greater adversaries, increasing the possibility that the factional strife will result in irreparable breakdown of community.

Because the adversarial process increases social tension and factionalism in conflict areas like environmental protection where our society suffers from a lack of shared values, I agree with May that what truly follows from radical legal critique is not simply minor reform of the adversarial system of dispute resolution so as to reduce its institutionalized bias. Rather, certain areas of law call for replacing adjudication with a method of dispute resolution that seeks to ameliorate, not exacerbate, conflict. Yet I want to emphasize that I see this need arising because of a lack of shared values, not the opposite. And I want to endorse a particular method of alternative dispute resolution: mediation.[5]

Unlike adjudication, mediation does not pit parties *against* each other or treat their respective points of view as positions necessarily in tension, one of which must fall as the other prevails. Rather, in mediation, the mediator acts not as a judge but as a facilitator of dialogue. The presumption throughout is to effect a fair resolution, not a compromise "decision" or "ruling" imposed on the parties from an authority figure but an *agreement* created and adopted by the parties.

The most important aspect of the mediation process, what Lon Fuller once referred to as the "central quality" of mediation, comes about through the *reorientation* of the parties toward each other.[6] Instead of concentrating on the technical legal positions advanced by each party, the mediator focuses on their respective *interests* and attempts to bring about a new and shared perception of their relationship. This attempted reorientation of attitudes and values marks the critical difference between mediation and adjudication. And it shows that mediation fits May's objective to find a method of dispute resolution that truly encourages *cooperation*.

Notes

1. See Roger Haydock and John Sonsteng, *Advocacy* (St. Paul, Minn.: West, 1994), 1: 4–5; James E. Moliterno and John M. Levy, *Ethics of the Lawyer's Work* (St. Paul, Minn.: West, 1993), 5–45, 254–59.

2. The fact that more than 90 percent of all lawsuits end in a negotiated settlement suggests that negotiation is not foreign to the adversarial system. See Moliterno and Levy, *Ethics of the Lawyer's Work*, 232. And the way legal texts address negotiation, using language of combat and competition, shows that within law, negotiation is not considered a nonadversarial practice. See Charles B. Craver, *Effective Legal Negotiation and Settlement*, 2d ed. (Charlottesville, Va.: Michie, 1993): passim (characterizing parties in negotiation as "adversaries"); 190–91 (discussing the negotiation tactic of "threaten[ing] dire consequences"); 243 (identifying strategies for "weakening an opponent's position of strength"); and Donald G. Gifford, *Legal Negotiation: Theory and Applications* (St. Paul, Minn.: West, 1989), 22 (discussing the importance of choosing the best "negotiation strategy"); 36–38 (stressing the need to assess the "relative bargaining power" of the parties); 79 (addressing the advantages and disadvantages of negotiating "on one's own territory"); 74–83, 99–109, 120–21, 141–52 (identifying various "competitive tactics" for negotiation). Although the authors do discuss "cooperative" negotiation techniques (Craver, 153–66; Gifford, 83–95, 111–18, 121–22, 152–62), they present them as tactics to be used, when strategically appropriate, in conjunction with competitive tactics.

3. 42 U.S.C. secs. 4321–4370a (1990).

4. 42 U.S.C. secs. 9601–9675 (1990).

5. I am encouraged that May has added to his chapter a section on mediation. Yet his discussion of divorce mediation, vexed by loose overlap between considerations of advocacy and dispute resolution, only further confounds his thesis. Mediation is not, as May suggests, a form of advocacy; it is a method of dispute resolution whereby a neutral third party (the mediator) seeks to help resolve a conflict through facilitated negotiation. Susan M. Leeson and Bryan M. Johnston, *Ending It: Dispute Resolution in America* (Cincinnati: Anderson, 1988), 133; John D. Rothman, *A Lawyer's Practical Guide to Mediation* (Kearney, Neb.: Morris, 1995), 85. May evinces a general misunderstanding of mediation practice when he suggests that mediators are advocates for the parties collectively, that they conduct mediations with a solution already in mind, and that medi-

ation works best when one party is willing to compromise first. At the very most, mediators are advocates for mediation as a process for resolving disputes. While they may in the process of mediating come to see various solutions to the conflict at hand, they have no authority to impose a settlement; they strive, rather, to help the parties develop a mutually agreeable solution themselves. See Stephen B. Goldberg, Frank E. A. Sander, and Nancy H. Rogers, *Dispute Resolution: Negotiation, Mediation, and Other Processes*, 2d ed. (Boston: Little, Brown, 1992), 104–5; C. Honeyman, "Five Elements of Mediation, *Negotiation Journal* 4 (1988): 153; Rothman, *A Lawyer's Practical Guide to Mediation*, 106. And although compromise is the goal of certain forms of negotiation, mediators try to facilitate a collaborative solution that satisfies the underlying interests of all parties.

6. Lon L. Fuller, "Mediation—Its Forms and Functions," *Southern California Law Review* 44 (1971): 325.

Part II

Feminist Political and Legal Theory

Chapter 5

Autonomy and the Encumbered Self

Emily R. Gill

Over the past two decades, many theorists have concluded that equality, at its best, embodies the ideals of universality and impartiality. More recently, however, some have questioned whether this vision in fact serves all individuals well. Frequently, detachment is attained "only by abstracting from the particularities of situation, feeling, affiliation, and point of view. These particularities still operate, however, in the actual context of action. Thus the ideal of impartiality generates a dichotomy between universal and particular, public and private, reason and passion."[1] Individuals do not exist prior to and in abstraction from their commitments, which are then only contingent. Rather, "a person's particular sense of history, affinity, and separateness, even the person's mode of reasoning, evaluating, and expressing feeling, are constituted partly by her or his group affinities."[2] The appearance of universality or impartiality, then, is an illusion.

Such critics question the traditionally modern "account of the subject as knower . . . standing outside of and opposed to objects of knowledge—autonomous, neutral, abstract, and purified of particularity. They [modern science and philosophy] construct this modern subjectivity by fleeing from material reality . . . to create a purified abstract idea of formal reason, disembodied and transcendent."[3] For Michael Sandel, this construction of the subject is a hallmark of liberalism. Only if we stand antecedently to the circumstances and conditions of our lives "can we view ourselves as subjects as well as objects of experience, as agents and not just instruments of the purposes we pursue."[4] The liberal self, to Sandel, is an "unencumbered self . . . prior to and independent of purposes and ends"[5] because only a self beyond the reach of experience and without constitutive ends and interests is free as an independent agent to *choose* its ends. "No role or commitment could define me so completely that I could not understand myself without it. No project could be so essential that turning away from it would call into question the person I am."[6]

For Sandel, however, the self without constitutive ends is also a self without continuity. "The self is disempowered because dissociated from those ends and desires which, woven gradually together into a coherent whole, provide a fixity of purpose, form a plan of life, and so account for the continuity of the self with its ends."[7] In his work as a whole, Sandel suggests that deontological theorists impoverish the self by emphasizing the voluntarist dimension of human agency, "in which the self is related to its ends as a willing subject to the objects of choice," at the expense of the cognitive dimension, "in which the self is related to its ends as a knowing subject to the objects of understanding" (58). We are not self-contained and impermeable beings, "individuated in advance and given prior to our ends, but must be subjects constituted in part by our central aspirations and attachments, always open, indeed vulnerable, to growth and transformation in the light of revised self-understandings" (172). Human agency requires the self not only to choose but also to reflect, "to turn its lights inward upon itself, to inquire into its constituent nature, to survey its various attachments and acknowledge their respective claims . . . to arrive at a self-understanding less opaque if never perfectly transparent, a subjectivity less fluid if never finally fixed, and so gradually, throughout a lifetime, to participate in the constitution of its identity" (153).

Contemporary theorists of difference like Iris Marion Young, for example, reassert the centrality of that which is experientially constitutive of the self as opposed to that which is chosen. This approach seems particularly appropriate in the area of sex difference, which is most often a matter of being, not of chosen affinity or commitment. In fact, Jean Elshtain, in her critique of androgyny, suggests that liberal environmentalists and androgynists "evade the possibility that human beings may have a 'nature' of some sort that is not exhausted with reference to the social forces that have impinged on it."[8] For Elshtain, the body is the primary locus of human identity, action, and accountability, rather than simply a vehicle with which the rational subject "enjoys a contingent relation" (147).[9] Identity and memory require "a *particular* history of having lived, as a body, in a social world" (147; emphasis in original). Thus, even "our knowing is essentially tied to our experiences of ourselves as bodies" (149).

Here a dilemma appears, however. In Sandel's terms, the experience of sex difference and its accompanying affinities may be interpreted as constitutive of the self, when the subject involved may wish to stand beyond the reach of experience to choose its ends. On the other hand, if particularities such as experience and affinity are inevitably constitutive of the self, as Young asserts, others' attempts to abstract from these particularities act to deny a part of the self that the subject may wish to affirm. Recent commentators on Sandel suggest that he exaggerates the dichotomy between choice and reflection, between the voluntarist and cognitive aspects of the self. Both individual choice *and* social experience shape the self. Preferences cannot be chosen in a vacuum. Yet "critical reflection needs an anchor—an individual standpoint marked by a set of endorsed preferences, traits, and so forth. Thus, voluntarism without some degree of situation and critical reflection without an independent base of choice are equally untenable."[10] Moreover, because in Sandel's view a self does exist that can reexamine its constituents and ends, individuals ought to enjoy "the conditions appropriate to that re-examining, as an indispensable part of leading the best possible life. And amongst those conditions should be the liberal guarantees of personal independence necessary to make that judgment freely."[11]

In this chapter I do two things. Using Sandel as a framework, I examine some theories of difference with a view toward their impact on agency in the voluntarist mode and in the cognitive mode as described by Sandel. I believe that the latter is necessary to and can enhance autonomy, but that it does so most clearly when it contributes to choice. Second, I examine the reaffirmation of particularity as it may contribute to what Will Kymlicka describes as a context of choice. "The decision about how to lead our lives must ultimately be ours alone, but this decision is always a matter of selecting what we believe to be most valuable from the various options available, selecting from a context of choice which provides us with different ways of life."[12]

I

According to some contemporary theorists of difference, much political thought that is apparently neutral in abstracting from the particularity of sex difference begins from a self-understanding that is historically male, and thus from a particularized understanding after all. This in turn implies a particularized understanding of the female, one that relegates her to particular roles and thus circumscribes, in Sandel's terms, both her choices and her reflections or self-understandings. More specifically, some theorists imply that political thought constructs the female in terms of particularities that afford too little detachment for willing in the voluntarist mode and also too little scope for reflection in the cognitive mode. Extrapolating from this line of thought, I suggest that human agency in its cognitive sense requires a *variety* of possible constitutive ends or constituents of identity if true autonomy is to exist, if one's self-understanding is to be other than automatically given. In this context, then, let us examine some of these theories of difference to see their impact on both reflection *and* choice.

The social contract has operated as the paramount metaphor for conditions of autonomy in much political philosophy. Yet Carole Pateman argues that voluntary contract often signifies an exchange of obedience for protection, generating "political right in the form of relations of domination and subordination"; specifically, sexual difference determines that women are not parties to the social contract but instead are the subjects of it.[13] Pateman interprets the history of political thought as revealing "that our social life is as if it were based on a sexual contract, which both establishes orderly access to women and a division of labour in which women are subordinate to men" (119).[14] In other words, "Contract is the specifically modern means of creating relationships of subordination, but because civil subordination originates in contract, it is presented as freedom."[15] The implicit sexual contract fades from view "because it is *displaced onto the marriage contract*,"[16] which remains like the Cheshire cat's grin when the cat's body is no longer apparent. Yet the missing elements reappear in the fact that the contract's scope and terms cannot be freely chosen by each couple but are limited to what the state authorizes. Hence "marriage is less a contract than a matter of *status*."[17]

Central to Pateman's account is the extent to which biology has been, and in many cases ostensibly still is, destiny for both men and women. Feminist constructions of an "ostensibly sex-neutral 'individual'" in reality force women to become replicas of men.[18] But "such an aspiration can never be fulfilled. The 'individual' is a patriarchal category. The individual is masculine and his sexuality is understood accordingly. . . . The patriarchal construction of sexuality, what it means to be a sexual being, is to possess and to have access to sexual property" (184–85). More generally, under patriarchy "the difference between masculinity and femininity is the political difference between freedom and subjection and . . . sexual mastery is the major means through which men affirm their manhood" (207). Thus, "the self is not completely subsumed in its sexuality, but identity is inseparable from the sexual construction of the self" (207).

Women, on the other hand, "have now won civil and juridical standing almost equal to men's, but they are not incorporated into workplaces on the same basis as male workers" (135).[19] They often are viewed and view themselves first and foremost as wives. "A wife who is in paid employment never ceases to be a housewife; instead she becomes a *working wife,* and increases the length of her working day."[20] Sexual harassment "helps maintain men's patriarchal right in the public world. . . . Sexual domination is part of the structure of subordination in the workplace," which is different for female than for male workers. "Women have not been incorporated into the patriarchal structure of capitalist employment as 'workers'; they have been incorporated as *women;* and how can it be otherwise when women are not, and cannot be, men?" (142; emphasis in original).

Since for Pateman the social construction of the self includes its sexual construction, patriarchal society asserts, in Sandel's terms, the centrality of experience and contingency, both biological and social, in the constitution of the self and of its resulting ends. Sandel observes, however, that the self may be disempowered not only when it is detached from its ends but also if it is without boundaries, if too *many* contingencies appear essential to its identity and function as constitutive ends.[21] "Unable to distinguish what is mine from what is me, I am in constant danger of drowning in a sea of circumstance" (57). On the other hand, Pateman describes the female self as constructed not with too many but too few constituents of identity. The "sea" is composed of only *one* circumstance, that of female sexuality and its attributes. The social construction of the female self places women in a particular structural position that shapes subsequent understandings of women and, most important, women's self-understandings. Thus the scope for reflection on the possible constituents of one's identity is too narrow for women to operate in the cognitive sense as knowing subjects to the objects of understanding.

If, however, subjects wish to and are able to transcend their structural definitions and to revise their self-understandings, Sandel's account allows for this move, "Reflexivity is a distancing faculty, and issues in a certain detachment. It succeeds by restoring the shrunken space between self and ends. . . . When I am able to reflect on my obsession, able to pick it out and make it an object of my reflection, I thereby establish a certain space between it and me, and so diminish its hold."[22] I shall leave aside the problem of how Pateman's socially constructed subjects, whose attributes function as constituents of their identities, manage this transcendence and revision. In any case, this distancing faculty facilitates the shift from the cognitive to the voluntarist dimension of agency, from the self's role as a knowing subject to the objects of understanding to its role as a willing subject to the objects of choice. In Pateman's account, however, women apparently cannot will the transcendence of their biological constitution to challenge their social construction, whether in patriarchal society or elsewhere.

First, the idea that all individuals own property in their own persons, in their capacities and attributes, empowers neither women nor men, in Pateman's opinion. The subject of any employment contract is the worker and his labor, not simply his labor power. "Since he cannot be separated from his capacities, he sells command over the use of his body and himself."[23] Thus "property in the person, unlike material property, cannot be separated from its owner" (2–3). The subject is never an unencumbered self but is always encumbered by the body. "The body and the self are not identical, but selves are inseparable from bodies" (206),[24] as is illustrated by the fact that "for self-protection, a prostitute must distance herself from her sexual use" (207).

Second, the concept of property in the person is a fiction for women even more than for men. The ultimate contemporary example of the connection between body and self can be found in the practice of surrogacy. Because sperm can be separated from the male body, as in artificial insemination, it is "the only example of property in the person that is not a political fiction" (217). But "the 'surrogate' mother contracts out right over the unique physiological, emotional and creative capacity of her body, that is to say, of herself as a woman" (215). The uterus is inseparable from womanhood, even as the latter is treated as irrelevant and as the gestational mother is considered a surrogate: "When the property of the 'surrogate' mother, her empty vessel, is filled with the seed of the man who has contracted with her, he, too, becomes the parent, the creative force that brings new life (property) into the world. . . . The story of the social contract is the greatest story of men giving political birth, but . . . thanks to the power of the creative political medium of contract, men can appropriate physical genesis too" (216–17).[25]

The biological construction of the female self, Pateman is implying, not only shapes the social understandings and self-understandings of women but also makes it impossible for the individual to step back from her ends or to exist outside them. She cannot employ freely, or deploy, property in her own person, in her capacities and attributes, because this property is constitutive of her personhood, and as a female person she cannot exist without these attributes. Whatever her self-understanding, then, her lack of detachment prevents her from exercising autonomy in the voluntarist mode. Women's difference from men is partly socially constructed but also partly a matter of biology that cannot be chosen or rejected.

Pateman's core objection to contract centers on her assertion that it allows relations of civil domination and subordination to masquerade as freedom. "Civil subordination depends upon the capacity of human beings to act as if they could contract out labour power or services rather than, as they must, contract out themselves and their labour to be used by another" (231). She concludes that "if political relations are to lose all resemblance to slavery, free women and men must willingly agree to uphold the social conditions of their autonomy. That is to say, they must agree to uphold limits." For mutual autonomy to replace mastery, "individual freedom must be limited by the structure of social relations in which freedom inheres" (232). Presumably, she means limits on what may be the subject of contract and a social framework that recognizes that both the social and biological construction of the female self have limited her self-understandings and her choices.

As we have seen, however, Pateman implies that the subject cannot completely transcend its biological constitution, whatever its social construction or the arrangements of the society in which it exists. "The individual as owner is separated from a body that is one sex or the other. A human body, except through misfortunes of birth, is not male and female at the same time, no matter how the body is dressed or positioned in the social structure" (223). Since, in Pateman's explanation, women cannot be "individuals" as men are, "to take embodied identity seriously demands the abandonment of the masculine, unitary individual to open up space for two figures; one masculine, one feminine" (224). Women should not strive to become "individuals" or replicas of men. Past feminists "demanded juridical equality and recognition *as women*" (45), claiming their private contributions as part of citizenship. In so doing, "they grappled with the political problem of expressing sexual difference; they did not attempt to deny political significance to womanhood" (227). Juridical freedom and equality can "help in the task of creating the social conditions for the development of an autonomous femininity," but "women's equal standing must be accepted as an expression of the freedom of women *as women*, and not treated as an indication that women can be just like men" (231; emphasis in original). But how do we treat women "as women"? The individual should be able to embrace attributes that, upon reflection, she takes to be constitutive of her selfhood. But she must also be able to detach herself from attributes she does *not* wish to claim as part of herself and to embrace others she may have chosen.

The social conditions of autonomy are addressed in more detail by Zillah Eisenstein. Like Pateman, she recognizes the social construction of the female self as society and culture convert biological sex into gender. "The supposition of *engendered* sex 'difference,' pretending differences between the sexes are natural, not cultural, homogenizes each sex and both genders— ostensibly, this supposition establishes gender on the basis of biology."[26] That is, by fusing cultural differences with biological ones, society *creates* gender from biology, engendering difference by enlarging the scope of biological distinctions. In this social construction, moreover, particularity is attributed only to women, not to men. "Men are the norm, so women *are* different (from men). But for women to be treated as equal, they must be treated *as* men, *like* men, because equality is premised on men" (54; emphasis in original). The law has treated legislative classifications involving pregnancy and veterans' preferences as nondiscriminatory because significant numbers of nonpregnant persons and nonveterans exist of *each* sex. "This is how an engendered discourse defines neutral law; it erases the presence of sex class at the same time it constructs it. Woman is made absent by the presence of the male standard, . . . which is supposedly sex neutral" (67). When present, women are defined as potentially pregnant bodies and thus as mothers, and "this viewing of women as others makes them their bodies" (83).[27] As we saw in Pateman, the sex-neutral "individual" is a man. Too often, "individuals with needs are men and . . . women are 'different'— women's needs are one and the same as the needs of the family. Hence, there is no conflict between individualism and familism. Individuals are men" (126–27).

The question, then, is one of how to treat difference. For example, viewing pregnancy as episodic, as a short-term disability, may minimize women's difference, but pregnancy exerts long-term effects on women's lives. Eisenstein writes, "To sever pregnancy from early infant care is to deny the way sex and gender operate in society today. Society need not operate so, . . . but the fact that it does . . . represent[s] the dilemma of the sex/gender system" (197).[28] Irrespective of society's operation, Barbara Katz Rothman asserts that pregnancy is not an episode but a relationship. "A baby enters the world already in a relationship, a physical, social, and emotional relationship with the woman in whose body it was nurtured."[29] Since the experience of the pregnant woman is open to no man, it is no wonder that "the individual" is a man! Even for the nonpregnant or never-pregnant woman, these theorists imply that the property in her person that makes her creatively unique in comparison with men is inseparable from her body and thus from her selfhood. How do we affirm particularity when this is appropriate and yet preserve autonomy?

On Eisenstein's account, "To recognize the particularity and specificity of woman's body need not be to define her as 'different.' . . . Differences must be reformulated so that diversity between the sexes is not incongruous with equality between them."[30] Thus, different treatment may not constitute unequal treatment. In *California Federal Savings and Loan Association et al. v. Mark Guerra et al.*,[31] the Supreme Court ruled that pregnancy leave was nondiscriminatory toward men and nonpregnant women because pregnancy constitutes a real difference requiring different treatment.[32] Eisenstein concludes that "sex/gender-specific legislation is not inherently problematic or progressive. It is made so by its aim and its political context."[33] Equality is the constitutive goal, she implies, whereas the choice of same or different treatment is derivative from this goal.

All of these theories assert that if, as Elshtain asserts, one's very knowing is a function of one's experience as a body, the particularities of the female self will structure both reflection and choice. If this fact is ignored, the female subject who wishes to embrace this understanding will fall short as a "sex-neutral" individual premised on male assumptions. If this fact is taken for granted in the social construction of the self, however, the female subject may lack opportunities to stand beyond the reach of experience to choose her ends. This is the "dilemma of difference" as described by Martha Minow. "When does treating people differently emphasize their differences and stigmatize or hinder them on that basis? and when does treating people the same become insensitive to their difference and likely to stigmatize or hinder them on *that* basis?"[34] Specifically, "the dilemma for decision-makers . . . is how to help overcome past hostilities and degradation of people on the basis of group differences without employing and, in that sense, legitimating those very differences" (47).

For Minow, the dilemma of difference results not from the fact of difference but, rather, from various unstated assumptions that underlie the manner in which difference is treated. First, differences are assumed to be intrinsic to individuals regarded as different rather than to result from social attitudes as we compare individuals and construct a relationship between some individuals and others with whom they are compared (53–56). Second, we assume unstated norms when we discuss difference "without explicit reference to the person or trait on the other side of the comparison" (56).[35] As we have seen, the "sex-neutral" individual is often one about whom typically "male" assumptions are made. Third, we assume that the impartial observer can make judgments unaffected by that observer's own experiences and particularities.[36] But if our knowing emanates from our experiences, and if our understanding is based on our constituent natures and possible constitutive ends, the observer will be constituted by experience and particularity that cannot be completely transcended. Fourth, we assume that the experiences and perspectives of those who are different are irrelevant (66–70). The patriarchal construction of women workers in Pateman's description exemplifies this point.

Finally, we tend to assume that existing socioeconomic arrangements are both natural and neutral in their operation on individuals. "It follows, then, that differences in the work and home lives of particular individuals arise because of personal choice. We presume that individuals are free, unhampered by the status quo, when they form their own preferences and act upon them."[37] In Sandel's terms, we assume that the subject can stand beyond the reach of experience and particularity and choose its ends, when this experience and particularity may already, in a structural sense, be constitutive of the self and its ends. Moreover, they may constitute the self in such a narrow fashion that the subject lacks both the detachment necessary for autonomy in the voluntarist sense and the scope necessary for autonomy in the cognitive sense. Now that we have examined some of the anomalies that can stem from the recognition of difference, I address "how far we can stress the (undeniably) socially constituted, relational character of personal autonomy without eroding autonomy's normative power in checking expansive claims for unchosen, ascribed social 'obligations.'"[38]

II

According to Sandel, "As long as it is assumed that man is by nature a being who chooses his ends rather than a being, as the ancients conceived him, who discovers his ends, then his fundamental preference must necessarily be for conditions of choice rather than, say, for conditions of self-knowledge."[39] This distinction results, in Sandel's opinion, in an impoverished conception of the self, not only for its impact on the individual but also because of its implications for community. In his strong, constitutive conception of community, the existence of community is determined not by cooperation in the pursuit of private ends or even by participation in the pursuit of certain shared ends, but whether community is "constitutive of the shared self-understandings of the participants, . . . not simply an attribute of certain of the participants' plans of life" (173). More specifically, "Community describes not just what they *have* as fellow citizens but also what they *are*, not a relationship they choose (as in a voluntary association) but an attachment they discover, not merely an attribute but a constituent of their identity" (150).[40]

Communitarians like Sandel suggest that there are shared, constitutive "ends that can serve as the basis for a politics of the common good which will be legitimate for all groups in society." But if we can discover these shared ends "in our historical practices and roles," we might also discover "that those practices and roles were defined by a small portion of the society—propertied, white men—to serve the interests of propertied, white men. These practices remain gender-coded, race-coded, and class-coded, even when women, blacks, and workers are legally allowed to participate in them."[41] Or to put it another way, the particularities that characterize propertied white males are defined as universal attributes of the human condition. Those who do not display these characteristics are marginalized, their own particularities denied legitimacy and ignored or else apotheosized in such a way that no *other* attributes are accorded legitimacy. Either way, critics like Kymlicka assert that much in communitarian politics conflicts with the aspiration to define one's own identity, "and can be used to restrict the ability of women and other marginalized groups to reject the aims and ambitions which have been defined for them by others" (87).

As we have seen, however, we need not necessarily choose between reflection and choice, between cognitive and voluntarist aspects of autonomy. We may discover attachments that we take as constitutive of our identities, yet detach ourselves from others to choose new values and relationships. To this end, I posit that if particularity is to function in a way that enhances autonomy, it must do so by contributing to a plurality of options that can enrich the scope for both self-understanding *and* choice. As Kymlicka asserts, we are "dependent on a cultural community for our self-development and for our context of choice," yet we may rightly claim independence, "as self-directed beings, from any of the specific roles and relationships that exist in the community" (127). Community may then have a constitutive role or be a constitutive value, insofar as it provides the cultural context for both reflection and choice. Again, "No particular task is set for us by society, and no particular cultural practice has authority that is beyond individual judgment and possible rejection. We can and should acquire our tasks through freely made personal judgments about the cultural structure, . . . which offers us possibilities we can either affirm or reject" (50–51).[42] Kymlicka is here suggesting that we do not value freedom of choice for its own sake but, rather, "as a precondition for pursuing those projects and practices that *are* valued for their own sake" (48).[43] I suggest, correspondingly, that neither do we value self-understanding, or the discovery of possible constituents of our identity, for its own sake or for what it tells us about ourselves. Rather, self-understanding, like freedom of choice, is a precondition for helping us decide what pursuits *are* intrinsically valuable.

For Kymlicka, the context of choice equates with the cultural context or cultural structure, or the background conditions providing the framework for individual reflection and choice. This framework, on his interpretation, can never eliminate difference or interpersonal conflict. Even when Marx asserts that capitalism creates conflict that communism will eliminate, "he is referring only to conflicts that arise between people *independently of their choices.* . . . But that leaves entirely open the question of whether conflicts will arise *as a result of people's choices.* Marx does not say that conflicts of *this* kind, that reflect differences in our freely chosen projects, are denials of our social nature, or that communist society will seek to eliminate them."[44] The only eliminable contradictions between and among our interests, then, are the conflicts that are structurally generated and independent of individual choice. In Engels's discussion of sexual relations under communism, for example, "what seems to ensure that non-exploitative relations will develop is that men lack any advantage in the social instruments of power, and women lack any economic vulnerability. . . . There is no correct socialist model of personal relations which is to be imposed on people regardless of their affections or goals" (120). The cultural context or structure, that is, does not disadvantage or impose costs on individuals as a result of unchosen constituents of their identities. Women, for instance, need neither reaffirm particularities from which they wish to detach themselves nor abstract from these particularities to deny constitutive attributes they wish to affirm. In Sandel's terms, the cultural context of choice penalizes neither attachments discovered nor relationships chosen but can enhance both the cognitive and voluntarist components of autonomy, which is itself the precondition for pursuits of intrinsic value.

Kymlicka's concern is with the rights of cultural minorities who may wish to carry on certain communal practices apart from the larger political community and who may, to that end, desire legal recognition as a distinct cultural community. I do not treat women as distinct in this sense, but I believe Kymlicka's emphasis on the importance of the cultural context or structure has implications for the autonomy of any who are different from what is considered the norm. Martha Minow implicitly addresses this issue in what she calls a social relations approach to difference, which "assumes that there is a basic connectedness between people, instead of assuming that autonomy is the prior and essential dimension of personhood."[45] In this approach, differences are not immutable and fixed attributers of individuals; they "are features of relationships rather than traits residing in the 'different' person" (86). The more traditional rights approach often prescribes equal treatment when individuals have mistakenly been treated differently when they were really the same, and sometimes prescribes special treatment or rights "either to remove the effects of past deprivation or to address some special characteristics of certain groups" (108). But the rights approach still presumes "that differences reside in the different person rather than in relation to norms embedded in prevailing institutions" (108). The social relations approach challenges the definition and description of individuals on a group basis, instead locating "difference as a comparison drawn—by somebody—between groups" (119). A conventional attribution of difference "locates the problem in the person who does not fit in rather than in relationships between people and social institutions. . . . From this vantage point, assertions of difference may be understood as statements of relationships. . . . I am no more different from you than you are from me" (111).[46]

Although Minow comprehensively addresses many kinds of difference, her treatment of the *California Federal* case mentioned above will serve as an example of the social relations approach. Women's rights groups have divided on the issue of pregnancy leave: should women be treated like men to prevent the perpetuation of stereotypes that exclude women, or should women be treated specially if they are not to be disadvantaged by the fact of pregnancy and new motherhood? The Supreme Court upheld the California statute allowing women to resume prior jobs after unpaid pregnancy disability leaves on the grounds that the law allows women *and* men to have families without risking their jobs. Any suggestion of discrimination "should be resolved by the extension to men of benefits comparable to those available to women following maternity or pregnancy leaves" (59).[47]

Minow suggests that too often, the issue of whether or not to afford special treatment to women "posits men as the norm and women as different or deviant from that norm" (58). In this case, however, "the Court used women's experiences as the benchmark and called for treating men equally in reference to women, thus reversing the usual practice" (59). "It continued to rely on the assumption that equality depends on sameness, but it changed the focus of what 'similarity' is relevant," in this instance "the status of each worker as both a public and a private person." The Court recognized that "both women and men may have parental roles and responsibilities. Thus, the 'difference' requiring 'special treatment' dissolves in the face of a larger similarity between male and female workers, each of whom has the task of juggling work and family obligations" (88). This solution still locates differences in persons rather than in relationships, neglecting "the interaction between individuals and social institutions that distributes responsibility for what is, after all, the basic mode of species reproduction, in which all persons—not just the pregnant person—have an interest" (88).[48] Minow "questions why the individual worker must bear responsibility for differing from the norm," when childbearing affects not only the individuals directly involved but also employers who may lose valuable workers and the larger community. A true social relations approach, then, would challenge the social arrangements in which differences matter (89). After all, both public and private power have been used "to construct the social meaning of a trait of difference and to erect and maintain structures of exclusion and discrimination on the basis of that difference" (282). Power, she implies, may also be used to deconstruct these social meanings.

Minow's account displays the virtue of showing that both the voluntarist and cognitive aspects of agency may contribute to autonomy, and that they do so by creating a cultural context or context of choice that enhances this autonomy. The rights approach appears appropriate to the self detached from and prior to ends among which it is exercising choice. As Minow notes, "Rights analysis offers release from hierarchy and subordination to those who can match the picture of the abstract, autonomous individual presupposed by the theory of rights" (147). But depending on how difference is defined, rights may not help people who cannot show they have been mistakenly excluded from the group of people to whom rights apply. "For those who do not match that picture, application of rights analysis can be not only unresponsive but also punitive. If an assertion of rights by an individual produces an individualized response, the remedy still leaves in place existing institutions that themselves define and burden difference" (147). The rights approach, then, may actually limit the voluntarist aspect of autonomy because certain affinities and particularities are treated as attributes constitutive of the self, which cannot then stand beyond the reach of experience to choose its ends.

The social relations approach, on the other hand, appears appropriate to the self with many possible constitutive ends who is pursuing self-understanding by focusing on some attachments or affinities over others. But there is a voluntarist as well as a cognitive component to this activity, one central to the cultural context for choice *and* for self-understanding. In her discussion of children's rights, Minow suggests that inquiry into the differences between children and adults "wrongly suggests that such differences are real and discoverable rather than contingent upon social interpretations and choices" (303). J. Donald Moon questions this contrast: "Obviously, what will count as a difference will depend on social choices and interpretations—on the kinds of categories we use, and on the purposes for which we introduce these distinctions. But they are *also* discovered. Once we have certain categories, we discover whether two objects, individuated in terms of these categories, differ in certain respects."[49] In my view, Minow never denies that the application of categories to objects will involve discovery. Rather, she is asserting that *what* we discover is contingent upon the categories we use, and that *these* are matters of social interpretation and choice. In other words, where the rights approach assigns social meaning to a given that we have "discovered" and understood, the social relations approach suggests that we *choose* when we construct or deconstruct the social meanings of sameness and difference, even though our understandings shape our choices. We can stand collectively beyond the reach of assigned social interpretations to choose new ones, and in so doing we may collectively create a cultural context that functions as an enhanced framework for both reflection and choice.

Minow suggests that at its best, even the language of rights "can reconfirm community."[50] In claiming rights, we invest our private outlooks with public meanings. "In a deeper sense, those claiming rights implicitly invest themselves in a larger community, even in the act of seeking to change it" (294). That is, "Rights provide a language that depends upon and expresses human interconnection at the very moment when individuals ask others to recognize their separate interests" (296).[51] At its best, then, the language of rights approaches the social relations model as we address the interaction between individuals and social institutions by debating the social meanings we have assigned to sameness and difference and perhaps by altering our shared understandings. Just as there is a voluntarist component in the social relations approach, there is a cognitive one in the rights approach. While in recognizing possible self-understandings we exercise choice, we may collectively discover new self-understandings of sameness and difference in our common enterprise.

We saw in the introduction that for Iris Marion Young, a person's selfhood is partly constituted by group affinities. "This does not mean that persons have no individual styles, or are unable to transcend or reject a group identity. Nor does it preclude persons from having many aspects that are independent of these group identities." Nevertheless, in her opinion poststructuralist philosophy has demonstrated that the subject is not "an autonomous original or an underlying substance to which attributes of gender, nationality, . . . and so on might attach."[52] Although the group differences emanating from these processes do not always result in exclusion, ignoring differences disadvantages groups that try to assimilate according to rules and standards already set by privileged groups, "allows privileged groups to ignore their own group specificity," and "often produces an internalized devaluation by members of those (disadvantaged) groups themselves" (165).

Young rejects a conformist ideal of assimilation, which assumes current institutions and norms as givens, in favor of a transformational ideal, which allows for group-specific policies if these are necessary to transform institutions "so that group membership really is irrelevant to how persons are treated" (165). A positive sense of group difference, however, may also require the "principle that members of oppressed groups need separate organizations that exclude others, . . . in order for these groups to discover and reinforce the positivity of their specific experience" (167). Whatever the specifics, what Young advocates contributes to the cultural context of choice that Kymlicka describes. Although the latter's primary concern is with the legal recognition of cultural minorities, much in his account is relevant to any who are different. "A government that gives special rights to members of a distinct cultural community may still be treating them as *individuals;* the provision of such rights just reflects a different view about how to treat them as individuals and as equals." With regard to group-specific policies versus group-blind ones, "neither view is more concerned with treating individuals as equals than the other. They just reflect different views of what individuals are, and hence what it is to treat them as equals."[53]

In Kymlicka's view, cultural membership is a primary good, and its recognition contributes to and expands the cultural context of choice.

"Cultural membership is not a means used in the pursuit of one's ends. It is rather the context within which we choose our ends, and come to see their value, and this is a precondition of self-respect, of the sense that one's ends are worth pursuing" (192).[54] In Sandel's terms, a cultural context that recognizes the largest number of possible constituents of one's identity provides the broadest scope for both reflection and choice. To ensure both reflection and choice, however, we must be clear about what is constitutive and what is derivative about the concept of recognizing difference as part of the cultural context. Otherwise, we risk an encounter with Minow's dilemma of difference, wherein individuals are penalized whether their differences are ignored or recognized.

Above I alluded to Kymlicka's discussion of differences or conflicts that arise independently of individual choice, as opposed to those that result *from* individual choice. For him, "a liberal needs to know whether a request for special rights or resources is grounded in differential choices or unequal circumstances" (186). Aboriginal rights in Canada, for example, can be defended on the basis of unequal circumstances, as a result of which such cultural minorities "have to spend their resources on securing the cultural membership which makes sense of their lives, something which non-aboriginal people get for free" (187). To put it differently, "People should have to pay for their choices, but special political rights are needed to remove inequalities in the context of choice which arise before people even make their choices" (190).[55] For instance, Young agrees with Christine Littleton's advocacy of gender-conscious policy, which "publicly acknowledges culturally based gender differences" but is "directed at rendering femininely gendered cultural attributes costless for women."[56] This approach accepts structured social gender difference—what Eisenstein calls engendered difference—but is unconcerned with whether differences are natural or not. Rather, the aim is to preclude either reward or punishment for following what would traditionally be considered a male or female lifestyle. The implication is that women choose neither their biological natures nor, in many cases, the structural roles in child rearing that they often assume. The cultural context, therefore, should take account of these circumstances so that individuals, as they reflect on the particularities and affinities that constitute their identities, can choose without penalty which possible constituents to affirm and which to reject. This parallels Minow's social relations approach, locating difference in relationships and in the interactions between individuals and social institutions.

On the other hand, although a culture-conscious or gender-conscious policy allows the subject to affirm its own experience and particularities, we must take care that it does not *confirm* those particularities. That is, the acceptance of structured social gender differences may relieve the tension that impels the subject to reexamine its affinities and attachments, to arrive at new self-understandings, and perhaps to make new choices. Kymlicka, for example, advocates preservation of a cultural *structure* or context of choice but not the preservation of any particular cultural *character*. Some who classify cultural membership as a primary good do so "not to protect the community as such, but to protect their particular preferred vision of what sort of *character* the community should have."[57] On his view, however, "the cultural community continues to exist even when its members are free to modify the character of the culture, should they find its traditional ways of life no longer worthwhile" (167).[58] In fact "on a liberal theory of equality, the very reasons to respect a principle affirming the importance of cultural membership to minority groups is also a reason to respect a principle affirming the rights of individual members of those groups" (197).

The constitutive goal of the recognition of difference, then, is to expand the scope for both reflection and choice, and thus to enhance individual autonomy. Recognition of difference is derivative from this goal, and therefore should not "be tied to the protection and promotion of . . . existing practices." For example, "Two people who share cultural membership may share no ends or projects at all. . . . Our reflections are reflections about the plans and projects that are present in our cultural structure, but no particular plans or projects are exempt from possible rejection on the basis of that reflection" (239).[59] If the recognition of difference *is* contingent on the protection of existing practices, these practices would then continue because of facilitated individual choices. And it is unequal circumstances, not differential choices, that should ground the recognition of difference. As Kymlicka notes, the "assumption of plurality" must be accompanied by attention to revisability (60).[60] To put it differently, emphasis on the cultural structure protects the context, but emphasis on the individual members protects the choice in the context of choice.

Conclusion

In this chapter I have attempted to show that both voluntarist and cognitive modes of agency, as outlined by Sandel, can contribute to autonomy in spite of some of the anomalies that can spring from the recognition of difference. We can admit the importance of community without being subsumed in its expectations, just as we can assert the importance of autonomy without denying its relational character. Young points out that although individualism and community appear as opposites, underlying their seeming polarity is a common logic.

> Each entails a denial of difference and a desire to bring multiplicity and heterogeneity into unity, though in opposing ways. Liberal individualism denies difference by positing the self as a solid, self-sufficient unity, not defined by anything or anyone other than itself. Its formalistic ethic of rights also denies difference by bringing all such separated individuals under a common measure of rights. Proponents of community, on the other hand, deny difference by positing fusion rather than separation as the social ideal. They conceive the social subject as a relation of unity or mutuality composed by identification and symmetry among individuals within a totality. Communitarianism represents an urge to see persons in unity with one another in a shared whole.[61]

I have tried to steer a course between these extremes. Liberals can admit the role of particularity in the constitution of the self without relinquishing their emphasis on individual choice, just as proponents of community can value the cultural structure or context of choice without insisting upon a particular cultural character. Individuals should not have to abstract from their specific affinities and particularities if they wish to affirm them or if they wish others to affirm their personhood. On the other hand, they should not be forced to define themselves by them, nor should others insist on viewing them as essential. That is, we should be able to affirm particularity without being trapped by it. Only thus can we understand the social meanings of sameness and difference and also choose which meanings will matter.

Notes

1. Iris Marion Young, *Justice and the Politics of Difference* (Princeton: Princeton University Press, 1990), 97.

2. Ibid., 45; also see Martha Minow, *Making All the Difference: Inclusion, Exclusion, and American Law* (Ithaca: Cornell University Press, 1990), 151.

3. Young, *Justice*, 125.

4. Michael Sandel, *Liberalism and the Limits of Justice* (Cambridge: Cambridge University Press, 1982), 10–11.

5. Michael Sandel, "The Procedural Republic and the Unencumbered Self," *Political Theory* 12, no. 1 (1984): 82.

6. Ibid., 86; also see Sandel, *Liberalism*, 62.

7. Sandel, *Liberalism*, 57.

8. Jean Bethke Elshtain, "Against Androgyny," in *Feminism and Equality*, ed. Anne Phillips (New York: New York University Press, 1987), 145.

9. Ibid., 147; see also 143–48.

10. Diana T. Meyers, *Self, Society, and Personal Choice* (New York: Columbia University Press, 1989), 94; see also 92–97.

11. Will Kymlicka, *Liberalism, Community and Culture* (Oxford: Clarendon Press, 1991), 55–56.

12. Ibid., 164.

13. Carole Pateman, *The Sexual Contract* (Stanford: Stanford University Press, 1988), 8; see 6–8.

14. Also see ibid., 109–11.

15. Ibid., 118; also see Minow, *Making All the Difference*, 148–56.

16. Pateman, *The Sexual Contract*, 110; emphasis in original.

17. Ibid., 164. See 165–66; and Minow, *Making All the Difference*, 275–83.

18. Pateman, *The Sexual Contract*, 187.

19. See ibid., 135–42; and Zillah Eisenstein, *The Female Body and the Law* (Berkeley: University of California Press, 1988), 82.

20. Pateman, *The Sexual Contract*, 140; emphasis in original.

21. Sandel, *Liberalism*, 57–58.

22. Ibid., 58.

23. Pateman, *The Sexual Contract*, 151; see also 59, 66, 148–53.

24. Also see ibid., 231.

25. Also see ibid., 86–90.

26. Eisenstein, *The Female Body*, 3; emphasis in original.

27. See also ibid., 79–87, 204.

28. See also ibid., 195–200.

29. Barbara Katz Rothman, *Recreating Motherhood: Ideology and Technology in a Patriarchal Society* (New York: Norton, 1989), 91; see also 90–105.

30. Eisenstein, *The Female Body*, 107.

31. *California Federal Savings and Loan Association et al. v. Mark Guerra et al.*, 107 S. Ct. 683 (1987).

32. Eisenstein, *The Female Body*, 178–79.

33. See also ibid., 201–10; Young, *Justice*, 175–78.

34. Minow, *Making All the Difference*, 20; emphasis in original.

35. See also ibid., 56–60; Young, *Justice*, 163–66.

36. Minow, *Making All the Difference*, 60–65.

37. See also ibid., 70–74.

38. Rogers M. Smith, review of Jennifer Nedelsky, *Private Property and the Limits of American Constitutionalism* (Chicago: University of Chicago Press, 1990), *Political Theory* 20, no. 1 (1992): 169.

39. Sandel, *Liberalism*, 22; also see 58, 121–22.

40. Emphasis in original. See also ibid., 147–54.

41. Kymlicka, *Liberalism, Community*, 86.

42. See also ibid., 48–51.

43. Also see Will Kymlicka, "Liberalism and Communitarianism," *Canadian Journal of Philosophy* 18, no. 2 (1988): 186–89.

44. Kymlicka, *Liberalism, Community*, 117; emphasis in original. See also 114–21.

45. Minow, *Making All the Difference*, 110.

46. See also ibid., 110–20, 214–15.

47. Referring to *California Federal*, 107 S. Ct. 694, 695; also see Minow, *Making All the Difference*, 87.

48. Also see Young, *Justice*, 175–76.

49. J. Donald Moon, *Constructing Community: Moral Pluralism and Tragic Conflicts* (Princeton: Princeton University Press, 1993), 169.

50. Minow, *Making All the Difference*, 293.

51. See also ibid., 291–303.

52. Young, *Justice*, 45.

53. Kymlicka, *Liberalism, Community*, 211; emphasis in original.

54. Also see ibid., 169–72.

55. See also ibid., 185–93, 237–42.

56. Young, *Justice*, 176–77.

57. Kymlicka, *Liberalism, Community*, 168; emphasis in original.

58. See also ibid., 165–67, 59–61, 87–89.

59. See also ibid., 238–41.

60. For a dialogue on the implications of cultural difference, see Chandran Kukathas, "Are There Any Cultural Rights?" *Political Theory* 20, no. 1 (1992): 105–39; Will Kymlicka, "The Rights of Minority Cultures: Reply to Kukathas," *Political Theory* 20, no. 1 (1992): 140–46.

61. Young, *Justice*, 239; see also 226–36.

With Respect to Gill's "Autonomy and the Encumbered Self"

Natalie Dandekar

Gill claims that she, ultimately, will show how apparently disparate approaches to social theory can be brought together around a revised concept of autonomy formulated in terms of a revised understanding of human agency and embodiment. This revision will make it possible for "liberals . . . [to] admit the role of particularity in the constitution of the self without relinquishing their emphasis on individual choice." By the same means, proponents of community can "value the cultural structure . . . without insisting upon a particular cultural character." Gill must therefore convincingly connect three apparently disparate perspectives: theorists who focus on responding to the dilemma of difference; the communitarian perspective of Kymlicka; and the liberal ideal of autonomy typified by Sandel. This is an ambitious project.

Four issues, I believe, need to be addressed before Gill's project can be considered a success. Are Sandel's efforts to add cognitive modes to the voluntarist modes of human agency so rooted in the Cartesian understanding of a human self as to be indifferent to embodiment? To what extent do differences in interpreting "rights" matter in defining or constructing an embodied autonomy? How are the concepts of socialized self-understanding and autonomy related to each other? Finally, what constitutes primary goods, and why should we think so? In discussing these four issues, I explain why they seem to be stumbling blocks that must be overcome in order to specify the connection of embodiment, autonomy, and personal freedom.

Sandel, Descartes, and Indifference to Embodiment

In adopting Sandel's inclusion of cognitive as well as voluntarist modes of human agency, Gill seems to suppose that restoring the modality of cognition will provide a basis for promoting the rights of concrete, embodied selves within a politically organized community. On the contrary, Descartes, who did understand human agency as compounded of both cognitive modes and voluntarist modes, found that understanding to be compatible with an atomic individualism so abstract that the question of whether or not the self was embodied could not be answered with any certainty. For example, in Meditation IV, Descartes notices that "my errors . . . depend on a combination of two causes: to wit, on the faculty of knowledge that rests in me and on the power of choice . . . —that is to say, of the understanding and . . . the will."[1] Both of Sandel's modes are here specified. Yet shortly thereafter, Descartes demonstrates the extent to which a self-definition in terms of these two modes is compatible with radical uncertainty as to whether embodiment is necessarily part of being himself when he concludes that on this question one must remain indifferent. "When I lately examined whether anything existed in the world . . . it followed very clearly that I myself existed, I could not prevent myself from believing that a thing I so clearly conceived was true. . . . on the contrary, . . . [when] I doubt whether this thinking nature . . . by which I am what I am, differs from this corporeal nature or is identical to it . . . I am entirely indifferent as to which of the two I affirm or deny."[2]

If it is possible that cognition and volition are both compatible with "indifference" as to whether or not embodiment is identical or otherwise necessarily involved with selfhood and agency, then reducing the impoverished self of deontological voluntarism by restoring the value of cognition may not suffice to promote a concept of the self as embodied. We may remain, though in an enriched sense, within the rationalist tradition, a tradition compatible with the postulate of atomically abstract individuals capable of rationally choosing a social contract even as they deny the importance of embodied circumstance.

Gill's further analysis does not lay this fear to rest since the supposition that, at least for some men, selfhood is separate from one's body seems to lurk behind the discussion of pregnancy in a puzzling way. As she puts it, "Even for the nonpregnant or never-pregnant woman, these theorists imply that the property in her person that makes her creatively unique in comparison with men is inseparable from her body and thus from her selfhood."

What I found important here, in terms of the modalities approach, was the implication that male selfhood is described as if it is separable from male bodies, rather than being correlated with the privileging of male bodies to the disadvantage of female bodies. If the modalities approach does suggest that cognition and will are independent of rather than correlated with any specific embodiment, it may thus continue to mask effectively the assumption that male embodiment is the standard by which women are defective. As with René Descartes, who ignores(?) the fact that he is a male when he philosophizes as if he is an abstract universal, philosophers may engage both modalities and still hold that embodiment is a matter of presumed indifference. The question asked by Gill, "How do we affirm particularity when this is appropriate and yet preserve autonomy?" becomes pointedly important. But unless the modality of cognition is itself to be changed so that embodiment must matter, I do not see how adding this modality bridges the necessary space so as to unite autonomy with particular embodiment.

Two Approaches to "Rights" in Resolving Dilemmas of Difference

I suspect that Gill attributes an unrealistic unity of interpretation to the group of feminist theoreticians whose work is focused on articulating corrective responses to the dilemma of difference. With respect to the problem, they do all generally agree; the supposedly neutral standard of reason supports discrimination. Often the standard simply assumes that males are the norm. In addition, the legal standard of a reasonable person generally works to discriminate against the economically deprived, the ethnically diverse, and the educationally impoverished regardless of gender.[3] When the reasonable-person standard is specifically modified, as in the reasonable-woman standard suggested by Shaw,[4] it supports discriminatory outcomes inasmuch as it elevates a normative notion of the economically secure, well-educated woman as the proper model of reasonableness.[5] Thus, the problem perceived by these theorists may be recognized as the problem of invidious discrimination.

However, when these theoreticians attempt to work toward solutions to the dilemma of difference, they differ in terms of whether they adopt what Greenawalt calls "the principled" or "the relational" approach to law.[6] This difference in approach shows up most strikingly in the disparate ways in which feminists use rights discourse. Minow openly seeks to replace standard rights analysis with a social relations analysis that would leave room for rights only to the extent that rights are recognized as interpersonal relationship claims.[7] Others seek, rather, to reconstruct equality among individuals, using law "to . . . make difference costless."[8] To this end, rights need to be corrected, but the standard analysis need not be scrapped.

Gill observes that this means "at its best, then, the language of rights approaches the social relations model as we address the interaction between individuals and social institutions by debating the social meanings we have assigned to sameness and difference." But what has happened to the value of the individual in this relationship formulation of rights? Who holds these rights when they are not specific to individuals but, rather, to the interrelationship? I think this issue needs to be specifically addressed if the effort to reconcile individualism, autonomy, socialized selfhood, and community is to succeed.

Women's Socialization and Our Understanding of Autonomy

The conceptual relationship between self-understanding, socialization, and autonomy seems prone to difficulties that need to be resolved. It seems to me Gill rightly acknowledges the ways in which differences that mark a person as belonging to an out-group may constitute a positive part of that person's self-understanding. In such cases, belonging will reinforce differences. The different norms of the powerful, politically privileged community will be negatively regarded by the less privileged community.

But this acknowledgment may not fit smoothly with even a revised understanding of autonomy. Three examples may help clarify what is involved in this problem. First, Bartky has written on the socialization process that in women produces docile bodies by way of normative prescriptions delivered, in part, by the mass-circulation women's magazines.[9] Women are thus socialized to regard themselves as needing to conform to an ideal image, so they excessively diet and, in so doing, come to regard the body as enemy of the self.

Second, Wignaraja describes some phenomena observed among the very poor women who benefit from microeconomic poverty-alleviation projects in such countries as Bangladesh and Nepal as "altruistic." That is, when these very poor women do finally gain access to cash, most spend their earnings in the following family-oriented pattern: first they buy food for the family; then buy shelter and clothing for the family; next they take steps to ensure the family's security by investing in family assets like poultry. Only after achieving these three goals do they ever, and then only rarely, spend some personal income on more personal goods.[10] Clearly, they are acting upon a self-understanding that involves affirming social prescriptions about their relationship to their family. What is less clear is how this self-understanding relates to autonomy.

Third, Hooks contrasts feminist analysis of the family as an oppressive institution with the socialized self-understanding of less affluent black women.

> Many black women find the family the least oppressive institution. Despite sexism in the context of family, we may experience dignity, self-worth and a humanization that is not experienced in the outside world wherein we confront all forms of oppression. . . . We wish to rid family life of the abusive dimensions created by sexist oppression without devaluing it. . . .
>
> Devaluation of family life in feminist discussion often reflects the class nature of the movement. Individuals from privileged classes rely on a number of institutional and social structures to affirm and protect their interests. The bourgeois woman can repudiate family without believing that by so doing she relinquishes the possibility of relationship, care and protection. If all else fails, she can buy care.[11]

Hooks seems to claim that both positions reflect social realities that have been internalized to become part of a woman's self-understanding. The question is, how do these socially constructed self-understandings correlate with autonomy?

How are theoreticians to discover or invent the means by which to formulate a new definition of autonomy/freedom as embodied? How shall we maintain a position sensitive to the affirmative self-construction of a self-understanding and retain the awareness that some perceptions are the product of socialization processes that co-opt a woman's embodied energies?

Is Enhanced Choice Intrinsically Valuable?

What constitutes primary goods, and why should we think so? If, for example, autonomy represents an independently valuable achievement, then it seems one has to refer to a possibility that whether I value your socialized commitments or not, whether or not I see them as instantiating a community that is better than otherwise, it is a source of independent value that you, for whatever socialized reasons, do value them. However, Gill writes as if this is not the case. In a gloss on Kymlicka she suggests that "neither do we value self-understanding, or the discovery of possible constituents of our identity, for its own sake or for what it tells us about ourselves. Rather, self-understanding, like freedom of choice, is a precondition for helping us decide what pursuits *are* intrinsically valuable."

In that case, and if as also seems probably correct, the self is not an autonomous original but an achievement constructed from interaction with social institutions, then although some pursuits must be intrinsically valuable (in terms of some absolute standards of value), our self-understanding and understanding of autonomy must be relative to our social context.

In Gill's chapter one possible suggestion about the intrinsically valuable seems to me to be potentially inappropriate to the demands of ecological sustainability. For example, while discussing Kymlicka, Gill writes, "The constitutive goal of the recognition of difference, then, is to expand the scope for both reflection and choice, and thus to enhance individual autonomy." It seems to me that this claim reflects a character preference that might need moral inhibition, as for example with respect to the ecological principles of accepting limits and living within them, rather than seeking continual expansion. I think we need to work with the awareness that some choices, such as those that can be made among the bewildering array of equally sugared cereals, do not per se enhance individual autonomy for embodied selves.

In conclusion, I found Gill's essay a worthwhile effort to put together a wide spectrum of theory in order to formulate a concept of autonomy that takes account of embodiment. Nevertheless, I think that the four issues discussed above must be given more explicit treatment before embodiment and autonomy can be shown to be connected in ways that enable us "to affirm particularity without being trapped by it."

Notes

1. René Descartes, "Meditations on First Philosophy," in *The Philosophical Works of Descartes,* ed E. S. Haldane and G. R. T. Ross, vol. 1 (Cambridge: Cambridge University Press, 1967), 174.

2. Ibid., 176.

3. See Robert C. Post, "The Social Foundations of Privacy: Community and Self in the Common Law Tort," *California Law Review* 77 (1989): 957, 961.

4. See Margery Shaw, "Conditional Prospective Rights of the Fetus," *Journal of Legal Medicine* 5 (1984): 63.

5. See Natalie Dandekar, "Fetal Abuse and Female Autonomy" (paper presented at NEH seminar, *The Nature and Value of Autonomy,* 1990), 10–15.

6. Kent Greenawalt, *Law and Objectivity* (New York: Oxford University Press, 1992), 155–59.

7. Martha Minow, *Making All the Difference: Inclusion, Exclusion and American Law* (Ithaca: Cornell University, 1990), 107–20.

8. Christine A. Littleton, "Reconstructing Sexual Equality," in *Feminist Legal Theory*, ed. Katharine T. Bartlett and Rosanne Kennedy (Boulder: Westview Press, 1991), 35–56.

9. Sandra Bartky, "Foucault, Femininity and the Modernization of Patriarchal Power," in *Feminist Philosophies, Problems, Theories and Applications*, ed. J. Kourany, J. Sterba, and R. Tong (Englewood Cliffs, N.J.: Prentice-Hall, 1992), 103–18.

10. Ponna Wignaraja, *Women, Poverty and Resources* (New Delhi: Sage, 1990), 124.

11. Bell Hooks, *Feminist Theory, from Margin to Center* (Boston: South End Press, 1984), 37.

Comment

Autonomy and the Encumbered Self:
A Response

Suzanne Duvall Jacobitti

Debates about the nature of the self or subject have become a common agenda item in contemporary American political theory. The current terms of debate seem to have been set by the charges made some time ago by Robert Nozick and then Michael Sandel that John Rawls, in his *Theory of Justice*, depended on an untenable concept of the self—a self that was abstract, "unsituated," and "unencumbered" by ends or purposes or community attachments. Sandel and other communitarians seemed to favor an account of the self as "thick" with particular characteristics and firmly embedded or situated in its community. This American debate parallels similar debates in Continental thought between those such as Husserl (who tried to make a transcendental ego the ground of philosophy) and Sartre (who insisted on the self as a nothing that created itself), on the one hand, and, on the other hand, Heidegger, who dissolved the self into a function of the *volk* or of Being, and later structuralists and deconstructionists who further dissolved the self or subject into a social construction. The latter approaches have been embraced by some American feminists and other defenders of "difference" who use it to affirm the claim that the self or individual subject in Western philosophy is really a social construction elevating the white male bourgeois self into the Self as such, a "myth" that works to perpetuate oppression of women and others whose experiences are "different."

As Emily Gill says in "Autonomy and the Encumbered Self," Sandel argues that the abstract construction of the self is a "hallmark of liberalism" (or at least of deontological liberalism)—a claim that relates to the general critique of

---

Suzanne Jacobitti's comment originally appeared in substantially different form in Larry May and Jerome Kohn, eds. *Hannah Arendt: Twenty Years Later* (Cambridge: MIT Press, 1996).

modernity and its abstract, atomistic universalism so common in Continental thought since Heidegger. Liberal theorists since Sandel have been struggling to meet these criticisms. Most now concede something to Sandel but do not go all the way to deconstruction of the subject. Liberalism requires the capacity of choice, of freedom; if individuals are wholly a function of their particularity, wholly a product of "socialization" and of biology, then the standard liberal priority of liberty loses its point and the liberal principles that individuals have dignity and are entitled to equal respect lose their validity. But of course not just liberalism is threatened from this point of view. All Western morality and law, as Nietzsche noted, are based on the assumption that individuals do make choices and can justly be held responsible for those choices.

Gill is well aware of this problem and would like to find a middle ground between those who emphasize choice and universal standards and those who emphasize situatedness and particularity. She worries about feminist theorists like Carole Pateman, Jean Elshtain, and Zillah Eisenstein, who seem to deny that women can transcend their biological givenness and the social construction of gendered identities. For such thinkers, because women are destined by their bodies to see or know the world as women, self-discovery or self-understanding for women is impossible in a liberal culture that requires them to think of themselves as individuals (i.e., males) or, because they are "different" from males, as a deficient sort of male. Only by abandoning the notion of "individual" or "person" and the universalistic norms associated with it, such thinkers argue, will women (and other marginalized persons) be able to find their identities and achieve justice.

Gill quite rightly fears the effects of carrying respect for particularity and situatedness this far. People should have opportunities to escape social predefinition. As she puts it, "We should be able to affirm particularity without being trapped by it." This leads Gill to favor a social order that allows for and indeed fosters choice, an order that contains a variety of ways of life, among which we may choose. I am fully in agreement with Gill in favoring a diverse, pluralistic society permitting a variety of styles of life. Like her (and Will Kymlicka, whom she cites in this context), I am frightened by the prospect of a close-knit community that marginalizes all who do not identify with the dominant "shared understandings." However, it still might be the case that the belief that "I" am capable of choosing among ends and ways of life may be a "myth," an illusion, and that who I am is the result of a combination of biology and socialization. As Gill says, many theories of difference simply deny the possibility of choice. This is also what is implied in the Continental thought that inspires many such thinkers. Gill is logically committed to rejecting this; her position presupposes that it is possible for individuals to transcend their social and biological conditioning. That is, she believes in individual freedom as a human capacity. I would like to push her in the direction of making her philosophical underpinnings more explicit.

I should begin by conceding that there may be good prudential reasons for not being more explicit about such matters, given the political desirability of winning support for liberal principles from citizens with widely varying philosophical and religious commitments. Thus John Rawls argues against embedding liberal political theory in more comprehensive philosophical positions, maintaining that it should rest on only the minimal philosophical assumptions needed to defend the basic principles of liberalism. Rawls particularly wants to avoid a substantive concept of human nature that would entail controversial notions of the human good.[1] His notion of the self, therefore, is restricted to the assertion of an abstract subject with the capacity to choose and no other inherent characteristics. Unfortunately, however, this account of the self, as we have seen, is hardly noncontroversial; indeed, the alleged capacity to choose is exactly what is at issue between the more radical theorists of difference and liberals. It seems, then, that liberals cannot do without a more philosophically rich notion of the self.

There are the beginnings of a fuller account in Gill's chapter. She argues persuasively that personal identity is in part a function of discovering oneself and in part a matter of choosing who one wishes to be; this leads her to argue that subjects can "transcend their structural definitions" and "revise their self-understandings." To explain this, she uses Michael Sandel's distinction between "agency in the voluntarist mode" and "agency in the cognitive mode." "Agency" here is used as Sandel defines it, as "the faculty by which the self comes by its ends."[2] Sandel says that a self can "come by" its ends in two ways. On the "voluntarist" account, the self is entirely distinct from its ends. The bounds of the self or subject are "antecedently given and finally fixed"—that is, the self is what it is before it acquires any characteristics or purposes. The latter are chosen by the self by means of "the faculty of will," which "allows the self . . . to transcend" itself. Such choices of ends do not change the identity of the self; hence on this account the self does not participate in shaping its identity (152).

On the "cognitive" account, by contrast, the self is not predefined or defined at all but is at first undistinguished from its situation; it finds itself, in Sandel's words, "unbounded," "awash with possible purposes and ends." Here, "agency" involves "seeking self-understanding," Sandel says, and this requires not the faculty of will but the "capacity for reflection," a capacity that enables the subject to "survey its various attachments and acknowledge their respective claims, to sort out the bounds . . . between the self and the other . . . and so gradually, throughout a lifetime, to participate in the constitution of its identity" (152–53). This reflective capacity involves an ability to distance itself from its discovered ends, so that the self possesses them as ends rather than being possessed by them (57–58).

Emily Gill, following Diana Meyers and Will Kymlicka, seeks a middle ground between liberals and communitarians. She argues that a proper account of self requires that we be agents in both the voluntarist and the cognitive senses. Thus we begin as situated selves and discover our existing attachments and desires and reflect on them "in the cognitive mode." We also, however, can choose to accept them or not—and even to choose other attachments and ends, not part of our original identities. The capacities to reflect and to choose will be fostered only in a pluralistic society that offers a variety of choices among ways of life. "True autonomy," Gill says, requires that one find oneself in a context that offers a "*variety* of possible constitutive ends or constituents of identity." (5) "The individual should be able to embrace attributes that, upon reflection, she takes to be constitutive of her selfhood. But she must also be able to detach herself from attributes she does *not* wish to claim as part of herself and to embrace others she may have chosen."

Like Rawls, then, Gill assumes that the self is capable of free choice of ends and hence is a "willing subject." However, unlike Rawls's self, this self is firmly situated in a body and in a particular cultural setting. It is capable, by virtue of being a "knowing subject," to discover facts about that setting and about its own initial constitution and, through its faculty of reflection (a "distancing faculty") to step back from the traits and desires and purposes it initially finds in itself (at least the socially constituted ones, if not the biological ones) and consider them as separate from itself. It can then, by virtue of the will, choose whether to retain these as a part of itself or not.

I find this approach to the self very promising and want to raise some further questions: Does it embrace "free will" in the traditional Christian sense? How does this faculty of the will relate to the faculties of knowing and reflecting? How do these relate to action? And how do all these faculties fit together into a single self? While I certainly do not claim to have answers to such questions, I would like to suggest that Hannah Arendt has a good bit to offer in this respect. Her position was in many ways like the one Gill proposes in acknowledging that we are situated in a particular body and society but insisting on our capacity to transcend that situation. Arendt also struggled with the problem of how to fit various faculties like will and reflection and cognition and action into a coherent account of the self (her account of judgment, in particular, resembles Gill's account of the distancing function of reflection), and her thoughts on these matters (as I am arguing in a larger work) are a good bit more coherent than some have maintained. A full account of Arendt's views on these matters is beyond the scope of this paper,[3] but I do wish to suggest briefly how Arendt's account of how we form our character might contribute to the position Gill is developing.

In *The Origins of Totalitarianism*, in her discussion of the Nazi efforts to destroy the "human person," the "unique identity" of an individual, Arendt refers to our "individuality" as "the uniqueness shaped in equal parts by nature, will and destiny."[4] Explicating this a bit (for Arendt does not do so), we may assume that the part shaped by nature is our biological inheritance, the part shaped by "destiny" is the socially constituted part of the self, and the part of the self due to "will" is that part which, through deliberate choices, the person herself has shaped and for which she can be held responsible. What explains the aspect of the self that we *are* responsible for? Arendt's clearest discussion of this is in *The Life of the Mind*, where she compares how animals and humans "appear" in the world. We, like animals, she says, simply appear in the world when we are born; we have no choice in the matter. In addition, both animals and humans engage in "self-display"—that is, they actively do things that are seen by, attract the attention of, other sentient creatures. However, while animals do whatever they do by instinct (apparently), humans, "*up to a point* . . . choose how to appear to others," and this involves an "intervention of the mind," a "deliberate choice."[5] The difference between "self-display" by an animal and the "self-presentation" of a person is "active and conscious choice of the image shown" (36). When I show anger, for example, unless I am simply swept away by rage and hence act utterly without conscious choice, my action reflects a decision about "what is fit for appearance." Arendt makes clear here that the *feeling* of anger is not a matter of choice; this springs from our "soul." But the *show* of anger is deliberate (31–32). Similarly, when a person displays courage, it does not indicate absence of the emotion of fear but a decision that "fear is not what he wants to show" (36).

It is by choosing, repeatedly and over time, how we wish to appear that we shape our character. Thus, one who repeatedly shows courage becomes a courageous person; courage has become "second nature or a habit" for that person (36). Out of many such acts of self-presentation, Arendt says, "arises finally what we call character or personality, the conglomeration of a number of identifiable qualities gathered together into a comprehensible and reliably identifiable whole, and imprinted, as it were, on an unchangeable substratum of gifts and defects peculiar to our soul and body structure" (37). The individual is "fashioned by the will and aware that it could be different from what it is (character, unlike bodily appearance or talents and abilities, is not given to the self at birth)."[6]

This discussion of character formation sheds some light on Arendt's discussions elsewhere of the role of motives and principles in action. Our choices of how we wish to appear are, she says

> determined by various factors; many of them are predetermined by the culture into which we are born—they are made because we wish to please others. But there are also choices not inspired by our environment; we may make them because we wish to please ourselves or because we wish to set an example, that is, to persuade others to be pleased with what pleases us. Whatever the motives may be, success and failure in the enterprise of self-presentation depend on the consistency and duration of the image thereby presented to the world.[7]

This passage warrants careful attention. If we wish to please others, then our choice is "predetermined" or "inspired" by the environment. How can a "choice" be "predetermined"? In the sense that what my action "means" to others is determined by their culture, their "opinions," and hence to please them my action must conform to these preexisting categories.

If, to take Arendt's classic example, Achilles wants to be a hero (that is, wants to be remembered by others as courageous, what a hero ought to be), Homeric culture offered him only one course of action—to die in battle. And this of course is what he chose.[8] To take a more ordinary example, if a teenager wants to be "popular," current teen culture makes rather rigorous demands on how that teenager must present herself. In both cases, we can say action is "inspired" by the dominant opinion in the culture. Even the romantic "individualists," in their determination to be "unique personalities," had to choose outrageous or bizarre appearances, that is, what would appear bizarre to their contemporaries. Hence they too were negatively determined by opinion. In all these cases, individuals choose how they wish to appear, but their choices are constrained by their desire to please (or displease) others and hence by existing categories and roles of the particular culture.

What about the person who does not care to please others? One might think, for example, of a woman who wishes to free herself from dominant social definitions. Arendt suggests two possibilities. First, there is the woman who simply wants to please herself, not caring what others think. Her choices are much less constrained, though still limited by her particular given nature and self-shaped character (and the danger of being judged insane). Second, there is the woman who may not care to please others but who does want to set an example for others, to be a role model, as we say today. Such a woman must be cognizant of existing social definitions, so that she may communicate with those she wants to influence and still carefully and deliberately deviate from some of those definitions.

While not directly addressing the issue of gender definition, Arendt's approach is sensitive to that problem in other ways. First, she was utterly impatient with psychological approaches that attempt to reduce individuals and their actions to underlying motivations and desires (which are so easy to stereotype). Because motives lie buried deep in the soul, Arendt said (they *never* appear), they remain unknown to actor and observers. Any attempt to force them into the open is likely to raise suspicions about the actor's integrity or hypocrisy. This problem is rooted in the very fact that we "present" or "show" ourselves. How does the observer know that the person is not merely "making a show," that the action is not a disguise for some underlying motive? In any particular case, Arendt says, we cannot know, and inquiring into motives will not shed any light. The only way we know a person's true character is by whether that person presents regularly, over time, a consistent appearance. "Only self-presentation [and not animal self-display] is open to hypocrisy and pretense . . . and the only way to tell pretense and make-believe from reality and truth is the former's failure to endure." When I choose to present myself to the world in a certain way, Arendt says, it is a sort of promise to continue to act in that way; the hypocrite is one who breaks that promise.[9]

Second, the fact of individual uniqueness, she argues, makes descriptions of an individual person very difficult. It "confounds all efforts toward unequivocal verbal expression. The moment we want to say *who* somebody is, our very vocabulary leads us astray into saying *what* he is," that is, we use general descriptive terms (tall, handsome, smart, clever, etc.), all of which refer to traits that this person shares with others. We end up describing a "type" and "his specific uniqueness escapes us."[10] This is why Arendt argues that a narrative, a story, is the best way to describe who someone is. And such a story can best be written (and only definitively written) at the end of the person's life. "The unchangeable identity of the person, though disclosing itself intangibly in act and speech, becomes tangible only in the story of the actor's . . . life, but as such, it can be known . . . only after it has come to its end" (193). Obviously, such a story is not written by the actor but by others. Thus, "nobody is the author or producer of his own life story." The stories that result from one's words and deeds "reveal an agent, but this agent is not an author or producer" (184).

In Arendt, then, we find a strong enough concept of the self—as both situated and free—to allow for individual dignity and for moral and legal responsibility. It is also a concept that should complement the efforts of liberal feminists.

Notes

1. See especially, John Rawls, "Justice as Fairness: Political not Metaphysical," *Philosophy and Public Affairs* 14 (1985): 223–51.

2. Michael Sandel, *Liberalism and the Limits of Justice* (Cambridge: Cambridge University Press, 1982), 57–58.

3. See my "Thinking about the Self," in *Hannah Arendt: Twenty Years Later*, ed. Larry May and Jerome Kohn (Cambridge: MIT Press, 1996), for a fuller account.

4. Hannah Arendt, *The Origins of Totalitarianism*, new ed. (New York: Harcourt Brace Jovanovich, 1968), 454.

5. Hannah Arendt, *The Life of the Mind*, 2 vols. (New York: Harcourt Brace Jovanovich, 1978), 1: 34–35.

6. Arendt, *Life of the Mind*, 2: 195.

7. Ibid., 1: 36.

8. Hannah Arendt, *The Human Condition* (Chicago: University of Chicago Press, 1958), 179, 193–94.

9. Arendt, *Life of the Mind*, 1: 35–36.

10. Arendt, *Human Condition*, 181.

Chapter 6

Feminist Legal Critics: The Reluctant Radicals

Patricia Smith

Feminist legal criticism began not as a radical critique but as a liberal argument for the universal application of traditional legal categories.[1] The early campaigns for universal suffrage are the first obvious examples. The arguments for women's suffrage were radical only in the sense that they tended to limit traditional patriarchal power and to equalize the political power of women in a very limited way. Women's suffrage was in that limited sense socially radical, but this fact was hardly recognized at the time. That is, giving women the vote was not widely expected to change the social, legal, or political situation of men or women in any radical way at all.

And conceptually, the arguments for women's suffrage were not radical in any sense; they were liberal. It was not necessary for them to be radical. This was because of an interesting contradiction between universal liberal rhetoric and patriarchal social structures that depended for its resolution on unsustainable factual assumptions about the differences between the basic nature of men and women. These assumptions were explicitly built into law in the form of overt prohibitions against the participation of women in various aspects of public life.

In the case of voting, for example, the prohibition against women's voting was most generally based on the view that women were incapable of understanding political issues. Women, it was thought, were politically incompetent. Incompetence (along with danger, including moral danger) has, in fact, been the most common argument against women's doing almost everything for most of human history. The incompetence argument has struck contemporary feminists as ironic in the face of apparently powerful counterexamples, such as Cleopatra and Queen Elizabeth I, to name

Chapter 6 originally appeared in David S. Caudill and Steven Jay Gold, eds. *Radical Philosophy of Law: Contemporary Challenges to Mainstream Legal Theory and Practice* (Atlantic Highlands, N.J.: Humanities Press, 1995).

only two powerful female leaders who seemed to understand not only political issues but political strategy quite as well as any man. But human beings have never allowed powerful but inconvenient counterexamples to stand in the way of powerful and convenient theories, and we still do not. We call them exceptions, and early political thinkers called them exceptions too. Queens did not count. But eventually, as women gradually became more generally educated, the exceptions overpowered the rule of incompetence as to voting, and the prohibition was overcome.

This development was based on a liberal rather than a radical view. The liberal view is that all human beings are presumptively entitled to equal treatment, or equality before the law. Eighteenth-century political rhetoric speaks this way about human rights, often referred to as the "rights of man." Now, the fact is that a significant portion of the human population was excluded from these "human" rights. Apparently you had to prove you were human. Native Americans, Chinese immigrants, and African American slaves, of course, had no more rights than women; the justification was that these groups of individuals were *different.* (Different from *what* was left unspecified, but the assumption was that they were different from the norm, which was basically male and European, and was taken as given.) The presumption of equality was overridden as to women and minorities, or did not apply to them because of supposedly intrinsic differences of race and sex.

Thus, the great liberal debate of the nineteenth and twentieth centuries has been over who gets included in the ranks of personhood, citizenship, and humanity. Over time the circle was expanded to include more and more groups that had previously been considered unfit for rights: non-property owners, common working men, different nationalities, different races, and finally even women. In all these cases the decision to include these groups was based on the conclusion that differences that were previously thought significant were not significant after all. For purposes of law, it was decided that the differences between the excluded groups and the included group were largely irrelevant. What never changed was the norm: the standard of evaluation or the standard of comparison. That standard was based on the status quo and founded in the assumptions of those in power. The standard was never questioned because it was assumed to be necessary, neutral, and universal—simply a description of the world. Thus, the great liberal debate was over which classes of people are factually or materially equal. If you could prove (or convince those in power) that you were materially equal (that is, psychologically, dispositionally, and intellectually equal to the norm), then and only then you were entitled to formal equality or equality before the law.

That was the forum entered by liberal feminists, and it is in fact the forum of greatest advance in the cause of women's rights. One thing that shows is that much of the liberal ideal is correct—most differences between groups of people should be considered irrelevant to law. But in recent decades women have discovered that the liberal program has serious limitations, and that discovery has led many feminists to a more radical evaluation of law and also to some of the greatest intellectual contributions feminists have made to legal analysis, namely, the serious challenge made to traditional discriminatory norms. Nowadays, feminists are asking why as a matter of justice, those in power are entitled to formulate standards that favor themselves by which to measure all others. As a matter of power, this is easily understood. As a matter of justice, it is quite puzzling. The answer to the puzzle is that the norms formulated by those in power are not characterized as favoring themselves but as neutral descriptions of necessary features of the world. So the current challenge for feminist scholars is to show how norms traditionally considered neutral are actually biased. The feminist critique of equal protection law provides the clearest illustration of both the liberal approach and its limits, and some recent work of feminist legal critics in this area and others demonstrates the new and radicalized challenge feminism now presents to previously unexamined discriminatory legal norms. In the next two sections I consider each of these to illustrate the development of feminist legal analysis as a certain form of radical legal critique.

The Evolution of Sex Discrimination in Equal-Protection Law

The 1950s and 1960s marked the first serious consideration among the American people that a legal system overall might be biased against an entire class of people, and in particular an entire race of people. (Of course, the Marxists had been making the class argument for years, but it had very little impact in the United States.) With the struggle for civil rights for American blacks came the realization that law itself was at least sometimes used systematically to disadvantage an entire group with no apparent justification that anyone could find, since by the 1960s it had become embarrassing to argue that blacks are not human beings, or not human "in the relevant sense."

It is interesting that it took more than a decade for any serious analogies to be drawn between the legal treatment of blacks and the legal treatment of women, but at least by the 1970s effective arguments were being made that sexism was in some sense analogous to racism. In 1971 the Supreme Court struck down for the first time a sex-based classification as a violation of the equal protection clause of the Fourteenth Amendment.[2] The arguments made in this case and others of the time were analogous to the liberal arguments being made against race discrimination. For example, in 1973 ACLU counsel Ruth Bader Ginsberg argued in *Frontiero v. Richardson* that sex-based classifications, like racially based classifications, should be recognized as constitutionally suspect on three grounds. First, historically women have been subjugated and restricted as a class. Second, women ought to be judged on their individual merits rather than on the basis of stereotypes that are often inaccurate, and even if accurate in general may be inaccurate as applied to a particular individual. (In other words, if an individual woman meets the standard norm, she ought not to be eliminated by a blanket prohibition against women as a class.) Third, sex is an immutable characteristic that often bears no relation to the ability to perform or contribute.[3]

Thus, the typical argument for the advancement of women's rights in the early 1970s was the liberal argument that challenged the dominant power to make good on its universal claims for impartiality and justice by opposing historical oppression, recognizing the value of individuality, and avoiding the individual unfairness of frequently inaccurate stereotypes. This argument worked well initially, at least in blatant cases of overt discrimination, and well it should because it employs the dominant ideology of the classical liberal tradition, which is central to Western legal thought. However, it did not take long for problems to crop up.

Because the basis of sex discrimination claims was the traditional idea of similarly situated persons being differentially treated on irrelevant grounds, the Court saw no basis for deciding cases in which persons were not similarly situated. Thus, when *Roe v. Wade* was decided shortly after *Frontiero*, the woman's right to choose abortion was based on the right to privacy with no mention of a foundation in equal protection law based on sex.[4] Similarly, when mandatory unpaid maternity leaves for schoolteachers were challenged in *Cleveland Board of Education v. LaFleur*, the Court avoided the sex discrimination claim by striking down the policy on other grounds.[5] Having thus hemmed itself into an analysis of sex discrimination based only on the differential treatment of similarly situated persons, when the Court was faced squarely and unavoidably with the sex discrimination claims of pregnant women in *Geduldig v. Aiello* in 1974, it reached the stunning conclusion that discrimination based on pregnancy does not involve a sex-based classification.[6] *Geduldig* does not represent one of the Court's shining hours. It generated an enormous wave of critical commentary. The extension of the reasoning in *Geduldig* to a Title VII case prompted a swift amendment (the Pregnancy Disability Act) by Congress repudiating the Court's reasoning. And the Court itself in more recent decisions has backed away from this holding, but it has not changed its general rationale for sex discrimination under the equal protection clause.[7]

The problems caused by the general rationale that bases a discrimination claim solely on the differential treatment of similarly situated persons shows that it cannot deal with questions of fair treatment where differences are real. There is something so obviously wrong with the idea that where differences are real, equal protection of the law cannot apply that a raft of critical commentary has been generated that has led to a more radical feminist critique of law. What feminists have realized is that equal protection law itself, although characterized as neutral, in fact assumes a male standard of what is normal. For example, the average working woman will be pregnant twice during her working career. Pregnancy is abnormal only for a working man. Thus, the standard of normality for working persons is male. The question, of course, is why should that be the standard?

Christine Littleton has summarized the feminist critique of current equality analysis in the following three points that demonstrate its male bias. First, it defines as beyond its scope precisely those issues that women find crucial to their concrete experience as women (such as pregnancy). Second, differences between men and women that are created by the relationship of women to particular and contingent social structures (such as home and work responsibilities) are taken as natural (that is, unchangeable and inherent) and as located solely in the woman herself (women are naturally domestic). Third, it assumes (without evidence) the gender neutrality of social institutions, as well as the notion that practices must distinguish themselves from "business as usual" in order to be seen as unequal.[8]

More briefly put, equality analysis is biased against women in three respects: it is inapplicable once it encounters a "real" difference from men; it locates the difference in women rather than in relationships; and it fails to question the assumption that social institutions are gender-neutral, and that women and men are therefore similarly related to those institutions.

This analysis made many feminists acutely aware of the arbitrariness of norms, and of the fact that the inability of the courts to deal with sex discrimination in many cases is directly related to the inability to evaluate biased norms. If the liberal presumption of neutral legal processes retards the ability to evaluate norms as biased, then the liberal approach is sharply limited in its ability to correct systematic injustice, such as that which grows out of systematic patriarchal norms. This is no longer a liberal but a radical view, and many feminists have moved to that form of analysis in the critique of law.

The Development of Feminist Legal Critique as Radical Reform

Feminists have recognized that a significant part of law is the legitimation of the dominant ideology and a significant part of the dominant ideology of most societies is patriarchal. This is the focus of much recent feminist legal critique. It is the embodiment of the observation that norms are often systematically biased in ways that reinforce the subordination of women to men by assuming a male standard of what is normal, or a male perspective of what is real, and then entrenching these assumptions by characterizing them as neutral. Many feminists have developed this position in a variety of ways.

Perhaps best known are the views of Catherine MacKinnon. In *A Feminist Theory of the State*, MacKinnon sets out a radical feminist thesis of law and jurisprudence.[9] She is concerned with the transformation of belief into reality. Law, she points out, is a crucial factor in that transformation. Virtually all societies, she notes, are organized in social hierarchies that subordinate women to men on the basis of sex, as well as subordinating certain people to others on the basis of race and class. These facts of social organization, which institutionalize social power, are embodied in the organization of states as law. That is, through law, social domination is made both legitimate and invisible. It becomes reality—just the way things are. Liberal legalism or positivist jurisprudence buries the embodiment of patriarchal dominance even further by insisting that the proper domain of jurisprudence is descriptive, not evaluative or normative. As MacKinnon puts it:

> Liberal legalism [i.e., legal positivism] is thus a medium for making male dominance both invisible and legitimate by adopting the male point of view in law at the same time as it enforces that view on society. . . . Through legal mediation, male dominance is made to seem a feature of life, not a one-sided construct imposed by force for the advantage of a dominant group. To the degree it succeeds ontologically, male dominance does not look epistemological: control over being produces control over consciousness. . . . Dominance reified becomes difference. Coercion legitimated

becomes consent. . . . In the liberal state, the rule of law—neutral, abstract, elevated, pervasive—both institutionalizes the power of men over women and institutionalizes power in its male form.[10]

There are many variations on this theme. Quite a number of feminists have suggested that legal standards often uncritically reinforce social disadvantages imposed on women. For example, Deborah Rhode[11] and Christine Littleton[12] have both suggested moderate versions of the radical thesis that recognize the need to address structural problems of patriarchy that entrench inequality, but argue for addressing them in terms of disadvantage rather than domination. Both are examples of feminist theories that call for accepting diversity in all its forms, using law to insure that diversity is not penalized. Both require the equal acceptance of cultural differences and concentrate on eliminating the unequal consequences of sex differences, whatever their origin or nature. One of the attractive features of this approach is that it makes no particular assumptions about the intrinsic psychological nature of men or women. It does not presume that we can know what the intrinsic differences or similarities might be, or what the sexes would be like if social conditioning were different. It holds only that no cultural position should be penalized—it should not be a disadvantage to be one sex or race or nationality rather than another. The idea, as Littleton puts it, is to embrace diversity and make difference costless.

In another interesting proposal from a rather different direction, Nadine Taub and Wendy Williams have suggested one way that the courts could formulate in legal doctrine the ideal that difference should not be penalized.[13] Taub and Williams advocate the expansion of what the Court has called the *Griggs* doctrine of discriminatory impact.[14] Very generally speaking, the *Griggs* doctrine says that if a norm or practice has a disproportionate impact on a suspect class (such as race or sex), then that norm or practice is subject to reevaluation. Unfortunately, the Court has chosen to restrict rather than expand the *Griggs* doctrine, but suggestions like that of Taub and Williams's show that equal protection could be made an effective device for the protection of disadvantaged classes if the dominant class saw fit to develop it in that direction.

Whether these critiques are formulated in terms of disproportionate impact, the domination of women, or their disadvantage, all represent a shift from liberal claims for inclusion in traditional norms to a radical critique of those norms as fundamentally biased. Martha Minow has generalized this position to a critique of the inability of courts (and particularly the Supreme Court's inability) to deal with the problem of differences in a pluralistic society.[15] Unexamined assumptions create what Minow calls "dilemmas of difference" for the courts. She points out that the Supreme Court is often faced with the apparent dilemma of reinforcing disadvantage no matter which choice it makes. If it recognizes a disadvantage so as to correct it, it may reinforce stereotypes that perpetuate it. On the other hand, if the Court ignores the difference so as to counter the stereotypes associated with it, then there is no way to address the disadvantage attached to the difference.[16] This is a serious problem for all classes that are systematically disadvantaged because the "neutral" (that is, disinterested and detached) application of biased standards simply reproduces systematic disadvantage, thus calling into question the very meaning of neutrality. Minow suggests that courts could defuse these dilemmas by recognizing the unexamined assumptions that generate them.

First, Minow points out, we commonly assume that differences are intrinsic rather than relational or comparative. Women are considered intrinsically different rather than different as compared to men. Jews are intrinsically different rather than different as compared to Christians, and so forth. As she remarks, men are as different from women as women are from men; Christians are as different from Jews as Jews are from Christians. The question is why the norm should be male and Christian. Second, we typically adopt an unstated norm as a point of reference in evaluating others. This norm is not neutral or inevitable, but it seems so when left unstated and unexamined. It is taken as given rather than recognized as chosen. It is assumed to be universal rather than recognized as particular. Third, we treat the perspective of the person doing the judging as objective, even though in fact no one can see fully from someone else's point of view or without a point of view. Fourth, we assume that the perspective of those being judged is either irrelevant or already covered by the supposedly objective and universal perspective of the judge. Fifth, it is assumed that the status quo—the existing social and economic arrangement—is natural, neutral, inevitable, uncoerced, and good. Thus, departures from the status quo risk nonneutrality and interference with individual freedom. Minow believes that making these assumptions explicit will require judges to examine the foundations of their own perspectives, which are often not recognized as perspectives at all. Once recognized as perspectives, the views must be defended as compared to other perspectives rather than being erroneously assumed universal.[17]

The above examples illustrate that many feminists today recognize that a significant part of law is the legitimation of the status quo, which is to say, the dominant power or ideology, and that a significant part of the dominant ideology of our society (and most others) is patriarchal. Thus, standard traditional norms must be examined and defended in terms of the interests of all people rather than assumed to be inevitable and neutral.

However, a fact that many feminists do not mention but most presume is that patriarchy is not the only or the entire dominant ideology of this society. Our society is also individualist, committed to justice and freedom, committed to the ideals of impartiality, the rule of law, and equality before the law. These are not patriarchal ideals as such.[18] They are universal, humanist ideals. Actually, they are not particularly compatible with patriarchy, and this contradiction between what is often called liberal ideology—but what might be called humanist ideology—and patriarchy can still be exploited in the cause of justice for women. That is, the contradiction between patriarchy and humanistic liberal ideals, which are both embodied in Anglo-American law, enables even radical feminists to advocate reform rather than revolution. Thus, even radical feminists are radical only in the sense of advocating far-reaching reforms.

The view of Taub and Williams illustrates this clearly. On the one hand, the proposal they make is very moderate: a simple and reasonable extension of a doctrine already formulated by the Court and regularly used in one form in Title VII cases. In another respect, the proposal is a radical one because the effect of it would be to counteract the disadvantages imposed on certain classes of people by social organization itself. Yet, the rationale is perfectly compatible with humanistic ideals verbally expressed in the Anglo-American liberal tradition for two hundred years.

Similarly, Minow's suggestions would have a radical impact on the process of judging itself, yet on the other hand, all she is really arguing is that those in power should be accountable to examine their own assumptions. This is so reasonable a requirement one wonders how anyone committed to rational thinking could argue against it. Certainly, a liberal would not.

Even MacKinnon, one of the most radical of feminists, utilizes the distinction between humanistic liberal rhetoric and patriarchal practices. In a recent essay on equality, MacKinnon argues that the law of equality provides a peculiar opportunity for challenging the inequality of law on behalf of women because law does not usually guarantee rights to something that does not exist. Equality in law is understood formally, and so it is supposed that by and large women already have it. Many if not most formal legal barriers for women have been dismantled. Women can now own property, execute contracts, attend universities, engage in businesses and professions without formal prohibition. But, as many feminists have observed, this formal equality does not eliminate informal discrimination, nor does it provide equal opportunity in fact. MacKinnon argues that it is up to feminists to make equality law meaningful for women by defining it in terms of the concrete experience of women's lives, and challenging the male forms of power that are affirmatively embodied as rights in law. MacKinnon recognizes that equality is not about character traits or even human nature. It is not about "sameness and difference," as it is so often construed, but about domination and subordination. Equality and inequality are about the distribution of power. To confront that distribution of power directly, recognizing it for what it is, and to remove the mask of legitimacy raised by its legalization is the critical task of feminist jurisprudence, according to MacKinnon.[19]

The positions just discussed recognize implicitly or explicitly that there are serious contradictions between the universal values that we profess and the patriarchal institutions that we practice in fact. This is a consistent factor in feminist legal analysis that connects recent work with early liberal feminist views. But early liberal feminist criticism was effective only when it was directed at explicitly patriarchal legal doctrines. These patriarchal legal doctrines made the contradiction explicit and clear.[20]

Many feminists today argue that the form of the contradiction has changed. It is no longer an explicit contradiction between two clearly articulated legal rules. At least much of the time the contradiction is now between two (or more) rather vaguely understood legal norms that are the embodiment of traditional social standards. Thus, traditional standards cannot simply be taken as given. Rebutting false claims of factual difference between men and women is not enough. The contradictions between universal values and patriarchal practices cannot be effectively utilized for freedom and justice for women until the bias of certain norms is recognized.

These problems are far from over, and a major aggravating factor in their solution is the common claim that they have already been solved.[21] I believe that the remaining problems can be usefully characterized in the form of two remaining hurdles.

The first hurdle is simply a development of the original liberal battle: how to keep the discrimination that used to come in overtly through the front door from sneaking in covertly through the back door. Old stereotypes die hard, and despite our best efforts to combat unfounded and untestable assumptions about differences between men and women, these assumptions seem able to constitute themselves like chameleons in new forms. But discrimination must be opposed in whatever form it takes.

The second hurdle is how to get those who occupy positions of power to see that the norms they use are, after all, just the norms they choose, and that many traditional norms in fact benefit men at the expense of women and/or reinforce traditional social arrangements that restrict the freedom of women.

The case of *EEOC v. Sears* provides a rather familiar example of the issues involved in the first hurdle.[22] This case involved a Title VII class action lawsuit charging Sears Roebuck and Co. with employment discrimination against women in hiring and promotion. The charge was based on statistical evidence that women were greatly underrepresented in higher-paying commission sales positions although the pool of applicants was more or less equal, and lower-paying jobs were predominantly filled by women. This approach relied on a typical focus of Title VII class action suits that utilizes statistics that indicate a disproportionate impact from facially neutral practices as presumptive evidence of discrimination. In other words, if a disproportionate impact is shown, Title VII presumes that discrimination is the reason for it. This, then, shifts to the defendant the burden of proof to provide nondiscriminatory reasons for the differences shown by the statistics.

To meet this burden of proof, Sears argued successfully that women were underrepresented in the higher-paying commission sales jobs not because of discrimination but because women as a class really are not interested in such jobs.[23] In fact, Sears used the language of certain feminist scholars to support its claim that women dislike competition and value good relationships more than money. Thus, they tend to sacrifice monetary advancement for less stressful working conditions and limited hours that enable them to meet their responsibilities at home. Hence, disparities in higher-paying jobs are due not to discrimination but to women's own choices. This argument was accepted by the court, even in the face of contradicting testimony from actual women who had applied to Sears for commission-sales positions.[24]

Joan Williams has done a good job of pointing out that this reasoning simply reenshrines old stereotypes of women as passive, domestic, and self-sacrificing, stereotypes that are powerful and entrenched.[25] It is always easier to fall back on them than it is to get rid of them. What is particularly distressing about the *Sears* case is that it inserts sexist stereotypes into precisely the legislation that was enacted to counteract them. Even if the stereotypes are true as generalizations, Title VII was designed to protect women who do not fit that generalization, specifically women such as those who applied for the commission-sales positions at Sears. Sears simply discounted those women and so did the court. That is, Sears assumed that those women really did not want the jobs they applied for; they were padding their applications to increase their chances of getting hired.[26] Because most women applied for low-level clerking jobs, Sears reasoned, that must be what women (all women) prefer. That outrageously invalid argument is the argument that the court accepted as the basis of its interpretation of Title VII. This will disadvantage all future claimants. Furthermore, if actual testimony cannot rebut the Sears argument that women are not interested in competitive work, how could any plaintiff overcome that argument on the part of any employer? One wonders how any woman can ever win a Title VII claim based on disproportionate impact again? Cases like *Sears* show how easy it is to go backwards, even with regard to the old liberal argument that we are all human and entitled to equal treatment based on our individual merits. We have far to go before men and women will be presumed equal and before discriminatory assumptions about the "intrinsic" differences in male and female disposition and intellect are overcome.

There are no easy examples of the issues connected with the second hurdle because in the evaluation of traditional norms what seems normal is what everyone is used to, and that is the status quo. The challenge always carries the burden of persuasion, always seems at least initially less plausible than the norm, and that is true whether or not the norm is just.[27] Feminists have found that norms are most difficult to challenge where the differences (physical or social) between men and women are real, and the interests of men and women are perceived to be at odds. In such cases it is the status quo itself that disadvantages women, and it cannot be corrected unless the norm is changed. This involves new evaluations at very fundamental levels.

Consider, for example, the formulation of harm or injury. What constitutes an injury is central to legal action. It has long been a truism that justice and law require interpersonal respect, at least to the extent that we may not intentionally harm or defraud other individuals or interfere with their freedom. We are not entitled to cause injury. Virtually all moral and legal theories agree that this is the core of interpersonal responsibility. One person's freedom ends with the freedom and bodily integrity of another.

Any individual's rights are limited by the basic rights of all other persons. Thus, coercion, intimidation, fraudulent deception, and bodily injury are prohibited by justice and law without question. That is the settled core of liberal jurisprudence, but it does not specify what counts as harm or injury.

Somehow injury does not apply the same way to women as to men, particularly with respect to men who are related to them or who know them. If assault is prohibited, why are husbands so often not prosecuted for beating their wives? If exploitation is wrong, why are employers so often not prosecuted for pressuring their employees into sexual relations? If rape is illegal, why are men so often not prosecuted if they are acquainted with the women they coerce into sex? If bodily integrity is a fundamental right, how could decisions regarding pregnancy rest ultimately with anyone other than the woman whose body is involved? All these are areas that involve real differences between men and women, and they are areas in which the interests of men and women can now be interpreted as possibly conflicting.

As Minow has pointed out, contrary to assumptions of universality, all law is formulated from a perspective, and we can hardly be surprised if it turns out to be the perspective of those who formulated it, which is to say, the perspective of powerful men—the traditional patriarchs. It is difficult to assume the perspective of someone else. It takes a level of self-awareness that is truly rare. Nor is it more common for people in power to recognize the limits of their own views and the value, let alone the significance, of understanding and accommodating the views of others.

Until almost the twentieth century women were not considered to have interests or views of their own. Women were not independent or free. In fact, they were not separate individuals legally. A woman could not have an interest that conflicted with the interests of her husband or father. Thus, she could not be harmed or injured by her husband or father (unless he killed her). The man to whom she was related was responsible for her.

So it is hardly surprising that wife beating was construed as discipline, which is not a harm. It is not surprising that rape, unlike any other crime, was defined from the perspective of the perpetrator rather than the victim. Nor is it surprising that until recently sexual harassment simply did not exist, and procreation (both in terms of contraception and abortion) was controlled by government rather than by women. Women did not have separate interests; their interests were defined by men, from the perspective of men, in terms of the interests of men, because that is who formulated the law. This was not a commitment of liberalism. It is not even compatible with liberalism. It was an assumption embodied in a patriarchal society that was left unexamined because it was the norm that women had no interests separate from their husbands or fathers, and that the law should not intrude into family matters. The challenge for feminists is how to change such norms and others like them, which have been taken as given—as normal—for hundreds or even thousands of years.

The very fact that such issues are now being addressed, that such topics are being publicly discussed is the first sign of progress. Yet we have far to go before women are recognized as entitled to bodily integrity that cannot be coercively usurped by men who know them and by legislators who presume to define their interests. The great divide between the protection of women from strangers, and the nonprotection of women from men who know them reflects old and deeply embedded notions of male supremacy, domination, and the ownership of women. Until recently, these views were supported by overt acceptance of male authority and supremacy. Today many people say that these old presumptions of patriarchy no longer hold. Today we say that women are entitled to determine their own physical integrity by their own voluntary choices.

Yet these abstract ideals have serious concrete limits. Powerful forces have mobilized to oppose reproductive freedom for women on the assumption that women are not entitled to make such choices. The physical integrity of women does not include the right to control their reproductive capacities. Pregnancy is not a harm; it is a blessing. Thus, the norm is still that women are essentially mothers, first and foremost. The choice not to be a mother (i.e., to be in actual control of one's reproductive capacities), although formally acknowledged in law, is still highly controversial and is flatly rejected by many. The long-standing commitment to individual autonomy is a fundamental norm of our society that has never been and still is not applied equally to men and women. That is because (a) men and women are different, so deciding what an equal commitment to autonomy means is not a simple matter; (b) autonomy was never considered important for women in the past; and (c) those who decided legal, moral, and religious policy about motherhood and procreation were not the same people who were subject to the disadvantages of such policies. So the fight over who should be in control of women's bodies is still far from settled.

And old patterns of social interaction based on norms that subordinate women are perpetuated, largely by denial and by blaming the victim. If a woman gets raped or beaten not by a stranger but in the course of normal life, then she must have brought it on herself. If she is harassed by her employer, she must have led him on. And anyway, date rape has to be rare. Wife battering is surely uncommon. Sexual harassment must be largely imaginary. We do not want to hear about these problems.

Statistical surveys clearly indicate that women are harmed much more often by men who know them than by any other cause. For example, four million women are battered in their homes in the United States each year. Women are harassed, beaten, raped, and killed by men who know them far more often than by strangers. Yet these offenses, with the exception of killing, are still largely unprosecuted. Why? Because we the people excuse the abuse of women as a form of control or an outlet for frustration. The old joke is "If you can't beat your wife who can you beat?" This attitude and behavior is a hangover from an earlier and more overtly sexist day, and we don't want to know about it. So we pretend that it is a rarity committed by a few outlaws, as are ordinary crimes. But it is not.[28]

The pervasiveness of these abusive practices attests to the worst features of the continuing sexism of our society. Old norms die hard. Physical coercion and violence remain an option for male domination in personal relations as a last resort. The more women struggle for freedom and equality, the more some men will respond with violence. The more women compete, the more they will be harassed by those who feel threatened or offended by the changing status quo.

And the failure to prosecute attests to the continuing sexism of our law.[29] This will not change significantly until traditional norms are changed that condone it. Until police and prosecutors, judges and juries recognize such injuries as serious harms and stop making excuses for them, women will not be protected. But police and prosecutors, judges and juries by and large reflect the attitudes of the general public.

So long as overpowering your date is not the same as raping a stranger, and beating your wife is not as serious as assaulting someone on the street, and pressuring your secretary into sex is just the way life is, and pregnancy is characterized by Supreme Court justices as an inconvenience, the physical integrity of women will not be determined by their own voluntary choices. Thus, many women today are still dominated by physical force and restrictive legislation, denied the most basic protections of justice by a society and a legal system that pretends that some physical coercion is not real harm, and in any case that women can avoid it by "proper behavior," by understanding their limits. Such a view is not compatible with the liberal commitment to freedom and equal treatment, as liberal feminists have argued for many years. It can be made compatible only by assuming the normative commitments of patriarchy as a fact of life. And that is not actually hard to do (in fact it is actually harder not to do) because patriarchal assumptions have set the standard of normal social relations, religious ideals, moral expectations, and legal standards for thousands of years. Patriarchy is the norm—or more accurately, it is an enormously complex network of norms. It is challenging those norms and that network that constitutes the radical agenda of modern feminists. It is an agenda that does not conflict with liberal values; it does not require overthrow of the government, or even amending the Constitution, but it does require the eventual transformation of our most fundamental institutions, including extensive legal reform.

Notes

1. "Radical" and "liberal" are terms of multiple definition and use. I consider a radical critique to be one that calls for revolutionary or fundamental change of some sort, but not necessarily military overthrow, or political upheaval, or even immediate social change. That is, on my view, a radical critique can call for incremental or evolutionary change, so long as the ultimate goal is monumental or profound. "Liberal" is harder to define because it standardly encompasses a broad swath of views ranging from communitarian to libertarian. But usually liberals are thought to fall somewhere between those two poles. I believe that all liberals are committed to freedom, justice, and the significance of individuals, although they may interpret these values in very different ways. Thus, on my view, it is possible for a radical critique to rest on liberal values. The two positions are not categorically antagonistic. However, whether a particular radical critique is compatible with a particular liberal view depends on the particulars of both. I will use the term "liberal" to stand for a commitment to freedom, justice in the form of equal treatment, and the significance of individuals.

2. *Reed v. Reed*, 404 U.S. 71 (1971).

3. 411 U.S. 677 (1973).

4. 410 U.S. 113 (1973).

5. 414 U.S. 632 (1974).

6. 417 U.S. 484 (1974).

7. See *Newport News Shipping and Dry Dock v. EEOC*, 103 S. Ct. 2622 (1983). The general rationale is that individuals cannot be treated differently on the basis of sex unless there is some clearly specifiable difference that justifies different treatment. Thus, so long as the sexes are similar, they must be treated the same.

8. Christine Littleton, "Reconstructing Equality," *California Law Review* 75 (1987): 1279.

9. Catherine MacKinnon, *Toward a Feminist Theory of the State* (Cambridge: Harvard University Press, 1989).

10. Ibid., 237–38.

11. Deborah Rhode, *Justice and Gender* (Cambridge: Harvard University Press, 1989).

12. Littleton, "Reconstructing Equality."

13. Nadine Taub and Wendy Williams, "Will Equality Require More . . . ?" *Rutgers Law Review/Civil Rights Developments* 37 (1985): 825.

14. See *Griggs v. Duke Power*, 401 U.S. 424 (1971).

15. Martha Minow, "Justice Engendered," *Harvard Law Review* 101 (1987): 10.

16. The common formulation of the early debate over women's rights illustrates the problem. It was asked whether women, being different, should argue for equal rights or for special rights. Equal (i.e., identical) rights seemed to disadvantage women sometimes (e.g., as to pregnancy benefits), and so some argued that special rights were needed to accommodate women's special needs and circumstances. Others argued that only equal (i.e., identical) rights should be claimed because any special needs or differences acknowledged by women are always used to limit women in the long run, and special rights will be viewed as special favors that accommodate women's deficiencies. The problem is that if that is the way the issue is formulated, then women lose either way because the (unstated) norm is male. After all, who is it that women are different from? Whose rights (if equality is the standard) should women's rights be equal to? And if women's rights should sometimes be different from men's, why is it women's rights that are characterized as special? Why not formulate rights in terms of women's needs and characterize men's rights as special? One way makes as much sense as the other. The question is, who is the norm?

17. Minow, "Justice Engendered."

18. Some feminists consider all these principles to be patriarchal, but most feminists either do not specify their position on this point or hold a more contextually based view, rather like that expressed here.

19. MacKinnon, *Toward a Feminist Theory.*

20. In *Reed v. Reed*, for example, it was held that a woman could not be barred from being the executrix of an estate on the basis of her sex, since there was no demonstrable difference between men and women in regard to administering an estate. The (patriarchal) state law that excluded all women as a class from that activity was clearly contradicted by our supposedly universal commitment to freedom and equal treatment and by our constitutional commitment to equal protection of the law.

21. See, e.g., Deborah Rhode, "The 'No Problem' Problem: Feminist Challenges and Cultural Change," *Yale Law Journal* 100 (1991): 1731.

22. *EEOC v. Sears*, 628 F. Supp. 1264 (N.D. Ill. 1986).

23. It is worth noting that in *Castro v. Beecher*, 334 F. Supp. 930, 936 (D. Mass. 1976), an almost identical argument that the underrepresentation of blacks in law enforcement was due simply to their lack of interest was rejected by the court as racist. And in

Glover v. Johnson, 478 F. Supp. 1075, 1086–88 (E.D. Mich. 1979), the argument that women did not need vocational training because women preferred unskilled jobs anyway was also rejected as prejudice. Thus, in the past the courts have rejected justifications of disparities based on supposed lack of interest.

24. The court also ignored expert testimony from a historian who argued that history shows that women accept more competitive jobs whenever they become available. See Joan Williams, "Deconstructing Gender," *Michigan Law Review* 87 (1989): 797.

25. Ibid.

26. The Sears managers, the statistical analyst, and the guidebook for hiring all systematically discounted applications of women for traditionally male positions (such as commission sales.) The statistical analyst explained on the witness stand exactly how she went about discounting all applications of women for "male" jobs. Yet the court accepted this approach as appropriately reflecting the (supposed) interests of women, despite conflicting testimony by actual women that they had in fact wanted commission sales positions. This demonstrates the power of stereotypes, once accepted. See ibid., 813–20.

27. For example, in *Plessy v. Ferguson*, 163 U.S. 537, the case that established the legitimacy of racial segregation under the equal protection clause, the Court said (among other things): "The object of the amendment was undoubtedly to enforce the absolute equality of the two races before the law, but, in the nature of things, it could not have been intended to abolish distinctions based upon color, or to enforce social, as distinguished from political, equality, or a commingling of the two races upon terms unsatisfactory to either." Segregation was the norm. A mere constitutional amendment requiring racial equality could not rebut the presumption of the legitimacy of the status quo, hence the Court's interpretation of "equal protection" allowed the norm to stand. It appears clearly unjust to us today, but at the time it seemed perfectly reasonable, which attests to the strength of the status quo. How many reasonable and defensible sexist judgments of the 1980s and 1990s will seem similarly outrageous fifty years from now? We haven't the distance to tell.

28. During the Vietnam War, 59,000 soldiers were killed, causing a storm of public outrage. During the same period 54,000 women were killed by their male partners, without so much as a whisper of public protest. We can say we didn't know. (That's what the Germans said about the Jews.) But why didn't we know? It was public record. We didn't want to know. And we still don't. Women's voices are louder now, but we still mostly ignored the recent Senate report (S. Rept. 197, 102d Cong., 1st sess. October 1991) that noted that both rape and domestic violence have sharply increased in the past decade. Four million women are severely battered every year, the leading cause of injury for U.S. women (much greater than assault by strangers.) From two to four thousand women are now murdered by their male partners yearly. In 1990 more women were beaten by their male partners than were married that year. Nor can the increase of rape

and battery be fully explained by better reporting because the government systematically underestimates the numbers of such victims. See S. Rept. 197.

29. Again using domestic violence as my example, women cannot escape this harm without legal intervention. Three-fourths of all reported domestic violence assaults occur after a woman has left her partner, and the majority of murdered battered women are killed after they leave. Between 1983 and 1987 battered women shelters reported more than a 100 percent increase in women seeking refuge, and one million were turned away each year for lack of space. Yet funding in the past five years has been decreased. Half of all homeless American women in the past decade were refugees of domestic violence. But legal response has been slow; only fifteen states have laws that prosecute batterers and protect victims. See generally K. Culliton, "Domestic Violence Legislation in Chile and the U.S." (unpublished manuscript).

Chapter 7

Law and Social Exclusion

Diana Tietjens Meyers

The Problem of Difference

Martha Minow's *Making All the Difference* offers a sweeping and detailed analysis of social exclusion. As her title implies, the book is about social change—making a difference. But the double entendre in the title is that Minow's book focuses on a particular but pervasive social problem: the problem of difference. Formerly understood as the problem of prejudice or bigotry, that is, mass contempt for and concerted discrimination against individuals simply because they belong to a minority or powerless social group, recasting the wrong of social exclusion as the problem of difference brings out the complexity of this injustice. Thinking of social exclusion solely in terms of the prejudice of the excluders reduces the problem to the despicable attitudes of a dominant group and leaves out two important dimensions of the problem: the institutionalization of exclusion, and the viewpoint of the excluded. Minow steadfastly refuses to simplify the problem of social exclusion. Nevertheless, she is guardedly optimistic that it can be overcome, for the central thesis of her book is that the problem of difference is not as intractable as it often seems. To make her case, she pursues a pair of interrelated strategies: one aimed at the way in which people think about difference; the other aimed at the way institutions respond to difference.

For Minow, the problem of difference is partly a problem about how we think about people. Instead of noticing individuals, we tend to consign people to exclusionary categories—sex, race, sexual orientation, disability, ethnicity, religion, and so forth—and then dismiss the people thus classified as inherently defective. In this way, difference—the neutral fact that peo-

Chapter 7 originally appeared as "Social Exclusion, Moral Reflection and Rights," *Law and Philosophy* 12 (1993): 115–30, and is reprinted here with the kind permission of Kluwer Academic Publishers.

162

ple look different, act different, and choose different affiliations—degenerates into "difference": the censorious freighting of the facts of difference. Against this invidious drift, Minow maintains that difference always involves a reciprocal comparative judgment. If you are different from me, I am different from you. Moreover, she claims that there is no objective standard from which deviation constitutes difference, that is, norms are always conceived from a perspective, and no perspective is privileged.

But thinking about people in more fluid terms will not eliminate the problem of difference, for "difference" is memorialized in entrenched social practices. When established institutions and the policies they implement are taken to be natural and fair, any change that accommodates "different" people will disrupt the settled expectations of members of the dominant group, the people for whom these arrangements were designed and who accept them. As a result, such change will appear to interfere with these individuals' freedom and will be regarded as departing from neutrality in bestowing undeserved benefits on a new group of claimants. Yet, as Minow observes, the status quo is not neutral for members of excluded groups; their free choice and prospects for self-realization are obstructed by the very institutions and policies that serve others so well.

When unilateral ascriptions of "difference" are institutionalized in this way, the double bind of the "dilemma of difference" arises. As Minow points out, "The stigma of difference may be recreated both by ignoring and by focusing on it." By ignoring difference and treating everyone as the same, government may "freeze in place the past consequences of difference," but, by creating programs that acknowledge difference, government "make[s] those differences matter and thus symbolically reinforces them."[1] By pretending that women in the United States today are no different from men, equal opportunity guarantees that many women who have children and who take time off to care for them will be left behind in their careers. They have chosen, goes the familiar rationale, to put family ahead of professional advancement and thus to sacrifice work experience, which is a legitimate factor in promotion decisions. However, if government were to provide affirmative action for women who leave career tracks to care for preschool children and who later wish to rejoin the workforce,[2] the cri de quota would be raised. Women would be stigmatized as freeloaders, taking "vacations" to raise kids and returning to unearned advantages in the workplace. Either way, women who become mothers in the context of traditional relations with men lose. As equals, they do not measure up; as recipients of special favors, they would be despised.

What is to be done? According to Minow, we need to approach legal analysis innovatively. We need to jettison abnormal persons analysis and rights analysis and to adopt social relations analysis. As Minow expounds, social relations analysis covers quite a lot of intellectual territory: wherever there are relationships, social relations analysis instructs us to take them into account. People should expose and scrutinize conceptual relations. They should be cognizant of various sorts of social and political relations: the relations between society and the individual, between the state and individuals, between individuals, and between branches of government. They should be aware of power relations between themselves and people whom they are seeking to understand and help. They should become sensitive to the relations between their unconscious anxieties and needs and their moral judgments. They should use relational methods to respect particularity, that is, they should engage in dialogue with others, and they should take the perspective of the other. They should examine and evaluate the quality of political and interpersonal relationships. Roughly, what Minow is rejecting is a model that construes moral and legal deliberation as a monologic, objective application of abstract, absolute values.

Minow believes that the potential of social relations analysis is far-reaching and salutary. Social relations analysis makes it possible to transcend the dilemma of difference by demonstrating that claims of difference do not mark intrinsic divisions between people and by generating responses to "difference" that reconcile rights with a social conception of the person and thus reconcile rights with community.

Difference and Social Relations

Denying that difference is real, social relations analysis locates difference in power relations that enable some people to regard themselves as the norm, to label others as different, and to establish institutions that consolidate their power by making difference a social and economic liability. If we analyze "difference" in this way, Minow contends, we give "the basic connectedness between people and the injuries that result from social isolation and exclusion" their due (379). The advantages of recognizing the role of power in the creation of difference are obvious, but this line of thought is troubling in two respects. First, the scope of Minow's thesis is not always clear. Is it difference or "difference" that is socially constructed through power relations? Second, it is doubtful that Minow is giving the viewpoint of the excluded sufficient weight, for her account reduces their subjectivity to the effects of domination.

Although Minow sometimes seems to assert that both difference and "difference" are entirely socially constructed, her diagnoses of various problems of social exclusion hint at a more subtle view. Her best formulations allow that a tangled knot of physiological facts, institutions and practices, and value judgments constitute difference. Thus, Minow grants that nothing we could do would change the fact that severely mentally retarded people need extra help. But she also insists that differences are socially constructed "to a significant degree." They are exaggerated by optional social arrangements—most people's ignorance of sign language heightens the difference between people who can hear and people who cannot. Moreover, they are transformed into "differences" by prevailing values—deaf people have often been deemed abnormal and incompetent. Minow calls for creating social arrangements that include "different" people as full participants, and she rejects the contrasts between normality and abnormality and between competency and incompetency.

Surely, there is no gainsaying Minow's claims that choices about our physical and social environment limit some people unnecessarily and that too many people have been falsely judged abnormal and incompetent. However, her zeal to deny the justifiability of ostracizing people as "different" sometimes comes perilously close to erasing difference. There are various cases of difference, and it is important both to recognize misfortune where it exists and also to recognize values that have arisen from the experience of difference.

Many differences are not figments of a dominant group's malign collective imagination. Some differences are disabilities, if not afflictions, and would remain disabilities regardless of our social arrangements. Consider blindness. Suppose that your doctor told you that you will be blind tomorrow but assured you that there was no reason to be upset. Happily, you would be able to walk safely because traffic signals would be equipped with audio directions; you would be able to travel freely because Congress had voted to furnish blind people with full-time chauffeurs; you would be able to read anything you wanted because all published materials would be available in braille; and so on. Speaking for myself, I might be slightly relieved to learn that my condition would not be as crippling as blindness is today, but I would still despair. Not only is seeing wonderful, but I would find many tasks that I now manage easily much harder. Regardless of how lavishly my society compensated me for my blindness, I would become less able to enjoy life and less able to function. If socially constructed at all, that residue of difference is socially constructed only on the view that everything is socially constructed.

In this kind of case, there is a reality of reduced competence and a privileged perspective. Walt Stromer, who was blinded at the age of twenty-six, catalogues reactions to the experience of being blind as follows: "Blindness is merely a nuisance, according to some. For most of us it is worse than that, at least on some days. For a few people it is devastating."[3] Because it is better to be able to see, social programs for the blind properly concentrate on minimizing the disadvantages of blindness. It would be obtuse to pretend that any reconceptualization of the norm could do away with this difference and hypocritical to valorize blindness. Indeed, many disabled people resent euphemistic labels, such as "physically challenged" or "differently abled." Marilyn Golden of the Disability Rights Education and Defense Fund objects to such terms on the grounds that they "mask reality and [are] therefore demeaning and offensive."[4] Likewise, "challenged" and similar language was resoundingly eschewed in a survey of the national readership of *The Disability Rag,* a journal devoted to the concerns of the disabled.[5] Here, Minow's preoccupation with changing the social meaning of difference misses the point.

In contrast, the case for the social construction of difference is well illustrated by race, a difference that is entirely socially constructed.[6] Though there are no physical or mental disabilities regularly correlated with African descent, there are in the United States legions of social and economic liabilities associated with this ancestry. The abolition of slavery did not end the injustices inflicted on African Americans, nor is an end in sight. To rationalize this treatment, whites manufactured failings of character and intellect, authoritatively ascribed these failings to blacks, and solemnly censured blacks. Thus, the history of African Americans in the United States chronicles centuries of enforced marginalization punctuated by frequent episodes of overt brutality.

Here, the clear imperative of justice is to expose myths that link incompetence to skin pigment for what they are and to reverse the exclusionary practices that took up where slavery left off. However, racial justice cannot properly be construed as guaranteeing African Americans the right to assimilate to white culture through integration. If integration is the goal, it must be understood in a way that respects racial difference insofar as individual African Americans choose for reasons of culture and solidarity to identify with this classification. Drawing on African cultures antedating the European slave trade as well as experiences of defiance and unity during slavery and its aftermath, African American culture is for many a wellspring of values and a foundation for community. Vile as other-defined racial "difference" is, self-defined racial difference demands respect. Minow seldom acknowledges the positive standing of self-assigned difference, and, when she does, she insists that such difference must be independent of institutionalized domination. Thus, it is hard to avoid inferring that she does not fully appreciate this crucial dimension of the problem of difference.

On the one hand, when difference stems from an irremediable disability, it cannot be dissolved through a more egalitarian conceptual schema. Indeed, focusing on our categorization of such disabilities may distract attention from the urgent need to provide ameliorative services. On the other hand, when difference stems from the proud appropriation of a cultural identity despite its roots in oppression, it cannot be dissolved without compounding the injustice to those who have been oppressed. Although oversolicitousness of race, ethnicity, gender, sexual orientation, and the like can be an insulting display of noblesse oblige, so, too, ignoring such identities can be an arrogant exercise of privilege: I am so secure in my position that your difference is beneath my notice. Still, there are cases in which difference can be dissolved by altering dominant standards and adjusting social policy and where doing so would not trample on self-avowed difference. But, I shall urge, not all of these cases support the conclusion that remedial action should be taken.

Consider mild mental retardation, a condition that does not require constant supervision or institutionalization but that does significantly limit people's intellectual development. How debilitating this condition is depends on the sort of world we create. In a simpler society—one without advanced technology, mass dissemination of information, and complex political and economic systems—these people would not be especially disadvantaged. However, making society fully negotiable for the mildly retarded would mean that others would have to accept a relatively primitive, stultifying existence. It seems doubtful that they should. Why should people not hold chess tournaments, invent and market faster computer chips, or read *Finnegan's Wake?* Though industrial civilization brings along notorious problems, societies with sophisticated culture and science—societies that render mildly retarded adults less competent than the vast majority of their contemporaries—are desirable in many respects. Indeed, it seems clear that living in an environment that they cannot fully comprehend benefits the mildly retarded because, for example, medical treatments that help these individuals would not otherwise be discovered.[7] Thus, it would be a mistake to condemn the institutions and practices of industrial societies as examples of a dominant group's wielding power unfairly to disadvantage a group of socially defined outsiders and to advocate a policy of leveling that would nullify those differences for the mildly retarded.

The way other people structure and embellish their lives is a major factor determining how disabling some differences are. Yet, that the adverse impact of some differences is largely a byproduct of optional social institutions and practices does not entail that measures should be taken to neutralize them. Only insofar as different people are denied suitable opportunities for fulfillment, preyed upon, or ridiculed, that is, only insofar as cruel and unwarranted value judgments are made about them, does the social construction of such differences become pernicious. There are kinds and degrees of competence as well as incompetence. Judgments of competence and incompetence are objectionable only when they are regarded as absolute—groups of people are either altogether competent or altogether incompetent—or when relative incompetence gives rise to scorn. Moreover, whether we should endorse social institutions and practices that magnify the impact of differences requires weighing countervailing considerations: the hardship to those who are disabled versus the hardship to those who are enabled. Because reducing the social and economic impact of difference typically requires reallocating limited resources, it is not always clear that society's only conscionable course is to invest whatever it takes to minimize or eliminate the consequences of difference.

Social Relations Analysis

Before the question of whether society should undertake to combat difference can profitably be raised, however, it is necessary to figure out what measures would be needed and how those measures could be defended. That there are different kinds of difference suggests that there are different ways to resolve the dilemma of difference. Yet, for purposes of generating and justifying solutions to this problem, Minow relies exclusively on social relations analysis.

Though social relations analysis, as Minow presents it, is an eclectic potpourri of deliberative strategies, she offers this approach as an alternative to impartial reason, the logic of consistency and universality that grounds the rights tradition associated with Locke, Kant, and recently John Rawls. In what follows, I shall urge that Minow's rejection of impartial reason is misguided, for she implicitly and, I think, rightly relies on impartial reason to develop a solution to one variant of the dilemma of difference. But I shall also urge that we can extract an account of a second moral capacity from Minow's sketch of social relations analysis—I shall call this capacity empathic thought—and that this capacity is the key to dealing with a second form that the dilemma of difference takes. I doubt that we can "make all the difference" if we channel moral reflection into any single modality.

To see the relevance of impartial reason to the dilemma of difference, it is helpful to begin by examining a model of a successful public policy response to difference: Social Security in the United States. The institutionalization of Social Security has not eliminated prejudice against elderly people; employers resist hiring them, and purportedly humorous images of doddering old fools remain in currency. However, this persistent prejudice does not taint Social Security, a transfer payment program in which funds are redistributed from younger wage earners to the elderly. (I leave aside Social Security's less publicized missions, such as providing disability payments and providing income for the minor children of deceased participants in the program.) Why aren't Social Security pensioners grouped together with welfare mothers and resented for the same reasons?

It seems to me that three major factors have contributed to the acceptance of Social Security. First, it is not perceived as a transfer payment program. The illusion that Social Security is an insurance program into which workers pay premiums and from which they eventually draw their fair share of dividends has been successfully maintained. Thus, receiving Social Security checks is not likened to taking charity from welfare. Second, Social Security appears to relieve adult children of financial responsibility for their parents. Believing the Social Security taxes they are now paying to be savings for their own eventual pension, wage earners do not see that they remain indirectly responsible for their parents' economic well-being. Yet, it is doubtful that general recognition of the redistributive structure of Social Security would bring the system into disrepute, for, third, old age is a universal problem. Though some people will not reach retirement age, everyone must anticipate this eventuality. Thus, Social Security is perceived as universally beneficial.

Accommodating difference does not perpetuate the stigma of difference when the interests of the "different" coincide with the interests of others and when no "different" group is explicitly targeted to receive special benefits. Some of the solutions to the dilemma of difference that Minow endorses follow this pattern. For example, she concurs with the U.S. Supreme Court in framing the issue of maternity leave in terms of the gender-neutral standard of being entitled to have a family and a job. Until family relations have been reconceptualized in a way that assigns men equal responsibility for children and the elderly, laws conferring the right to take family leave and to return to work without penalty will benefit women primarily. Yet, the gender-neutral language in which these laws are cast prompts people to understand the problem of caring for dependents, like the problem of old age, as a universal one. Moreover, because two incomes have ceased to be a luxury for many U.S. families, feminist demands for maternity leave may eventually converge with everyone's household needs.

Now, it seems to me that this type of resolution of the dilemma of difference is most perspicuously explicated not in terms of social relations analysis but, rather, in terms of impartial reason. For impartial reason, the guiding question is, What if everyone did that? Or, in political terms, Would you want to live in a society in which everyone had [did not have] that freedom or in which everyone could [could not] claim that benefit? Answers to this question are presumed to yield answers to the questions What do we all have in common? and What conduct befits our common humanity? Justice is achieved through the consistent application of nondiscriminatory categories that capture universal human capacities and basic interests. The aim is to set up a social structure that protects these shared interests while affording all members of society the opportunity to realize their potential. Although people are expected to avail themselves of their rights in ways that suit their particular talents and aspirations, the conceptual infrastructure of impartial reason is homogenizing. What is valued in people and what is regarded as essential to them is what they have in common.

Consider Rawls's impartialist defense of his difference principle, the principle requiring that inequalities of income and wealth should benefit the least-advantaged members of society. Rawls urges his readers to leave aside all knowledge of their personal situation and to project their basic interest profile into a different socioeconomic niche, namely, that of the least-advantaged member of society.[8] If I think that were I among the least advantaged, I would find material inequalities unacceptable unless they improved my lot in life, then I should endorse the difference principle. Underlying Rawls's impartial rationality is the assumption that people's basic interests are uniform. His conception of the original position does not allow middle-class deliberators to entertain the possibility that a disadvantaged member of society might have interests markedly different from theirs. For Rawls, one lone person performing the deduction from the original position can represent everyone: my conclusions about justice will be duplicated by anyone else.[9]

For impartial reason, difference, if it is not superficial and accidental, violates the regnant paradigm of the person.[10] To accommodate difference impartially, then, is to make it vanish morally by assimilating it to established categories or by expanding established categories. Social Security and family leave finesse difference in this way.

But, of course, opening economic and political life to "different" people often conflicts with the interests of the dominant group, and many differences resist absorption into neutral categories. As we have seen, some people suffer from disabilities that will not obligingly disappear, morally or otherwise, and that require extra consideration. Other people have identities that reflect their experience of segregation and oppression but that they could not strip away without betraying themselves. Now, it might be pointed out that impartial reason is equipped to address cases of this kind, as well. The converse of the impartialist dictum "Treat like cases alike" is "Treat different cases differently." This backup precept handily disposes of situations that are covered by well-established principles of fairness: parents have rightful authority over their minor children; victims of force or fraud should be compensated; the punishment should fit the crime. However, the dilemma of difference arises only when difference is not generally believed to warrant special moral consideration. When this skepticism prevails, treating "different" people differently calls attention to their historically despised difference and reinforces exclusionary tendencies.

Impartial reason can countenance departures from the moral norm of uniform treatment, but such departures are usually conceived as addressing exceptional predicaments or temporary conditions. The presumption is that for moral purposes, people are alike and ought to be treated the same way. Consequently, impartial reason is not well adapted to envisaging moral responses to irremediable or cherished differences.

But there is another moral capacity that neither ignores nor abhors difference, namely, empathic thought. To think empathically, one must ask,

"Who are you?" and "How can I best respond to your needs?" Empathic thought requires people to attend to others in order to learn to see the world from their point of view—in Elizabeth V. Spelman's apt phrase, to apprentice themselves to others.[11] One's own point of view may ultimately prove to be a permutation of another group's basic interest profile, but it may not. What I imagine I would care about if I were blind, African American, lesbian, or male may not be what members of these groups in fact care about. Although empathic thought relies on the deliberator's accumulated experience of people and human relations, it assumes no standard case. Rather, it pays attention to individuals and seeks to understand and respond to each individual's distinctive ensemble of strengths and weaknesses, hopes, and fears. Difference is presumed to be the norm—every person is unique—and the task of moral reflection is to devise action that is gauged to particular persons. Thus, making allowance for difference carries no connotations of favoritism or exploitation. Rather, empathic thought relishes and honors difference.

Whereas impartial reason relies on comprehensive moral categories and thus minimizes the number of moral categories, empathic thought allows moral categories to proliferate in proportion to its perception of moral variation. Different people require different treatment. Impartial reason celebrates the value of universal humanity through fidelity to abstract principles; empathic thought celebrates the value of human diversity through concern for other individuals. Impartial reason and empathic thought diverge in the way in which moral deliberation is conducted, in the form of their moral recommendations, and in the values they privilege. They differ, then, with respect to their aptitude for dealing with issues of "difference."

Susan Moller Okin's discussion of the traditional woman reveals how impartial reason's insensitivity to difference can go awry. The housewife and mother who is economically dependent on her husband seldom has equal standing in major family decisions, such as whether to relocate to pursue career opportunities and how income is to be allocated. By the standards of impartial reason, such subordination is demeaning and demands rectification. Okin traces the traditional woman's subservience to her economic dependence and fashions a dual-paycheck remedy.[12] The idea is that because the person who is performing unpaid domestic services is making as valuable a contribution to the family economy as the person who is working for a wage, it is right that the worth of this contribution be officially recognized. This recognition should take the form of a paycheck; the wage worker will receive checks for half of his salary, and the domestic worker will receive checks for half of the wage worker's salary. Through this device, the domestic worker is not only duly compensated for her labor but also freed of the liability of economic dependence. With an income of her own, she gains an equal voice in major family decisions.

Now, it seems obvious to me that this scheme will not bring about the results that Okin seeks.[13] What is the homemaker going to do with her checks? Probably, like me, she will deposit them in the couple's joint checking account. Surely, we cannot legally require couples to maintain separate finances. But, even if we did, the traditional woman's status would hardly be transfigured, for she would remain economically dependent on her spouse. If he leaves her, she loses her income. Should we prohibit divorce? What is missing, I believe, in Okin's plan is any empathic understanding of the traditional woman. Maybe Okin thinks the traditional woman is just like many academic women: give her professional status and economic rewards, and in time she will blossom into a self-assertive agent. But I doubt that this portrait is accurate. The traditional woman believes that her husband is the head of the household and that her proper role is that of helpmeet. A symbolic paycheck will not change her values and consequently will not make her an equal partner in her marriage.

The futility of Okin's proposal is not its worst failing, however. More serious still, it fails to respect the traditional woman. No doubt, there are many women who are stuck in the traditional feminine role and who badly want to escape from it or would want to escape if escape were feasible. Impartial reason, as Okin interprets it, holds that basic human interests dictate that no woman fulfilling this role could reasonably feel otherwise.[14] But, if there are women who sincerely embrace this role, and, though I wish it weren't so, I suspect that there are, it is morally repugnant to visit an alien ideal of marital equality upon them. Only through empathic thought can difference be acknowledged and given due respect.

But, of course, respecting difference through empathic thought entails neither accepting others' wishes uncritically nor granting others whatever they demand. Empathic thought asks, "How can I best respond to your needs?" not "What do you want me to do?" Thus, once one understands another's point of view, one needs a deliberative filter to fashion a moral response. That filter is constituted by a further pair of questions: Who am I—what capacities are at my disposal, and what sort of a person do I aspire to be? What sort of a person would doing that [not doing that] make me?

Empathic thought takes into account the agent's strengths and weaknesses along with that individual's moral ideals, and it commends action that responds to others in a manner that is consonant with that self-concept.[15] Needless to say, these questions can be framed from a political standpoint, as well: What sort of a society are we—what resources are at our disposal, and what sort of a society do we aspire to bring about? What sort of a society would implementing that policy (not implementing that policy) make us? Empathic thought is an interactive mode of moral reflection. It invites others to voice their needs, and it invites deliberators to articulate their capabilities and their values. The aim of empathic thought is to reconcile the integrity of individuals or societies with people's expressed needs.

Minow's treatment of special education supplies striking examples of the empathic approach to the dilemma of difference. Her description of the elementary school class that coped with the enrollment of a deaf pupil by learning sign language illustrates this approach. It is undeniable that the deaf child is different, but by entering her world the teacher and the other students succeeded in bringing her into their community, thereby enriching everyone's classroom experience and affirming the value of acquainting oneself with an unfamiliar point of view. But special education has sometimes had much more far-reaching consequences, for it has brought about a curious deconstruction of "difference" in some U.S. schools. Various statutory mandates have entitled a whole range of pupils to demand "appropriate" public education. Thus, as the types of pupils have multiplied—deaf, hyperactive, dyslexic, gifted, bilingual, and so forth—and as the numbers of "different" students have soared (in some school systems 80 percent of the student body is considered learning disabled) difference has ceased to be deviant. With the normalization of difference comes empathic response to it. Teachers tailor pedagogical methods and educational services to meet individual students' needs. Mainstreaming is effected without homogenization, and delight in diversity supplants grudging tolerance of difference.

There are, then, at least two forms that the dilemma of difference takes. In one form, blindness to commonality where it exists or where it could exist creates artificial boundaries between groups of people that work to the detriment of all but the most powerful of those groups. Through more skillful and imaginative use of impartial reason, this form of the dilemma can be resolved. As Minow puts it, the idea is to expand the definition of who is the same. In the other form, contempt for genuine difference is invoked to justify a powerful group's indifference to or exploitation of others. Here, the dilemma of difference will persist until empathic thought pierces the cocoon of contempt and enables people to appreciate human diversity. In Minow's words, the solution is to broaden the definition of difference. The intractability of the dilemma of difference is an artifact of routinized and unidimensional moral reflection. As long as impartial reason is captivated by a rigid set of categories and as long as impartial reason monopolizes moral reflection to the exclusion of empathic thought, differences will be stigmatized and penalized.

Rights in Relationship

Though Minow maintains that social relations analysis provides an adequate basis for defusing all charges of difference, she acknowledges that solutions to the dilemma of difference can take either of two distinct forms: expanding the scope of sameness or multiplying acknowledged differences. Still, she reverts to monoconceptualism in contending that both of these solution types can be captured in the language of rights. To sustain her view, she undertakes a reconstruction of rights language along lines designed to satisfy the solutions' communitarian critics.

Minow's reasons for seeking to rescue rights are familiar. Enforced rights restrain arbitrary power, and the wrongfully dispossessed can appeal to rights to press their demands. But, if rights are considered to be timeless and absolute, they may threaten the interests of excluded groups. University admissions procedures have traditionally recognized the right to be judged solely on your academic qualifications unless you are a talented athlete, the son or daughter of a wealthy donor, or a resident of a distant, sparsely populated state. Unless the exceptions to meritocracy that this right countenances can be amended to include membership in a disadvantaged racial minority, it is clear that this right raises a formidable barrier to educational advancement for many African Americans. To prevent such calcification, Minow proposes that we reject the idea that the rights we recognize are transcendent moral truths and, instead, embed rights in relations.

Political discourse and, especially, legal discourse in the United States are conducted by claiming rights. Rights talk is the lingua franca in which we articulate our sense of justice; in which we set forth what we believe is our due and what we owe to others; in which we seek access to those who wield political power and fight against injustice. Because rights talk is the road to empowerment, I, like Minow, would be reluctant to deprive any excluded group of the rhetorical impact of rights claims. However, Minow's argument for a more catholic account of rights is not persuasive.

She advocates shifting from analyzing the concept of a right—are rights claims? entitlements? trumps?—to describing the role rights play in social and legal life. She characterizes rights as "features of interpersonal connection" (289), as "a vocabulary used by community members to interpret and reinterpret their relationships with one another," (306), and as "a language for describing and remaking patterns of relationships" (383). That rights function in these ways is hard to deny, but that these functions are not peculiar to rights is equally undeniable; the functions Minow attributes to rights could be ascribed equally well to responsibilities or emotions. It remains an open question whether it is wise for theorists to join in the reduction of our variegated and nuanced moral vocabulary to a single rhetorical mode. I shall return to this question shortly, but first I want to look at Minow's other major point in defense of rights discourse.

Not wanting to surrender the value of community, Minow seeks to incorporate it into her account of rights. Rights, according to Minow, are a medium for expressing and strengthening communal relationships." Unfortunately, the price of this synthetic project is the impoverishment of the conception of community that is retained in rights theory. In Minow's theory of rights, a community is nothing more than a collection of people who live according to a common set of rules of order, that is, who agree to settle their conflicts by arguing about their rights instead of by assaulting one another. Of course she is right that participating in this process of adjudication presupposes a community that has created the necessary cultural backdrop and legal apparatus. Likewise, she is right that participating in this process affirms and strengthens liberal, juridical communities. But this is by no means the kind of community communitarians have in mind when they maintain that rights-based relations subvert community. Rights establish moral boundaries around people and an adversarial system for redressing violations of those boundaries. Whether recognizing rights always impedes the development of harmonious, warm communal bonds is an empirical question that I am in no position to answer. However, that rights do not presuppose such a community is indisputable. I suspect, then, that proponents of communitarian ideals are unlikely to be won over by Minow's attempt to consolidate rights and community.

To cast all moral values in the language of rights is to conceal, perhaps to cancel out, the plurality of moral reasons. Thus, compartmentalization—

keeping the language of rights distinct from the languages of communitarianism, care, welfarism, and so forth—is appealing, for it preserves the richness of moral discourse. Yet, it does not follow that rights can be derived only through impartial reason. On the contrary, empathic thought can justify rights claims, as well. This, I believe, is the truth that is buried in Minow's avalanche of redescriptions of rights. However, it is important to recognize that impartial reason and empathic thought generate rights in different ways and therefore that the rights they yield need not exactly coincide. Indeed, in view of the disparities these two modes of moral reflection produce, I shall suggest that rights theory would do well to see rights as a collaborative product of impartial reason and empathic thought.

Consider the right to education. Impartial reason asks, "Would I want to live in a society that did not provide free public elementary and secondary education?" It proceeds deductively from the ignorance into which humans are universally born and thus the universal need for formal intellectual training to the equal right to educational opportunity. Like everyone else, I would not want to be deprived of that right. In contrast, empathic thought begins by noticing this person's distinctive potential and urgent need, that person's distinctive potential and urgent need, and so forth and then asks, "What kind of a society would withhold free public primary and secondary education?" If we agree that we want no part of a society that lets many people's potential languish and that rules out upward mobility, and if we combine that aversion with our inductive grasp of people's various needs, we will conclude that we have a responsibility to supply appropriate education for each child.

The deficiencies of these two approaches are complementary, as are their virtues. Impartial reason resists customizing rights to fit actual people's diverse needs, but empathic thought resists generalizing to a broad pattern of need that would warrant the recognition of a universal right. In other words, abandoning impartial reason invites capriciousness, and rejecting empathic thought invites rigidity. Accordingly, if the right to education were understood as grounded in a collaboration between impartial reason and empathic thought, we would secure a universal right that guaranteed education geared to the capacities and limitations of each child, a right that would not substitute formal equality for substantial equality.

If this view of the foundations of rights is correct, it follows that the temptation to divide the moral realm between issues of rights and liberty and issues of welfare and aid, with impartial reason governing the former and empathic thought confined to the latter, should be resisted. Not only can sensitization to others' distinctive needs supply ample grounds for not interfering with others but also, as we saw earlier, impartial reason can come to the defense of welfare programs like the Social Security system. Moreover, because commitments to liberty constrain welfare initiatives, and because welfare-enhancing programs impinge on liberty, this dichotomous pairing of moral issues and moral capacities is bound to break down. Impartial reason and empathic thought do not hold sway in conveniently separate domains, nor are their normative prescriptions invariably rivals.

It would be foolish, as Minow contends, to give up on the dynamic of rights-based social protest and litigation for fear of the stasis of rights-based judicial reinforcement of existing social hierarchies. But it would also be foolish to elevate rights to the status of an all-consuming, all-purpose moral currency. The goal, I think, is to expand the compass of rights without nullifying other moral values. To achieve this balance, it is necessary to recognize not only that impartial reason and empathic thought do not exhaust our moral capacities but also that each of these reflective modes sustains a repertory of moral concepts that is not confined to rights; impartial reason is traditionally associated with duties that are not correlated with rights, and Carol Gilligan links empathic thought to responsibilities, to mention a couple. Furthermore, it is necessary to recognize the complementary contributions of impartial reason and empathic thought to arguments for rights.

Though grounded in impartial reason, traditional rights theories address the generic human unity discernible in the diversity of individuals and indirectly the diversity of individuals that flourishes within the unity of common humanity. Basic liberties were justified by appeal to universal human traits, but individuality was expected to thrive through the exercise of these liberties. The challenge Minow levels at contemporary rights theory is to extend this double perspective to a broader spectrum of rights and to the full spectrum of right-holders. I have argued that this can best be accomplished through an account of rights that draws on both impartial reason and empathic thought.

Notes

I am grateful to Daniel Ginsberg, Eva Feder Kittay, and Joel Kupperman for their helpful comments on earlier drafts of this chapter.

1. Martha Minow, *Making All the Difference* (Ithaca: Cornell University Press, 1990) 20, 42.

2. Virginia Held, "The Obligations of Mothers and Fathers," in *Mothering*, ed. Joyce Trebilcot (Totowa, N.J.: Rowman & Allanheld, 1983), 19.

3. Walt Stromer, "On Being Blind," *New York Review of Books* 38 (1991): 61.

4. Anne Matthews, "Cultivating the Cruelty-Free Can Get a Person Zapped!" *International Herald Tribune*, July 10, 1991, 5.

5. Ibid.

6. Anthony Appiah, "'But Would That Still Be Me?' Notes on Gender, 'Race,' Ethnicity, as Sources of 'Identity,'" *The Journal of Philosophy* 87 (1990): 493–99, at 496, 499.

7. It should be noted that the mildly retarded are by no means the only people who are baffled by many aspects of modern society. Most people easily comprehend monthly bank statements and electronic banking machines, but many must turn to professionals for investment advice. Likewise, most people have at best a rudimentary grasp of medicine. Yet, few would want to forgo the benefits of complex economic and scientific establishments in exchange for simpler systems that would never mystify them.

8. John Rawls, *A Theory of Justice* (Cambridge: Harvard University Press, 1971), 153.

9. Ibid., 139.

10. This is not to say that impartial reason denies that people care deeply about their personal projects. In fact, it is often this very involvement with individual life plans that serves to justify robust individual liberties (e.g., ibid., 206–8). But notice that what justifies these liberties is the universal human interest in conceiving and carrying out one's own life plan, not each individual's commitment to his or her particular life plan.

11. Elizabeth V. Spelman, *Inessential Woman* (Boston: Beacon Press, 1988), 178.

12. Susan Moller Okin, *Justice, Gender, and the Family* (New York: Basic Books, 1989), 181.

13. I want to stress that my criticisms of Okin's dual-paycheck proposal do not extend to her helpful suggestions about ensuring the economic well-being of women and children in the aftermath of divorce.

14. Okin, *Justice, Gender, and the Family*, 175.

15. For further discussion of this approach to deliberation, see Diana Tietjens Meyers, *Subjection and Subjectivity: Psychoanalytic Feminism and Moral Philosophy* (New York: Routledge, 1994), 119–69.

Differences, Universality, and the Radical Critique of Law: Reflections on Smith and Meyers

Carol C. Gould

The radical critique of the law derives from several sources, among them the feminist emphasis on difference, the Marxist critique of domination, and the communitarian argument concerning concretely situated social and juridical relations. The chapters considered here may be located in both the feminist and communitarian contexts and make important and useful contributions to this discussion. The thrust of my comments centers on two points: first, that the discussions of difference and empathy would benefit from a more theoretical grounding, without which the accounts remain somewhat ad hoc; and related to this, second, that these authors do not yet have a generalized account of difference that would permit the systematic recognition of differences by the law. An additional point, which may only be suggested here, is that the critiques these authors offer, as effective and important as they are, may not be radical enough in that they do not address the question of social change as a condition for a serious transformation of the legal norms that they discuss.

Perhaps the major theme in feminist critiques of the law concerns how differences, especially those of gender, can be incorporated within a legal tradition that is claimed to be based on impartiality and neutrality, and that stresses equal treatment for similarly situated persons. One feminist approach would be to argue for the recognition and protection of those interests that are different from the standard interests usually considered in the law. Along these lines, Uma Narayan provides a helpful analysis of what she calls "nonstandard interests" and points to the need for special protections in the law for interests that fall outside the perception of "the standard interests of standard persons."[1] Narayan takes a critical view of the notion of standard interests and uses the term with scare quotes to indicate that the "standard" is often exclusionary and discriminatory by tending to be identified with the interests of white males or other dominant social groups. However, her useful classification of nonstandard interests and vulnerabilities[2] and her recommendation that they are worthy of legal protection still retains the distinction between the standard and the nonstandard and leaves in place a conception of standard interests as those by reference to which the nonstandard interests are defined. This approach seems to retain an idea of the standard as the normal despite her wariness of such a view. Yet, Narayan also proposes to rethink the concept of standard interests such that "we accord protection to *all* interests that are morally legitimate and serious enough to warrant protection."[3] But this remains somewhat vague and ad hoc, as does her distinction between standard and nonstandard interests itself.

What is needed, I think, is a more fundamental rejection of the framework that suggests a distinction between standard persons and interests on the one hand and nonstandard ones on the other. I propose that individuals be recognized as pursuing differentiated modes of self-development but that each has a prima facie equal right to the conditions for this self-development.[4] These conditions may be seen to include certain basic ones without which no activity would be possible and certain nonbasic ones that are required for fuller and individually differentiated self-development. In this sense, one may want to say that each individual has both standard (i.e., basic) and nonstandard interests, but the standard here no longer functions in the exclusionary way that it does when it functions as a mask for domination.

This approach contrasts with the common liberal one that defends a conception of basic interests, the securing and enhancing of which are seen as the primary function of government. Such a liberal approach leaves out too much. It omits any claim that individuals can make for societal provision of certain nonbasic conditions for their individuated modes of self-development—for example, certain forms of education and training. I have argued that in this case there are rights not to the same conditions but rather to equivalent conditions.[5]

It has sometimes been suggested that the differentiated interests that feminists have emphasized can in fact be accommodated by a reasonable liberalism and that in this way the ideas of the neutrality and impartiality of the law can be preserved. Such an approach would take issue with the claim that the feminist critique of the law from the standpoint of the validation of differences is a radical one. According to such an approach, this critique can be incorporated within a universalistic liberal framework.

It seems to me, however, that this would be to miss a crucial point, namely, that the feminist critique of the law demands an acknowledgment of difference as a means of achieving equality. This can be distinguished from the classic liberal view in which differences such as gender or race are recognized as irrelevant to equal treatment, which requires that there be no discrimination in the law based on such differences. This classical view may be characterized as the toleration of differences or as impartiality. In an early feminist essay, I characterized this view as abstract universality and argued for a conception of concrete universality or "universality with a difference." On this conception, concrete social and historical differences, such as those associated with gender, need to be recognized if individuals are to be treated equally and it is not simply the sameness of these individuals that is the basis for their equal rights. The recognition of differences among individuals thus becomes a positive requirement for the achievement of equality.[6]

In her chapter in this volume, Patricia Smith is right to stress that the feminist critique retains a liberal universalistic element in its appeal to "humanist ideals," as she puts it, or to what I prefer to call a conception of equal agency or equal freedom.[7] Yet, although the classical liberal position remains content with a principle of negative liberty and formal equality, I would add that some feminist theories, like certain other socially critical approaches, tend to appeal to a conception of positive freedom as well in which what is required is not merely the absence of impediments, or impartial treatment for all, but also the provision of specific and differentiated means to satisfy the requirements of difference. This move gives such feminist theories a more radical edge.

The radical character of the feminist critique of the law also emerges, as Smith astutely observes, when it is seen to be based on a critique of domination. This domination involves an idea of unequal or differential power in the concrete social relations between men and women, which is reflected and institutionalized in the law. (One may add that the norm implicit in the critique of domination is not only that of equality but also that of reciprocity, which involves an idea of the equivalence of the relations of each individual to the other.)[8]

However, in Smith's account, the feminist critique of the law is radical only insofar as it recognizes that the stated liberal universalist norms are not only contradicted by patriarchal practices but often serve to mask them.

The program that Smith describes of revealing this contradiction "to those in power" and thereby hoping to transform the law is characterized by her as essentially reformist and thus falls within the liberal tradition of the law.

We may observe that this approach retains the liberal conception of difference as something to be shown to be irrelevant and overcome as a ground for exclusion from the equal treatment required by liberal principles. It does not theorize difference as also having a positive value and as a basis for differential, though equivalent, claims within a framework of basic equality. Further, we may suggest that traditional liberalism provides insufficient grounds for the critique of systemic social relations of power, in the form of domination or of economic exploitation, even if it ameliorates discrimination based on irrelevant differences. Again, if the project of the radical feminist critique of the law is to reveal that present norms of equality often disadvantage women unfairly and that they are contingent and require change, then getting those in power to see this, as Smith puts it here, would be a quixotic task because it neglects the role of social change and the interest that those in power have in their present interpretation of the norms.

Diana Meyers, in her contribution to this volume, does not focus on the critique of domination but rather calls up another major aspect of feminist thought that we may characterize as sensitivity to the concrete differences of the other, and to his or her particular needs. This draws (though not explicitly) on the perspective of care, in contrast to the perspective of justice, a distinction developed in Carol Gilligan's earlier work and in the feminist literature more generally. In her useful and thought-provoking discussion of Martha Minow's social relations approach to the law, Meyers proposes "empathic thought" or empathy with the distinctive other, as the complement to the traditional approach of impartial reason. She holds that empathic thought generates rights in political and legal contexts differently from impartial reason, which bases such rights on universal claims. Her emphasis on the differentiated other and her argument for the rights claims that derive from such distinctive needs is similar to the argument referred to earlier concerning the recognition of concrete differences among individuals as a basis for achieving equality (a notion of equality that incorporates and does not exclude difference); and also as a basis for rights claims.

However, it is not yet clear how empathic thought as described may be said to generate rights. If empathic thought is an identification with a *particular* other who is unique, is Meyers claiming that there are unique or singular rights, that is, rights applying only to a single individual? Surely not.

More plausibly, we may speak of one's (equal) right to develop one's unique potentialities (as suggested in the concept of equal positive freedom). But this conception applies to each individual and is in this respect impartial. That is not to say that such impartiality is not informed by the moral and affective understanding of particular others that helps to justify the recognition of the right. The concept of impartiality need not be so formal, empty, and rigid as to leave out its own motivation in a concern for others (though it has functioned that way in much of the tradition).

Generally speaking, we have a fairly good understanding of how empathic thought works in personal and moral contexts, but considerably more needs to be said about its applicability to law. Meyers would need to give a fuller account of how we move from empathy with an individual to the justification not only of rights for disadvantaged groups or those with distinctive needs (the particular cases Meyers discusses) but also of rights for everyone. Further, we can conceive of political or legal relations based on care, for example, concern for the vulnerable embodied in welfare and also certain types of reciprocal relations that play an important role in democratic community, and in these cases empathy may well be involved, but here too its role merits a more detailed exploration.

Reflecting on the feminist critiques of the law more generally, one may observe that they have tended to be somewhat limited in scope, applying to certain areas of law, most especially to questions of equal protection and the role of differences in that context, and to the legal recognition of specific rights and gender-directed crimes and harms, for example, rape, wife battering, and sexual harassment. It is perhaps surprising that there are not more systematic critiques of the law from a feminist standpoint.

In conclusion, I would like to call attention to one aspect of a radical critique of the law that has been very little discussed in any of the chapters in this volume. That is the question of the legal protection and enhancement of common interests beyond the idea of the universal interests that all individuals have. By "common interest" I mean an interest that several individuals share in the realization of a common goal that they have jointly chosen and that requires their joint or common activity to achieve. There are aspects of the law that do address some such common interests, for example, in the case of regulations concerning corporations, public institutions, and the government itself; and in addition there is a body of law concerning the related notion of public goods, for example, clean air, clean water, national forests, and so on. But there is an open area of economic and social cooperation and common activity for which there is as yet only minimal, if any, legal protection or regulation. I am thinking here of what might be called rights to participatory self-management by workers with or without shared ownership; or again, rights of democratic participation in decision making in social or cultural institutions. But this could probably be the subject of another volume, perhaps on social cooperation, law, and the common interest.

Notes

1. Uma Narayan, " 'Standard Persons' and 'Nonstandard' Vulnerabilities: The Legal Protection of 'Nonstandard' Interests," in *Law, Justice, and the State,* Proceedings of the IVR 16th World Congress, ed. M. M. Karlsson et al. (Berlin: Duncker & Humblot, 1993), 377–86.

2. Ibid., 379–83.

3. Ibid., 385–86.

4. An extended discussion of this is in my *Rethinking Democracy: Freedom and Social Cooperation in Politics, Economy, and Society* (Cambridge: Cambridge University Press, 1988), esp. chaps. 1, 5.

5. Ibid., chap. 5.

6. Carol C. Gould, "The Women Question: Philosophy of Liberation and the Liberation of Philosophy," *Philosophical Forum* 5, nos. 1–2 (fall-winter 1973–1974): 5–44. Reprinted in *Women and Philosophy*, ed. C. Gould and M. Wartofsky (New York: G. P. Putnam's, 1976).

7. Gould, *Rethinking Democracy*, chap. 1.

8. Carol C. Gould, "Beyond Causality in the Social Sciences: Reciprocity as a Model of Non-Exploitative Social Relations," in *Epistemology, Methodology, and the Social Sciences*, Boston Studies in the Philosophy of Science, ed. R. S. Cohen and M. W. Wartofsky, vol. 71 (Boston: D. Reidel, 1983), 53–88.

Liberalism, Impartiality, and Difference: Commentary on Smith and Meyers

Bruce M. Landesman

Radical criticisms of the law often go like this: an idea or practice is criticized, often astutely. In the course of this, the idea or practice is labeled as liberal; or as involving rights analysis or equality; or as resting on impartiality or universality or reason; and so on. The critic then takes himself or herself to have criticized not only the view under consideration but also liberalism, or rights, or equality, or universality, or impartiality. I find this objectionable for at least two reasons. First, it is difficult to say how liberalism or rights or equality or impartiality should be understood. These are matters of continuing debate. The critics show insufficient respect for the complexity of these ideas and for the traditions that have developed them. Second, proponents of liberalism or rights or equality or universality often think that the criticism can be made from within their view, and not necessarily outside it. They do not recognize themselves in the limitations perceived as inherent in liberalism or rights or equality or impartiality.

Patricia Smith's chapter is this kind of critique. Smith argues that two different strategies have been used to promote the just treatment of women. The first is based on the principle that like cases should be treated alike and that unequal treatment is justifiable only when there are relevant differences. Women were held to be different from men in some fundamental way that justified a denial of rights possessed by men. The strategy is to challenge the claim of difference, a strategy that has been effective in countering both sexism and racism in recent decades. The differences cited are rationalizations created by prejudice.

There are, however, some real and important differences between women and men, for example, pregnancy and physical vulnerability. Here the notion of equality as treating similar cases similarly and different cases differently disadvantages women. Because women really are different from men, it is assumed that they are justly disadvantaged. The second strategy is to show that the role of these differences in justifying disadvantage presupposes an implicit, biased, and male norm of what is normal and abnormal. Not giving birth is normal, giving birth abnormal, so "abnormal" women are rightly disadvantaged with respect to career advancement. But this male norm is neither "necessary, neutral [nor] universal." On a different norm women's "differences" are normal and fail to justify unequal treatment. This is the strategy being pursued by feminists these days.

I basically agree with Smith's analysis. Notice, however, that I have formulated her views without any reference to liberal or radical ideas, universality or reason, or any strong notions about rights and equality. Further, I find nothing inconsistent between her ideas and my own basically liberal political outlook. But Smith is insistent that the first strategy is liberal, the second radical; the first involves equality analysis, the second presumably does not. I do not think that these claims add anything to the basic argument.

What for Smith is the difference between liberal argument and radical critique? Near the beginning of the chapter it appears to be a difference between mere reform and more fulsome, that is, "radical," change. But surely the liberal idea that there are no important differences between men and women, or whites and blacks, that can justify unequal rights has led to fundamental change in this society since the 1960s. Of course the change is not all that is needed; poverty, racism and sexism, explicit and implicit, still exist. But surely something quite important, quite radical, has happened.

At another point Smith, commenting that the inclusion of women until recently was based "on a liberal rather than a radical view," asserts that "the liberal view is that all human beings are presumptively entitled to equal treatment, or equality before the law." Does she mean to hold that the radical view rejects this? If so, such radicalism has no appeal. In fact, when Smith wants to appropriate this idea for her own "radical" purposes, it becomes "humanist ideology" or "humanist ideals" rather than liberal. She says further that most feminists, even the most radical (such as Catherine MacKinnon), adhere to this ideal, whatever else they may hold. Even the radicals, then, are also liberal. So what is the difference?

There is a third possibility Smith mentions, that radicals engage in a critique of the status quo and its fundamental norms, and that liberals assume that such norms are neutral and just, and the status quo legitimate.

Do liberals fail to question norms? This is hardly plausible. There is no bar in liberal discourse to questioning any social norm in pursuit of liberal ends, and the history of liberal theory and practice amply illustrates this. (What, after all did John Stuart Mill do, if he did not question all kinds of norms?) Even if liberals think that government must be neutral (a contentious claim about the nature of liberalism), they certainly are not committed to holding that *existing norms* are neutral. If, according to liberals, norms *should* be neutral, then norms should be scrutinized and nonneutral norms replaced.

I therefore find little of substance in the appeal to liberal versus radical feminism, at least as Smith presents it. In fact, her substantive claims can be put straightforwardly if we make explicit the following formal principle of equality underlying them:

> People should be treated equally when there are no relevant differences between them, and treated unequally when there is a relevant difference between them that justifies unequal treatment.

This is an uncontroversial (perhaps tautologous) principle often cited in discussion of equality. The so-called liberal critique focuses on the first part. It holds that on certain fundamental matters there are no relevant differences between men and women that justify unequal treatment. The so-called radical critique focuses on the second part. It is the claim that certain differences, though real, do not justify unequal treatment. The two critiques are different sides of the same idea. One emphasizes the similarities that require equal treatment; the other focuses on differences that fail to justify unequal treatment. The critique of norms inherent in "radical" practice is merely a critique of certain claims of relevance used for justifying inequality. But there is nothing particularly radical, as opposed to liberal, in this. (Perhaps in practice and in law, only the first side has up to now been emphasized. This may be so, but in principle there is not much difference, certainly not enough to warrant one as liberal, the other as radical.)

The second or "radical" critique also makes use of another fairly obvious idea, that similar treatment is not always equal treatment, and different treatment is not always unequal treatment. People whose needs, wants, abilities, and circumstances differ can be treated unequally if treated the same, and equally if treated differently. For example, similar medical treatment is unequal treatment for the healthy and the sick, and different education can be equal education for the able and disabled. Thus treating women and men equally can mean treating them differently when there is a real difference between them. This point is inherent in the "radical" critique. There is a real difference between women and men in that women get pregnant and men do not. This difference, however, does not justify disadvantaging women with regard to the opportunity to advance their careers. But there is a question of just what *constitutes* equal treatment in the face of this difference. Some hold that it should be different treatment, that women should get time off for pregnancy, which men do not. Others hold that it makes more sense to consider women and men alike in having various kinds of family responsibilities. Thus both should receive family leave and be treated in this regard similarly, although women will use this leave differently from men when they use it to give birth. Once again there is nothing particularly radical or liberal in these points. There is nothing here a liberal need reject.

I now turn to an analogous duality in Diana Meyers's discussion, between "rights analysis" and "social relations analysis." Meyers is critiquing Martha Minow's important book *Making All the Difference*. With respect to the book, I find Meyers's remarks shrewd and sensible. Both her sympathy with Minow and the correction of Minow's exaggerations seem to me astute. But I take issue with the difference between "impartial reason," which presumably underlies rights analysis, and "empathic thought," which is Meyers's notion of what is most helpful in Minow's social relations approach.

Impartial reason is apparently Meyers's term for that important idea about morality that Kant tried to capture with the notion of the universalizability of valid moral maxims, and that others (e.g., Baier, Hare) have tried to capture in other ways. Meyers says that "the guiding questions" of impartial reason are What if everyone did that? Would you want to live in a society in which everyone had [did not have] that freedom or in which everyone could [could not] claim that benefit? And these are connected to What do we all have in common? What conduct befits our common humanity? These questions, however, are neither well formed nor open to clear answers:

1. To "What if everyone did that?" we must first ask, Did what? because actions are describable in many ways.
2. To "Would you want to live in a society . . . ?" people with different wants and values will give different answers.

3. To "What conduct befits our common humanity?" we have to decide whether to interpret "befits" in utilitarian/Hobbesean terms, or in Aristotelian/Kantian terms that make reason our essential characteristic, or use natural law ideas of what is most fitting for humans.

But I would rather leave this, since I think that what Meyers is getting at is the notion that there are characteristics that people have in common, have equally, and those characteristics require not only equal but similar treatment. I suggest this for two reasons. The first is a number of things she says about impartial reason: that impartial reason is "homogenizing," its focus is on "what people have in common"; it accommodates difference by making it "vanish morally"; and it presumes that "for moral purposes, people are alike and ought to be treated *the same way*" (emphasis added). The second reason is that her foil to impartial reason, "empathic thought," focuses on what is different and requires people "to attend to others in order to see the world from their point of view" and "to devise action that is gauged to particular persons."

Interpreted this way—impartial reason attends to what is common, empathic thought to what is different—these two certainly contrast. But Meyers also admits that impartial reason "can countenance departures from the moral norm of uniform treatment," and that the converse of " 'treat like cases alike' is 'treat different cases differently.' " So to "protect universal human capacities and basic interests," impartial reason can respond to differences. However, says Meyers, "Such departures [from uniform treatment] are usually conceived as addressing exceptional predicaments or temporary conditions. . . . Impartial reason is not well adapted to envisaging moral responses to irremediable or cherished differences." This is certainly true of impartial reason if one defines it as having a presumption in favor of uniform treatment. But why should impartiality be defined this way? Impartiality is at root a concern for everyone and that concern certainly must be cashed in as the concern that, other things being equal, everyone do equally well, lead equally good lives. When people have different needs, desires, and abilities, impartiality will then call for different treatment so as to promote a deeper equality. Surely, to understand what impartiality requires when there are such differences, empathic thought is essential. Not only is there is no conflict between impartiality and empathy, impartiality requires empathy.

Perhaps Meyers confuses impartial reason with the bureaucratic reason used by state authorities, which treats people uniformly out of concern for simplicity, efficiency, and perhaps some notion of fairness. Bureaucratic reason may well be inattentive to difference and biased in favor of uniformity, and insofar as Meyers and Minow critique it and its practice in modern liberal societies, they are on target. Bureaucratic impartiality may well overlook difference or construe it as abnormal and so turn difference into tendentious "difference." There needs to be careful thought about such "reason," its merits as well as its faults, and Minow has done a great service by raising the issue. But I see no reason to identify bureaucratic impartiality with moral impartiality itself, and many reasons to keep them separate. Nor—to extend these remarks to rights, which are supposed to underlie impartiality but not empathy—must rights inevitably entail uniformity. If there is a fundamental right to an equal opportunity for leading a good life, and people are different in essential ways, then what particular acts or means people have a right to in order to have this opportunity equally will be different. There is nothing in rights that prevents this, although this might be a difficulty with bureaucratic and legal instantiations of rights at a particular historical moment. These are criticizable from the point of view of a deeper understanding of rights themselves.

In sum, I have little objection to Smith's and Meyers's (and Minow's) substantive views about the importance of attending to and normalizing difference in order to treat people justly. I wish only to defend liberalism, impartiality, and rights of the charge of such neglect. It may serve an ideological purpose, but I do not think people need to criticize these things to be on the side of the angels. Liberalism, impartiality, and rights can be allies, not opponents, in the cause.

Part III

Liberal Responses to
Feminist and Critical Theory

Chapter 8

Are Feminist and Critical Legal Theory Radical?

Richard T. De George

Critical and some feminist legal theorists claim to be radical. Are they? The question may appear trivial or beside the point or simply a matter of semantics. Yet getting clear about the answer to this question is necessary if one is both to understand and evaluate their projects.

The term "radical" may be used in many ways. In any of its senses it implies fundamental change. How fundamental is a question we shall pursue. Part of the claim of both the legal and radical feminist legal critics is that they are radical because they wish to overthrow and replace liberalism and the liberal theory of law. Whether they wish to overthrow liberal society as such and the system of liberal free enterprise with which the liberal society is intertwined is problematic. To get some grasp on what it means for a theory to be radical, and how we can approach radical theory, it is useful to turn to what I shall consider the historically appropriate paradigm of radical theory, the writings of Karl Marx.

Marx's radical critique had three component parts. The first consisted in identifying economic, political, religious, or other social problems and analyzing them in such a way as to show that their solutions did not and could not lie on the surface level at which the problem appeared. Religious problems could not be solved at the level of religion, nor even at the level of politics; political questions masked vested interests that led to the economic level; and basic to all of them was the human level. A radical critique for Marx meant going to the roots, and for him the root was humankind itself.[1] Central to the critical process is rooting out the cause of the problem at hand at its deepest level.

Once the cause of the problem is correctly identified, the next step in a radical critique involves devising an alternative to the problem that not only solves it but presents the positive condition that results from solving it. Thus if the cause of exploitation is private property, then the solution to exploitation is to get rid of private property, and the resulting kind of society is one of common property, which brings with it a host of other changes. To the kind of society in which there would be no exploitation Marx gives the name communism. That is an alternative to the existing capitalist structure.

The third step is to outline the means of solving the problem by getting from where we are to the proposed new and desirable state of affairs. To stop at stage two is to follow the route of the utopian socialists. A necessary component is a theory of revolution that informs actual social practice. For a revolution to succeed, it must appeal to those who suffer the ills described, and who are willing to do what is necessary to achieve the better alternative. For Marx, this meant creating a class that suffered the ills of humankind and that in freeing itself would free humankind.[2] He identified that class as the proletariat, which had nothing to lose but its chains and which had a world to win.[3] Marx did not complain that the bourgeoisie did not pay attention to him. He did not care about the bourgeoisie. He did not address his critique to the rich and powerful, to the establishment, but to those who had nothing, to the proletariat. He did not complain that the professors at the University of Berlin or Oxford did not hire proletarians or did not incorporate his critique into mainstream philosophy or law. His aim was not to be accepted by those in power but to change the whole system and replace those in power. He did not seek piecemeal change but radical change, which he saw as incompatible with piecemeal change.

Once the new society was formed, the theory informing it would of course no longer be radical. A theory is radical only when it is deeply opposed to the existing theory and reality. Once it becomes the dominant position, it can no longer be radical, even if its content does not change at all from what it was when considered radical. Hence a theory is radical not by virtue of its content but only insofar as that content is considered in relation to the dominant theory or practice.

If we take Marx as the paradigm of radical critique, are present-day radical feminist and critical legal theory radical? From the chapters in this volume, as well as from the broader literature, it hardly appears so. The fact that both of these types of critique appear in scholarly journals and books makes them suspect from the start. How radical can a theory be if its intent is primarily to change the minds of professors, politicians, lawyers, judges, legislators, or others in power? Feminist and critical legal theorists have for the most part taken upon themselves the first of Marx's three tasks. Some feel they are radical because their critiques, if taken to their logical conclusion, would call for so great a change in the system that it would no longer be the same system. Those radical feminists who see the problems they analyze rooted in patriarchy should, if they are to be consistent, call for the replacement of patriarchy. Those who see the problems as rooted in the tax system, should call for the end of that system. Those who see the problem rooted in racism, should call for the end of racism. And a good number of the radical critics are willing to go this far.

However, going this far falls short of what Marx envisaged as the goal of critique and of radical theory. Raising consciousness was admittedly part of Marx's project, and the aim of feminist and critical legal theory is at least in part to raise the consciousness not only of legal theorists, judges, and lawyers but also of the ordinary citizen. Yet Marx, as I described his project, did not simply attack legal theory on the level of theory. He did not simply attempt to replace bourgeois legal theory with proletarian legal theory. His view was that simply changing legal theory did not cut deep enough. After all, legal theory and law itself are all reflective of the power relations and especially the economic relations present in society. Those with economic power control the legal system and use it to their benefit. Simply pointing this out will not produce any significant change. Even if the ordinary citizen becomes conscious of this, what can that citizen do? Politics and the legislature are filled with those who represent the vested interests of the economically dominant class. Even if conscious of this fact and fully aware of it, the ordinary citizen is not motivated to do anything about it because the ordinary citizen at the level of legislation can in fact do little if anything.

What is the hope of the feminist and critical legal theorists? Is it that if enough women become conscious of the inequalities built into the law, they will protest and demand changes in the law? Is it that if judges are made aware of the biases built into the law, they will change their decisions or their decision procedures? Is it that if members of the legislature come to see the inequalities or injustices in the law, they will, out of goodwill or out of fear of not being reelected, ignore the vested interests of lobbying groups and do what they have come to see as right? For Marx, any of these changes were both unlikely and insufficient. According to his view, law reflects the social realities of a society. Hence, attacking law and attempting to change law or legal theory is treating the evil at the level at which it is superficially found. But can one really change legal theory or the law without changing the reality that they reflect? Of course, if one thinks that ideas change reality, rather than vice versa, one may operate at the level of theory or law. But for Marx, this is an idealistic approach and will produce no significant effects.

Even if we accept the position that a view or theory can be radical if it attacks the dominant theory or law at the level of theory of law, how deep do the feminist or critical legal theorists go? The answer is difficult to generalize. Few, if any, in the United States seem to call for the overthrow of the U. S. Constitution and for its replacement by another one or by some other legal and political system. If they do not wish to do away with the Constitution, do they wish to amend it or change it? The answer is often yes. But does amending the Constitution or changing the way it is interpreted constitute radical change? Such changes may be deep and important, but why call them radical? And why claim that the changes are incompatible with liberal theory? I shall return to these questions.

The second of Marx's steps is a more difficult one, and one that some, but fewer, feminist or critical legal theorists have been willing to take. What exactly is to replace the patriarchy, the tax system, the racism, the universalism present in the existing system? Simply saying that the changed legal theory or the changed law or even that the changed society will no longer contain these is not enough. What is necessary is serious thought about all the changes that result and the kind of new and different system of law or kind of society that emerges. If the change is truly radical in Marx's sense, the new society will be significantly different from the old. The details of what one hopes to achieve are necessary. What will a society that is no longer based on patriarchy be like? Will it be based on matriarchy? If so, why is that preferable? Will it be based on neither? If so, has there ever been such a society? What will it look like? How will it be different in specific detail from our present society? What are the dangers it brings with it? If it is profoundly different from our present society, is it so much more preferable that it is worth risking what we have achieved in a great many areas in order to achieve it?

Becoming conscious of what is profoundly wrong with our society leads naturally to asking what the alternatives are. But both feminist and critical legal theory have failed thus far to present a very full or attractive picture of the society that is supposed to result from the deep changes they propose. Marx presented us with a view of what society without private property and hence without classes, without exploitation, without alienation, and with democratic control and the possibility of the all-around development of the individual might look like. He did not attempt to paint the picture of future society in great detail, but at least there was enough detail to let the workers know what they were being asked to suffer and fight for. The future that feminist and critical legal theorists have in mind is not as clear, in part because the proposals are more piecemeal and lack an overarching theory that enables the theorists to paint the alternative in positive and the present system in negative terms.

It is the third component of Marx's radical theory on which most critical and radical feminist theorists falter. Having described the ideal, how does society get from where it is to where the theorists want it to be? Who is to be the engine of change? What will motivate them? Do they have so much more to gain than to lose that it is worth the struggle for them? This third component is the acid test of a radical theory. To think that one can make radical change without overthrowing those in power and to think that those in power will give up their power without a struggle is to dream utopian dreams.

Seizing control of the Harvard Law School may be a dream of the critical legal theorists. But what will such control actually gain them? They may produce some students who think as they do, and who eventually become legislators or judges. Is this the route of radical change? The aims of the feminist critics are even harder to determine in this regard. Is their aim to break the glass ceilings that prevent women from rising to positions of power and to replace men in those positions, or is it somehow to restructure the social order so as to eliminate positions of power? How can they do the latter? Is it by violent or by nonviolent means? Who is to do this? All women? Women and men who come to share the consciousness they are promoting? That these questions remain unanswered is an indication of the partial development of these theories.

But perhaps the stated aims of many of the radical feminists and critical legal theorists are not really radical. And, if not, perhaps they can be accommodated by a liberal society, and calling themselves radical confuses rather than clarifies the issues and the solutions.

If women and minority members want not a new system, which they have yet to describe, but an economic, political, and social system similar to the one we have in the United States but without discrimination and racism, that is a goal that can be articulated, defended, and aimed at within our present structures. In fact, that is what the critical theorists are doing. They are not in jails for their writings, they are not leading rebellions. Achieving even the amount of racial equality we have today took protest, some violence, and a good deal of suffering. But the movement for greater

racial equality in the 1960s took place within the system. It was a movement for equal rights within the system, not for a different system.

Many feminist critical theorists seem to want their voices heard within
the academy, they want women to hold high offices in universities, corporations, and government, and they want women to have the same chance as
men to achieve such positions. That also is a goal to be achieved within
"the system," not by the overthrow of the system. If patriarchy is truly at
the heart of the evil that feminists attack, the question of how central that
is to the economic, political, legal, and other systems of our country is the
question. To claim that these systems would not be the same if they were
not built on patriarchy requires a detailed account of what the differences
would be without patriarchy, how the *system* would be changed, and what
the new system should look like. Capitalism, for instance, can be defined
in terms of an accumulation of industrial capital, a free market, and private
property.[4] That patriarchy necessarily is part of that model is certainly not
obvious. If it is, and if capitalism must be replaced, then the question is by
what? Similarly with the Constitution of the United States. Must that be
replaced because it is inherently patriarchal? If so, what kind of a constitution or what kind of nonconstitutional system is being proposed?

If on the other hand the feminist critique does not call for replacing
capitalism or for replacing the Constitution, then although it undoubtedly
involves serious and important changes, that they cannot be accommodated by liberal theory and practice is not at all clear, and the opposite
seems to be the case.

Hence, the question arises as to why both feminist and critical legal theorists attack liberalism, as if liberalism is a definite, clearly stated theory
that political or other groups have explicitly adopted as a platform. The
German Social Democratic Party and the Russian Social Democratic Party
adopted Marxism as their official ideologies. Neither the Republican nor
the Democratic parties in the United States have adopted any specific philosophy or ideology as their platform. They can both be described in some
ways as liberal, as can the American legal system and the economic system.
But that liberalism necessarily involves some version of universalism that
is incompatible with concern for particular differences is a characterization
of liberalism that seems to have been constructed by some feminist critiques
only to be attacked.

Some may object that my rejection of the claims of feminist and critical
theory to be radical is simply an attempt to put them down or to divert atten-

tion from them. Is it a way to defuse their claims or trivialize them? I claim not. But raising that question raises in turn the question of why they call themselves radical. Is it to call attention to themselves rather than to their specific claims? Is it to defuse criticism that may be launched against them?

I suggest that whether they are called radical or not is not an important point either way. But contrasting their claims with Marx's helps us explicitly raise the questions of exactly how deep they wish to go and of how to evaluate their theoretical and practical goals.

Both feminist and critical legal theory have a good deal to teach us. If one separates their specific attacks and the changes they propose from their rhetoric and claims to be radical, many of the former can be evaluated and acted on. A great many of the changes are changes that many of those who think of themselves as liberals can accept and to which they can devote their energies. Why either the feminist or critical legal theorists seek to distance themselves from the large support they can garner from self-styled liberals who support many of their specific proposals is at best puzzling.

The chapter by Patricia Smith in this volume is a case in point. Smith calls the feminist legal critics "reluctant radicals," yet it is difficult to see in what way the views she describes are not liberal, unless "liberal" is taken narrowly to mean whatever has resulted thus far in law in the United States, and hence that any further change is by definition radical. Surely, that would be an almost arbitrary sense of "radical." Nor is it clear what alternative to the liberal system of law she or they envisage, how it would be achieved, and who would do the achieving. If there is an action program of social revolution, are women as a whole to rise up and change the system? And if so, which system or systems and how? To portray these writers as radical implies some deep change. But what is to replace the patriarchal society, and exactly what that involves remain mysteries.

If we look at the changes that can be considered paradigms of feminist criticism, most of them make perfectly good sense and are changes that can be embraced by liberals, male or female. In fact, most them are embraced by most liberals. Smith's formulation of the radical critique centers on "why as a matter of justice, those in power are entitled to formulate standards that favor themselves by which to measure all others." This is certainly a valid question to raise. But what is missing is any demonstration that such an entitlement is a necessary constituent of liberalism or of liberal theory. Showing how the norms are biased seems perfectly consistent with liberal theory. Littleton and others argue that equality analysis is biased against women. It may well be; and if the argument is made out, it is not clear why the law cannot be changed to make it unbiased. If the argument is truly radical in the sense that the present system of law is incapable of being made unbiased, then the second step is to describe the system—it would seem not only of law but necessarily of politics, economics, and so on—that is capable of being unbiased and that continues to provide all the benefits and protections that liberalism has achieved. What such systems would look like remains puzzling, as does the means for bringing about the required changes.

Similarly, the claim that in legal doctrine difference ought not be penalized is perfectly intelligible and makes a good deal of sense. Why is this incompatible with liberal theory? The answer seems to be that liberalism means inclusion under universal norms, not recognition of differences. But if this is correct, and if for some reason liberalism cannot recognize differences, what does a legal system look like that does not recognize universality? It would seem that liberalism's universality can be enlarged to recognize that all people are different in some important ways while being similar in other important ways. Minow, a radical representative, wants judges "to examine the foundations of their own perspectives."[5] Getting the justices to examine their own perspectives is important and represents an important change. But this seems to imply that the system of courts and law as established under the Constitution will remain under this supposedly radical reform.

All this is not radical in Marx's sense, and it is not clearly nonliberal or antiliberal. For one of the liberal tenets (if we take Mill's *On Liberty* as a classical text of liberalism) is the revisability of one's beliefs and perspectives when the evidence demands it. For feminists to write or act as if wife beating is justifiable in every male perspective and is somehow necessarily part of liberal legal theory is to do justice neither to males nor to liberal theory. That rape or sexual harassment are similarly acceptable to men and justified by liberal theory is surely bombast to make a point. That to be either pro or con on the abortion issue is either male or liberal is patently not accurate; many men and many liberals are pro-choice, and a considerable number of women are pro-life.

The conclusion to which I am drawn is that many of the substantive positions for which feminist legal theorists, as well as many critical legal theorists, argue are positions that are reasonable, liberal, and possible to achieve within the existing system. To that extent they are not radical, even though if the changes are adopted the system will be importantly different from what it is today.

On the other hand, if most laws are bad or if the existing system is inherently immoral and unjust, then it cannot be changed piecemeal. If this is so, unless we overthrow such tyranny we are cowards or slaves. Yet that claim has a false ring to it; especially in this postcommunist era. Perhaps Marx has not been shown to be wrong by the events of the Soviet Union and Eastern Europe because his views have not yet even been tried. Nonetheless, the events since 1917 should not be entirely discounted. Before we mount the barricades and sacrifice ourselves, our generation, and perhaps the generations that will come after us, we should have a clear idea of what we wish to accomplish and a reasonable expectation that what we shall achieve will be significantly better than what we have and are able to achieve by piecemeal, peaceful, or minimally violent change.

Many liberals, as well as many ordinary citizens, both male and female, who consider themselves neither liberal nor radical believe that they achieve more of what they want by living with the existing system and modifying it piece by piece than by any radical overthrow. They also believe that government is to some significant extent by the people, and that laws, even if they often favor the rich, also protect the interests of the poor, at least to some extent.

These considerations exemplify what seems to me to be the general case: that most of what goes under the name of radical critical legal theory is not very radical and that the varying aims that most of the so-called radicals espouse can be adequately handled under existing liberal legal theory and practice. The critical theorists have adopted some of the vocabulary of radicalism, but to change things at the roots means revolution, not piecemeal change. Arguing for radical change from the comfortable security of a university position, and arguing one's case to others holding similar positions, is hardly the stuff that radical theory in its historical sense requires. From that viewpoint, the various radical social theorists are presenting variants of the liberal ideology and the liberal system under which they flourish. To so designate them is not to show or even to claim they are mistaken in what they propose. But it is to keep their claims in proper perspective and to allow us to join with them in their real task of changing the system in ways that liberals can agree will make it better.

To a significant extent both feminist and critical legal theorists have helped raise the consciousness of many in the academy about realities in the existing laws and legal and social structures. They have pointed out needed reforms. Perhaps those insights could not and so would not have been achieved by those comfortably in the liberal tradition. To this extent the critics have served and continue to serve an important function. Perhaps unless they characterized their views as radical and unless they attacked liberalism they would have been ignored or would not have achieved the degree of consciousness-raising they have achieved. And surely my evaluation of the degree to which they are radical when compared to Marx will not move them to change their vocabulary or their claims. Nonetheless, such a comparison can help both them and others who agree with some of their specific proposals to clarify the depth of the changes they propose, the kind of society that will emerge if they are successful, the kinds of actions needed to achieve the changes, and the degree to which we are willing to sacrifice what we have for the promise they hold before us.

Social change importantly affects the lives of people. Dramatic change, such as to constitute revolution, should neither be proposed nor undertaken lightly. At least that much we should have learned from Marx and from those who claimed to have acted in his name.

Notes

1. Karl Marx, "Contribution to the Critique of Hegel's Philosophy of Right," *Early Writings*, ed. T. B. Bottomore (New York: McGraw-Hill, 1964), 52.

2. Ibid., 58.

3. Karl Marx, *"Manifesto of the Communist Party,"* in *The Marx-Engels Reader*, Robert C. Tucker, 2d ed. (New York: Norton, 1978), pt. 4.

4. For a fuller discussion of this, see my *Business Ethics*, 4th ed. (Englewood Cliffs, N.J.: Prentice-Hall, 1995), chap. 6.

5. Patricia Smith (in this volume) cites Marthow Minow, *Making All the Difference* (Ithaca: Cornell University Press, 1990).

Chapter 9

Liberalism and Radical Critiques of the Law

Wade L. Robison

Daniel Defoe's heroine in *Roxana, The Unfortunate Mistress*, gave up her children after her husband left her so they could survive. So she could survive, she became a prostitute and eventually the mistress of a prince of France. When he became king, she left and took up with a Dutch gentleman who, on the third night of their sleeping together, said, "Tho' I have push'd this Matter farther than ever I intended; or than, I believe, you expected from me, who never made any Pretences to you but what were very honest; yet to heal it all up, and let you see how sincerely I meant at first, and how honest I will ever be to you, I am ready to marry you still, and desire you to let it be done to-Morrow Morning; and I will give you the same fair Conditions of Marriage as I wou'd have done before."[1] Roxana had saved more than twenty thousand pounds in her dealings with her previous lover and she "believ'd, if it had not been for the Money, which he knew I had, he wou'd never have desir'd to marry me after he had lain with me: For, where is the Man that cares to marry a Whore, tho' of his own making?" (145). When she told him that marriage "was the *only thing* [she] cou'd not grant," he was "surpriz'd" and "confounded," not finding it believable that she should sleep with him and then not marry him. Guessing her reason for refusing, he offered "not to touch one Pistole of your Estate, more, than shall be with your own voluntary consent" (143, 146–47).

What follows in *Roxana* is an object lesson both in how far one can go to meet some current objections to the law without critiquing it radically and what is necessary to go that far. For Roxana says, in response to that offer,

> I told him, I had, perhaps, differing Notions of Matrimony, from what the receiv'd Custom had given us of it; that I thought a Woman was a free Agent, as well as a Man, and was born free, and cou'd she manage herself suitably, might enjoy that Liberty to as much Purpose as Men do; that the Laws of Matrimony were indeed, otherwise, and Mankind at this time, acted quite upon other Principles; and those

205

such, that a Woman gave herself entirely away from herself, in marriage, and capit-
ulated only to be, at best, but *an Upper-Servant*. . . .

That the very Nature of the Marriage-Contract was, in short, nothing but giving up Liberty, Estate, Authority, and every-thing, to the Man, and the Woman was
indeed, a meer Woman ever after, that is to say, a Slave. (147–48)

Her lover, misunderstanding her theoretical point and so surprised that she
apparently thinks so ill of him, explains that he will let her be the pilot of
their ship. Roxana replies, "It is not you, *says I*, that I suspect, but the Laws
of Matrimony puts the Power into your Hands, bids you do it; commands
you to command; and binds me, forsooth, to obey; . . . all the rest, all that
you call Oneness of Interest, Mutual Affection, *and the like*, is Curtesie and
Kindness then, and a Woman is indeed, infinitely oblig'd where she meets
with it; but can't help herself where it fails (151).

If you hear John Locke here, it is no surprise. *Roxana* was published in
1724, and in the passage quoted, Roxana is arguing that the marriage contract ought to be like the contract from the state of nature. No rational persons in a state of nature would agree to live under an absolute monarch
since they would then "put themselves into a worse condition than the
state of Nature, wherein they had a Liberty to defend their Right against
the Injuries of others. . . . Whereas by supposing they have given up themselves to the *absolute Arbitrary Power* and will of a Legislator, they have dis-
armed themselves, and armed him, to make a prey of them when he
pleases."[2] Similarly any woman who marries, under the law of matrimony
then current, gives up her liberty to enforce her natural rights and is wholly
dependent upon the will, and thus upon the goodwill, of her husband, "but
can't help herself where it fails." Everything good that comes to her comes
as a matter of "Curtesie and Kindness" alone.

What is required, Roxana implies, is a change in the "Laws of Matrimony" that reflects the truth that "a Woman [is] as fit to govern and enjoy
her own Estate, without a Man, as a Man [is], without a Woman."[3]

We have here, in this exchange between Roxana and her Dutch friend,
Defoe's recognition that (a) conceptual space exists within the theoretical
framework of the law for compelling arguments that the law give equal status to women as well as to men. The substance of many critiques of the law
that call themselves radical can be mounted by liberal critics. Defoe was one.

But Roxana is able to mount such an attack on the laws of matrimony
only because she has real independence, created by her wealth, accumulated
through past real dependence. Defoe thus also implies that (b) appeal to the

theoretical basis of contract law is of little use to effectuate real change without real power within the existing social order. Were Roxana intent on effecting real change in the law, she would need more than the force of right on her side and need more than the capacity to marshall it eloquently for an attack on existing law. She would need real existing power.

Each of these truths deserves further comment.

Bias and Universalizability

Many laws are no doubt biased, some against women, some against other identifiable groups, and some of the forms of bias are so deeply entrenched in our common ways of thought and patterns of behavior that they seem natural. Neither of these truths should surprise us. People are often biased and biased in ways that, once noted, may surprise them, and us. We cannot reasonably expect laws to be made by anyone who does not share the socialized prejudices of the age. It should thus cause no wonder that law often reflects such prejudices and invites such criticisms as Defoe's.[4]

Roxana's arguments were as out of keeping for the early 1700s as they may be for too many today because, among other things, her position implies, as she puts it, that a woman, "if she had a-mind to gratifie herself as to Sexes, she might entertain a Man, as Man does a Mistress."[5] Locke's arguments in Book 1 of *The Treatise on Government* were equally out of keeping with the prejudices of the late 1600s, for, in attacking the position of Sir Robert Filmer, he argues for the following principle: "No natural difference ought to be the basis for any difference in 'politick capacity.' "[6] It is this principle, I suggest, that animates Defoe's arguments and this principle, and principles such as this, that can be used to sustain attacks on a variety of biases built into the law at various levels, from particular pieces of legislation to such general norms as equal protection. It is a principle of liberalism, and it allows for such attacks because of two features of it and one of liberalism:

(i) Such a principle can be variously interpreted.

The point is Rawls's about the distinction between the concept and various conceptions of justice.[7] Some think that equal protection requires in educational matters equal funding for all students, and others think that it requires only a certain minimum. These are competing conceptions of the concept of equal protection. Similarly, Locke's principle can be interpreted in a variety of ways depending upon what one takes to be natural differences, for instance, or upon what one takes to be a "politick capacity."

Lighting upon a conception that is not biased in some way is complicated not only because those in power share the prejudices of the day but because of another feature of such principles:

(ii) Their essential concepts are essentially contestable.

For many interpretations, we have no decision procedure to decide which is the correct one, morally or otherwise, and so even the most principled arguments for change can be met by other principled arguments. The effect on present arrangements of appeal to principle is thus diminished, and in any event, those present arrangements, whatever they are, have a dead weight difficult to move and a momentum difficult to alter. Defoe might well be astonished to know how long it has taken Roxana's arguments to begin to penetrate the body politic.

But liberalism allows for such change. It is one of its strengths that it accommodates change when powered by reason and principle. The *scope* of this claim needs to be made clear. One can provide substantive constitutional arguments at three different levels—about legislative acts, executive decisions, judicial opinions, and so on within the framework of an existing constitution not put into question by these arguments; about the provisions and implications of a constitution itself; or about the very conditions of having a constitution (about, e.g., the constitutive conditions of having a constitution, the equality of the contracting parties, for instance, a matter of concern in, e.g., *Dred Scott*).[8] That is, everything within a legal system is open to question on liberal principles, though it can matter to the success of the question at which level it is raised.

That equal protection takes the male status to be the norm, as it is claimed occurs regarding laws that discount pregnancy, is one conception that can be replaced by another. That we can attack norms that are deeply embedded in the system—like that of equal protection—does not make our critique a radical one *if* the machinery for that attack exists within the system itself. And it does, I argue, for a great deal of the current criticism directed against it.

For instance, Patricia Smith's arguments in her chapter are, I suggest, right on the mark *except* for the claim that the criticisms are somehow radical. If "norms traditionally considered neutral are actually biased," nothing about the liberal tradition prevents that point from being made. Quite the contrary. It is part of the liberal tradition that such concepts as equal protection can be realized in competing conceptions, with different groups arguing for different conceptions of what it is to have equal protection and letting the process sort itself through to determine which conception ought to be realized. Liberalism means to *encourage* such criticism and change. Even if the process itself is biased, as it is, that does not change the theoretical point that the liberal tradition allows for and encourages just such criticisms—even of the process itself.

Consider objections to the rape law. Some of these may come as a surprise to someone trained in the law. For instance, Susan Estrich enlightens when she points out that the traditional American "doctrines of consent, defined as nonresistance, and force, measured by resistance . . . [mean] that the trial focuses almost entirely on the woman, not the man. Her intent, not his, is disputed. And since her state of mind is key, her sexual history may be considered relevant, even though utterly unknown to him."[9] Such an effect ought to disconcert those trained in law who had not seen such implications, but crafting a different way of looking at rape law does not require a radical shift in any legal concepts. Estrich considers negligent liability for rape, transporting a concept used elsewhere in the law to rape law.

There are no doubt problems here. We need to concern ourselves that in changing rape laws so that they are not biased against women, we not bias them in yet another way. One cannot legally rape a man in Great Britain; such offenses must be treated as buggery or indecent assault. They are on the rise, with more than four thousand reported cases there in 1989 and with underreporting probably more likely in regard to it than in regard to rape of women.[10] And in many states in the United States rape is defined in a way that makes penetration of the vagina a necessary condition. But men can be raped, and clearly any rape law ought to include men, whatever the incidence of rape against men. It may be difficult to craft a law that accommodates such a feature of some humans as the incapacity for pregnancy, but that should cause no more difficulty than the problem of accommodating such a feature of some humans as the capacity for pregnancy—or of crafting a law that accommodates both contingencies. But to change our laws to accommodate pregnancy or to craft a rape law that is neutral regarding the sex of who is being raped, we need not alter the conceptual landscape of the law. We may need to change legislators in various states to make the needed changes, but that is a different matter and hardly requires a radical change in the law. Just as Locke's principle has conceptual space for the sort of change Defoe has Roxana argue for, so conceptual space exists for change in such principles as equal protection that some may think impede change.

Critiquing the Existing Legal System

Defoe saw what Locke does not mention, namely, that one can make use of the conceptual space he created for change only if one is empowered. Roxana was empowered by her money. She could refuse the offer of her lover and survive. But changing the system is harder.

It is not contract theory or "sexual difference [that] determines that women are not parties to the social contract but instead are the subjects of it."[11] The problem is that real change is effectuated in the law by real people with particular ends and whatever prejudices they may have, whether shallow or deep. It is this that causes the appeal to theory to fail even when it falls upon receptive ears, for those hearing it will reflect the deep prejudices common to the social system, and, even if they do not, they will be unable to move the system effectively beyond those prejudices in any but small increments because others, including those who must administer the law, will share deep prejudices. Even what some might consider major legal earthquakes are likely to move the system only glacially.

I was in Berkeley when the Rodney King decision came down, and I heard the riots and saw the destruction. I did not see, as Bill Martin says, "that at least a little piece of liberated territory was opening before our very eyes."[12] I found it depressing that unmarked black cars with four policemen apiece were stalking the streets to stop, question, and sometimes frisk young black males—leaving us white folks alone. I found it even more depressing to think that those without power were so constrained by the system, and perhaps so socialized by it, that they could have thought that they were liberating anything at all. The riots, however a seismic event they may have seemed, have not fundamentally altered the social positions of those who rioted. They are as powerless as they were before. They are only worse off economically and socially, living in neighborhoods more blighted and with relations between them and the authorities more contentious and fragile.

Emily Gill quotes Minow as saying, "Rights analysis offers release from hierarchy and subordination to those who can match the picture of the abstract, autonomous individual presupposed by the theory of rights." Yet it was not Roxana's appeal to Lockean contract theory to critique existing "Notions of Matrimony" that gave her the liberty to refuse her suitor and not give "herself entirely away from herself, in Marriage."[13] It was her independent wealth. Appealing to contract theory and to the rights essential to it will not alter that structure or any of the legal relations within it if the appeal is only to individuals abstracted from their real existence in a particular social structure—especially given the essentially contestable nature of the principles upon which claims to rights are founded. An abstract appeal to rights can have rhetorical power, but what is required for real change in a democracy in which rights compete as well as interests is that those who want their rights realized have political power. The appeal must be to the rights of real people with real power in an existing social structure.

Roxana's critique of the existing form of marriage contract in England in the 1720s is a metaphor for what is essential for any critique of any political structure to be successful. At a minimum, one must be so positioned, by wealth or power, as not to be significantly harmed if one's critique fails.

Contract Theory

All this fits nicely within the framework of contract theory—Locke's principle and Roxana's critique. Defoe is taking Locke's contract theory and simply applying its principles to the legislation that governs marriage law. We may imagine him asking, with Roxana, "Would I agree to such laws were I in a state of nature?"

The question is almost rhetorical, given the similarity of the relationship between an absolute monarch and his or her subjects and a husband and his wife. And so Roxana's argument, however puzzling to her Dutch lover, ought to strike us as powerful. But nothing about what I have to say about principles and their use in altering our laws without radical changes depends upon contract theory. Contract theory is a way of justifying certain principles, and the point I am making turns on the principles, not the mode of justification. Indeed, I think we will be misled if we concentrate upon contract theory.

David Hume was correct in attacking contract theory both because it fails to provide any moral leverage on the problem of justifying political authority and because it fails, empirically, to account for how individuals come to have political obligations and, I would add, any other political relations, including those marked by the concept of political rights. It also fails in other ways.

For one thing, contract theory fails to provide those within an existing legal framework with the means to use the principles upon which it is founded unless those are embodied in the existing legal framework *or* courts have the power to appeal beyond the existing constitution to the original position, or state of nature, from which the constitution was, it must be argued, supposed to have been chosen. The decision in *Dred Scott* that blacks could not be citizens was founded on a not implausible reading of the contractual basis of the United States. Either the states contracted into a United States, or individuals did, and in either case, neither gave up the preexisting right of individuals to own slaves. Because the Supreme Court in *Dred Scott* was constrained by an appeal to existing positive law, and could not appeal beyond the confines of the legal system to natural law, it could not properly subject the Missouri Compromise, which was at issue in *Dred Scott*, to criticism not founded on the Constitution.

It could not *properly* do so for two reasons. First, the Court's job is to interpret the law, not make it—where that means, or came to mean in American constitutional theory, constraining its decisions by preexisting and publicly known law. Second, if the Court were to appeal beyond the contractual conditions that are constitutive of the political system, it would not be abiding by a fundamental principle of constitutionally founded systems, namely, that the principles that govern the relations of citizens be chosen by the citizens. It is, in short, not just contract theory that is at issue here but principled concerns about the appropriate role of a supreme court in adjudicating questions of high moment in a democratic state. Given those principled concerns, contract theory forces us to take seriously the real contracts people do agree to and gives them a normative force that must be overcome even if they embody immoral principles. A court is not in a position to appeal to any principles outside the constitutional framework to provide a counterweight to any immoral principles a constitution may embody—especially when the constitution is founded upon a contract and the political ideology gives moral weight to the state's being founded on contract.[14]

The appeal to contract theory also fails to account for how change in political relations can be effectuated because the appeal to rights is ineffectual, no matter how principled, when unaccompanied by the practical conditions essential to creating change. To quote Emily Gill, liberals *can* "admit the role of particularity in the constitution of the self" if an appeal to rights is to have a real effect on changing an existing system. Doing that does not require any radical critique of legal theory, or of liberalism, I suggest, only of its supposed contractual foundations.

Notes

1. Daniel Defoe, *Roxana, The Fortunate Mistress, or, a History of the Life and Vast Variety of Fortunes of Mademoiselle de Beleau, afterwards called the Countess de Wintselsheim in Germany Being the Person known by the Name of the Lady Roxana in the time of Charles II* (New York: Oxford University Press, 1988), 143.

2. John Locke, *Two Treatises of Government*, ed. Peter Laslett (Cambridge: Cambridge University Press, 1963), pt. 2, sec. 137, 377.

3. Defoe, *Roxana*, 149.

4. As Patricia Smith puts it in her chapter in this volume, "We can hardly be surprised if [the perspective from which law is formulated] turns out to be the perspective of those who formulated it, which is to say, the perspective of powerful men—the traditional patriarchs." It is perhaps no more surprising if a regulative ideal is construed in biased ways that prevent it from functioning as a regulative norm. Such ideals ought to function as heuristic devices to try to guarantee objectivity and impartiality, but our understanding of them may be faulty. For instance, some Southerners argued before the Civil War that maintaining slavery was the only way to achieve "the great democratic principle of equality among men" (William Lee Miller, *Arguing about Slavery* [New York: Knopf, 1966], 439). That such an ideal might be so perversely understood as to ensure that some must be slaves that others might have equality only means that the meaning of the ideal is contestable. That some understand the ideal one way, and some another, is no evidence that the ideal should not be maintained. It only means that besides being contestable, the ideal is contested.

5. Defoe, *Roxana*, 149.

6. The phrase is Defoe's, drawn from a passage where we should hope that Roxana, and Defoe, are speaking ironically rather than, as may appear, getting caught up in the patriarchal system, saying that "while a Woman was single, she was a Masculine in her politick Capacity" (*Roxana*, 148).

I realize that my committing Locke to this principle is itself contentious because, many have argued, Locke thinks that there are natural differences between the sexes. I will not here argue for my position, but its main claim is that even if Locke is committed to there being natural differences between the sexes, he is also committed to those natural differences making a political difference. For one thing, women are as much within the state of nature as men for Locke, and they have as much to preserve. For another, he was attacking Filmer's theory of patriarchy, and, I argue, one mode of attack was to insist that if anyone were naturally empowered over another, it would be mothers over their children. He no more draws from this claim the conclusion that matriarchy is the correct political theory than the conclusion that because women are naturally different from men, men are politically their superiors. But I leave the details of this argument for another day. It will suffice for my purposes if Locke *could* have held the principle I attribute to him.

7. John Rawls, *A Theory of Justice* (Cambridge: Harvard University Press, 1971), 5.

8. See my "Constitutional Argument and Contract Theory," in *Praktische Vernunft und Theorien der Gerechtigkeit*, vol. 2, special edition of the *Archives for Philosophy of Law and Social Philosophy* (Stuttgart: Franz Steiner Verlag, 1992), 185–94.

9. Susan Estrich, *Real Rape* (Cambridge: Harvard University Press, 1987), 95–96.

10. "Confronting Last Taboo of Male Rape," *Guardian*, August 24, 1992, 6. Dr. Gillian Mezey, identified as a psychiatrist at St. George's Hospital in south London, is quoted as saying that "the perception is that only gays bugger each other, so a heterosexual man will be frightened of being accused of being gay." And he may, Dr. Mezey adds, "be criminalized himself if he approached the police."

11. Gill in her chapter in this volume, laying out the position of Carole Pateman.

12. Bill Martin, "Some Things I Learned In Berkeley" (paper presented at the 1992 AMINTAPHIL Conference, Allentown, Penn.), 2.

13. Defoe, *Roxana*, 147–48.

14. I have in mind here the concerns that Robert M. Cover investigates in questioning why it was that even abolitionist judges prior to the Civil War did not take advantage of what may appear, in retrospect, to be openings for abolitionist rulings. The judges seem more constrained by the immoral principles of the system than one might abstractly think they ought to be. See Cover, *Justice Accused* (New Haven: Yale University Press, 1975), esp. 197ff. In this regard it is worth examining a similar thesis about German judges prior to World War II. See Ingo Müller, *Hitler's Justice: The Courts of the Third Reich* (Cambridge: Harvard University Press, 1991), esp. pt. 2.

Chapter 10

Liberalism, Radicalism, Muddlism: Comments on Some New Ways of Thinking About Legal Questions

Joseph Ellin

Many of the chapters in this volume distinguish between what they regard as old and new ways of thinking about legal questions. The "old" way is said to be discriminatory or unfair or exclusionary or male-biased, and the "new" way is advocated as the "old's" truly fair and equitable replacement. Sometimes the "old" way is identified with liberalism and the "new" with radicalism, multiculturalism, and perspectivism. The old way deludes itself into thinking that its norms are impartial, universal, fair, and objective; the new way knows that norms merely reflect power relations.[1] The old way favors established perspectives and standard interests; the new way favors the excluded. In general, the chapters advocate what the authors seems to regard as a significant change in thinking and social policy.

I think that there is more rhetoric than substance in most of these claims. Differences between old and new are not vast; where they are important, as in certain views of rape law, the old is preferable. The belief that two major patterns of thought are being contrasted is a muddle, supported by various lesser muddles. Hence, I call it all "muddlism."

Liberalism, Bias, and Perspectivism

Radical critics of the law tend to take liberalism as their target (no doubt thinking that conservatism and libertarianism are too benighted to merit attention). They claim that liberalism has serious limitations: The "[liberal] standard of evaluation . . . was based on the status quo and founded in the assumptions of those in power. . . . It was assumed [incorrectly] to be necessary, neutral, and universal. . . . [Liberal] norms traditionally considered neutral are actually biased." What is called for is "a shift from liberal claims for inclusion in traditional norms to a radical critique of those norms as fundamentally biased" (Smith, this volume). This radical critique is often allied with multiculturalism or "perspectivism," which holds that there are no universal and objective principles but that human reasoning always occurs in some situated perspective.

Perspectivism itself is a muddle, and its alliance with radicalism a double muddle. As just described, perspectivism is self-contradictory because it holds that the reasoning behind it is objectively true, and not merely from some situated perspective. This is indicative of a serious muddle. The alliance between radicalism and perspectivism must be a muddle because radicalism's claim is not that there are no neutral and objective principles but that liberal principles are not neutral and objective. If there were no neutral and objective principles—if all principles were biased in someone's favor—there would be no reason to adopt radical principles over liberal ones. And if, as radicals insist in their multiculturalist moods, "no cultural position should be penalized" (Smith, this volume), then the cultural position of dominant white males should not be penalized.

Perspectivism—as found for instance in much-discussed Martha Minow, who wants us to recognize that purportedly neutral principles actually reinforce the status quo and are only assumed to be universal—may be a strategy but is not a philosophy. As a strategy, it tries to get us to acknowledge biases where biases may have existed unrecognized. But as a philosophy, perspectivism is self-contradictory because the very idea of a bias implies the existence of some objective standard from which the bias deviates. Nothing would be a bias if there were nothing but biases.[2] If it were necessarily true, as Minow believes, that "all law is formulated from a perspective" (Smith, this volume), then there would be no way to determine from whose perspective law should be formulated.

Of course, standards can be biased while seeming neutral and often are. Buildings and public facilities lack handicapped access. Accessing buildings by stairs may seem neutral but really isn't. Making doorways six and a half feet high or putting rows of passenger seats three feet apart in airplanes may seem correct to most people, but it inconveniences very tall people. Airplane seats are just wide enough for most of us to squeeze into, but very fat people slop over uncomfortably into their neighbors' seats. No question that important differences like these between people are often not taken into account in formulating social policies. To what extent deviations from the norm should be taken into account in formulating policy is a question whose importance perhaps is not sufficiently recognized, for example, consider medications that produce a major allergic reaction, but only in a tiny fraction of the people who might take them. But it is unfair to accuse liberals of being insensitive to this problem, and it is not typically liberals who take a view favoring the dominant group.

Many nonstandard interests could be taken into account without excess expense: airlines could provide a few seats larger than the norm; motels could provide a few extralong beds. Unfortunately, not all problems can be so easily resolved because interests conflict. Suppose a feminist wants protection for the woman who is offended by girlie pinups in the workplace. Would she also protect her fundamentalist neighbor who is offended by the people next door who live in sin? It is not clear that "neutral" principles by which these conflicts could be resolved fairly will not at some point have to refer to "reasonable people" or "standard conventions" and so on. Certain teenagers have a nonstandard interest in playing their portable stereo at maximum volume as they career down the street. Is this an intrusion into one's private space? If so, how can one explain why such noise pollution may be suppressed, other than by appeal to the tastes of "standard" (i.e., typical middle-aged, middle-class) people? However, if one does not object to painfully loud "music," how do we distinguish between such noise and girlie pictures?

The substantive positions advocated by radicals—that no cultural position should be penalized simply for being different, that biases should be recognized and removed, and that "difference should be costless"—are readily recognized as classical liberalism. Conflicts between values should be resolved by appeal to neutral principles so as to foster maximum liberty for all. Inevitable but, it is hoped, residual clashes may be resolved fairly on the basis of mutual respect and tolerance. Perhaps radicals think that somewhere there is a perfect world in which all conflicts can be resolved to everyone's complete satisfaction, but insofar as they admit some skepticism about this ideal, radicals embrace principles long advocated by liberals, and so cannot regard liberal principles as biased unless they regard principles they also accept as biased.

Discrimination

Let us turn to discrimination. Radicals think that the Supreme Court has "hemmed itself into an analysis of sex discrimination based only on the differential treatment of similarly situated persons" and blame this on the liberal interpretation of discrimination (Smith, this volume). How can we understand this criticism and the radical corrective to it?

Any view of discrimination depends on the idea that illegitimate differences are introduced; certain people are unfairly advantaged or disadvantaged and others are not. The liberal interpretation of discrimination sees this occurring, first, through illegitimate classification; the basic idea is that absent relevant differentiating characteristics, treatment accorded one group must be accorded everybody. Certain classifications must not be used, or used only when strictly necessary, in formulating policies. But second, liberals have also formulated the idea of discriminatory impact, according to which policies that disadvantage historically discriminated against groups may be discriminatory, even if they do not employ discriminatory classifications. For example, if only men get hired as firefighters, or whites as police officers, there is a presumption that the employment criteria are discriminatory, whatever they are; this presumption can be overcome, but only by showing that the criteria have a reasonable (or necessary) relation to the job. (Questions about burden of proof and what is to count as legitimate business purposes were hotly debated in the context of the 1991 civil rights bill.)

To see what inadequacy radicalism imputes to liberalism, let us distinguish four ideas:

1. The logical axiom that what is true of one thing is true of everything equal to it
2. The principle that all people must be treated equally unless there is a relevant difference between them that justifies differential treatment
3. The idea of suspect categories
4. The principle of differential impact

Now, (1) is an axiom of logic, a principle that all rational people must accept, but (2) is nothing but the application of that principle to conduct, so everybody must accept (2) as well. Because (2) is the classical liberal principle of nondiscrimination, liberalism is no more controversial than basic logic. Hence, it cannot be liberalism's principle that only relevant reasons justify distinctions or (what is the same thing) that similarly situated people must be treated similarly that is under attack.

In itself, (2) cannot lead to any specific results; what counts and what does not count as a rational reason to treat people differently has to be independently specified. The classical principle is comparative: it says only that certain groups must be treated alike but does not say how any group ought to be treated. We agree that murderers may be treated differently than car thieves, but black murderers may not be treated differently than white murderers. A criminal's race is not relevant to how he or she should be punished. Ultimately, the reason for this exclusion of race is that there is no acceptable theory of punishment that would allow its inclusion. But "acceptable" means morally and not only factually: in the end, all arguments about what is and is not a relevant reason are circular, or appeal to already-accepted values. The theory that one of the functions of punishment is the suppression of disfavored races (so that a black man who rapes a white woman is severely punished, and a white man who rapes a black woman is not punished at all) must be rejected not on the grounds that race is not relevant to punishment but on the grounds that such a theory is morally unacceptable. It is true that distinctions between the races, sexes, and so on are simply not relevant to most social activities, for example, to administering an estate, so a policy that gives preference to a man over a woman as the administrator of an estate would be discriminatory.[3] But ultimately what makes an end legitimate cannot be determined apart from considerations of what is to count as discriminatory.[4]

Two more ideas are needed to complete the contemporary liberal theory of discrimination. Suspect categories, principle (3), acknowledges that certain classifications have been used in an invidious manner in the past, and that this history creates strong grounds for suspecting their use in the present. A suspect category found in legislation invites "strict scrutiny" and requires "compelling" interest. The final idea, differential impact, builds on the idea of suspect categories. Discrimination can occur not through the use of illegitimate categories ("differential treatment") that disadvantage one group but as a result of seemingly neutral and otherwise legitimate policies that impact one group significantly more than another. Differential impact alone cannot brand a policy as discriminatory because any policy that draws classifications imposes burdens selectively: the income tax burdens only people with incomes, for example; regulation of barber shops, or of motor vehicles, burdens only barbers, or car owners. This is not discriminatory and subject to strict (or heightened) scrutiny unless the impacted class is protected. High upper-body strength criteria for firefighters, though reasonable and neutral, is said to be de facto discriminatory, not because it burdens physically weak people (preventing weak people from becoming firefighters is the legitimate goal of the policy) but because it burdens women, in that significant numbers of women cannot meet these criteria. Similarly it would be discriminatory to make wearing a beard a criterion for some job (other than rabbi perhaps; sex discrimination is permissible on religious grounds, as in the Catholic Church, the state not yet being willing to impose moral restrictions on God), just because this criterion necessarily makes women ineligible.

These are the principles of liberal discrimination. The question, then, is whether radicals (who do not disagree with any of this as far as it goes) are proposing anything additional to these. Clearly, the radical interpretation of discrimination is not so distant from the idea of discriminatory impact; radicals want to focus on "real differences," "disproportionate impact," and "equal opportunity in fact," which ought to be taken into account in considering what is discriminatory. There is a difference, though slight. It is this. Consider the policy mandating maternity leave for pregnant teachers.[5] Technically, the policy does not employ the distinction between men and women, even covertly, because its effect is not to burden women while not burdening men; the people burdened are only the subclass of women teachers who are pregnant and do not want to quit working. Women as a class are not burdened because although all pregnant teachers are women, most of the nonpregnant ones are women as well. Hence, "pregnant women who do not want to quit working" is not a sex-defined class.

Nonetheless, the policy is discriminatory in that only women are burdened; necessarily, men cannot be affected by mandatory maternity leaves. To capture this concern with policies whose discriminatory impact consists not in disadvantaging a group but in burdening exclusively some of its members, we could formulate a fifth principle:

5. The principle of exclusive burdening holds that when a policy (or possibly an action) burdens members of a protected group exclusively, it is regarded as discriminatory and in need of compelling justification. A stronger version would hold that the burden fall not exclusively but predominantly on members of the group.

Now, radicalism demands adoption of (5) and excoriates liberalism as the obstacle to its adoption. But in light of the fact that historically liberals have added (3) to (2), and then added (4) to (3), it does not seem too much to suggest that they might also be persuaded to add (5) to (4). In fact, liberals may have already done so because something like (5) could be said to be the idea motivating recent legislation, notably the Americans with Disabilities Act. Radicalism seems especially muddled in identifying liberalism as antagonistic to (5).

It is another question whether principle (5) is in itself desirable. There seem to be certain anomalies and limitations that should be noted:

1. Principle (5) appears to apply to situations such as the following, all of which might turn out to be sex discrimination:

(a) "Fetal abuse" occurs when, for example, a pregnant woman uses drugs and thus damages the fetus. "Fetal neglect" occurs when the pregnant woman refuses to have in utero surgery to repair a fetal defect. Liberals might oppose both on grounds of privacy, but (as Smith, in this volume suggests about abortion) principle (5) would regard both concepts as sex discrimination. It is certainly not clear that this categorization advances clarity of thinking on the problem of whether fetal abuse or neglect ought to be regarded as an offense. Should it be a reason to allow fetal mistreatment, that only women can do it?

(b) Is blocking access to an abortion clinic a form of sex discrimination? The 11th Circuit has ruled it is not, but in dissent one federal circuit judge said: "The majority's insistence that Operation Rescue opposes a 'practice' that has nothing to do with women brings abstraction to a new level of absurdity. It is impossible to sever the link between abortion and gender."[6] Because women are the only victims of Operation Rescue, principle (5) does seem to regard interference with abortion clinics as sex discrimination. If so, perhaps it is not clear why even legal antiabortion protest might not be so regarded, thus setting up an equal protection versus First Amendment conflict.

(c) Only minorities and other victim groups like homosexuals are injured by abusive speech and other abusive but otherwise (and hitherto) legal acts, now sometimes prohibited as harassment.[7] If these are discriminatory under (5), a second example of First Amendment conflict is generated.

2. Because principle (5) requires that all (or most?) of the disadvantaged be members of a certain class, its effect would likely be limited. For example, (5) would evidently not apply to religious discrimination problems, such as Indians who smoke peyote in violation of the drug laws, or employers and schools that prohibit religious garments on the premises, because the policies in question do not burden the religious group exclusively or even predominantly. Freedom of religion problems are probably best handled by balancing religious freedom against society's "compelling interests" (to combat drugs, for example).

3. By definition men are not a protected class. Hence mirror-image discriminatory policies that exclusively burdened men would not be regarded as sex discrimination under (5). Suppose, for example, a work environment contains chemicals that pose a danger to male reproductive capacity but not to female. A law or company policy that no man is allowed to work there unless he agrees to be sterilized burdens only those unsterilized men who wish to father children. A parallel policy regarding women would be discriminatory under principle (5), but not the policy aimed at men.

"Minow's Dilemma"

Minow's dilemma is discussed extensively in several chapters in this volume. If women are treated the same as men, consequences of past discrimination are not addressed. If they are treated differently, the stereotyped differences between the sexes are strengthened rather than eliminated. Not to initiate certain policies that appear to give preference to women condemns women to remain behind male colleagues. To initiate the policy stigmatizes women for gaining unfair advantage through special policies. Women lose either way.

It is not clear whether this is meant to be a problem of perception or of reality,[8] a moral problem or a tactical one. Whether women should spurn extra help, bear their double burdens (career plus family), and demand an end to social pressures that make them the child raiser, or advocate policies such as free day care, which would shift the child-care burden elsewhere, is a question of tactics. Whether women are entitled to the help because of the social pressures is the moral question of whether advocating and accepting the help makes them freeloaders (to follow Meyers's characterization in this volume).[9] Is it freeloading if women have the right to interrupt their careers in order to raise a family and then resume the careers with seniority and other perks on a par with men who have been on the job continuously? With regard to matters of salary, promotions, and so on, should x years on the job plus y years of family raising for a woman be equal to $x + y$ years on the job for a man? If yes, then why not x years on the job plus y years devoted to community service, political activity, or other useful nonemployment, for men *or* women? Family leave policies are facially sexually neutral, but the beneficiaries would be predominantly women. If this is legitimate to counter social pressure, perhaps the policy ought to be designed as a "social pressure" policy. (Imagine some town where there is great social pressure on fathers to participate in community activities such as Little League, scouting, religious-school teaching, and so on; should this entitle fathers to take "community activity" time off?) It is difficult to construct such policies in ways that are not discriminatory against someone. Family leave policies evidently discriminate against employees who do not have families, as well as against the self-employed, who cannot take leave without sacrificing income. Why should they not have the opportunity to be absent from their work for many years, doing something else that they prefer to working, without penalty? Perhaps what is wanted is simply a policy that gives everybody x years off the job, paid for by the government if need be. (But if there were such a policy, would the paid leave have to be mandatory, lest those refusing the leave obtain a sneak hidden advantage over those who go on leave?)

There is an obvious solution to the family problem that avoids these conundrums. Women who want family and a career can put their kids in day care. Day care in European countries is available from age three months (also in the United States but harder to find). Proponents of day care want the government to pay for it, but on the face of it, this is no more reasonable than expecting the government to pay for other important things wage earners can buy for themselves. As with food, housing, and health care, government subsidies might be available for low-income family raisers. Government financial support for mothers with children should be eliminated and replaced by subsidies for day care, so that all mothers and not just middle-class ones can liberate themselves from the antifeminist, welfare-perpetuating illusion that mothers must stay home and mind the kids. Given this obvious solution, the claim that there exists some sort of intractable dilemma in which women are trapped seems classical muddlism.[10]

Rape

Liberals are civil libertarians: they approach rape aware of its potential for provoking civil liberties violations. Radicals claim to represent the oppressed, in this case, rape victims. They want to punish rapists, and are not too scrupulous about standards of proof or definitions of the crime.

Hence, radicals tend to deny or ignore that sex involves deep and powerful emotions that distort thinking. The fact that it does is why the law until recently has trod carefully when charges of rape are made. The assault on civil liberties of rape-reform legislation is muddled, however, only when it comes in the guise of being itself civil libertarian. The elimination of the corroboration requirement and prohibition of victim's previous sexual history are motivated explicitly to produce more rape convictions. Under "new-thinking" rape-law reform, the prosecution no longer has the burden of proving every element of the crime beyond a reasonable doubt; absent corroboration, the jury is invited to guess which party is the greater liar. Evidence of past sexual history,[11] especially previous relations with the defendant, is relevant to impeach the complainant's (uncorroborated) testimony with regard to whether or not she consented, that is, with regard to whether or not the crime took place. Under rape-law reform, the defendant no longer has the right to use all relevant evidence in his defense; rape is now the only crime where the defendant is prohibited from putting before the jury evidence that might show the crime did not occur. The fact that a woman has had previous lovers does not mean that she was not raped by this one, but it does mean that a jury has grounds to regard her testimony as less credible than otherwise, just as the fact that a witness has lied in the past does not mean that he is lying now but is relevant to the assessment of whether he is lying.[12] It is true that a woman who has had lovers will need a proportionally stronger case to win a conviction against her rapist; this is as it should be, not because someone wants to be nasty toward women with lovers but because conviction should be more difficult when there is reason to believe that the crime did not occur.

Similar points apply with respect to corroboration. When there is a colorable defense of consent (acquaintance rape), the question is not who did it but whether the crime occurred at all. If I claim you stole my car and you claim I gave it to you, no civil libertarian would countenance that you might be convicted on nothing more than the jury's guess about which of us might be lying. I would be at the least expected to show that my claim is more plausible than yours; I might show, for example, that I had never met you before so I would not have been likely to have given you my car, or that I am not the kind of person who gives away possessions. If I cannot produce any corroboration, there is a reasonable doubt whether the crime occurred, and the defendant gets the benefit. Radicals who advocate conviction without corroboration in effect repeal the principle of the benefit of the doubt.

As for the definition of the crime, civil libertarians should be clear (but of course often are not)[13] that rape is a crime of nonconsent, so coercion should not be sufficient for the crime to occur. This is why date rape is propaganda, not philosophy (this is not to say that men do not rape their dates; when they do, it is rape of a date, not some special category of rape). The question in regard to rape is whether she consented, not why she did. Coerced consent is consent nonetheless, even if obtained by threats.[14] What negates consent is the overcoming of the will: sex takes place even though she does not consent to its occurrence. This, however, does not mean that only physical overmastering—the actual application of irresistible force, as in beating or forcibly holding down—should qualify as rape. The will can be overcome by threats that are terrifying. Thus, if the man produces a weapon, or grabs her violently, or in general acts or appears violent in such a way that the woman through fear is psychologically unable to resist, the crime is rape. Given this, it is clear that the former requirement that the woman actively resist, ideally (for purposes of prosecution) displaying bruises to prove it, was excessive. Resistance is virtually conclusive evidence that she did not consent, but it should not be necessary for conviction. Where the defense is consent, supported by a colorable argument, the prosecution has the burden of proving otherwise, but what needs to be proved is only reasonable fear overwhelming the will to resist, not actual physical violence.

This is another reason that acquaintance rape should be more difficult to prove than stranger rape. If a stranger jumps at you from the bushes, you are naturally terrified and your will to resist may desert you. It is less plausible that you can be so terrified by someone you have been voluntarily dating, so more proof is needed.

As for the mens rea of rape, there is nothing improper about founding rape on recklessness. Reckless rape occurs when the defendant ignores obvious signs that the woman does not consent, as in the *Morgan* case.[15] Whether reckless rape should be punished as severely as intentional rape is open to debate: reckless murder (second degree murder) is regarded as less serious than intentional murder (first degree murder). Negligent rape is another story. Negligent rape presumably would occur when the indications that the woman does not consent are unclear or are easy to misunderstand. Creating such a crime would presumably send the message (insofar as the criminal law can be relied on to send messages at all) that it is risky to have sex unless the woman's consent is unmistakable. The concept of negligent rape is therefore consistent with the fashionable "no means no" campaign;[16] whether it is consistent with the facts of human psychology (which one might think to be a more important restriction on criminal law) is another matter.

As for MacKinnon's proposal to make rape a crime of strict liability (reported by McGregor in this volume), this proposal can only reinforce the suspicion that the target of certain radical reformers is not rape but sex.[17] Making rape a crime of strict liability does not achieve the legitimate goal of providing an incentive for a man not to have sex unless he is confident the woman consents because such confidence, no matter how well founded, cannot be a defense to a strict liability crime. By definition, under strict liability the only way to be certain that you escape liability for the crime is to avoid committing the underlying act. Because in this case the act is sex, making rape a crime of strict liability provides an incentive only to refrain from sex altogether. Hence, a man would be running the risk of committing rape whenever he slept with a woman; no matter what she says and does, he cannot be confident that he has avoided the crime just because he thinks it is obvious that she consents. A jury that later is convinced that she did not in fact consent will be required to convict him of rape, no matter how evident it is to the jury that he would not have had sex had he reason to believe she was not willing. That is what strict liability means. The situation is only slightly better were rape to be predicated on negligence; negligent rape means that even if the jury accepts that the man would not have had sex if he had understood that the woman did not consent, it must still convict him if it thinks that he was unreasonable in assuming she consented.

No person with any regard for civil liberties could support such proposals. No person with any regard for the interests of women would support them either, for if—contrary to what certain radical reformers seem to believe—it is in the interests of some women to have consensual sex with men, then it is not in those women's interests that men be put in danger of rape conviction even when the men do not wish to have unconsented-to sex and would not have it if they were aware of the lack of consent; still less when they have taken every reasonable precaution to determine that consent occur. (To repeat, this does not exclude that rape can be founded on willful disregard or gross negligence.)

Finally, to return to the nondiscrimination principle, numbered (5) above, because virtually the only people charged with rape are men, were it not that (5) cannot apply to men, policies designed to sacrifice civil liberties in order to procure more rape convictions seem to violate (5) and thus could be regarded as sex discrimination. Hence, these two thrusts of radicalism seem to be inconsistent.

Notes

1. This is a favorite theme of Martha Minow, *Making All the Difference*. It is taken up favorably in several papers but criticized by Diana Meyers, who in this volume defends impartial reason. Meyers's defense, however, seems to me to be somewhat compromised by her appeal to tactical rather than logical grounds. Thus she argues the people support Social Security because it "is perceived as universally beneficial," even though in fact it involves transfer payments. But, as Meyers does not quite come out and admit, the only morally defensible argument in favor of impartial reason is that impartial principles really are fair to everyone, not merely perceived as being fair. Though "perspectivists" are hopelessly confused about this, presumably their view is that there is no such thing as really being fair. When this philosophical principle is combined with multiculturalism, the view that all cultures are equally worthy of respect, the result is an obvious muddle.

2. This obvious point may be overlooked because perspectivists confuse two senses of "perspective." If someone has an idea about something, then necessarily that idea, being his and not another person's, reflects his way of thinking, and so may be called his perspective. In the second sense, "perspective" means bias, that is, distortion of the truth. Perspectivists think that because any idea reflects the thinker's perspective, every idea must be biased. But this does not follow: the fact that my idea is mine, and thus dependent on my point of view, does not necessarily mean that my idea is biased or a distortion of the truth because my point of view might be the correct point of view. I might be able to prove this to an unbiased observer (who will nonetheless be looking at the evidence from *his* point of view; his perspective in the first sense of "perspective").

3. *Reed v. Reed*, 404 U.S. 71 (1971), one of the earliest sex discrimination cases, declaring the statute so providing a violation of equal protection.

4. A statute that excludes blacks from living in a certain area would be discriminatory because the goal of the statute is itself discriminatory, and not because the difference upon which the scheme is based, namely, race, is irrelevant to the end—residential segregation by race—the statute seeks to achieve.

5. *Geduldig v. Aiello*, 417 U.S. 484 (1974). Smith objects to the ruling that this policy is not sex discrimination, but without making clear just what she does regard as sex discrimination.

6. *Lucero v. Operation Rescue of Birmingham*, 41 F.3d 1493 (11th Cir. 1992) (Phyllis Kravitch, dissenting).

7. Especially in major liberal universities, where attacking capitalism, Christian religion, and the family have long been regarded as sacred free speech rights of students and faculty.

8. Meyers (this volume) makes a similar point when she wonders whether Minow's book is about difference or "difference."

9. "If government were to provide affirmative action for women who leave career tracks to care for preschool children and who later wish to rejoin the work force, the "cri de quota" would be raised. Women would be stigmatized as freeloaders, taking 'vacations' to raise kids and returning to unearned advantages in the workplace" (Meyers, this volume). The problem is this: women who take time off from work to raise children could return to work at the level they left it, that is, behind their male peers, in which case they presumably would not rise as high in their profession as they might have otherwise, or as would comparably qualified males who do not take leave. The alternative is that they could reenter the work force at the level they would have attained had they not taken leave; in this case they would be accused of getting something (career advancement) for nothing, that is, of freeloading.

10. This solution assumes that children do no worse in day care than they do at home, cared for by their mothers. This assumption may be false, but I cannot think of any plausible a priori reason that it should be. I must confess ignorance of empirical evidence, if any; my own evidence is purely anecdotal, based on a very small sample of kids (European) who have been raised in day care all their lives and seem rather better adjusted, more secure, and happier than most American kids raised at home. A second solution, favored by some, is that work be restructured so that both parents are free to tend to the kids without penalty. This would mean fairly flexible working hours, which might suit some industries better than others (universities can give people flexible working hours, but it is not clear that the same could be true of, say, symphony orchestras). It seems that at best the significant restructuring of work should be seen as a long-range goal. But even suitable work arrangements might occasionally break down, leaving the child—or the mother—high and dry. And even the most favorable restructuring of work can be undermined by men's expectations, that is, the man's reluctance to make adjustments necessary to assist his wife's career. In any event, the restructuring of work seems better suited to the needs of two-parent families than of one-parent families, so cannot be thought of as the ideal solution to the problem of women's double burden.

11. A former girlfriend recently sued Robin Williams, alleging he gave her genital herpes and demanding $6.5 million. His defense was that she might have gotten the disease from some one of her other lovers. Past sexual history was the essence of his defense. (Williams settled for an undisclosed sum; he called the case "Financial Attraction.") *New York Times*, 9 August 1992, sec. 9, 8. If past sexual history is relevant here in order to protect the defendant, why should it not be allowed in a rape case when the defense is consent of the woman?

12. Against this it might be pointed out that the defendant's past criminal convictions are not allowed to be presented to the jury on grounds of prejudice, even though such evidence might be regarded as relevant to whether the defendant has committed the crime charged. But such evidence *is* allowed for purposes of impeaching testimony,

which is one reason defendants with prior criminal records do not take the stand in their own defense.

13. Official civil libertarians do not have much of a track record regarding sex crime. In my county in Michigan recently, a man was sentenced to four years in prison for fondling the breasts of a teenage girl at an amusement park. No civil libertarian protested this ferocious punishment.

14. Those who think rape can be founded on coerced consent should try working this out: What counts as coercion sufficient to establish the crime of rape? If I tell my girl-friend that I won't love her anymore unless she goes to bed with me, is that coerced rape? If I tell her I won't take her on the promised trip to Hawaii, or won't pay the rent, or will tell her husband about our affair?

15. *Regina v. Morgan*, 2 All ER 347 (1975). And see e. m. curley, "Excusing Rape," *Philosophy and Public Affairs* 5, no. 2 (1976).

16. Columnist Mike Royko reports that a record by singer Holly Dunn was withdrawn from the market by Warner Bros. after certain feminists protested these lyrics: "When I say no, I mean maybe. Or maybe I mean yes." (Warner Bros. refused on grounds of artistic freedom to withdraw the Ice-T record allegedly glorifying cop killing.) *Kalamazoo Gazette*, August 7, 1992, p. A7.

17. There are of course authors who profess not to understand the distinction.

Part IV

Critical Views on Criminal Punishment

Chapter 11

Feminism, Women, and the Criminal Law

Joan L. McGregor

Have feminist theorists made substantive contributions to our understanding of the criminal law? They have. Yet despite the existence of a wide variety of feminist literature concerned with changes to the criminal law, no systematic evaluation of that literature from a philosophical standpoint has yet occurred. This is regrettable for at least two reasons. First, although these critiques and challenges have exposed injustice and proposed significant solutions, much of the literature has not received sufficient attention. Second, the proposed solutions often lead to "paradoxes" of their own, which unfortunately fail to protect the autonomy and welfare of women. For instance, the use of evidence to support the "battered woman's syndrome" to prove self-defense in homicide cases may be thought to have a good result because the killing may have been justified in response to sustained terror on the part of the husband. On the other hand, the use of the defense may deepen the individual woman's sense of powerlessness and lack of control over her life. Further, it may reinforce stereotypes about women as being more prone than men to psychological problems. Other examples arise with the work done by feminists who have focused on equality. One persistent problem is that in some cases treating women the *same* as men disadvantages women. On the other hand, treating, for example, women's sexuality as different from men's, as something that women view as special or "sacred," disadvantages women by making them seem in need of protection, as more vulnerable. Regrettably, I will not be able to provide a systematic evaluation of feminist contributions to our understanding of criminal law; rather, I will focus on a few of the problems raised by feminists against the rape laws.

Consider the history of feminist discussions of the law. In the 1970s feminist theorists advocated reforms in family law, employment, and rape, areas of law recognized as having a special impact on women.[1] Subsequent feminist critiques have challenged law's own account of itself as rational, fair, and objective by pinpointing its inadequacies in the treatment of women. Among these challenges, some theorists (Albie Sachs, Joan Hoff Wilson) focus on the "male monopoly of law," concerning themselves with women's struggle to achieve equality within the present system while confronted with male efforts to maintain their dominance within the legal profession and within the general public realm. Other theorists (Catherine MacKinnon, Robin West) focus on what is seen as a deep-seated male orientation in law that imbues all its practices. The law, it is said, embodies a male culture, a male way of doing things. MacKinnon, for example, argues that the law sees and treats women the way men see and treat women. Thus rape, prostitution, and obscenity laws have little to do with the physical security of women and everything to do with preserving men's rights over female sexuality. Other feminist theorists (Frances Olsen, Carol Smart) attack at the conceptual level; they attempt to demonstrate that sexism informs the analytical categories from which law constructs itself as "impartial." Feminist theorists may differ in many respects, yet they share in challenging the very concepts law invokes to define itself as a just and fair system, particularly in regard to the treatment of women.

Rape law provides the perfect illustration of the problems in the criminal law that concern feminist theorists. The blatant sexist assumptions and standards in rape law raise serious questions about the notion that law is rational, objective (meaning neutral), or even fair. The problems inherent in contemporary rape laws and the prosecution of rapes stem from the fact that statutes and the courts employ assumptions and standards about rape, consent, force, reasonable belief, and resistance that fail to account for the perspective of women. Unfortunately, those assumptions and standards are employed against women to their detriment. Feminists have criticized standard doctrines in rape law—for example, "utmost resistance," the corroboration requirement, or routine introduction at trial of past sexual histories in rape cases—as not being objective, as not being rational for the legitimate ends of criminal law, and point to the blatant unfairness the law has perpetrated and continues to perpetrate against women.

Historically rape was defined as "carnal knowledge [by a man] of a woman forcibly and against her will."[2] These laws were not designed to protect only women's interests.[3] Deborah Rhode in *Justice and Gender* claims: "Historically, rape has been perceived as a threat to male as well as female interests; it has devalued wives and daughters and jeopardized patrilineal systems of inheritance. But too stringent constraints on male sexuality have been equally threatening to male policymakers. The threat of criminal charges based on female fabrications has dominated the history of rape law."[4] The result was that to prove "forcibly" and "against her will," courts (and some statutes) required victim resistance. Expressed first as "utmost resistance," this requirement reflected the view that it was better for a woman to die than be "dishonored." The requirement on the victim was then reduced to "earnest resistance" and later to "reasonable resistance." Further, it was the practice to instruct the jury that it is unsafe to convict on the uncorroborated evidence of the purported victim. Glanville Williams, a leading twentieth-century English authority, said, "There is a sound reason for it [the instruction to the jury], because these cases are particularly subject to the danger of deliberately false charges, resulting from sexual neurosis, phantasy, jealousy, spite or simply a girl's refusal to admit that she consented to an act of which she is now ashamed."[5] It was the opinion of John Wigmore, author of the nation's most influential treatise on evidence in the 1960s, that "no judge should ever let a sex-offense charge go to the jury unless the female complainant's social history and mental make-up have been examined and testified to by a qualified physician."[6] Williams worried that psychological approaches, namely, having a physician question the complainant, to determine whether she is having fantasies, is neurotic, and so on may not be sufficiently probative and hence suggested that all female complainants take polygraph tests.[7] The legacy of the earlier cases is epitomized by the warning given three centuries ago by the English Lord Chief Justice Matthew Hale: rape is a charge "easily to be made and hard to be proved, and harder to be defended by the party accused, tho' ever so innocent." (This was for a long time and up until very recently, recited to juries before their deliberations.) Distrust of female victims was incorporated into the definition of the crime and the rules of proof.[8]

There are at three least major criticisms from feminists about criminal rape laws. First, the laws are designed to protect men's interest in their women, their daughters or their wives. For instance, the utmost resistance requirement reflected the belief that a woman should protect her chastity with her life instead of conceptualizing the laws as protecting women's sexual autonomy.[9] Second, the laws protect men's interest in sexual access and thus in avoiding criminal charge and conviction. The baseline assumption of consent, the routine introduction of the victim's sexual history, the force and resistance requirements, and the marital exception illustrate the protecting of men's interests in sexual access. Third, the laws themselves, particularly the force and resistance requirements, embody typical male perceptions, attitudes, and reactions rather than female ones.[10] Feminists claim that their concerns go beyond the ones of normal due process. Moreover, some feminists have argued that far from protecting women, the rape laws, through their expectations of proper female behavior and their high expectations of impermissible force, actually served to enhance male opportunities for sexual access, to increase women's dependence on a male protector, and to reinforce social relations of male dominance.

The Male Orientation to the Law

In the 1970s and again in the early 1980s in light of feminist theorists' critiques, there were significant reforms to rape laws. Nevertheless, contemporary laws are still plagued with problems. Consider the following case. In *State v. Rusk*, 289 Md. 230, 424 A.2d 720 (1981), the victim gave the defendant a ride home from a bar where they had met through a mutual friend. The defendant invited the victim up to his apartment, but she declined. After he took her car keys, she reluctantly accompanied him to his apartment. The defendant started to undress the victim. Before intercourse the victim said to the defendant, "If I do what you want will you let me go without killing me?" The victim started to cry and then the defendant, according to the victim, started lightly choking her. The appeals court argued that she had not been raped because she had not been *forced*.

The standards used in this case exemplify what feminists call the male orientation to the law. "Prohibited force" is defined in terms of the victim's response to the situation. That response must be resistance, and resistance is interpreted to mean physical resistance, not merely verbal protests. If the law were simply interested in protecting the autonomy rights of the victims of rape, then it would consider verbal protests as resistance. Moreover, if it were interested in protecting the autonomy rights of women, it would drop altogether the resistance requirement and see verbal protests as a sufficient condition for nonconsent. The physical "force" and physical "resistance" requirements in rape law appear to embody a male perception of threatening situations and a male way of responding to a threatening situation, namely, with physical force. Force translates into "physical force" rather than various power relationships to which women might feel vulnerable. Being isolated, without transportation, with someone you hardly know, who is physically more powerful than you are, possibly someone who is in a role of authority, all could contribute to feeling threatened and thereby being "forced" into sex. However, the law's standard "reasonable person" is one who fights back, not cries. As Estrich says: "The reasonable woman, it seems, is not a school-boy 'sissy'; she is a real man."[11] Also worth noticing is that the woman's behavior, not the defendant's, is the behavior subject to evaluation.[12]

When the "physical" resistance requirement is applied to women, the results have been disastrous because many women do not respond with phys-ical force to a threatening situation. One reason for not so responding may be the normal differential in strength between men and women. Other rea-sons for women's lack of resistance are unclear, but social conditioning prob-ably accounts for a large part of the explanation. For a rape conviction, a victim's not resisting must have originated, the courts have argued, in a *rea-sonable* fear that if she (the victim) had, her attacker would have visited great harm upon her. In *Rusk,* the victim's fear was based upon being isolated in an unfamiliar part of town late at night, without her car keys, and with a man she didn't know. The court declared her fear not reasonable. "She may not simply say, 'I was really scared,' and thereby transform consent or mere unwill-ingness into submission by force. These words do not transform a seducer into a rapist." Again a court had enshrined a standard of *reasonable fear* that is not based upon the experiences of women. To whom is the fear reasonable? For some (many?) women, to be situated as was the complainant in *Rusk* was cause enough to fear. Just as a lone man in a dark alley might be afraid of a taller, bulkier man making demands of him and comply without resistance, for many women such an intimidating male presence may be enough.

Consider the Wyoming Supreme Court's reversal of a conviction in *Gon-zales v. State.* As in *Rusk,* the defendant and victim met in a bar and the de-fendant requested a ride home. The victim refused, but the defendant got into her car anyway. The victim repeated her refusal, but after unsuccessfully trying to get him out of her car, she started to drive. He asked her to turn down a road and stop so that he could urinate. Before getting out of the car, he removed her keys from the ignition. When he returned, he told her he was going to rape her; she tried to talk him out of it. "He told her he was get-ting mad at her and then put his fist against her face and said, 'I'm going to do it. You can have it one way or the other.'"[13] The Wyoming Supreme Court ruled that the trial court's standard of subjective fear was in error: the court should not place the determination "solely in the judgment of the prosecutrix and omit the necessary element of a reasonable apprehension and reasonable ground for such fear; and the reasonableness must rest with the fact finder." The reasonableness test is appropriate, but the reviewing court should have found the lower court committed harmless error because a fact finder should (if asking whether the reasonable woman would have been afraid) have found that the fear was reasonable. The upper court seemed to suggest that a trier of fact might not find the fear in this case reasonable.

The requirement of responding with physical force not only embodies a male orientation toward the situation but also relies upon entrenched suspicion and distrust of the female victim. Unless the victim can prove that she physically resisted, what reason do we have to suppose that she is not lying? Moreover, in some cases, even resistance has not been sufficient to establish nonconsent. In contemporary cases we see the lingering effects of the attitudes explicitly expressed in the 1950s and 1960s in academic works, for example, in Williams's classic text on criminal law, where he warns that women often welcome a "masterly advance" and "present a token of resistance." A 1966 note in the *Stanford Law Review* argues that although a woman may desire sexual intercourse, it is customary for her to say "no, no, no" while meaning "yes, yes, yes."[14] A 1952 comment in the *Yale Law Journal* suggested that women do not know what they want or mean what they say and often require *force* to have a "pleasurable" experience.[15]

Force is defined in terms of the victim's resistance; if she did not resist, there was no force—therefore, no rape. And if the reason for not resisting is fear, then the situation must be one that is objectively threatening, that is, one that a man would find threatening. Consider *State v. Alston*, in which Alston and the victim had had a "consensual" relationship over a period of some months, during which Alston had behaved violently toward the victim on many occasions. A month after the relationship ended, Alston came to the school where the victim was a student, attempted to block her path, and demanded to know where she was living. When she refused to tell him, he grabbed her arm and said that she was coming with him. At one point he told her he was going to "fix her face" and that he had a "right" to have intercourse with her again, and then took her to the house of a friend of his. Alston asked if she was "ready," and she said she did not want to have sexual relations. He thereupon pulled her up from the chair, undressed her, pushed her legs apart, and penetrated her. She cried. The court agreed that she had not consented, but because there had been no "force," the action was not deemed to have been rape.

For the court to conclude that there had been no "force" in the situation is, according to Estrich, "to create a gulf between power and force and to define the latter strictly in schoolboy terms. Alston did not beat his victim—at least not with his fists. He did not have to. She had been beaten, physically and emotionally, long before."[16] Estrich goes on:

> The definition of force adopted by the *Alston* court, like the definition of noncon-
> sent adopted by earlier courts, protects male access to women where guns and beat-
> ing are not needed to secure it. The court did not hold that no means yes; but it
> made clear that, at least in "social" contexts like this one with appropriate victims,
> a man is free to proceed regardless of verbal nonconsent. In that sense Alston was
> right. He did have a "right" to intercourse, and his victim had no right to deny him
> merely by saying "no."[17]

Feminists have argued that rape should be reconceptualized as the product of power, which can be exercised in ways other than physical force. The legal understandings of coercion need expanding.[18]

Most statutes define rape as intercourse with force or coercion and without consent. This definition, argues Catharine MacKinnon, assumes a sado-masochistic definition of sex: intercourse with force or coercion can be or become consensual. This definition has a history. For instance, the Supreme Court of Nebraska said in 1889: "Voluntary submission by the woman, while she has power to resist, no matter how reluctantly yielded, removes from the act an essential element of the crime of rape. . . . If the carnal knowledge was with the consent of the woman, no matter how tardily given, or how much force had therefore been employed, it is no rape." Without this view of legitimate forms of sex, why include both the elements "with force and without consent"? This appears redundant. Reconsidered, it seems logical to assume that if force is present, it is because consent is absent. Rape cases finding insufficient evidence of force reveal that accept-able sex, in the legal perspective, can entail a lot of force. MacKinnon argues that the level of acceptable force is adjudicated starting just above the level set by what is seen as normal male behavior rather than the vic-tim's point of violation.[19] And what is an unacceptable level of force is rarely addressed directly.[20]

Consent is another aspect of rape statutes on which feminist theorists have focused attention. Estrich has pointed out that the consent standard for rape is unique. The law requires victims of rape, unlike victims of any other crime, to demonstrate their "wishes," that is, demonstrate their nonconsent, through physical force. Rather than requiring an explicit sign of consent and worrying about the circumstances in which the alleged consent was given (e.g., were the circumstances threatening, was the victim intimidated, were implicit threats made), the courts have interpreted silence and nonresistance as signs of consent. Even in cases where there is clearly overwhelming force, courts have pursued the issue of consent. In *People v. Burnham*, 222 Cal. Rptr. 630 (Cal. App. 1986), a woman was severely beaten and then forced to engage in intercourse with her husband and a dog. The court held out the possibility of consent, or at least that the defendant might reasonably believe that she was consenting.[21] For practical purposes, the baseline apparently is one of consent rather than nonconsent. Why do the courts and the law presume consent until proven otherwise? Why not err on the side of less sex and more control on the part of the woman victim? If the law assumed that there was not consent, then the law would require proof of actual affirmative assent for a defense of consent. MacKinnon argues: "If rape laws existed to enforce women's control over access to their sexuality, as the consent defense implies, no would mean no, marital rape would not be a widespread exception, and it would not be effectively legal to rape a prostitute."[22]

Guilt for the crime of rape, along with most serious crimes, requires the defendant to have a specific mental state, or mens rea. The defendant's mental state refers to what he actually believed or understood at the time of the crime. For rape, the defendant must have believed that his victim was not consenting or believe that she might not be consenting. Standard mens rea doctrine may not apply because, as MacKinnon has pointed out, it is in the interest of men to remain oblivious to women's desires, signs, sensibilities. The law "allows one person's conditioned unconsciousness to contraindicate another's violation."[23] As long as men continue to believe the stereotypes about women, for instance, that no means yes, that women require some force, that women have rape fantasies, and so on, then it may be true in many cases, particularly the so-called acquaintance rape cases, that the defendants will lack the mens rea for the crime. *Rusk* illustrates what some feminists contend is a standard of "reasonable belief," based on what men in a sexist society would believe reasonable in the circumstances, namely, that because he did not use "excessive" force and she did not strenuously resist, she was consenting. That standard fails to consider what women would reasonably believe in those circumstances. MacKinnon claims: "The problem is that the injury of rape lies in the meaning of the act to its victim, but the standard for its criminality lies in the meaning of the act to the assailant. Rape is only an injury from women's point of view. It is only a crime from the male point of view, explicitly including that of the accused."[24] The episode is considered a rape, a violation, only if the defendant thought that the woman was not consenting. Doctrinally, this means that the man's perspective of the woman's desires determines whether she is deemed violated.

MacKinnon suggests that a change is required: the defense of a mistaken belief in consent should not be acceptable. Mistake-of-fact defenses in common law vitiated the mens rea for the crime of rape. The argument for this was "if D commits the *actus reus* of an offense with a factual misunderstanding he should not be blamed for the social harm he caused unless he deserves blame for making the mistake."[25] It is, however, controversial whether those mistakes must be reasonable or not.[26] With the mistake defense, MacKinnon argues, the law measures whether the rape occurred from the standpoint of the (male) perpetrator, who is allowed to see sexual violence against women as acceptable.

Rape, contends MacKinnon, should be defined as sex by compulsion, of which physical force is one form. Lack of consent is redundant and should not be a separate element of the crime. Rape is not like other crimes of subjective intent "because sexuality defines gender norms." So, the only difference

> between assault and what is socially defined as a noninjury is the meaning of the encounter to the woman. Interpreted this way, the legal problem has been to determine whose view of that meaning constitutes what really happened, as if what happened objectively exists to be objectively determined. . . . As a result, although the rape law oscillates between subjective tests and objective standards invoking social reasonableness, it uniformly presumes a single underlying reality, rather than a reality split by the divergent meanings inequality produces. . . . When a rape prosecution is lost because a woman fails to prove that she did not consent, she is not considered to have been injured at all.[27]

What standard of culpability MacKinnon wants to adopt is unstated. Possibly proof of the *actus reus* would be sufficient, making rape a "strict liability" offense. Most twentieth-century theorists have argued against jettisoning the requirement of mens rea in serious criminal offenses, pointing out that it is wrong to hold a person responsible for something for which he had no conscious awareness of wrongdoing. Alternatively, MacKinnon might want to focus on the "compulsion" aspect of the episode and subsume these cases under assault, with the requirement for similar mental states.

Estrich takes a more moderate position and argues that mistaken belief should exonerate but only if the belief was objectively reasonable. Nevertheless, Estrich recognizes that it depends upon how we define "reasonable."

She posits that the reasonable man in the 1980s should be held to the knowledge that "no means no." For Estrich, the imposition of rape liability for negligent conduct, that is, a man's actions grounded on an unreasonable belief in the woman's consent, promotes deterrence and entails no injustice. The "key question" for Estrich is what we should expect and demand of men in ambiguous situations. Estrich argues that the law should require a man to understand that "no means no," and, if the woman's words are ignored, that should be adequate to ground a conviction of rape.

Making rape subject to the negligence standard has been criticized. The negligence standard does not require subjective awareness of wrongdoing, only that the reasonable person would have known. Crimes negligently done usually result in significantly reduced amounts of punishment. In our system of criminal justice, it is supposed that individuals are subject to severe punishments only if their behavior was a product of something that they intended, planned, or at least consciously disregarded a risk about.

What we have seen throughout is that the rape laws embody standards that are based on male perceptions or reactions, and male expectations of women. The rules are favorable to men. The model of behavior and beliefs are derived from male models. These rules fail to display the kind of neutrality and fairness that we should expect from the law.

Equality and Difference

Fairness is an essential characteristic of a just legal system. The problem for women of getting fair results out of supposedly neutral law is compounded by the fact that women repeatedly find themselves judged by a male standard of behavior when they try to invoke their formal equal rights. In almost all areas of law, women find their actions assessed according to male rather than female life patterns. Equal treatment for women, therefore, becomes treatment like that accorded a man. What purports to be equal treatment of the sexes in the actual operation of the law does not amount to equality of result.[28] Introduction of the sexual history of a woman during a rape trial is not helped by suggesting that the same evidentiary practices would be applied for men who assert that sexual relations have been forced upon them. Equality is a problematic foundation for legal reform because equality requires a standard of comparison, and the standard for comparison tends strongly to reflect existing societal norms. White men are usually the basis of comparison.

Treating women the same as men, equally in the simple sense, often disadvantages women. The standard rules of self-defense, for instance, do not help a woman who is terrorized by her husband and feels she can defend herself only at a time when she is not being directly threatened. The rule, however, permits the self-defense justification only when the person is being immediately and directly threatened. Or the rule that an assault victim cannot respond with deadly force unless she fears death may disadvantage women because many women may not feel that they can effectively defend themselves with nondeadly force. On the other hand, treating women as different often translates as in need of special protection, more vulnerable. Women, then, find themselves with many more social controls on their behavior.

Feminists who work on these issues find that there are often conflicts between short-run and long-run solutions. For instance, some women seemingly accept stereotypical gender roles and thereby present themselves as timid, passive, nonconfrontational, and/or afraid of men. If we design laws to protect these women from exploitation and harm, are we then sending the wrong message about women and encouraging women to behave in accord with those gender stereotypes? It may be in the long-run interests of women to be encouraged to give up those stereotypical gender roles. In the short run, however, it is in the interest of women to be protected from exploitation and harm. Vivian Berger, reviewing Estrich's *Real Rape*, worries that a too "understanding" attitude toward the [passive women] of the world by the legal system may backfire and ultimately damage the cause of women in general. She argues that we do not want the law to patronize women: "To treat as victims in a legal sense all of the female victims of life is at some point to cheapen, not celebrate, the rights to self-determination, sexual autonomy, and self- and societal respect of women."[29] Berger worries that Estrich's desire "to empower women in potentially consensual situations with the weapon of a rape charge" may in fact backfire and instead enfeeble them. Whether the "equality" or "difference" approach is adopted, these long- and short-run concerns will surface.

Concern for equality leads some states to design gender-neutral statutes. Replacing traditional statutes, which punished the rape of a woman by a man, reform statutes are gender-neutral (for example Michigan's, and by 1980 over half of the U.S. American jurisdictions had gender-neutral statutes).[30] Support for gender-neutral statutes also arises out of the following concerns: "Men who are sexually assaulted should have the same protection as female victims, and women who sexually assault men and other women should be liable for conviction as conventional rapists."[31] Gender neutrality is seen as a way "to eliminate the traditional attitude that the victim is supposed to resist earnestly to protect virginity, her female 'virtue' or her marital fidelity."[32]

A number of problems arise from the making of rape statutes gender-neutral. Indeed, it may address one set of problems by creating others. Because women do not necessarily react the same as men, as we saw earlier with, for example, the resistance requirement, women will be disadvantaged by making the standards the same for all. Further, rape is typically something that happens to women, by men. Rape is not a gender-neutral crime; women are overwhelmingly its victims. Making rape gender-neutral obscures this fact.

Another move has been to relabel rape a form of assault. The purpose of the change was to rid the offense of "its common law baggage of unique rules . . . of resistance and proof," to refocus attention away from the victim to where it properly belongs—with the defendant. Relabeling rape "sexual assault" assumes a position in the debate as to whether rape should be considered a crime of sexual desire or violence. Some feminists argue that rape is motivated by desire to dominate, to have power, not by uncontrollable sexual desire. Focusing on the violent aspects of rape makes it clear that the law is not trying to prohibit all sex and that violent men must be incapacitated as dangerous criminals, not treated as only sexually aberrant. Moreover, to see rape as violence is to recognize that sex should be inconsistent with violence.

Other feminists want to drop the term "sexual" from the designation of this crime, assimilating the crime into assault law. The advantages of this, according to Rosemary Tong, are that "(1) it eliminates residual corroboration rules; (2) it lowers the overly high age of consent for sexual intercourse; (3) it eliminates as admissible evidence the victim's past sexual history; (4) it eliminates the marital-exception rule; and (5) it reduces the penalties for rape."[33]

Reconceptualizing rape as assault has prompted some to question the seriousness of rape, particularly nonaggravated rape.[34] How serious an assault is rape? Assaults are normally graded in terms of level of bodily injuries. Supporters of the change recognized that equating rape with assaultive conduct may obscure the unique meaning and understanding of the indignity and harm of rape.[35] Rape is different from other assaults. The reasons for the difference are complex. But sex is different from other kinds of touching.[36] It is understandable that feminist law reformers should seek to eliminate from the law the rules that have made rape prosecutions more difficult than prosecutions for other crimes. Their intentions, however, have sometimes been misinterpreted.[37] Feminists are concerned that more rapes be prosecuted and hence argue that penalties for rape be reduced, recognizing that juries are unlikely to convict when the defendant faces a long sentence for a nonaggravated rape. Moreover, not all rapes are the same. Rapes that involve aggravated assault are worse than so-called simple rapes—that is not to suggest that the latter are not serious offenses and worthy of some punishment.

Problems with conceptualizing rape as a form of assault or an act of violence can include that fact that a man can force sex against a woman's will without physical violence; having power over the victim will do. The definition of "violence" needs to be clearly articulated and not confused with exclusively physical assaults. Many feminists argue that threats short of physical violence should be sufficient for rape. However, not all threats undermine a person's freedom, for example, "If you don't sleep with me, I won't give you a fur coat." So which threats are sufficient? This is a tough and tricky question. Other problems with conceptualizing rape as assault are that assault is not consented to in law; either assault cannot be consented to or consensual assault remains assault. Yet sexual assault consented to is intercourse, no matter how much force was used.

Feminists who argue for the rape as *sexual* assault want to reinforce its violent character *and* its sexual nature. Some argue that the so-called power rapists' and anger rapists' "choice of the vagina or anus as the object of aggression is not accidental, but essential. . . . The rapist seeks to spoil, corrupt, or even destroy those aspects of a woman's person that should be a source of pride, joy, and power for her rather than a source of shame, depression, and humiliation."[38]

On the other hand, rape as sexual assault focuses on women's sexuality as being particularly susceptible to attack and hence in need of special protection. This may reinforce the myth of rape "according to which the invasion of sexual integrity is so traumatic that the victim's psychic wounds never heal."[39] The sexual assault approach may unwittingly cast women back into the position of victim, a role that many feminists would like to move beyond.

Attempts to reconceptualize rape to accommodate the equality of men and women have proved more difficult than initially thought.

Sex and Sexuality

A central issue in the debate about rape and sexuality, claims Frances Olsen, is that women are oppressed by moralistic controls society places on women's sexual expression.[40] Yet women are also oppressed by the violence and sexual aggression that society allows in the name of sexual freedom. Sexual freedom, for instance, as interpreted by courts, translates into an expansive notion of seduction. Consider, for instance, a threat to a fourteen-year-old girl living with the defendant and his wife with return to a detention home if she refused to engage in intercourse, as a case of seduction.[41] Then there was a case where a man posing as a talent scout lured a high school student into his "temporary studio" with the prospect of helping place her as a model. Using fear and intimidation, he had sex with her.[42] In another case a man posing as a psychologist conducting a sociological experiment lured a young girl into his "office" and intimidated her into having sex with him.[43] The last two were deemed instances of seduction by the courts. Sexual freedom permits seduction, which, according to the courts, may involve a combination of fraudulent misrepresentation, intimidation, and threats.

On the other side, for example, statutory rape law prohibits any "act of sexual intercourse accomplished with a female not the wife of the perpetrator, where the female is under the age of 18 years."[44] This rule not only controls the sexual freedom of young women but also reinforces the sexual stereotypes of men as the aggressors and women as passive victims. Olsen argues that "the restrictive aspects of statutory rape laws are particularly objectionable because they exalt female chastity and treat women as lacking in sexual autonomy."[45] Further, statutory rape laws suggest that young men are not in need of protection and are able to control their sexual autonomy.

Many theorists have seen sexuality as a matter of where social controls should end and sexual freedom should begin. Libertines and moralists draw those lines at different extremes—more sexual freedom versus more social control. Olsen declares that "sexual freedom turns out to be freedom for men to exploit women [and] the burden of social control falls primarily upon women." The important question of sexuality is not where to draw such a line "but the substance and meaning that we give to sexuality." Isolated sex, promoted by pornography and advertising, and sex in exchange for love, promoted by romance magazines, have both been eroticized, but this does not mean that either is good, natural, or inevitable." Both of these conceptions alone are incomplete and possibly destructive. We need to look for alternative paradigms to conceive of sexuality. Olsen supposes that the best we have to start with is sex as an expression of an equal, sharing relationship.[46]

Leaving behind the sadomasochistic definition of sex, wherein the male is the aggressor and the female is passive and reluctant, the law needs an alternative conception upon which to rely. One proposed by Lois Pineau is the model of what she calls "communicative sexuality"; in intimate situations we have an obligation to take the ends of others as our own.

> Assuming that each person enters the [sexual] encounter in order to seek sexual satisfaction, each person engaging in the encounter has an obligation to help the other seek his or her ends. . . . But the obligation to promote the sexual ends of one's partner implies the obligation to know what those ends are, and also the obligation to know how those ends are attained. . . . In the practice of communicative sexuality, one combines the appropriate knowledge of the other with respect for the dialect of desire.[47]

Pineau further believes that communicative sexuality should be viewed as the norm for sexual encounters with which reasonable women would agree. Following from this view, "The guilt of date rapists [is located] in the failure to approach sexual relations on a communicative basis."[48]

Surely, this cannot be correct. The crime of rape cannot be analyzed as not approaching a sexual encounter on a communicative basis. "Communicative sexuality" may be an ideal for sexuality, but we would not want to say that failing to engage in it is rape. So that, for example, I could be convicted of rape for not performing some sex act that I know my partner wants me to perform. What is important is consent of the parties involved. If communicative sexuality has a role, it is an evidentiary one in helping establish that the victim did not consent. Furthermore, might one communicate that one desires a kind of sex that is not in line with what Pineau envisions as the ideal, say, sadomasochistic sex? If the partner went along with this, even though not liking it, would that be a case of rape? Moreover, I suspect that it is not true that every time individuals have sex each does it for personal enjoyment or sexual satisfaction. There may be other reasons that make individuals willing to consent to sexual encounters. Again, the fact that the person does not consent for sexual reasons should not lead to conclusion that the encounter is necessarily rape. Isn't this another form of control by the state? Is there merely *one* method of sexual expression? If sexual expression is one of the important ways of expressing oneself, then should not individuals be left free to explore those parameters?

New Directions

Feminists have been successful in showing that some legal rules, although they may appear objective in the sense of being neutral between relevant groups, may operate to disadvantage women as a group. Some other rules unfairly burden women more than men; and some rules are not rational as judged by the legitimate ends of the criminal law. After exposure of these problems, the question becomes how best to reconstruct the rules so that they are not riddled with gender biases, and such that they protect the other values we want protected (for example, ensuring that defendants have the ability to bring in relevant evidence). Although the legal system is a conservative institution, it should not be permitted to perpetuate gender stereotypes that seriously diminish the status of women and that foster and sanction harmful and disrespectful treatment. Criminal law has, according to Stephen Schulhofer, a number of salient characteristics; one is that it is "demanding,"[49] even to persons who find it difficult to comply. In this spirit, the law should always demand that persons respect the bodily integrity and property of others. When "crossing borders," agents should be demanded to proceed with caution, ensuring that consent is obtained and recognizing the risks entailed by imprudent behavior. A second central characteristic of the criminal law is that it is "judgmental." "In the event of conviction, it does not . . . forgive. Rather, it condemns, it blames, and it punishes."[50] Schulhofer says that these are "male" characteristics, ones that feminists would object to. This is, I think, inaccurate; many feminists would be happy to embrace demanding and judgmental traits. The point that many feminists have made is that the law has not demanded enough of men's behavior toward women and that it has been too ready to excuse, condone, and sympathize with that behavior.

I cannot spell out all the desirable changes to rape law that feminists' critiques suggest, but I will briefly set forth some suggestions. First, rape should be defined as sexual contact without consent. The force requirement should be dropped; introducing force as evidence of nonconsent is sensible, but force should not be a necessary condition for nonconsent. Furthermore, the law should specify the circumstances in which consent may be vitiated, where a yes does not mean yes. What consent means should be made clear in the statute, as in Washington's: "'Consent' means that at the time of the act of sexual intercourse there are actual words or conduct indicting freely given agreement to have sexual intercourse."[51] This type of specification of affirmative consent, and not merely the absence of resistance or some indication of nonconsent, makes mistaken belief more difficult to prove. If the victim did not say yes or indicate affirmative assent in nonthreatening circumstances, then sexual intercourse is rape. The expectation is that the reasonable man realizes that engaging in sexual intercourse without consent is a grave harm and hence, acts in accord with such knowledge. With consent specified in the statute, the mens rea standards of knowing and recklessness will capture many more cases. If the victim says no or does not say yes, then the defendant would know that the victim was not consenting. The range of "mistake of fact" cases would be greatly narrowed.

Nevertheless, there is still a need to differentiate levels of the crime, from aggravated rape with subjective culpability to lesser forms of sexual assault negligently done. If we assume that most people have the capacity to act reasonably and make judgments consistent with respecting the moral rights of others, then persons should be held culpable for failure to do so. Where there is the risk of grave harm to another, agents should be culpable for ignorance. If the individual is generally a careless and inattentive person, he is held accountable for failing to control a character defect that can cause him to act in a negligent manner. Some will argue that it is not fair to hold a defendant liable for behavior that he did not know was criminal. A few things should be said about this. First, it has always been known that it is wrong to engage in sexual contact without consent. Second, what is new is the recognition that many situations are ambiguous and hence subject to misunderstandings or worse. Laws can and should change when found inadequate to accomplish legitimate ends. Not all changes are unfair. What is unfair is not warning agents or making the information about the changes inaccessible.

One problem emerging from many feminists' discussions of law is the assumption of "gender essentialism," the idea that there is some essential way women are, some way women experience the world that transcends their race, class, education, social history, and whatever else goes into who we are. Gender essentialism distorts the situation and inclines us to adopt rules on the basis of this monolithic woman, when, in fact, women react in many ways and experience the world in many ways. Criminal laws, however, are designed to prevent harm to individuals, all individuals, including those who are timid, weak, gullible, and easily exploited. Given that the criminal law's job is to protect all individuals, I prefer criminal laws that deter individuals from harming those who are least capable of defending themselves. For me, then, arguing over whether women are this way or that is not relevant to the task of reforming criminal statutes. Rather, recognizing that some women are weak, timid, gullible, and that these are characteristics that can be exploited by unscrupulous persons is sufficient to design rules to prevent such harms.

The solutions proposed by feminist theorists need to be evaluated in light of a consistent and coherent view of the purpose of criminal law: respecting and protecting autonomy rights. This organizing principle correctly articulated will truly reflect women's concerns and protect their interests. Accomplishing this purpose requires rules that respond to relevant differences among individuals, while not disadvantaging agents on the basis of those differences.

In this chapter I have addressed only a small fraction of the contributions feminists have made to our understanding of the criminal law. What I hope comes through this brief exploration of the substantive critiques of rape laws is the depth and the power of feminist scholarship.

Notes

1. See Ngaire Naffine, *Law and the Sexes* (Sydney: Allen & Unwin, 1990), for an excellent discussion of the different types of feminist jurisprudence.

2. William Blackstone, *Commentaries on the Law of England* (1765–1769).

3. Deborah Rhode illustrates this point by noting that in many ancient societies the punishment was not directed solely at the aggressor; in some, the victim was required to marry the assailant, and her father was entitled to rape the aggressor's wife or sister. *Justice and Gender* (Cambridge: Howard University Press, 1989), 225.

4. Ibid., 244–45.

5. Glanville Williams, *The Proof of Guilt* (London: Stevens & Sons, 1963), 159.

6. John Henry Wigmore, *Evidence in Trials at Common Law*, rev. ed., ed. James Chadbourn (Boston: Little, Brown, 1970), vol. 3A, sec. 924a.

7. Williams, *The Proof of Guilt*, 162.

8. Susan Estrich, *Real Rape* (Cambridge: Harvard University Press, 1987), 29.

9. The fact that rape of any kind was considered one of the most serious crimes, with punishments similar to homicide, reinforced this attitude.

10. The crime of rape centers on penetration; sexuality is defined in terms of penetration, male-defined loss. Rape also centers upon one way men define loss of exclusive access—crime against female monogamy. Women's view of when they are violated often is different from men's, and yet men's view is determinative.

11. Estrich, *Real Rape*, 65.

12. Another example is the introduction of the victim's past sexual history.

13. *Gonzalez v. State*, 516 P. 2d 592, 593 (Wyo. 1973).

14. "Note, The Resistance Standard of Rape Legislation," *Stanford Law Review* 18 (1966): 680–89.

15. "Comment, Forcible and Statutory Rape: An Exploration of the Operation and Objectives of the Consent Standard," *Yale Law Journal* 62 (1952): 55–83. This note has been cited many times, including commentaries in American Law Institute, *Model Penal Code and Commentaries* (Philadelphia: American Law Institute, 1985).

16. Estrich, *Real Rape*, 62.

17. Ibid., 63.

18. Rhode, *Justice and Gender*, 252.

19. Catharine MacKinnon, *Toward a Feminist Theory of the State* (Cambridge: Harvard University Press, 1989), 173.

20. Note the recent South Carolina marital rape case, in which the husband tied his wife to the bed, hit her, and used a knife on her, none of which was sufficient to be ruled unacceptable force.

21. The convictions were reversed because of the judge's failure to give consent instructions.

22. MacKinnon, *Toward a Feminist Theory of the State*, 175.

23. Ibid., 182.

24. Ibid., 180.

25. Joshua Dressler, *Understanding Criminal Law* (New York: Matthew Bender, 1987), 132.

26. There is precedent for the view that unreasonable mistake of fact negates the mens rea required for rape. See *Regina v. Morgan* [1976] A. C. 182 (House of Lords).

27. MacKinnon, *Toward a Feminist Theory of the State*, 180.

28. Naffine, *Law and the Sexes*, 49.

29. Vivian Berger, "Not So Simple Rape," *Criminal Justice Ethics* 7, no. 1 (1988): 75.

30. Estrich, *Real Rape*, 81ff.

31. Comment, "Rape and Rape Law: Sexism in Society and the Law," *California Law Review* 61 (1973): 941.

32. Leigh Bienen, "Rape III—National Developments in Rape Reform Legislation," *Women's Rights Law Reporter* 6 (1980): 174–75.

33. Rosemary Tong, *Women, Sex, and the Law* (Towata, N.J.: Rowman & Allenheld, 1984), 113.

34. See, for example, Michael Davis, "Setting Penalties: What Does Rape Deserve?" *Law and Philosophy* 3 (1984): 61–110.

35. Estrich, *Real Rape*, 81ff.

36. See my "Rape, Consent, and the Reasonable Woman," in *In Harm's Way: Essays in Honor of Joel Feinberg*, ed. Jules Coleman and Allen Buchanan (Cambridge: Cambridge University Press, 1993), for a discussion of the wrong of rape.

37. For instance, Michael Davis mistakes a strategic maneuver for a conceptual point about the nature of rape. See note 34, above.

38. Tong, *Women, Sex, and the Law*, 117.

39. Ibid., 118.

40. Frances Olsen, "Statutory Rape: A Feminist Critique of Rights Analysis", in *Feminist Legal Theory*, ed. Katharine Bartlett and Rosanne Kennedy (Boulder: Westview Press, 1991), 305–17.

41. *Commonwealth v. Minarich*, 498 A. 2d 395 (Pa. Sup. 1985).

42. *Goldberg v. State*, 41 Md. App. 58, 395 A. 2d 1213 (1979).

43. *People v. Evans*, 85 Misc. 2d 1088, 379 N.Y.S. 2d 912 (1975).

44. California Penal Code, sec. 261.5 (West Supp., 1981).

45. Olsen, "Statutory Rape," 307.

46. Ibid., 312, 306, 314.

47. Lois Pineau, "Date Rape: A Feminist Analysis," *Law and Philosophy* 8 (1989): 235.

48. Ibid., 240.

49. Stephen J. Schulhofer, "The Gender Question in Criminal Law," *Social Philosophy and Policy* 7, no. 2 (spring 1990): 112.

50. Ibid.

51. Washington Revised Code Ann., sec. 9.01(6) (1981).

Chapter 12

A Radical Critique of Criminal Punishment

James F. Doyle

I considered using a more provocative title for my chapter, such as "Learning to Live *with* Crime and *without* Punishment." If you think this is a bizarre position to try to defend, I hope to show you that it is not as bizarre as it may seem. My goal is even more ambitious: I hope to show you that this position is more defensible than our present philosophical approaches to criminal punishment.

To achieve this goal, I first need to persuade you to think about punishment in a new and, I find, a more fruitful way. I think Richard Rorty is right when he says that the sort of philosophy needed for this purpose, whether about punishment or other issues, does not work piece by piece, analyzing concept after concept, or testing thesis after thesis. Rather, it works holistically and pragmatically. It says things like "Try thinking of it this way," or more specifically, "Try to ignore the apparently futile traditional questions by substituting the following new and possibly interesting questions."[1]

Following Rorty's advice, I am asking you, "Try thinking of punishment in a more holistic and pragmatic way that may lead not to making the practice of punishment better but to stopping punishment and doing something else instead." If this way of thinking proves to be fruitful, then we may be able, in Rorty's words, to *dissolve* inherited problems rather than *solve* them.[2]

It will help if we recognize that we face many obstacles in trying to think about punishment in a new way. Among these are practical and emotional obstacles such as those described by Nicola Lacey: Because we are so used to living with a system of punishment, and doubtless also because punitive responses are a salient feature of our emotional lives (this, of course, may change), the idea of being without a penal system, or even with

Chapter 12 originally appeared as "A Radical Critique of Criminal Punishment," *Social Justice* 22 (1995): 7. James F. Doyle gratefully acknowledges permission to republish this article in a revised form.

one far less extensive than our current one, tends to throw us into a state of alarm and anxiety. This in turn feeds into the arguments for punishment.[3] If we acknowledge in ourselves and others this deeply felt need for punishment, and then begin to question what this need is based on, I believe we can begin to overcome such practical obstacles, difficult though it may be.

Paradoxically, another obstacle is the tendency of most people to think of punishment as a peripheral rather than central feature of social life. Philosophers have helped reinforce this abstract stereotype of punishment as a more or less discrete practice operating at the margins of society to secure legal and moral compliance. This is not a true picture of punishment even in its formal legal sense. It is much less true of punishment as a pervasive network of institutions, practices, agencies, and social relations. To overcome this intellectual obstacle to thinking about punishment in a new way, we need to take to heart the criticism of David Garland and Peter Young: "A whole tradition of philosophical writing and debate conspires to present 'punishment' as something we can talk of and refer to in the singular, whilst disregarding the plurality and complexity of its empirical supports."[4]

This simplistic notion of punishment reinforces the view that what makes punishment most problematic—its central normative problem—is the state's coercion of individuals found guilty of a crime (usually, let us not forget, because they have been persuaded to *plead* guilty). The more grievous the effects of this coercion, the more problematic punishment becomes, on this view. The solution offered for this problem is a general rationale strong enough to justify the state's coercion of individuals. Much of the philosophical debate is about which of various possible rationales of punishment makes the strongest case for it: for example, rationales of deterrence, reform, rehabilitation, incapacitation, just deserts, retribution, restitution, exculpation, or some combination of these.

This philosophical approach to criminal justice makes the notion of punishment itself tendentious and question-begging in a variety of important ways. First, by identifying all punishment with formally authorized *state* punishment, this approach creates a presumption in favor of punishment, especially where the state is subject to democratic and constitutional controls. Second, the focus on the punishment of *individuals* reinforces a strongly individualistic view of responsibility for crime and its social consequences. Social responsibility—whether of groups, agencies, corporations, associations, institutions, or other social policy makers—is ignored or at most is acknowledged as a secondary problem, not the primary problem of punishment. Third, by treating all punishment as a necessary and fitting response to *crime* and *guilt*, this approach prompts us to think of punishment as inherently retributive and for this reason at least just in principle, if not in practice.

Because it is difficult to avoid these implicit connotations of the word "punishment," Garland and Young have argued for a more neutral substitute such as "penal practices" (wherever we find them), or simply "penality." I will follow their recommendation and use these alternative terms from time to time, just to remind us of the need for a broader, more neutral notion that can accommodate all the rich variety and complexity that punishment actually exhibits in our society. Consider, as one telling example of this need, an observation made by drama critic Frank Rich in the *New York Times*: "The world has become a place where no *good* deed, let alone bad one, goes unpunished."[5] As I hope to show, this observation expresses a profound insight into the contemporary institution of punishment in our society that would be unintelligible (or at least wildly metaphorical) unless we think of punishment in a way that is very different from the inherited philosophical notion of it.

I should mention one other serious obstacle to thinking about punishment in a new way, for which social scientists and especially criminologists are probably more responsible than philosophers. Among the many who have tried to explain and justify punishment, there has been a strong predilection to seize on some aspect or other of punishment as the theoretical key that will unlock all its mysteries. This has led to the identification of all punishment with incarceration and especially with the prison as an institution, with class conflict, with instilling discipline in the work force, with maintaining social control over deviant groups, and with many other aspects of penal practices. Such theories have contributed to our understanding of past and present penal practices, but at the cost of encouraging ways of thinking about punishment that are distorted and reductive.

It is safer to assume that there is no unifying theoretical approach to punishment that will provide the long-sought solution to the normative problems it poses. What *is* possible is to think about punishment in a way that will reveal why this is so, and this is what I hope to persuade you to do.

Obligation versus Social Relations

It will help to overcome the obstacles I have sketched—and they are by no means the only ones—if we think about penal practices in light of two very different ethical approaches to personal and social life. I follow the example of many other contemporary philosophers in calling one of these broad approaches the "ethics of obligation" and the other the "ethics of social relations," though these are at best crude shorthand labels for very complex and subtle moral philosophies. These two approaches are comparable to what Kent Greenawalt has contrasted as "principled" and "relational" normative approaches to law.[6] According to Greenawalt, the most radical challenge to the normative view of law as principled and objective is the alternative view that law is or should be relational and to some degree subjective. While I agree with Greenawalt's claim about these two approaches to law, I am concerned here about their implications for penal practices. I will give more attention to the ethics of social relations, partly because it is not as widely understood as the ethics of obligation, but more importantly because it suggests a new approach to penal practices in general and to criminal punishment in particular. I believe this will be clearer after we contrast these two ethical approaches.

The Ethics of Obligation

It is safe to say that the ethics of obligation, broadly conceived, has been the dominant ethical approach in modern so-called Western philosophy. The exemplars of this approach most often cited are Kant and, in our own time, John Rawls, though the label is also applicable to many other modern moral philosophers. What distinguishes this approach is that it makes obligation the central explanatory and normative concept in ethics, along with cognate concepts such as duties, rights, rules, principles, justice, and individual autonomy. This is what all versions of the ethics of obligation have in common, though they differ widely in their explanations of the sources of moral obligation. Examples of these sources range from the categorical imperative and Rawls's principles of justice to the principle of utility, inherent fundamental rights, and basic human needs. In addition to these secular theories are various religious accounts of the source of moral obligation.

For present purposes I will emphasize the typical features of the most influential secular versions of the ethics of obligation. These versions offer a universal or at least general theory of morality as governed by obligations that are rationally derivable from fundamental principles, rights, rules, or attributes of human nature. The ethics of obligation offers a model of personal and social life in which people confront one another as independent, autonomous equals, motivated by self-interest but capable of reaching a rational consensus about the moral obligations they must share. Traditionally this model applied only to men because philosophers did not consider women to be capable of independent, rational moral agency. Of course this belief tended to be self-fulfilling as long as women as a group had little opportunity to act independently. Mary Wollstonecraft and John Stuart Mill were very much ahead of their time in arguing that the model was no less appropriate for women than for men.[7]

Some but not all versions of the ethics of obligation have relied on the practice of promising or, more formally, on a kind of contractual agreement among equals, as a way of reconciling both the freedom of independent, autonomous individuals and their rational assent to the moral obligations they must share as members of the same society. The individualism that is characteristic of the ethics of obligation has been limited only by the minimal moral community required to sustain the practice of promising or contracting through which shared obligations are created. From these obligations are derived the rights and duties, standards of goodness and justice, and methods of rational criticism and justification that the ethics of obligation relies on to explain and justify morality.

Bernard Williams's critical interpretation of the ethics of obligation sheds light on several of its more implicit but important features.[8] He points out that the distinguishing mark of the ethics of obligation is not its appeal to obligations (which it shares with many other ethical approaches) but its reliance on a special and complex notion of obligation. This is a notion of moral obligation as part of a moral system that makes as many different ethical considerations as possible into obligations (179). To the extent that this transformation is successful, moral obligation becomes inescapable, even for people who reject its application to themselves. This moral system also gives obligations (and correlative rights) precedence over all other kinds of considerations of what is ethically desirable or admirable. According to the ethics of obligation, the way people determine moral obligations that apply to themselves and others is through rational deliberation (175).

To explain how people conceived as separate and independent members of society are able to cooperate with one another in determining the moral obligations that govern them, the ethics of obligation posits what Williams calls "the fiction of the deliberative community" (193–94). Members of such a community are supposed to treat one another as agents for whom relevant ethical considerations (i.e., obligations) are overriding reasons for action. If we think of Kant's community of the kingdom of ends as an example, we can understand why Williams calls this a fiction, though perhaps a necessary fiction for Kant's version of the ethics of obligation.

Another and closely related fiction on which the ethics of obligation relies is the view of people as agents who can act voluntarily and make relevant ethical considerations that are their reasons for acting. Clearly, this view is often belied by the facts. This fiction underlies what Williams calls "the blame system," which operates to reinforce shared moral obligations by blaming violators of these obligations as if they are free agents, not only with regard to their actions but also their character and their physical, psychological, and social circumstances. The blame system focuses on individual responsibility for actions, guided by "the ideal that human existence can be ultimately just" (195). This inspiring ideal is integral to the ethics of obligation, but it, too, is a fiction in conflict with the factual generalization that "most advantages and admired characteristics are distributed in ways that, if not unjust, are at any rate not just, and some people are simply luckier than others" (195). In short, it is an illusion to think that justice or any other value can be beyond moral luck, whether good or bad.

The inescapable contingencies of moral luck and the changing complexities of human social life call into serious question the various fictions on which the ethics of obligation depends. It is plausible to think of these fictions as secular "residues" of the traditional belief in divine or natural providence. They are closely related to other residues of providence such as the ideas of the self-regulating free market guided by "the invisible hand," the harmonious community bound together by shared assumptions and values, and the objective, principled system of criminal law and punishment. The continuing powerful influence of these fictions on our thinking supports Williams's observation, that "if obligation is allowed to structure ethical thought, there are several natural ways in which it can come to dominate life altogether" (182).

We can see the influence of these fictions, and of the ethics of obligation they reinforce, all around us and throughout our history. For example, the fiction of the deliberative community continues to be an implicit basis for excluding white women, black Americans, American Indians, and other groups from full membership in public and private institutions while at the same time making them (us) subject to the same obligations as white men. While this paradoxical blend of social exclusion and inclusion is no longer formally sanctioned by the U.S. Constitution and legal system, it persists as an informal and pervasive structural feature of public and private life. Also worth mentioning in connection with the fiction of the deliberative community is the growing emphasis on what is called "community policing." Proponents of community policing make the questionable and often false assumption that socially cohesive communities actually exist to support such a policy.

Another example of the influence that continues to be exerted by the ethics of obligation—and especially the fiction of the deliberative community—is the persistent identification of Arab Americans and other groups with terrorism. Not only does this policy of social exclusion impose obligations on some people while depriving them of the rights other people enjoy, it also risks imposing blame, guilt, and punishment by association. The blaming system that is an integral part of the ethics of obligation also influences the growing demand to reduce or eliminate the minimum age at which juveniles can be criminally prosecuted and punished for felony charges. Policies adopted in response to this demand in effect extend the reach of adult obligations, blame, and punishment to immature juveniles and even children.

One of the main functions of law as an institution has been to turn ethical and other kinds of interests into obligations, and then to enforce these obligations. The intended or unintended effect of this process is to preserve or change existing distributions of economic, political, and other kinds of power in society. Familiar though this function of law may be, its dependence on the ethics of obligation as a source of legitimation is much less obvious. In law as well as in ethics, giving special weight to obligations as overriding normative considerations tends to yield reductive decisions that fail to do justice to a variety of other ethical considerations. A notable example of this reductive oversimplification is the series of legal decisions intended to guide public policy on abortion. Obligations and rights by themselves cannot provide a satisfactory ethical or legal basis for resolving this complex issue. This criticism can also be made of the way other complex issues of justice have been addressed, such as guaranteed health care, protection from discrimination and oppression on the basis of sexual orientation, affirmative action, protection from crime, the widening gap in quality of life, and many other issues calling for more sensitivity to the broad variety of ethical and other considerations involved.

Particularly in the area of criminal justice, one finds pervasive insensitivity to relevant ethical considerations of racial, ethnic, and class bias in criminal legislation, law enforcement, prosecution, conviction, victimization, blame, and punishment. This is confirmed by (among many others) Michael Tonry in *Malign Neglect: Race, Crime, and Punishment*, where he points out the trend toward attaching the death penalty to more and more crimes, enacting new mandatory penalties, and restricting prisoners' habeas corpus rights.[9] The policies resulting from this trend are, according to Tonry, the very opposite of what criminal justice needs, which is to *cause less harm*, especially to black Americans and their struggling families, institutions, and communities. This is how Tonry describes the implications of this needed policy for sentencing: "A policy that directed judges to impose the least restrictive appropriate alternative would have the rare property that every legitimate consideration would be advanced."[10]

The Ethics of Social Relations

Much more could be said about the ethics of obligation and its influence, but I hope the preceding sketch will suffice to show how it contrasts with the ethics of social relations. Growing dissatisfaction with the ethics of obligation has been one of the motivations for developing an alternative ethical approach to personal and social life and to such institutions as law and punishment. Another motivation has been the strongly felt need for an ethics that more adequately reflects the experience of women and children as well as men and of people representing different groups and cultures.

Martha Minow has eloquently expressed the dissatisfaction many have felt with the ethics of obligation. Her interpretation of this approach helps us understand why it places so much reliance on force and penal practices.[11] She criticizes the ethics of obligation—which she refers to as "rights analysis"—for its emphasis on process at the expense of substantive moral and legal values. Even thinkers who have employed the idea of a social contract as a heuristic device to arrive at fundamental obligations, rights, and responsibilities governing a society tend to emphasize process over substance. "These thinkers," Minow argues, "treat legal rights as the principles and norms that people would agree to if we all engaged in the kind of process signified by the image of the social contract." Asking what rational people would consent to—what the "rational consensus" would be—becomes the touchstone for analysis of this sort, as developed by such theorists as John Rawls, Robert Nozick, Ronald Dworkin, and Bruce Ackerman. Because people are likely to disagree about many important values, the rights established by reference to the hypo-

thetical "rational consensus" will be basic ground rules for ordering society—
and for conducting future disagreements (149).

What is obscured by these hypothetical procedures is the need to encourage the sharing of some substantive values by members of society while also
encouraging the diversity of substantive values to which they subscribe, especially in a society as culturally pluralistic and rapidly changing as the United
States. Another shortcoming of these hypothetical procedures is that they
give the appearance of including all members of society as equal participants
when, in fact, they exclude or subordinate many members who are considered to be "different" in ways that affect their competence to participate.
This is how Minow explains the exclusive and inegalitarian implications of
such ethical theories: "Social contract theories do not exclude only those
people who lack the requisite mental competence and capacity for reason;
any who would identify themselves as members of groups first, rather than
as autonomous individuals first, would also find their point of view excluded"
(151). As she points out, it is not only that any sign of difference such as
being disabled, female, gay, deviant, or a member of a racial, ethnic, or religious minority may threaten exclusion, subordination, or even degradation;
some types of people and their points of view are tacitly adopted as the norm
for society, and all others are assigned the status of being different. The allocation of rights and obligations reflects these patterns of socially assigned
similarity and difference, of inclusion and exclusion.

From this social relations perspective, there are two pretenses created
by the ethics of obligation. Minow characterizes these as the pretense that
people are already free and equal, and the pretense that we can be neutral
and impartial between individuals (389). When we consider individuals
not in isolation but in the context of their complex and changing social
relations to one another, we can see that some of these are relations
between or among equals, but others are inherently relations of unequals.
For example, friendship or marriage is often a relation between equals, but
there are inherent inequalities in social relations between parents and their
young children, mature children and their aging or infirm parents, teachers and their students, present and future generations, and many others.
Both kinds of social relations exhibit changing patterns of dependence,
mutual dependence, inclusion, exclusion, differential power, vulnerability,
trust, distrust, care, love, hostility, and partiality.

Among the dangers of pretended impartiality is an intolerance for real
differences among people and points of view. Intolerance masquerading as

impartiality is related to another danger, namely, that the state and law will claim to act in the name of the community or the public without being subject to any challenge of this claim. Without effective challenge and, if necessary, rejection of such claims made by governmental officials, what is lacking is a community, in Minow's words, "that acknowledges and admits the historical uses of power to exclude, deny, and silence—and commits itself to enabling suppressed points of view to be heard, to making a covert conflict overt" (389). Not only must members of such a community learn to take the point of view of others who have been defined as socially different; they must come to acknowledge the relational character of people's selves and their social connectedness to one another through their fundamental similarities as well as real differences. Among the many real differences are those of gender, ethnicity, and sexuality that are important in people's self-definition of their own identity.

While criticizing the ethics of obligation, Minow recognizes that rights are an indispensable part of any adequate ethical approach to law. Thus she advocates an ethics of rights-in-social-relations that emphasizes the moral responsibility to take the point of view of others, and especially of those who have suffered the various forms of exclusion, subordination, or degradation resulting from socially defined difference. In negative terms, this is a moral responsibility not to view members of society either as independent subjects of relatively fixed rights or as individuals lacking this status. More positively, it is a responsibility to recognize that all members of society may have claims of right that grow out of their social relations to one another and to their community. These claims of right are no less real for being subject to change and to varying degrees of recognition and legitimation by the community. Minow suggests that we think of these claims of right as a valuable form of discourse that "affirms a particular kind of community; a community dedicated to invigorating words with power to restrain, so that even the powerless can appeal to these words" (299). Here it is good to remind ourselves that the category of the powerless encompasses a wide spectrum of people, including children.

Taking the point of view of others thus involves placing oneself in their position within patterns of changing social relations reflecting socially defined difference among people. This imaginative exchange of social positions and even social selves involves critical reflection as well as empathy. It enables one to appreciate the force of the question Why should these socially defined differences make a difference? To take this question seriously is also to take seriously claims of right to freedom and protection from the injurious effects of these socially defined differences. In this way members and officials of a community can acknowledge and help to overcome the effects of these socially defined differences without employing and thereby reinforcing these very differences in the process. They can reject the assumptions of immutable categories, fixed status, and inherited traits that have provided the basis for defined differences and, at the same time, recognize the rights claims of those who have suffered the effects of these differences.

Not only does the ethics of social relations provide a more defensible account of our moral responsibilities to others than does the ethics of obligation; it also compares favorably in its account of the development of individuality and personal autonomy. Annette Baier, another well-known advocate of the ethics of social relations, rejects the individualistic view that self-identity and individuality are achieved in opposition to society. Baier argues instead that as distinctive persons we are all social creations, for better or worse, depending in part on our moral luck. Individuality, she writes, "is not something a person *has*, which she then chooses relationships to suit, but something that develops out of a series of dependencies and interdependencies, and responses to them."[12] The more these relations of dependency and interdependency are sustained by active concern and care for the well-being of the people involved, the more conducive they are to lifelong development of individuality, self-knowledge, and moral character.

In like manner, the ethics of social relations rejects the individualistic approach to personal autonomy offered by the ethics of obligation. Minow argues that what has traditionally excluded women, children, and members of various minority groups from the category of autonomous persons is a conception of autonomy as independence of others and rational impartiality in moral decision making. As she points out, this individualistic and rationalistic conception neglects the kind of social relations and community that are preconditions for anyone's development of personal autonomy. She contends that such a conception distorts not only autonomy but the competence to exercise rights: "Autonomy, if defined as the condition of an unencumbered and independent self, is a not a precondition of any individual's exercise of rights."[13] She argues instead for a view of the self and personal autonomy as relationally constructed, and dependent for their development on a community that "is willing for the individual to make claims and to participate in the defining and redefining of personal and social boundaries" (301). This view is compatible with the recognition that "people's actions and motives are formed not autonomously but in rela-tionship to others and may even result from failure of others to attend to a person who lands in trouble" (221). Thus judgments of personal responsi-bility for people's character and conduct should be based on how much individual freedom and control, if any, they have been able to exercise within the patterns of social relations that have shaped them.

The upshot of this argument about individuality and personal auton-omy is to give due weight to *social* as well as individual responsibility for people's actions and omissions. These two loci of responsibility are com-plementary rather than being mutually exclusive, and both are necessary components in explaining, evaluating, and responding to our own and other people's conduct. Contrary to the fiction supported by the ethics of obligation that existence can be ultimately just, the view supported by the ethics of social relations emphasizes *equity* rather than justice. A world based on equity is, according to Martha Nussbaum, "a world of imperfect human efforts and of complex obstacles to doing well, a world in which humans sometimes deliberately do wrong, but sometimes also get tripped up by ignorance, passion, poverty, bad education, or circumstantial con-straints of various sort."[14] In such a world, equity in turn opens the way for mercy when this is an appropriate response.

Before we consider how to think about penal practices in light of the contrast I have drawn between the ethics of obligation and the ethics of social relations, it may be useful to explain briefly some of the practical implications of the social relations approach. These implications, as we should expect, are very different from the practical implications of the ethics of obligation. As already indicated, normative concepts such as rights, obligations, individual moral agents, social relations, individual autonomy, communities, and justice may appear to be similar in the two approaches, but in fact they are quite distinct in their meaning and practi-cal implications.

For example, rights and the obligations correlated with them figure in the ethics of social relations as only two of several different kinds of ethical con-siderations, and other kinds may be more relevant or important in many sit-uations. A case in point is an empirical study cited by Michael Tonry, showing that the probability of being arrested for a nontrivial crime by age eighteen ranges from 80 percent or higher for some groups to 5 percent or lower for other groups.[15] As he points out, citing the offenders' bad moral character is a glib and patently inadequate basis for explaining these differential rates of crime or allocating responsibility for crimes. In this case, emphasizing the rights and obligations that have been violated and the blame and punishment that should be imposed would leave out a much more important ethical consideration. This consideration is the prevailing patterns of social relations that result in very unequal chances among the young of being criminalized, often for life. Insensitivity to this ethical consideration obscures the widening gap between the freedom, quality of life, and social prospects of the more powerful and less powerful groups in society.

This example also shows why the social relations approach does not face the practical dilemma confronting the ethics of obligation, of trying to justify both equal and special treatment of people in such practices as affirmative action, prosecution, and criminal sentencing. The relational approach is based on the assumption that all people live within networks of social relations that determine how they as individuals and groups are treated. Prevailing social relations have many beneficial or adverse effects, one of the latter being to reinforce people's prejudices about other people who differ from them. This has the further effect of making people's status and prospects in society seem fixed and their socially attributed differences seem inherent and unchangeable. The strength of the ethics of social relations is that it encourages us to challenge social structures based on beliefs in people's fixed status and inherent differences as if these were beyond all choice. By recognizing that these social relations and the institutions that incorporate them are results of cumulative individual and collective *choices*, we can demand more than incremental changes toward merely formal equality that leave most social inequalities still in place. The ethics of social relations points the way to overcoming social inequalities based on socially attributed differences that are made important by human choices.

Penalty and Obligation

As I have already suggested, penal practices find their strongest normative support in the ethics of obligation. This approach to ethics makes the upholding of relatively fixed obligations and rights the central defining feature of morality and law. Compared to the ethics of social relations, the ethics of obligation is more "principled" and "objective" in the sense that it is based on more abstract, impersonal, simplified, and idealized conceptions of what people are like, how they as agents are related to their conduct, and how they are socially related to one another. Where the ethics of obligation is the dominant ethical orientation, one of the practical and cultural consequences has been reliance on penal practices in efforts to maintain moral, political, and legal authority in societies. Especially evident has been an escalating reliance on criminal punishment in many societies for at least two reasons. One is the growing challenge to moral, political, and legal authority in societies that are becoming more culturally conscious and diverse and, partly for this reason, also more perceptibly unequal in socioeconomic and political terms. A second and related reason for increasing reliance on criminal punishment is the social imperative to control crime—especially the kinds and rates of crime that call into question the effectiveness if not the legitimacy of existing authority.

An important cultural effect as well as cause of this growing reliance on punishment is the development of a punitive social climate. This was confirmed by the astute observation of Frank Rich cited earlier: "The world has become a place where no *good* deed, let alone bad one, goes unpunished." We live in a world where more and more people are threatened by some kind of formal or informal punitive response if they act in ways they reasonably consider to be morally best, or good, or right. This includes being a whistleblower, exhibiting creative work, being dedicated to children and their upbringing, getting an abortion, acting out of concern for the quality of life of future generations—and this list can be extended indefinitely. It has become a commonplace in our society to blame and punish the victims of moral, civil, and criminal wrongs. This is a consequence in part of reliance on a blaming system together with a belief that human existence is ultimately just. This makes it seem necessary in the case of every wrong for *someone* to be blamed and punished. Moreover, as more and more people experience the erosion of protection from crime and other violations of obligations and rights, the zeal to punish impels them to engage in practices that penalize the innocent as well as the guilty. Accompanying this expansion of punitive practices is a greater willingness to express publicly what David Garland has referred to as "punitive passions," which, he writes, "are elicited and evoked, trained and organized, by the very institutional practices which they come to support."[16]

From the perspective of the ethics of social relations, reliance on individualistic criminalization and punishment to maintain authority and counteract crime gives rise to a complex institution that is at war with itself and with the larger society it is expected to serve. The more powerful and pervasive this institution becomes, the more it isolates and excludes individuals and thereby weakens the moral and social influence of intermediate groups between the individual and the state.[17] This in turn makes the apparent need for expanded punishment self-fulfilling, as intermediate groups, from the family and schools to the community as a whole, lose their capacity to induce social cooperation among their members. Commenting on this paradox at the heart of the reliance on criminal punishment, David Garland points out that "it is only the mainstream processes of socialization (internalized morality and the sense of duty, the informal inducements and rewards of conformity, the practical and cultural networks of mutual expectation and interdependence, etc.) which are able to promote proper conduct on a consistent and regular basis."[18] As a result, he argues, "punishment is fated never to 'succeed' to any great degree because the conditions that do most to induce conformity—or to promote crime and deviance—lie outside the jurisdiction of penal institutions" (289). From this argument Garland draws the practical conclusion that a society "which intends to promote disciplined conduct and social control will concentrate not upon punishing offenders but upon socializing and integrating young citizens—a work of social justice and moral education rather than penal policy" (292).

Justifying a reliance on criminal punishment is made even more difficult by two other paradoxes that appear to be inherent in this institution. From the perspective of the ethics of obligation, punishment is considered to be practically necessary to the maintenance of moral, political, and legal authority. However, punishment cannot *create* authority that does not already exist in a society. The weaker these kinds of authority in a society, the more it relies on punishment to bolster that authority and maintain social control. As it happens, these are the social conditions in which punishment is least effective in achieving these social purposes. Indeed, reliance on punishment may only exacerbate the problems of weak authority and social control. Paradoxically, a society that enjoys strong and legitimate authority has little actual need to rely on punishment.[19]

A second paradox is that punishment can be, at the same time, practically necessary for the maintenance of a form of authority and yet very limited or even self-defeating as an institution for controlling crime. Garland argues that this combination of traits is what makes punishment *tragic*.[20] He claims that attempted philosophical justifications of punishment—whether based on the Enlightenment belief that punishment can perform a positive, utilitarian role or the retributive belief in a redemptive moral community—have obscured this intrinsically tragic character of the institution. Thinking about punishment as intrinsically tragic helps us appreciate Garland's description of it as a civil war in miniature between a state and its citizens. The lesson he draws is this: "However well it is organized, and however humanely administered, punishment is inescapably marked by moral contradiction and unwanted irony—as when it seeks to uphold freedom by means of its deprivation, or condemns private violence using a violence which is publicly authorized" (292). He might have added the further ironies that punishment condemns killing by authorizing execution and excludes and deprives mostly those who are already victims of social exclusion and deprivation.

Thinking about punishment in the way defended in this article should make us, at the very least, as open-minded about its justifiability as Nicola Lacey was when she wrote: "I *do* suppose that we can reach a threshold where the arguments for punishment have become too pale a reflection of the ideal conception to provide a justification, or indeed where they have run out altogether, and where punishing and even threatening to punish become straightforwardly morally wrong."[21] I argue that we have already reached this threshold, and that the various arguments for punishment have been strained to the breaking point by the relentless expansion of penal practices far beyond any reasonable limit of practical necessity. We need to consider, along with criminal punishment, other less harmful and costly ways in which a community or society can respond to the whole spectrum of violations of people's changing claims of right. This spectrum should include and give due weight to all categories of criminal violations, and especially categories that have been persistently neglected in the past. These include violations directed against people's sex, gender, race, class, ethnicity, sexuality, age, religion, and other social differences. Due recognition must also be given to the seriousness of white-collar, corporate, and governmental criminal violations. The relative neglect of these categories of criminal violations helps explain why punishment has been used disproportionately against the poor, the powerless, the marginalized, and the uneducated in our society.

David Garland argues that any *justifiable* social response to the complex problems of maintaining authority and controlling crime must conform, as far as possible, to people's "deeply held conceptions of what kind of people they are, how they wish to be governed, and what kind of society they wish to create."[22] Even if we assume diversity among these deeply held conceptions, as we should, they are very much in conflict with the institution of criminal punishment, and especially with its increasing reliance on imprisonment (not to mention capital punishment in the United States). Gar-land sheds further light on this conflict by explaining the tacit complicity through which penal institutions are able to sustain public support for even the most degrading forms of punishment: "In an era when corporal pun-ishment has become uncivilized, and open violence unconscionable, the prison supplies a subtle, situational form of violence against the person which enables retribution to be inflicted in a way which is sufficiently dis-creet and 'deniable' to be culturally acceptable to most of the population."[23] This explanation also shows how the state's authority to punish its citizens is subtly transformed into the authority to oppress them. Criminal punish-ment inevitably tends to weaken the standards we expect the state to meet in its exercise of power over its citizens.

Conclusion

Even if I have shown—or at least raised serious doubts—that the institution of criminal punishment is ethically, politically, and legally unjustifiable, the question remains whether this institution is a *necessary* evil in practice. To respond to this challenging question in the manner it deserves would require at least another chapter. Here I can only point the way to responding to this question by offering a few concluding suggestions. One of the strengths of the ethics of rights-in-social-relations is that it locates the responsibility for most of our social successes and failures in people acting and living within established patterns of social relations—especially within institutions such as the law, families, the various agencies of the state, and various corporate entities. This ethical approach asks us to question institutional practices based on norms used to classify people as socially different, deviant, less valu-able, or expendable. Further, this approach asks us to take the social posi-tion and perspective of other people, and especially of others who are adversely affected by institutionalized practices of exclusion and inclusion. The argument of the relational approach is that only in this way can we rec-ognize our own and other people's partiality and distinguish between bene-ficial and harmful partiality in our social relations to one another.

If we adopt the ethical perspective of rights-in-social-relations we can see more clearly why a society concerned about protecting all of its members from violations of their claims of right should rely on institutions other than crim-inal punishment. Changing and strengthening families, health-care institu-tions, child-care institutions, preschool and more advanced educational institutions, economic institutions, and community governance institutions will clearly pay much higher personal and social dividends for the same social investment than will the attempt to expand and strengthen the institution of criminal punishment. If this approach does not in practice reduce the incidence and harm of criminal violations to socially acceptable levels, the ethics of rights-in-social-relations would challenge us to devise new institutional arrangements and communities through which nonpunitive, nonviolent, and restorative criminal justice can be achieved.

As an alternative to the institution of criminal punishment and penal practices generally, volunteer- and publicly supported mediation between convicted offenders and victims or survivors of crime holds much promise as a practical application of the ethics of social relations. Institutions offering this kind of mediation can be effective only if participation in them is completely voluntary, but—unlike prevailing criminal justice institutions—they offer real opportunities for the people most affected by a crime to gain an understanding of the motivations and the social context of the crime, its personal and social consequences, and the kinds of individual and social redress that are most appropriate as responses to the crime. Advocates of these institutions offer two main reasons that they should be available everywhere as genuine alternatives to punitive responses to crime. The first is that criminal punishment is largely a symbolic, negative response to crime that "allows offenders to escape true responsibility for their crimes by allowing them to repay their so-called debt to society in a worthless currency of personal deprivation."[24] The second reason is that "mediation is also about the responsibility of communities for consuming their own smoke; by dealing with both victims and offenders it lets both of them play proper parts in the communities in which they live." Even if these institutions offering the alternative of mediation are not applicable to all crimes and the people affected by them, they give us good reason to think that institutions inspired by the ethics of social relations can effectively replace the institution of criminal punishment. They provide a model for giving due weight to ethical considerations of rights in contexts of social relations that are essential to understanding, explaining, and responding appropriately to criminal conduct. They also provide a model for tempering criminal justice with equity and, when appropriate, with mercy.

Strong support for this approach comes from other quarters as well. For example, in a rare collaboration between a criminologist and a philosopher, John Braithwaite and Philip Pettit have argued that "most human action which fits criminal categories is best dealt with by refraining from invoking a punitive response."[25] To support this claim, they defend a holistic and pragmatic theory of criminal justice that shows how we can gradually free ourselves from reliance on penal practices. They offer independent confirmation that the institution of criminal punishment, far from being justifiable, is not even a necessary evil.

Notes

1. Richard Rorty, *Contingency, Irony, and Solidarity* (Cambridge: Cambridge University Press, 1989), 9.

2. Ibid., 20.

3. Nicola Lacey, *State Punishment* (London: Routledge, 1988), 198.

4. David Garland and Peter Young, "Towards a Social Analysis of Penality," in *The Power to Punish*, ed. David Garland and Peter Young (London: Heinemann, 1983), 1–36, at 11.

5. *New York Times*, October 27, 1989, 13 (my emphasis).

6. Kent Greenawalt, *Law and Objectivity* (New York: Oxford University Press, 1992), 155–59.

7. In this regard Plato, though not a proponent of the ethics of obligation, was even more ahead of his time. How much more is revealed by John Rawls's assumption that the typical family will have only one "head of household," a lapse pointed out by Annette Baier, in "The Need for More than Justice," in *Science, Morality and Feminist Theory*, ed. Marsha Hanen and Kai Nielsen (Calgary: University of Calgary Press, 1987), 51.

8. Bernard Williams, *Ethics and the Limits of Philosophy* (Cambridge: Harvard University Press, 1985), chap. 10.

9. Michael Tonry, *Malign Neglect: Race, Crime, and Punishment in America* (New York: Oxford University Press, 1995), 180.

10. Ibid., 192.

11. Martha Minow, *Making All the Difference: Inclusion, Exclusion, and American Law* (Ithaca: Cornell University Press, 1990), esp. chap. 6.

12. Annette Baier, "What Do Women Want in a Moral Theory?" *Nous* 19 (1985): 49 (her emphasis).

13. Minow, *Making All the Difference*, 301.

14. Martha Nussbaum, "Equity and Mercy," *Philosophy and Public Affairs* 22 (1993): 91–92.

15. Tonry, *Malign Neglect*, 139.

16. David Garland, *Punishment and Modern Society* (Chicago: University of Chicago Press, 1990), 67.

17. See John Braithwaite, *Crime, Shame, and Reintegration* (Cambridge: Cambridge University Press, 1989), 88, for a discussion of this point.

18. Garland, *Punishment and Modern Society*, 288–89.

19. See ibid., 59–61.

20. See ibid., 80–81.

21. Lacey, *State Punishment*, 197.

22. Garland, *Punishment and Modern Society*, 291.

23. Ibid., 289.

24. Philip Priestly, "Crime without Punishment," *Guardian*, August 24, 1994, 12.

25. John Braithwaite and Philip Pettit, *Not Just Deserts* (Oxford: Clarendon Press, 1992), 2.

Chapter 13

Punishment and Inclusion: The Presuppositions of Corrective Justice in Aristotle and What They Imply

Randall R. Curren

There is a view of Aristotle's conception of corrective justice that has enjoyed some following among tort theorists in recent years, according to which corrective justice is *distinct* from distributive justice and entirely *independent* of it.[1] The distinctness of the two is, of course, asserted by Aristotle in a well-known passage in the *Nicomachean Ethics,* and no one could seriously doubt that he does take the *forms* of these two kinds of justice to be distinct: "What is just in distributions of common assets will always fit the [geometrical] proportion mentioned above. . . . On the other hand, what is just in transactions is certainly equal in a way, and what is unjust is unequal; but still it fits numerical proportion, not the [geometrical] proportion of the other species."[2] He goes on to say that justice in transactions, or corrective justice, "treats the people involved as equals, when one does injustice and the other suffers it," looking "only at differences in the harm," and ignoring the differences in merit between the two parties that would be determinative in distributive justice (1132a3–6).

It seems to be widely assumed that this formal distinction between distributive and corrective justice precludes any substantial relationship between the two, and various conclusions are then drawn from this. The authority of this Aristotelian notion of corrective justice is invoked in one way or another in support of a private law conception of tort liability, in opposition to any vision of it as an instrument of public policy through

Chapter 13 originally appeared as "Punishent and Inclusion: The Presuppositions of Corrective Justice in Aristotle and What They Imply," *Canadian Journal of Law and Jurisprudence* 8 (1995): 259–74.

which larger distributive aims might be promoted. "Aristotle's account stands opposed to . . . the utopianism of the social reformer, the economic calculations of the maximizer of efficiency, and the romantic nihilism of those who proclaim that law is dead," says Weinrib,[3] referring in turn to Unger,[4] Posner,[5] and Kairys.[6] Not so far removed from this is Richard Epstein's well-known attempt to invoke the notion of corrective justice on behalf of a private law conception of torts, with the apparent aim of sharply limiting corporate liability.[7] Posner, in turn, has argued that Aristotle's view is in fact essentially compatible with his own economic theory of law,[8] but his scholarship has not been compelling enough to alter the impression that Aristotle's notion of corrective justice implies a private law conception of torts and stands opposed to a progressive politics of law.

What is rather remarkable about all of this, apart from the generally cavalier and, in the case of Weinrib, obscure treatment of the Aristotelian texts, is how little it has been recognized that Aristotle's formal distinction between distributive and corrective justice does not preclude his holding that there are varieties of corrective justice that presuppose forms of distributive justice. It is generally *assumed* that formal distinctness entails normative independence, but clearly it does not. For all Aristotle says about the nature of corrective justice, he might nevertheless hold that imposing at least some kinds of sanctions is inappropriate unless certain forms of distributive justice have been attained.

Weinrib's argument is that "the irreducible unity of a transaction disqualifies the possibility of an instrumental understanding of private law,"[9] but this assumes incorrectly that what may be interpreted as a transaction can never also be interpreted as a distribution. The argument is, in any case, neither Aristotle's nor Aristotelian in spirit, and it ignores the larger context of Aristotle's legal thought and the purposes he thinks law should serve. It ignores the fact that for Aristotle *all* law is an instrument of political rule, and none of it *private* in the modern sense that Weinrib intends. Indeed, it is clear that Aristotle had no such distinction in mind as the modern one between criminal law and torts, and that everything he says about corrective justice might just as reasonably be applied to our criminal law.[10] It is a bit odd, then, that recent attention to Aristotle's remarks about corrective justice has occupied itself so single-mindedly with applications in the law of torts.

Although Aristotle would not have called corrective justice an "instrument of public policy," he did regard law in general as one of the two fundamental tools of the legislator's craft, and he thought that legislators should exploit its full potential in pursuing the state's natural aims. He took those aims to be the resolution and elimination of conflict,[11] including most particularly the ever-present conflict between rich and poor, and the pursuit of the goodness and well-being of all citizens.[12] He assumed that those aims could be promoted in part through laws that were implemented or enforced, as the Athenian homicide code was,[13] through privately initiated actions. Thus, if my purpose here were to develop a theory of torts consistent with Aristotle's view of the larger purposes of the law concerned with "involuntary transactions" or interpersonal harms, I would connect the idea of restoring "equality" between the two parties to an involuntary transaction not with the troubled notion of making the aggrieved party "whole again" through compensation but, rather, with the goal of resolving conflict, and with the ancient notion that anger may be appeased and "vengeance bought off."[14] I would also press the claim that the notion of "restoring equality" was itself a quite progressive one not long before Aristotle's time, inasmuch as it introduced a range of protected rights held by rich and poor alike, and thereby rejected forms of aristocratic privilege that had been common before the democratic reforms of Solon. This is a project for another occasion, however.

My concern here is not with torts but with criminal law, and what I will try to show is that Aristotle did not regard corrective and distributive justice as entirely independent, and that his view of the connections between them provides the materials for a radical critique of criminal law as we know it. A reasonable case can be made for his having adopted the view of political and legal authority developed by Plato in the *Laws*, and for his recognizing the conditions for just punishment imposed by that view. It is a view on which corrective justice in what we would call the criminal domain is morally grounded in a kind of distributive justice.

My aim here is thus partly interpretive, but I shall be concerned as much with the implications of the view that I attribute to Aristotle as with the grounds for attributing it to him. Given this division of labor, and the space that a thorough treatment of the interpretive issues would fill, I will confine myself to arguing the historical case in a more summary fashion than I would ordinarily wish to. Ideally, I would wish to demonstrate that one can mount on Aristotelian premises a radical and plausible critique of present systems of criminal punishment, but a more realistic hope for the present is to show that it is plausible that Aristotle held beliefs that could sustain such a critique. By a "radical" critique, I mean one that reveals deficiencies in the foundations of a fundamental social institution or practice, those deficiencies being serious enough to at least threaten the legitimacy of its continuing to exist without significant modification.

I

Michael Philips pointed out, in "The Justification of Punishment and the Justification of Political Authority," that "the theory of punishment is importantly connected with the theory of state authority" because "the moral justification of punishment by the state is obviously importantly connected to the moral justification of the state's authority."[15] He noted, quite aptly, that the full significance of this has received little notice in recent work on the justification of punishment. It was recognized by Kant, Hegel, Marx, and other eighteenth- and nineteenth-century thinkers, however, and I'll argue here that it was recognized by Plato, and in turn by Aristotle, to a remarkable degree.[16]

Law and education were intimately linked in Greek thought,[17] and in Plato's hands they are both linked to a theory of legitimate state authority. The rule of law must be established as much through education as through mechanisms of oversight and public accountability, in Plato's view, and to claim this is for him not only to acknowledge the practical impossibility of establishing compliance with law through the mechanisms of law enforcement—of coercion—alone but to recognize something important about the foundations of legitimate state authority. I'll summarize what I take that important something to be before turning in the remainder of this section and the next to the grounds for thinking that Plato and Aristotle recognized it.

The threat of punishment may be required to create and preserve the rule of law, but punishment also *presupposes* a rule of law and thus a background of good-faith effort to establish a rule of law through such noncoercive and largely educational measures as may be reasonably thought sufficient to establish civil order.[18] In the absence of those measures, the legitimacy of speaking of the enforcement *of law* would be in doubt, and so there arise issues of fundamental importance regarding the content and scope of distribution of the education that is necessary to establishing the norms of public life and inducing individuals to comply (or initiating them into compliance) with those norms. Since compliance with law is ineluctably a de jure condition for uninterrupted enjoyment of a range of important goods and rights, and since compliance is likely to be substantially causally influenced by preparation for compliance, the distribution of such preparation or education must be viewed as an important issue of distributive justice. Thus, corrective justice may presuppose a form of distributive justice, that is, a just distribution of goods of a sort that are essential to becoming and remaining a full member of the society bound by the law to be enforced. Putting it bluntly, the suggestion is that there may be failures to include individuals in full membership in society, to initiate them into the compliance with law that is a condition for full membership, that are so serious as to make *punishment* morally improper even in the face of serious violations of law.

The argument of Plato's *Laws* begins with a view of the foundations of legitimate authority. The grounds on which authority is claimed are several, Plato says, but the most widespread is the claim of the stronger to rule the weaker (690B), and the most in accordance with nature is the "natural rule of law, without force, over willing subjects," administered by men and women (804e–805a) of practical wisdom.[19] The conclusion that the latter is the only legitimate ground of political authority is defended with an argument (running from 683B to 693D, and repeated in a somewhat different form at 693D–702A) grounded in purportedly empirical claims about what is conducive to preserving constitutional order. Conduciveness to constitutional stability serves here as a test of what is natural, and naturalness serves as the test of legitimacy.

A few pages later in Book IV Plato poses the question of whether it is not the case that when the stronger rule by superior force, they punish those who fail to do the things they have named as just (714D), and he announces in response a few lines later (715B) that those who rule in this way and stipulate laws that are not in the common interest produce ordinances that are just in name only. The clear implication is that these so-called laws have no legitimate claim to be obeyed or enforced. What follows then, by way of spelling out what is involved in legitimate rule, must be understood in part as an elaboration of the necessary conditions for just enforcement of law, even though Plato's view of punishment is that it is most often (though not always) intended to be educative or a "therapy for the soul." As he says at 718B, the laws themselves will show one how to order one's life through persuasion, and *when noncoercive forms of persuasion fail*, "when dispositions are recalcitrant–[they] will persuade by just and forceful punishment."

It is in describing what is involved in proper persuasion that Plato then reveals his view of the place of public instruction in proper legislation. The first element of this view is built on the idea that rational self-control develops only under certain favorable conditions, and so cannot be presupposed but instead must be conscientiously cultivated if legislation is to have any social effect. At *Laws* 644–645 he suggests that it is the work of education to make people generally receptive to reason and law, and he suggests that without proper education it is *unlikely* that conformity with reason and law will be very widespread.

The second major element of his view is the claim that laws should be presented and prefaced in a way that will "make the one who listens . . . more agreeable and a better learner." This idea is pursued in Book IV through the elaboration of two models of medicine and legislating, and the notion that the laws should be preceded by "preludes." These two models of medicine correspond to the two grounds for claiming authority already invoked, and serve to sharpen the contrast and make it more vivid. The kind of doctor who does not follow nature, he says, does not "give or receive any account of the illness afflicting" the patient, whereas the better kind "investigates [illnesses] from their beginning and according to nature, communing with the patient himself and his friends, and he both learns something himself from the individuals and, as much as he can, teaches the one who is sick. He doesn't give orders until he has in some sense persuaded; when he has on each occasion tamed the sick person with persuasion, he attempts to succeed in leading him back to health" (720D).

This superior "double method" of the doctor who acts from knowledge and with the informed consent of the patient is then illustrated in the domain of legislation by contrasting (at 721A–D) a law set down as a simple command and threat of punishment, the threat being the only reason of any kind given for obeying, with a law preceded by a "prelude" that explains the rationale for it, "so that he who receives the law uttered by the legislator might receive the command—that is, the law—in a frame of mind more favorably disposed and therefore more apt to learn something" (723A–B). These preludes must precede not only the laws as a whole but each of them individually, Plato insists (723B), and it seems to be largely through this means and the education for conformity to reason already mentioned, that the legislator will endeavor to earn the consent of the citizens to his or her rule.

The laws and their preludes will not be merely announced and written down, however. Plato envisions the instructional dimensions of legislating as appropriately carried out by publicly appointed teachers (804C–D), who will evidently inherit much of the burden of the good legislator to "commun[e] with [each youth] himself and his friends, . . . learn[ing] something himself from [them], and . . . taming [each] with persuasion," in order to induce a sympathetic acceptance of law, and self-discipline in accordance with law. The teacher's job, in a sense, is to make the case for a youth's becoming a member or citizen of his or her community, bound by the norms of that community, and the teacher is to do this by "communing"—by creating the personal bonds of friendship and trust that must inevitably precede an acceptance of those norms.[20]

Plato provides us in this way, and through the ideas of judicial oversight and governmental accountability, with not only a natural law account of the proper substance of law but also, and more interestingly, a structural or formal account of the elements of a true rule of law, one aspect of this being a model for how to take the notion of rule by consent seriously. On this model hypothetical consent, if that means only the worthiness of law to command respect and assent, is not enough to create a just rule of law, if people are not at least moderately rational and well-informed about the rationales for laws and the probable consequences of compliance, or if they are unable to *trust* those who would so inform them. Indeed, the idea seems to be that a legitimate rule of law rests in *real* and *ongoing* consent, if only tacit, arising from informed and reasoned choice. He reiterates at several junctures the necessity of putting persuasion before threats and punishment (718B; 727C; 783D; 880A; 907D), and indicates most explicitly in his "prelude" to the law of capital offenses and the remarks following it (853B–854E) that punishment presupposes reasonable efforts on the legislator's part to provide suitable education.

II

The tone of Aristotle's "philosophy of human affairs" is, as Weinrib suggests, not utopian, but it is reformist and very practical in its insistence that proposals for reform be feasible and presented in such a manner that the leaders who are being advised will be easily persuaded (*Pol.* 1289a1–4). He divides regimes, just as Plato does in his arguments from stability (683B–702A), into those that govern by consent and aim at the common good, and those that rule by force and aim at the private good of those in power (*Pol.* 3. 6–9, and *Pol.* 3–5 generally; cf. also *NE* 1129b15–20), and he offers to each an argument for reform that engages the ends it has. To the morally serious, who do or intend to rule in the common interest, he offers arguments that connect reform with the promotion of *eudaimonia* or human well-being (in *Pol.* 1–3 and 7–8), and to those who may care only about promoting their own interests through staying in power, he offers arguments that connect reform with the preservation of rule (in 4–5).[21] These latter arguments are clearly directly inspired by Plato's arguments from what preserves the state in the *Laws*, and differ from them primarily in being grounded in Aristotle's systematic study of actual constitutions. They are seriously empirical, rather than essentially mythological, as Plato's are. They also lay out a series of increasingly ambitious reforms, which Plato's do not, but the similarities are striking, and it seems to be essentially the same view of legitimate rule that is being defended by these two very similar trains of argument.

Given the two distinct audiences Aristotle wished to persuade, and the corresponding motives presumed by his own two streams of argument, there would have been little point in his making much of the idea that the justice of punishment rests on morally weighty assumptions. Because he conceived of the form of inquiry he was engaged in as essentially practical in its intent, the point would have been of primarily theoretical—and thus secondary—interest, and mooted by a more fundamental insistence on reforms that would move unjust regimes toward a form of rule that is not only "moderate," or in the "middle" between forcible domination of the poor by the rich and forcible domination of the rich by the poor (*Pol.* 4.11; cf. *Laws* 693D–E), but in which consent, the common good, and the bonds of mutual trust and goodwill are effectively promoted (*Pol.* 1285a27–28; 5.11; *NE* 1155b31–34, 1155a23–28, 1157a21–25).

Nevertheless, in addition to the many signs of Aristotle's endorsing the Platonic view of legitimate state authority, he does explicitly acknowledge the futility of laying down law without educating children for acceptance of it (*Pol.* 1310a15–18), and he echoes, in his treatment of responsibility in *NE* 3.5, the Platonic acknowledgment that punishment presupposes a background of reasonable effort by the state. Aristotle's treatment of responsibility for character in 3.5 (1114a3ff.) has been criticized for ignoring the role of upbringing and education in its apparent insistence that people are all free to acquire voluntarily whatever state of character they wish, yet he makes it clear both in *NE* 10.9 and throughout the *Politics* that he regards proper nurture and education as *necessary* conditions for virtue.[22] In *NE* 3.5 itself (at 1114a15–16) he invokes the image of bringing ruin upon oneself through indulgent living in defiance of one's doctor's orders, and we must assume that he intends medical art as no less a model for legislative art in this instance than in others.[23] Occurring as it does in the context of a discussion of the appropriate conditions for blame, it is strongly suggestive of similar clauses in *Laws* 727C, in the prelude to the laws as a whole ("when he delights in pleasures contrary to the advice and praise given by the lawgiver"), and 853B, in the prelude to the law of capital offenses, with its specific reference to the education the accused is presumed to have enjoyed.

There are, in addition, a rather startling number of thematic elements shared by *NE* 3.5 and *Laws* 644B–646D, with the Platonic insistence that education is essential if people are to become rational, autonomous, and law-abiding, making 3.5 a rather good example of what commentators have had in mind in suggesting that Aristotle wrote his moral and political works "with the *Laws* open at his fingertips."[24] Evidence of borrowing does not prove, of course, that Aristotle was happy with every aspect of what he borrowed from, but given his general eagerness to point out his departures from the views of his former teacher, a borrowing of this richness that lacks any overt departures from the original is reasonably good evidence of agreement.

This leaves untouched a rather dense thicket of interpretive issues that cannot be addressed here, but it suggests that Aristotle may well have accepted all of the essential elements of the view of political authority and just punishment that I have attributed to Plato. If indeed he did, which I think likely, then he did regard corrective justice as resting on a just distribution of a range of social goods that contribute to the acquisition of virtue and self-control.

III

What rationally compelling implications this Platonic, and arguably Aristotelian, view of legitimate punishment may have for contemporary law is not altogether clear, of course, given the uncertain identity of the normative principles underlying it. The question for us now, therefore, is what those principles might be.

What is left of the two principal components of the view of authority I have described here, when we set aside for present purposes the natural law test of the substance of law, is a rather rich notion of consent, and the idea that consent of this sort is a requirement for legitimate law and enforcement of law. We must assume that the view is that moral responsibility for a legally proscribed wrong is not sufficient grounds for the state's imposition of punishment, and there is nothing remarkable about this because the right to punish, as it is normally claimed by governments, is patently relational to begin with. It applies only to actors and conduct within the jurisdictional authority of the laws to be enforced.

A reasonable course for us to take, then, is to consider how much of this notion of consent might be salvaged, supposing that we might be able to agree that consent is necessary for the law to have authority. A sympathetic line to take would be to try to identify the conditions that would be necessary for consent to be genuine, or free, or properly informed, and taking this line, one might well agree that meaningful popular authorization of law would require some of the very things Plato insists on. It might include not only publication of the reasons for the laws being as they are but also education that would by and large enable people to appreciate and assess the force of those reasons. Without the first condition, consent would not be properly informed, one might insist, and without the latter condition, consent would not be fully competent and not fully free, in one important sense of the word "free." It would not be free, in precisely the sense that one would lack the capacity to be rationally self-determining in the relevant domain of choice.

This line of thinking may be summed up by distinguishing three forms of consent. The first is "simple consent," or consent that is merely voluntary, in the sense of noncoerced. Consent theories in the classical liberal mold, when they rely on a notion of real consent, whether "express" or "tacit," might *seem* to have simple consent in mind, though it is not so clear that they really do. The second form of consent is "informed consent," by which I mean consent given to something that one knows not only the essential features of but also the reasons held to favor it, and with knowledge of the alternatives that there are known good reasons to consider. The typical supposition about adults negotiating an original contract is that these conditions are actually met, I take it. The third form of consent, with its assumptions of adequate information and rational ability, I'll call "rational consent." Rational consent would reflect people's interests with as much reliability as can be guaranteed by reasonable educative efforts, aimed not only to inform but to cultivate abilities to reason and judge.[25]

There is a good deal to be said for this notion of rational consent because it is a fair approximation of the kind of consent we should rationally prefer to be giving, when we give our consent. In some sense we would all like to be perfectly rational and to give our consent only when it is perfectly rational for us to do so, but only, I take it, if coming to be this rational were without cost. Surely it would not be, however, so the kind of consent we should rationally wish to give is consent that is as rational as it could be made to be by an education that enhances rationality up to, but not beyond, the point at which the marginal cost to us of that education ceases to pay for itself through the marginal gains in rationality it is likely to yield.

Moreover, on classical liberal assumptions about the natural course of development of a person's powers of reason, the conditions for this kind of consent would seem to be met by adult original contractors. The Platonic-Aristotelian view may then be rather more like a classical liberal view than it might first seem to be, the principal differences arising from the former's less optimistic view of the likelihood of a person's coming to possess a rational will without substantial educational efforts, and from its notion that authority rests in real, ongoing consent.

The notion that reason, virtue, and self-control are *attainments* that individuals do not have the wherewithal to secure through their own unaided powers is an aspect of the Platonic-Aristotelian account that may be understood to have significance beyond any connection it may have with the notion of consent, however. The view that these attributes are attainments of this sort seems to me correct, and it suggests a principle to the effect that if it is the community's fault that a person turns out badly, then the authority of the community cannot be invoked in blaming that person for the harms that come about owing to his or her badness. Neither Plato nor Aristotle *says* this in quite so many words, of course, but it has the advantage of being a morally sound principle, namely, a principle of "noncomplicity." Given the community's power to influence behavior, there is a burden of care it must bear in seeking to establish a rule of law. Its authority to blame must be *established* through its own good faith efforts, on this principle, and the scope of that authority may be considered to be limited to those it has taken reasonable care to incorporate into the life of the community, in accordance with its requirements but also in the enjoyment of those "condition[s] favorable to the practice of virtue."

We normally assume that moral responsibility is a sufficient condition for imposing the sanctions of moral censure, but this seems to me rather implausible in general, and the present claim in particular is that there is a speaker-relative constraint on the appropriateness of blame, and not just actor-relative constraints (the "actor" being in a legal context the defendant). Blame or moral censure is undeniably an important aspect of actual criminal proceedings and punishment,[26] and so criminal punishment as we know and practice it would seem to be precluded when blame is precluded. This is not to say that when the conditions for rational consent are met but the conditions for noncomplicity are not met, that our hands are completely morally tied and all effective avenues to security closed. It is to say, instead, that we need to find different ways of responding to and (better yet) preventing crime. If we are in no position to blame, and so no position to punish, we may nevertheless claim a right of self-defense and find alternative means through which to exercise that right. Even conceding this, however, might straddle us with a need for very extensive reform.

The principle of noncomplicity has enjoyed no small acceptance among philosophers of the Western tradition, though most notably in connection with the theological problem of evil.[27] The question that is of crucial importance in understanding its implications for secular moral judgments and the sanctions of both morality and law is what would properly count as a good faith effort, or by contrast, an effort that is so deficient that the individual's badness may be properly judged the community's fault. The Platonic-Aristotelian suggestion seems to be that initiation into compliance with law must not be left to chance, if the state is to have assurance that it is in the right in bringing criminal penalties to bear on its citizens and residents. More concretely, the view seems to be that those who are to undertake this initiation must proceed by attempting to "commune with" and create relationships of trust with the young, so as to create those conditions in which there is a reasonable chance that they will learn that compliance with law will serve *their* ends and not only those of others, and will accept the principles embodied in law as their own. The young must be drawn into and made part of the community bound together by common law, by a kind of attraction, on the assumption that many of them would be unlikely to become a part of it otherwise. To the extent that something like this is correct, and it does not seem to me very far off the mark, it does give us a measure, if only rough, of what is adequate.

Even in the absence of a well-defined threshold of adequate state investment in the foundations of consent and voluntary compliance, one can identify a problem of fairness in instances where such investments are made inequitably. In the face of seriously unequal efforts to enable those who are growing up to come to a rational acceptance of and compliance with law, what is most reasonable may be the view that it is unfair to let the burden of legal sanctions fall as heavily on those who were not properly prepared to accept law as on those who were. This might be developed through a general notion of "equal protection" of the law, understanding by this a principle of natural justice that might or might not be implied by the equal protection clause of the Fourteenth Amendment to the U.S. Constitution. To the extent that a government must engage in certain activities in order to institute a rule of law in the first place, one might consider it under a general duty to engage in those activities in ways that do not place some individuals more at risk of suffering criminal convictions than others. If it is wrong to police or prosecute one segment of the population more aggressively than another because it unfairly puts the members of that segment at greater risk of conviction, then there is reason to hold that differential investments in moral socialization that influence the likelihood of later criminal activity are also suspect.

IV

What this amounts to, then, is first of all the suggestion that the conditions for one's giving rational consent to the law must be met in order for it to have legitimate jurisdiction over one, and second that the state must not be at fault for one's inclination to engage in crime if one is to be properly punished. If these conditions have not been met, then there is a sense in which appropriate efforts have not been made to make one part of the society whose full privileges are formally and often substantially contingent upon compliance with law. This goes to the substance of public education in the broadest sense, though it does not demand publicly sponsored schools, as Plato and Aristotle both seem to argue, if there are other means of ensuring the universal provision of education with the requisite content. Moreover, it is surely true that a great deal of the burden rests with early upbringing and socialization,[28] so the provisions of family and welfare law, and forms of intervention to assure that every child receives adequate care and socialization are as much to the point as provisions for adequate schooling are. Nor should the importance of other spheres of socialization beyond home and school be ignored. In any case, where efforts to provide the foundations for rational acceptance of the legitimacy of law are widely or entirely absent there would be no law with any legitimate claim on anyone, and where they are lacking only with respect to particular individuals, one would have to regard those individuals as beyond its scope. Further, where people are allowed to turn out substantially less inclined to accept and comply with law than they might have been through reasonable state efforts, those of whom this is true cannot in good faith be blamed or consequently punished by the state. As we have seen, these two lines of thought converge in the idea that a proper acceptance of law supplies both the grounds for consent and the capacity to comply.

These principles are not far removed from those of classical liberalism, and the critique of punishment to which they give rise would rest on some of the same claims of fact that a Marxist critique of punishment would. Accepting Jeffrie Murphy's "Marxism and Retribution" as a suitable guide to the Marxist view, it is readily apparent that there are points of convergence pertaining to both consent and complicity. The latter is evident in Murphy's conclusion that it is unjust "to punish people who act out of those very motives that society encourages and reinforces," and in his suggestion that a good deal of crime may in fact arise from motives encouraged by society, such as "greed, selfishness, and indifference to one's fellows." More broadly, he suggests that "criminals typically are not members of a shared community of values with their jailers," and that this is owing to social and economic inequalities that undermine the social sentiments of sympathetic identification and reciprocity.[29]

Although I would not disagree with either of these claims, the latter seems to me particularly well taken. There is support for it in the substantial case that can be made through comparative criminological studies for the idea that crime rates are influenced both by work-force participation rates, and independently of that by the extent of inequality in a society.[30] Moreover, these are claims about the foundations of social learning of the sorts that are essential to establishing a broad acceptance of law, and I am sympathetic to the idea that at least some industrial nations are doing less toward securing those foundations than they could be reasonably expected to do. I would note, however, that this rests on claims about the prospects for reciprocal feelings of goodwill or sympathy extending across class lines, which is perhaps not directly relevant to the dominant pattern of violent crime in the United States, it being one nation in which aggressors and their victims share low socioeconomic status.[31] So it may be more directly to the point to focus not on the foundations for broad social reciprocity but on whether children have decent people in their lives who care about them enough to enable them to care about themselves and others, and thus to form a significantly motivating attachment to the social morality prescribed by the law. There are arguably many children in the inner cities of the

United States who now lack this, and are brought up not in accordance with the standards of "decent" society but in accordance with a brutal "code of the streets."[32] What can one say of the moral socialization of children in a world where the inculcation of that code does not stop even at killing a five-year-old for refusing to steal, as happened in a public housing project in Chicago recently?[33]

Quite apart from what might be done for such children through providing their parents with better opportunities and assistance, there is evidence of gross failure in the direct socialization undertaken by the state through the medium of public schooling. It is well established, for instance, that students of different socioeconomic status (SES) tend to be "tracked" into very different kinds of classrooms, and that those into which lower-SES students are tracked are distinguished by their lack of trust, cooperation, and goodwill. As Jeannie Oakes concludes in a major study of tracking, "[Observed] differences [in classroom relationships] have a strong potential for leading students differentially either toward affiliation with and active involvement in social institutions or toward alienation from and a more negative involvement in the institutions they encounter."[34] Indeed, there is reason to conclude that the higher incidence of misconduct and criminality among students assigned to lower tracks is in part a consequence of the more hostile climate of the classrooms they are assigned to.[35] This is arguably a good example of a rectifiable inequity in the provision of social goods that ground a rational acceptance of, and compliance with, law.

Turning now from complicity to consent, there are similarities between Murphy's Marxism and the Aristotelian view on this theme as well, but also significant differences arising from their somewhat different conceptions of consent. "Central to the Social Contract idea," says Murphy, "is the claim that we owe allegiance to the law because the benefits we have derived have been voluntarily accepted." They have been voluntarily accepted, the story goes, because "as rational [people], [we] can see that the rules benefit everyone ([ourselves] included) and that [we] would have selected them in the original position of choice," and seeing this we stay and accept those benefits.[36] The basis for critique consists, then, of two claims of fact: that the social classes that produce the larger numbers of criminals do not derive much benefit from the existence of law, and even if they did would lack any means by which to emigrate and thereby forgo those benefits. Thus, on two counts, they could not be properly said to consent to the authority of law by voluntarily accepting its benefits.

What is different in the Aristotelian critique is that it could, but need not, make use of the claim that the body of law in question does not benefit members of disadvantaged classes, and that it need not take emigration to be a necessary condition for withholding consent. Law must aim at the good of all citizens to be just, by Aristotle's standards, but on his account the substantive justice of law has nothing to do with whether anyone has given his or her consent to it. On his view it is not enough that *a rational person* would consent to a body of law, because *instituting* a rule of law requires far more than this. One does not earn consent simply by conceiving of laws that are substantively attractive. It is necessary, in addition, that people *be* rational, which they turn out to be only under favorable circumstances, and that they be appropriately informed. It is necessary, in other words, that they be in a position to give rational consent to the rule of law they are bound by, so even if the laws *are* beneficial to everyone, they lack authority on the Aristotelian view if people have not been prepared to see that. Thus, even without concerning ourselves with the benefits of law to the poor, or what one might accept as a refusal of consent, one can find a basis for critique in the existence of avoidable ignorance and incomprehension of the rational basis for the law. I would cite in this connection some of the same facts noted above, including those that point to a failure to cultivate trust in the credibility of authority figures, and add that deficiencies of intellectual development, low academic attainment, and the use of corporal punishment by parents are important predictors of who will commit criminal offenses.[37] The use of corporal punishment with children is significant in providing them with a model for aggressive behavior and also, insofar as corporal punishment is a style of behavioral management, with a model that *fails to cultivate a responsiveness to reason*.

Beyond this, and closely connected, is the Aristotelian thought, more radical than anything in Marx, that the acquisition of a rational will, of self-control, and of the capacity to comply with law is an attainment that requires timely and very substantial social investments that are far from being universally forthcoming. Several childhood traits predictive of later violent criminality may be described as deficits of rational self-control, namely hyperactivity, impulsivity, and deficits of attention, concentration, and ability to defer gratification.[38] Whatever role genetic factors may play in these traits, they are surely in part learned, and not only remediable through instruction but also preventable to some degree through parental training. Studies of experimental interventions have indeed shown success in improving the self-control and social skills of aggressive children, and in teaching them alternatives to the aggressive behavioral strategies they have typically learned quite early in their lives.[39] To the extent that we know or could learn how to promote effectively the development of rational self-control in children whose families are not up to the task, the burden of the Aristotelian argument is that there is a weighty moral imperative to do so, and that the legitimacy of our systems of criminal punishment rests on doing so.

It is possible, of course, to regard education that inculcates virtue, self-control, and a willingness to obey the law as an oppressive form of social control, but the fact remains that the privileges of full membership in a society governed by law are contingent upon conformity with that law, and conformity is itself an attainment of sorts, which becomes more likely when social investments of the right kind are made, and less likely when those investments are not made. When those investments are deficient or made in a discriminatory manner, and we are faced, as we are in the United States, with crime rates that far exceed those of other industrialized nations[40] and vary widely between the groups in whom we have invested quite differently, we must regard ourselves as faced with gross injustice that no appeal to individual choice can undo.

Notes

1. This corrective justice "school" of thought has included Jules Coleman ("Moral Theories of Torts: Their Scope and Limits: Part II," *Law and Philosophy* 2, [1983]: 5–36; and other works); George Fletcher ("Fairness and Utility in Tort Theory," *Harvard Law Review* 85 [1972]: 537–73); John Borgo ("Causal Paradigms in Tort Law," *Journal of Legal Studies* 8 [1979]: 419–55); Frederick Sharp ("Aristotle, Justice and Enterprise Liability in the Law of Torts," *University of Toronto Faculty of Law Review* 34, [1976]: 84–92); Richard Epstein ("A Theory of Strict Liability," *Journal of Legal Studies* 2 [1973]: 151–221); and most recently Alan Strudler ("Mass Torts And Moral Principles," *Law and Philosophy* 11 [1992]: 297–330). It is Ernest Weinrib, however, who has most studiously defended the idea that Aristotle regards corrective and distributive justice as independent. See particularly his article, "Aristotle's Forms of Justice," in *Justice, Law and Method in Plato and Aristotle*, ed. Spiro Panagiotou (Edmonton: Academic, 1987), 133–57; and "Legal Formalism: On the Immanent Rationality of Law," *Yale Law Journal* 97 (1988): 949–1016.

2. Aristotle, *Nicomachean Ethics*, trans. Terence Irwin (Indianapolis: Hackett, 1985), 1131b28–1132a3–6.

3. Weinrib, "Aristotle's Forms of Justice," 152.

4. Roberto Unger, "The Critical Legal Studies Movement," *Harvard Law Review* 96 (1983): 561–675.

5. Richard Posner, *Economic Analysis of Law,* 2d ed. (Chicago: University of Chicago Press, 1977).

6. David Kairys, ed., *The Politics of Law* (New York: Pantheon, 1982).

7. In Richard Epstein "A Theory of Strict Liability, Nuisance Law: Corrective Justice and Its Utilitarian Constraints," *Journal of Legal Studies* 8 (1979): 49–102; and other works.

8. Richard Posner, "The Concept of Corrective Justice in Recent Theories of Tort Law," *Journal of Legal Studies* 10 (1981): 187–206.

9. Weinrib, "Aristotle's Forms of Justice," 148.

10. In discussing Aristotle's notion of corrective justice, Weinrib writes in "Legal Formalism," 977–78, that "Aristotle observed that what we would now call private law has a special structure of its own." Because Aristotle recognized no category of law corresponding to our private law (rather, only, the sorts of harms that fall under our criminal code but that could be only privately prosecuted under Athenian law), it is quite unclear how he could have made any such observation.

11. There is evidence for this in his concern, evident throughout the *Politics*, that law unite, and not divide, cities, and also in his insistence in 3.1 of the *Nicomachean Ethics* (NE) that an expression of regret for an unintended harm is a necessary condition for escaping legal responsibility. The best explanation for his linking responsibility and regret in this way is that without the expression of goodwill conveyed by regret, even an unintended harm may incite antagonistic feelings and generate conflict.

12. It is clear through much of the *Politics* that having these aims is part of what distinguishes a legitimate form of rule or system of law from a corrupt one. See, e.g., 3.7.

13. It is worth noting that many features of what remains of this code suggest that its fundamental purpose was not to punish or compensate but to resolve conflict. See Michael Gagarin, *Drakon and Early Athenian Homicide Law* (New Haven: Yale University Press, 1981), chap. 8.

14. For a view of this sort, see Steven D. Smith, "The Critics and the 'Crisis': A Reassessment of Current Conceptions of Tort Law," *Cornell Law Review* 72 (1987): 765–98.

15. Michael Philips, "The Justification of Punishment and the Justification of Political Authority," *Law and Philosophy* 5 (1986): 393–416.

16. It was also recognized by Jeffrie Murphy, of course, in "Marxism and Retribution," *Philosophy and Public Affairs* (1973): 218. In the closing section of this paper I will note the points of contact between the Marxist critique, as he presents it, and the radical consequences of an Aristotelian view.

17. See Jacqueline de Romilly, *La Loi dans la penseé Greque* (Paris: Société D'Édition "Les Belles Lettres," 1971), chap. 11.

18. "Educational" measures should be understood here very broadly, so as to include formal schooling but also a great deal more. Noneducational measures might include a reduction in inequality, in order that compliance with law may be attractive to sufficient numbers of people. Plato and Aristotle both make provisions for this, but neither suggests any connection between measures of this sort and the legitimacy of punishment, except perhaps through the idea that legitimate law aims not at the good of one class of citizens but at the common good of all.

19. The translation here is R. G. Bury's (*Plato: The Laws* [Cambridge: Harvard University Press, 1984]). Generally, in what follows the translations of passages from the *Laws* are substantially those in Thomas Pangle, *The Laws of Plato* (Chicago: University of Chicago Press, 1988).

20. Rawls's description in *A Theory of Justice* (Cambridge: Harvard University Press, 1971), 490–91, of the way in which the development of a sense of justice depends upon personal attachments is probably substantially correct. (See Richard M. Ryan and J. Stiller, "The Social Contexts of Internalization," *Advances in Motivation and Achievement* 7 [1991]: 115–49.) His view suggests that social virtue is unlikely to emerge or prevail in the absence of a sense of justice, and a sense of justice is not likely to emerge in a child to whom authority figures (i.e., individuals who represent or manifestly adhere to acceptable principles of social life) do not communicate a clear intention to act for the child's good.

21. I develop this interpretation of the argumentative strategies of the *Politics* at some length in "Justice, Instruction, and the Good: The Case for Public Education in Aristotle and Plato's Laws, Part II" *Studies in Philosophy and Education* 12 (1993): 103–26.

22. As I have argued in "The Contribution of 'Nicomachean Ethics' iii 5 to Aristotle's Theory of Responsibility," *History of Philosophy Quarterly* 6 (1989): 261–77, and at greater length in "Education and the Origins of Character in Aristotle," in *Philosophy of Education, 1991,* ed. Margaret Buchmann and Robert Floden (Urbana: Philosophy of Education Society, 1992), 202–10.

23. On the general extent of his adoption of this Platonic metaphor and model of legislation, see Werner Jaeger, "Aristotle's Use of Medicine as Model of Method in His Ethics," *Journal of Hellenic Studies* 77 (1957): 54–61.

24. The idea is a common one, but the wording is Pierre Pellegrin's, in "On the 'Platonic' Part of Aristotle's *Politics*" (paper delivered at Boston University, January 19, 1992).

25. "Rational consent," as I'm using it here, is thus not *ideally* rational consent. The notion of "*reasonable* educative efforts" introduces some indeterminacy into the idea of "rational consent" that I will not be able to resolve here, given the complexity of what might constitute reasonable education.

26. See R. A. Duff, *Trials and Punishments* (Cambrige: Cambridge University Press, 1986), 39ff.

27. Not insignificantly, it is this theological problem that gave rise to the myth, which descended from Augustine into the Christian Enlightenment, of a radical and innate

"free will." The point I am concerned to establish here is that if we abandon this myth in favor of Plato and Aristotle's more plausible pre-Christian view of the efforts required to produce a good and rational will, then we are faced with a problem not only for theology but for secular human communities as well.

28. See Albert Reiss, Jr., et al., *Understanding and Preventing Violence* (Washington, D.C.: National Academy Press, 1993). Summarizing the findings of a large body of research, Reiss and his coauthors note that "violent offenders tend to have experienced poor parental child rearing methods, poor supervision, and separations from their parents when they were children. . . . In addition, they tend disproportionately to come from low-income, large-sized families in poor housing in deprived, inner-city, high-crime areas" (367).

29. Murphy, "Marxism and Retribution," 236, 237.

30. See Elliot Currie, *Confronting Crime* (New York: Pantheon, 1985).

31. See Reiss et al., *Understanding and Preventing Violence*, 5.

32. See Elijah Anderson, "The Code of the Streets," *Atlantic Monthly* 273 (1994): 80–94. Anderson, a prominent sociologist, observes:

> For [a significant minority of hard-core street youths] the standards of the street code are the only game in town. The extent to which some children—particularly those who through upbringing have become most alienated and those lacking in strong and conventional social support—experience, feel, and internalize racist rejection and contempt from mainstream society may strongly encourage them to express contempt for the more conventional society in turn. In dealing with this contempt and rejection, some youngsters will consciously invest themselves and their considerable mental resources in what amounts to an oppositional culture to preserve themselves and their self-respect. Once they do, any respect they might be able to garner in the wider system pales in comparison with the respect available in the local system; thus they often lose interest in even attempting to negotiate the mainstream system. (94).

33. "Children kill boy, 5, for refusing to steal," *Rochester Democrat and Chronicle*, October 15, 1994, page 1A.

34. Jeannie Oakes, *Keeping Track* (New Haven: Yale University Press, 1985), 134 .

35. Other factors associated with high crime rates in schools that point to the significance of student-teacher relationships for moral socialization are noted in California State Office of the Attorney General, *School Security Handbook* (Sacramento, 1981), 12.

36. Murphy, "Marxism and Retribution," 237.

37. See Reiss et al., *Understanding and Preventing Violence*, 7, 383, 388–91.

38. Ibid., 7.

39. Ibid., 385ff.

40. Ibid., 3–5; Currie, *Confronting Crime*, chap. 1.

Chapter 14

Jurisprudential Indeterminacy:
The Case of Hate Speech Regulation

Thomas W. Simon

Contemporary Legal Theory

Law schools have become unusually interesting places, intellectually and politically, for they are probably the only places in higher education where ideological factions, representing the right and the left, engage one another in serious intellectual and political dialogue. Proponents of Law and Economics, Communitarianism, and Critical Race Theory, to name a few, write critiques of one another's works. The Law and Economics movement has a conservative political bent; Critical Race Theorists openly proclaim their leftist allegiances; and Communitarians see themselves as occupying a middle range between the other two.[1]

These current legal theories derive from radically different philosophical assumptions and premises. Law and Economics accepts an abstract individualism that locates individual identity primarily within the socially isolated individual. Communitarianism challenges the economic view that individuals are rational utility or wealth maximizers and offers an alternative conception of the social self, whose identity is constituted by the very social relationships that Law and Economics proponents downplay. Critical Race Theorists, while having more sympathy with the concept of a social self from Communitarianism than with the abstract individualism of Law and Economics, posit a political version of the self. Within Critical Race Theory the self is constructed not only by the social dimension but also by the political dimension, where the forces of power operate against disadvantaged groups.

Chapter 14 originally appeared in *Democracy and Social Injustice: Law, Politics, and Philosophy* (Lanham, Md.: Rowman & Littlefield, 1995).

Given the identifiable political and philosophical elements in each theory, we would expect widespread disagreement over their respective practical recommendations and positions. On the few issues where these intellectually and politically divergent approaches converge, the agreed-upon position has a robustness seldom found in controversial issues. Surprisingly, Law and Economics proponents, Communitarians, and Critical Race Theorists all seem to favor hate speech regulation.[2] At the very least, it makes it more difficult to argue against hate speech codes when proponents from opposite sides of the political spectrum support regulation. Yet, appearances are deceiving. Upon closer analysis, it turns out that none of the approaches provides a definitive answer to the hate speech problem. The agreement among the approaches results from a looseness within each of the theoretical structures.

In short, all three approaches suffer from what another group, Critical Legal Studies advocates, terms "indeterminacy." Indeterminacy arises at two levels: at the level of legal rules and at the level of theories and principles used to justify legal rules. David Kairys describes the former sense of indeterminacy as operating when "legal reasoning does not provide concrete, real answers to particular legal or social problems."[3] As an example of the latter, theoretical sense of indeterminacy, Duncan Kennedy has argued that the cost-benefit analyses employed in Law and Economics do not produce determinant results in particular cases.[4] According to Kennedy, the values of the cost-benefit analyst are more determinative of policy outcomes than the cost-benefit analysis itself. I want to concentrate on a particular version of indeterminacy at the theoretical level. Despite appearances to the contrary, I contend that none of the theoretical frameworks underlying the approaches considered here is determinative enough to provide an answer to the hate speech regulation issue.

It is my contention that the indeterminacy that infects all three approaches highlights something fundamentally problematic with the approaches. The theories seem to support hate speech regulation. Yet, strong antiregulatory arguments can be constructed within two of the approaches, namely, Law and Economics, and Communitarianism. Neither of these jurisprudential approaches provides a definitive or a defensible position on the hate speech issue. Critical Race Theory manifests a slightly different kind of indeterminacy. It is not that a strong antiregulatory argument can be mustered within Critical Race Theory; rather, the theory does not provide a determinative answer on the hate speech issue, despite its claims to the contrary, because of vague and problematic concepts within the theory.

The failure of the approaches to provide a defensible and definitive position on hate speech suggests that something more fundamentally problematic lurks beneath the surface of these elaborately constructed theories. The inadequacies of these approaches, I contend, centers around their respective notions of harm. Regarding the first two approaches, neither Law and Economics nor Communitarianism provides a normative theory of harm to disadvantaged groups. The central concepts within each theory do not yield any definitive results on disadvantaged group harms, such as racism. A position on an issue like hate speech comes as a result of the introduction of extratheoretic values into the analysis. Without a normative commitment on the issue of disadvantaged-group harm, both approaches will continue to be vulnerable to the charge of indeterminacy on issues such as hate speech.

Critical Race Theorists, probably the most vocal supporters of hate speech regulation, also face a problem with the notion of harm. Unlike Law and Economics or Communitarianism, Critical Race Theorists give prominence to the harms suffered by disadvantaged groups, particularly racial groups. However, we can raise questions concerning their characterization of the type of harm they emphasize. Critical Race Theorists concentrate on the sensitivity interests affected by certain forms of speech. As a result, Critical Race Theorists emphasize harms that result from speech but not from social and economic conditions. Because of the vagueness of the concept of sensitivity harms, Critical Race Theorists find themselves committed to an inordinate amount of speech regulation. The notion of sensitivity harm is not refined enough to block the case for too much speech regulation, and as such it provides ammunition for the opponents of regulation.

So, the three jurisprudential theories that defend hate speech regulation are all found wanting in the analysis that I will provide. In what follows, I will characterize these three legal philosophies and demonstrate their inadequacies to the struggle against racism. This does not imply an abandonment of the fight against racism. On the contrary, it calls for renewed efforts, but not in the direction of hate speech regulation.

Law and Economics

Law and Economics analysts use the tools of economics largely in the areas of contract, tort, and property law. However, many have also ventured into discrimination law and constitutional law. By far the most venturesome is one of the founders of the movement, Judge Richard Posner, who has applied law and economics to a wide variety of issues.

Posner, wanting to give the "free speech icon an acid bath of economics," proposed the following algebraic recasting of the free speech formula that Judge Learned Hand used in *Dennis*:[5]

$$V + E < P \times L/(1 + i)^n$$
where
V is the value of the speech
E is the social costs of the harm
P is the probability that the speech in question will do harm
L is the legal error costs
n is the time between the speech and the harm
i is the discount rate[6]

V, the information loss from the suppression of the speech, depends upon the following factors: "(1) the nature and value of the speech suppressed and (2), the amount of speech suppressed, which in turn depends on (a), the method, scope, and extent of the regulation, and (b), the market robustness (versus fragility) of the speech suppressed."[7]

According to Posner, in *Collin* the value of V was quite low for the Nazis to march through the predominantly Jewish town of Skokie, a suburb of Chicago.[8] On the other side of the equation, Posner places a high value on the probability that the speech could cause harm to the people of Skokie, especially to the Holocaust survivors who live in Skokie.[9] Although Posner admits that the value of E, the cost of erroneous suppression of speech, might prove problematic in *Collin*, he opines that the formula provides enough conceptual force to distinguish "a Nazi march in Skokie from a civil rights march in Selma."[10] However, Posner's analysis does not provide a means of differentiating the Skokie from the Selma case because it lapses into a form of indeterminacy, depending more on Posner's value judgments than anything else.

Let us examine how hate speech might fare within a Law and Economics framework. The Posner formula seems to offer a determination on the question of the constitutionality of the hate speech regulations. Consider the following: the hate speech cases appear to mirror the Nazi case. If the Nazi march is unprotected, then so is hate speech because hate speech fares even less well under the formula. Hate speech has even a lower value (V) than the Nazi march. The Nazi march at least has some political overtones that could arguably qualify as worthy of protection, whereas hate speech has little or no political import. Individual, one-on-one outbursts of hate speech often have little or no connection with any organized political movement. Further, the hate speech is directed at specific individuals; the Nazi march, in contrast, had a more diffuse audience. Shouting an invective to a targeted individual is more analogous to the Nazis disseminating hate mail to known survivors of concentration camps[11] than it is to the Nazi march in Skokie, where potential victims could "divert their eyes." Finally, intended speech has a greater probability of causing harm than unintended activity. Hate speech seems to qualify to an even greater degree than the Nazi march as intentional speech. Arguably, the Nazis' primary intent could have been more to garner publicity for their cause than to cause harm to Holocaust survivors. In contrast, it is difficult to imagine what other intent could lie behind hate speech than the intent to harm the targeted individual. So, hate speakers would find it difficult to find a protection behind a Posnerian economic wall.

However, the economic analysis only seems to support hate-speech regulation. The economic analyst makes questionable assumptions that fit some intuitions, but the analysis does not fare well under closer scrutiny. The questionable assumptions concern the nature of hate speech, its targeted audience, and the intent of the speaker. The tenuous nature of these assumptions can best be seen in the context of the crude/sophisticated distinction.[12] Crude hate speech, by its very nature, appears not to have any redeeming features. In contrast, sophisticated hate speech at least has the redeeming feature that it is susceptible to examination within the marketplace of ideas. Intuitively, crude hate speech falls outside the realm of rational discourse, and sophisticated hate speech fits comfortably within the confines of debate and argumentation. A closer look, however, reveals that crude and sophisticated speech cannot easily be distinguished according to susceptibility to rationality.

Crude hate speech can directly and indirectly invoke rational deliberation. Even in the midst of a hate speech act, rational dialogue could emerge. The voice of reason can tame emotional outbursts. Less direct examples include those where the crude hate speech incident becomes a stimulus for later dialogue. The University of Michigan Enforcement Model, for example, has a provision for informal mediation before the initiation of formal procedures. A crude hate speech incident could serve as an opportunity to open dialogue over abusive speech.[13] This happened when students at Arizona State University reacted to a racist flyer containing crude hate speech by organizing open discussions whereby they could educate others about the harm inflicted by hate speech.[14]

Alternatively, sophisticated hate speech does not always leave room for informed rational debate between its proponents and representatives of vulnerable groups.[15] A presentation demonstrating the inverse relation between racial characteristics and intelligence within the classroom may leave little room for challenge, particularly from racial minority students. Students find themselves in a differential power relationship with their professors. For example, according to one report, "at the University of Washington, a professor called in campus police to bar a student from class who had questioned her assertion that lesbians make the best parents."[16] Situations like these do not lend themselves to rational and open dialogue within the classroom. So, the distinction between crude and sophisticated hate speech does not turn on whether rational dialogue applies to one but not to the other.

Not only does the economic analysis make unwarranted assumptions about the nature of the speech involved, presuming that crude hate speech harms in uniquely pernicious ways, it also assumes, with little argumentation, that targeted audiences warrant greater protection from hate speech than more diffuse audiences.[17] This presumes that a flyer targeted to specific Holocaust survivors causes greater harm than one generally circulated. Yet, the opposite may just as well be the case. The widely circulated flyer has the potential of harming more Holocaust survivors and of legitimating the hate felt by others toward the targeted group. Again, the crude/sophisticated hate speech distinction proves telling. A university professor may not have any specific individuals targeted by hate speech remarks in the classroom, but the reverberating effects of the comments could be immense.

Finally, the economic model unjustifiably takes for granted that intended hate speech is more harmful than its unintended kin. Crude speech, for some unexplained reason, is thought to be connected directly with intent. Yet, crude speech should not automatically qualify as the paradigm for intended speech. Sophisticated versions of hate speech can have their intentional aspects as well, and they can be arguably more so and more insidious.

Take the example of a professor in a class lecture designed to demonstrate the heritability of intelligence who contends that blacks have lower mean IQ scores than whites. Although the harmful aspects of the message may be more subtle in the scientific lecture case than in the more paradigmatic case of crude hate speech, sophisticated speech can have a persecutorial and hateful intent once fully analyzed. The speaker's intent is not as easy to determine as the distinction between crude and sophisticated hate speech might suggest. It may merely seem that crude hate speech clearly stems from racial animosity and that sophisticated hate speech does not—at least not without considerably more investigation. However, the intent issue is much more complicated than it seems on the surface in both the crude and sophisticated versions of hate speech. Someone may quite unintentionally utter a form of crude hate speech, whereas someone else may very intentionally adhere to a racist animus within the safer harbor (and thus more dangerous) of sophisticated hate speech. Moreover, sophisticated hate speech purports to be rational and scientifically acceptable. As such, it can have more pervasive and long-standing effects. Much bigotry has taken the form of "scientific" speech, and is damaging precisely because it comes clothed in respectable garb.

At Stanford University, a white student identified as "Fred" defaced a poster of Beethoven to represent a black stereotype and placed it outside the room of an African American student. Fred, a German Jew, could not understand why blacks did not react in the same way to teasing that he did to the anti-Semitism that ran rampant in the English boarding school he had attended.[18] This information about Fred raises questions about whether Fred's symbolic speech stemmed from racial animosity.

I cannot do justice to the debate over the relationship between race and IQ, but the intent underlying sophisticated hate speech seems just as complicated as that of crude hate speakers, such as Fred. When the seemingly innocent scientific pronouncements are fully analyzed, more racial animosity may underlie them than meets the eye. Compare any examples of crude hate speech with the following statement addressed to an African-American freshman at Stanford:

> LeVon, if you find yourself struggling in your classes here, you should realize it isn't your fault. It's simply that you're the beneficiary of a disruptive policy of affirmative action that places underqualified, underprepared and often undertalented black students in demanding educational environments like this one. The policy's equalitarian aims may be well intentioned, but given the fact that aptitude tests place African Americans almost a full standard deviation below the mean, even controlling for socioeconomic disparities, they are also profoundly misguided. The truth is, you probably don't belong here, and your college experience will be a long downhill slide.[19]

The intent behind this sophisticated hate speech seems fairly obvious.

An economic analysis of law does not provide a definitive position on hate speech regulation. It does so only if we grant some questionable assumptions about different types of hate speech incidents. Without those assumptions, we can make a strong case within the economic analysis against regulation. Basically, the antiregulator would need to show that the harms generated from crude hate speech are no worse than those generated from other types of speech that we would presumably want to protect.

Within a Law and Economics framework, the outcome of the debate between proponents and opponents of hate speech regulation would hinge on an assessment of the harm associated with hate speech. The debate over such harms can be decided only if Law and Economics constructs a normative theory of harms that would give greater weight to certain kinds of harms directed against certain kinds of groups. Because nothing within Law and Economics would provide an answer to the questions concerning the harms, Law and Economics is indeterminate as to the hate speech issue in that both the regulation and nonregulation of hate speech can be justified within the theory.[20]

Communitarianism

Communitarianism developed as an alternative to the individualism that underlies a number of theoretical perspectives, such as Law and Economics. In contrast to what Communitarian thinkers see as an impoverished view of the self defined apart from a social situation, they argue that a person's moral identity is defined, in part, in terms of social filiations, affiliations, and viewpoints. Communitarians emphasize a conception of community animated by a shared conception of the good.

Communitarians also provide a defense of hate speech regulation but on very different grounds from those of the Law and Economics cost-benefit approach.[21] They attempt to defend group libel laws.[22] Law and Economics tends to place its focus on individual harms; Communitarianism emphasizes community harms. Communitarians attack liberals, and by extension Law and Economics theorists, for their failure to give sufficient centrality to the notion of group identity. Each individual's moral identity is inextricably connected with her or his group affiliations, not merely those instrumental relations voluntarily chosen but, what is more important, those constitutive associations that define the individual within a social context.

> On this strong view, to say that the members of a society are bound by a sense of community is not simply to say that a great many of them profess communitarian sentiments and pursue communitarian aims, but rather that they conceive their identity—the subject and not just the object of their feelings and aspirations—as defined to some extent by the community of which they are a part. For them, community describes not just what they have as fellow citizens but also what they are, not a relationship they choose (as in a voluntary association) but an attachment they discover, not merely an attribute but a constituent of their identity.[23]

So, a person's identity is not simply a matter of what organizations she may choose to join but of what communities define her.

Given the importance of constitutive group identity, race and ethnic identity take on a central importance. The harms from hate speech run deep. Hate speech attacks personhood. A racial slur goes directly to the heart of the targeted individual's identity.

Hate speech not only harms individuals; it also harms all other members of the targeted group. Patricia Williams, for example, speaks of the "Beethoven injury."[24] By this she means the injuries she suffered from the hate speech hurled at another. Again, we return to the incident in which a white student (Fred) placed a poster of Beethoven drawn as a black caricature on an African American student's door at Stanford. Williams contends, "Even though the remark was not made to me or even in my presence, I respond to it personally and also as a member of the group derogated; I respond personally but as part of an intergenerational collective."[25] So, hate speech affects the sensitivity interest not only of the hearer but also of those associated with her or his group.

Communitarians rely on a constitutive sense of community and group identity; that leads them into a problematic situation of the valorization of group identity—at least of the stigmatized group. Is hate speech wrong because it adversely affects a person's racial identity or because, among other things, it wrongfully classifies a person? Communitarians locate the harm within the identity of the social individual. However, racial identity—indeed identity in general—proves to be a troublesome concept. Although African American pride may have positive aspects for some, for others, the pride may serve more as a defensive shield than as a positive value.[26] African Americans need not see their personhood at stake in the hate-speech issue. The hate speaker's "humanity" is at issue, not the targets'. To have society find hate speech an actionable offense, African Americans should not have to celebrate their seemingly unavoidable attachment to race.[27]

Without a positive valorization of community and group identity, Communitarians have no way of characterizing the harm involved in incidents of hate speech. There is no prior social self that receives the brunt of the harm from hate speech. Rather, the harm stems from noncommunitarian sources, from others trying to define someone in negative and harmful ways. Communitarian arguments in favor of hate speech regulation need a constitutive sense of group identity—race does not provide the Communitarians with a sufficiently robust sense of the social self. Communitarians need a strong justification for racial/gender/ethnic pride.

The failure to acknowledge fully or to discount completely the constitutive nature of race for personal identity creates an indeterminacy for Communitarians. If race is constitutive of the self, then that provides grounds for regulating hate speech; regulation can protect a self as socially constructed. If race is not constitutive of the self, then there is no prima facie need for regulative protection. One could argue that regulation of hate speech stifles the discovery of the constitutive self; the discovery of racial identity becomes more likely in the midst of hate speech and other forms of attack. Often one hears accounts of individuals who discover their racial or ethnic identity only in the midst of an incident wherein the racial or ethnic identity is made a central issue.

Indeterminacy also arises within Communitarianism in its failure to differentiate groups. Communitarians do not have a sufficiently rich theory to block placing all types of groups on par: blacks, neo-Nazis, members of the Klu Klux Klan, and so on. Iris Young, for example, tries to differentiate social (constitutive) groups from interest and ideological groups. Young defines a social group as "a collective of people who have affinity with one another because of a set of practices or way of life."[28] In contrast, on Young's view, interest groups, such as the National Rifle Association, aggregate around specific goals such as gun control, and ideological groups, such as the Nazis, share political and moral beliefs, including anti-Semitic and racist ones. Yet, the Nazis do qualify as social group because they do share cultural practices as well as political and moral beliefs.[29] Conversely, so-called social groups do not necessarily share cultural and social practices within the group. In short, a "common way of life" does not adequately differentiate social groups from other types of groups.

Without an adequate typology of groups, Communitarians cannot adequately differentiate among many types of group harms. Nazi vilification stands on the same platform as hate speech directed against racial minorities. Unlike

Law and Economics proponents, Communitarians have a clearly differentiated sense of harm, namely, harm that can affect the constitutive elements of the self. However, Communitarians fail to defend concrete instantiations of harms to the social self. Race remains indeterminate in Communitarianism. Race could just as easily qualify as a discovered constitutive identity as it could as a false identity constructed by others. By not fully explicating what it is to have a constitutive identity, Communitarians do not give a determinative answer to the question of hate-speech regulation. The tenets of Communitarianism leave plenty of room for someone to argue against hate speech regulation on the grounds that the harm in question does not really affect the constitutive identity of the targeted individuals.

Finally, I need not repeat the arguments I developed in the previous section, which showed that Law and Economics failed to distinguish adequately between crude and sophisticated hate speech. Communitarians run into the same problem. In fact, if we are to take group identity as seriously as Communitarians seem to want us to, hardly anything negative could be said about any group without undermining a person's identity.

Critical Race Theory

Critical Race Theorists chide Critical Legal Theorists for their failure to give race a central place in their analyses.[30] In keeping with its name, Critical Race Theory gives prominence to race, and its proponents have been at the forefront of the fight to institute hate speech regulations to combat racism.[31] Unlike those in the Law and Economics, and Communitarian camps, Critical Race Theorists have no difficulty in giving a definitive answer on the hate speech issue.

My disagreement with Critical Race Theory cannot be over the centrality of race. Rather, I object to its characterization of the harm at issue. I make this objection with a great deal of trepidation, for Critical Race Theorists represent voices of racial minorities. Certainly, we must listen to the voices of those who claim harm from hate speech.

Despite the importance of a victim perspective, problems arise with it. By demanding that the victims of hate speech determine the social meaning and harm of hate speech, Critical Race Theorists run into their own indeterminacy problem. Victims would need to become regulators. Otherwise, regulators would be guilty of paternalism because they would determine the potential harm inflicted upon victims from their own, nonvictim perspective. Here an indeterminacy arises, for who chooses the potential victims and on what grounds? Without a clear-cut ordering of potential harms, any number of groups could claim regulator status.

Moreover, although the power of words and the racist aspects of hate speech should not be underestimated, neither should they be overestimated. Speech, justifiably determined by the victims as hateful and harmful, remains speech. Hate speech deserves clear condemnation, but it does not thereby qualify for formal, legal sanctioning.

To accommodate the harms associated with speech, Critical Race Theorists have to construct a new type of harm to accommodate hate speech. They must establish that sensitivity harms[32] (defined relative to the hearer's attitude) as well as interest harms (defined independently of the hearer's attitude) merit legal recognition. Sensitivity harms are too broad and do not do the job for Critical Race Theorists. Sensitivity harms, while associated with more politically based interest harms, depend critically on individual psychological attitudes and sensitivities. The psychological base of sensitivity harms is diffuse enough to allow for members of almost any group to make their case for having been harmed by some form of speech. Even the mere mentioning of a hate speech slur for purposes of illustration could result in a sensitivity harm to someone.

Finally, sensitivity harms do not adequately protect racial minorities because they do not fully encompass political power dynamics. The implementation of the University of Michigan's hate speech code provides a good illustration of this. Whites brought charges against more than twenty blacks for racist speech, yet the university did not punish a single instance of white racist speech.[33] Hate speech codes can regulate and stifle the speech of racial minorities.

By leaving sensitivity harms largely undefined, Critical Race Theorists have fostered their own brand of indeterminacy. We cannot make a case against regulating hate speech within Critical Race Theory. Rather, the indeterminacy is that we can make a case for excessively expansive regulation within Critical Race Theory, which, in turn, undermines the case that Critical Race Theorists try to make. Further, a focus on sensitivity harms diverts intellectual energy away from the graver task of analyzing the interest harms at work in the political economy. Relative to the three approaches I have considered, Critical Race Theorists would have the easiest time adjusting the theory to take up some of the looseness.[34] The question arises, then, would they want to expend their efforts refining their position on hate speech regulation? With all the complexities of institutional racism facing our society, hate speech regulation may prove to be not only cosmetic but also diversionary.

Conclusion

I have chosen to analyze three jurisprudential approaches that fairly consistently have taken a stand in favor of hate speech regulation. All have provided justifications for their respective positions, but all fail to defend adequately the positions upon closer analysis. Perhaps, indeterminacy at the theoretical level should catch no one by surprise. Every theoretical orientation cannot yield definitive answers to every controversial issue. General theories always have policy underdetermination.

Nevertheless, when radically different theories provide the same or similar answers to a problem, that should at least give us pause. The agreement that we find from so many divergent sources provides some support for a policy. Law and Economics, Communitarianism, and Critical Race Theory make strange bedfellows because they have widely divergent political agendas and philosophical roots. Yet, they seem to agree on the issue of hate speech regulation. All of them favor some form of hate speech codes.

The agreement among the theories points to a gap common to all the approaches. Not only does the support for hate speech regulation break down upon closer examination in each case but the defenses run into problems for similar reasons. The theories have not supplied a normative theory of group harms. They have not adequately specified what kind of harms ought to be given primary attention. Should jurisprudential theories concentrate on harms stemming from the use of speech or on harms coming from other sources? Nor have the theories fully analyzed how the harms differently affect members of various groups. For example, do the harms have the same effect on affluent white males that they have on poor black females?

Law and Economics leaves a great deal of the analysis of harm to intuitive judgments that do not bear up under closer scrutiny. This results in treating Nazi marches through Skokie and civil rights marches through Selma on par. Communitarians try to localize the harm within a constitutive notion of the self, but they fail to provide any defensible analysis of how race fits into that picture. Finally, Critical Race Theorists give prominence to a sensitivity harm while paying relatively little attention to what some considered far more pernicious harms coming from economic status and the like.

The lesson from this exercise consists in redirecting jurisprudential efforts toward constructing a normative theory of group harm. If we design hate speech codes to counter racism, we need to reevaluate what we mean by racism. We need to understand how racism compares with other forms of group harm, such as sexism and homophobia. Analyses along these lines would make the debates within and between Law and Economics, Communitarianism, and Critical Race Theory more intellectually vibrant and politically relevant than they already are. Finally, we need to determine if group harm should be constitutionally cognizable.

Notes

1. By focusing on these three perspectives, I do not mean to imply that they represent the only or even the most prestigious positions in contemporary jurisprudence. Liberalism is notably absent from my analysis. Depending on the issue, liberals often ally themselves with one or more of the positions discussed in this paper. I have not included liberalism because liberals tend to reject hate speech regulations.

2. Unfortunately, I have not found representatives from each perspective who directly address the problem of hate speech regulation. So, I have had to reconstruct rationally parts of the positions.

3. David Kairys, "Law and Politics," *George Washington Law Review* 52 (1984): 243, 247. For a critique of this form of indeterminacy, see Lawrence B. Solum, "On the Indeterminacy Crisis: Critiquing Critical Dogma," *University of Chicago Law Review* 54 (1987): 462–503.

4. Duncan Kennedy, "Form and Substance in Private Law Adjudication," *Harvard Law Review* 89 (1976): 1685, 1700.

5. *United States v. Dennis*, 183 F. 2d 201, 212 (2d Cir. 1950), aff'd., 341 U.S. 494 (1951).

6. Richard Posner, "Free Speech in an Economic Perspective," *Suffolk University Law Review* 20 (1986): 1, 8.

7. Ibid., 9.

8. See *Collin v. Smith*, 447 F. Supp. 676, 700–701 (N.D. Ill.), aff'd., 578 F. 2d 1197 (7th Cir. 1978).

9. Posner, "Free Speech in an Economic Perspective," 31.

10. Ibid.

11. Ibid.

12. According to Matsuda, crude hate speech has the following characteristics: a persecutorial, hateful, and degrading message of racial inferiority directed against a historically oppressed group. Mari Matsuda, "Public Response to Racist Speech: Considering the Victim's Story," *Michigan Law Review* 87 (1989): 2320.

13. Alan E. Brownstein, "Hate Speech at Public Universities: The Search for an Enforcement Model," *Wayne Law Review* 37 (1991): 1451–68 (proposing an informal education as opposed to a formal enforcement model of hate speech regulation).

14. Nat Hentoff, "The Right Thing at ASU," *Washington Post*, June 25, 1991, A19.

15. See Henry W. Saad, "The Case for Prohibition of Racial Epithets in the University Classroom," *Wayne Law Review* 37 (1991): 1351–62. ("A minority that is the object of racial, sexual or ethnocentric epithets in the park may leave or engage in verbal combat. In the classroom, however, a student victimized by racial or ethnocentric invective should not be forced to resort to such activity" [1357]). Saad represented the University of Michigan in *Doe v. University of Michigan*, a successful challenge to the University of Michigan's hate speech code.

16. Henry Hyde and George Fishman, "The Collegiate Speech Protection Act of 1991: A Response to the New Intolerance in the Academy," *Wayne Law Review* 37 (1991): 1469–1524, at 1472; citing Sykes and Miner, "Sense and Sensitivity," *National Review*, March 18, 1991, 30–31.

17. Posner, "Free Speech in an Economic Perspective," 31. ("Focused or targeted harassment, as in the case of defamation, is apt to generate a greater, or at least a more readily quantifiable, harm.")

18. Patricia J. Williams, *The Alchemy of Race and Rights*, (Cambridge: Harvard University Press, 1991), 111.

19. As quoted in Henry Louis Gates, Jr., "Let Them Talk," *New Republic*, September 20 and 27, 1993.

20. I do not mean to imply that the distinction between crude and sophisticated hate speech is the only stumbling block for Law and Economics. It is one of many controversial assumptions made by proponents of Law and Economics. CLS theorists have been particularly forceful in their critiques of Law and Economics.

21. Communitarians have also defended hate speech regulation with a virtue rationale. For a critique of this approach, which I do not address in this chapter, see Suzanna Sherry, "Speaking of Virtue: A Republican Approach to University Regulation of Hate Speech," *Minnesota Law Review* 75 (1991): 933–44.

22. In *Beauharnais v. Illinois*, 343 U.S. 250 (1952), the Supreme Court adopted a group-libel analysis. However, many claim that *Beauharnais* is no longer good law. Nevertheless, a number of commentators have attempted to revive the group-libel approach. Hadley Arkes, "Civility and the Restriction of Speech: Rediscovering the Defamation of Groups," *Supreme Court Review*, 1974, 281–335 (advocating a group libel approach); David Kretzmer, "Freedom of Speech and Racism," *Cardozo Law Review* 8 (1987): 445–513; Kenneth Lasson, "Racial Defamation as Free Speech: Abusing the First Amendment," *Columbia Human Rights Law Review* 17 (1985): 11–55; Kenneth Lasson, "In Defense of Group-Libel Laws or Why the First Amendment Should Not Protect Nazis," *New York Law School Human Rights Annual* 2 (1985): 289–320; "Note, A Communitarian Defense of Group Libel Laws," *Harvard Law Review* 101 (1988): 682–701;

David Riesman, "Democracy and Defamation: Control of Group Libel," *Columbia Law Review* 42 (1942): 727–80. The University of Kansas has adopted a group-libel approach to hate speech (*University of Kansas Student Handbook*, 1990–1991, 28).

23. Michael Sandel, *Liberalism and the Limits of Justice*, (Cambridge: Cambridge University Press: 1982), 150.

24. Williams, *The Alchemy of Race and Rights*, 112.

25. Ibid., 112–113.

26. For a similar analysis as applied to homosexuality, see, e.g., Jed Rubenfield, "The Right of Privacy," *Harvard Law Review* 102 (1989): 737–807. People should be able to engage in sexual practices with members of their own gender "so that they may avoid being forced into an identity, not because they are defining their identities through the decision itself" (782).

27. See Marilyn Friedman, "Feminism and Modern Friendship: Dislocating the Community," *Ethics* 99 (1989): 275–90, at 282.

28. Iris Marion Young, "Social Movements and the Politics of Difference," *Justice and the Politics of Difference* (Princeton: Princeton University Press, 1990), 186.

29. See Kathleen Blee, *Women of the Klan* (Berkeley: University of California Press, 1991), for illustration of the deep–seated cultural practices and even some liberal beliefs among Klan members.

30. Richard Delgado, "The Ethereal Scholar: Does Critical Legal Studies Have What Minorities Want?" *Harvard Civil Rights-Civil Liberties Law Review* 22 (1987): 301–22; Mari Matsuda, "Looking to the Bottom: Critical Legal Studies and Reparations," *Harvard Civil Rights-Civil Liberties Law Review* 22 (1987): 323–99; Patricia Williams, "Alchemical Notes; Reconstructing Ideals from Deconstructed Rights," *Harvard Civil Rights-Civil Liberties Law Review* 22 (1987): 401–47; John Hardwick, "The Schism Between Minorities and the Critical Legal Studies Movement: Requiem for a Heavyweight?" *Boston College Third World Law Journal* 11 (1991): 137–64. Andrew Haines, "The Critical Legal Studies Movement and Racism: Useful Analytics and Guides for Social Action or an Irrelevant Modern Legal Skepticism and Solipsism?" *William Mitchell Law Review* 13 (1987): 685–736.

31. Richard Delgado, "Words That Wound: A Tort Action for Racial Insults, Epithets, and Name-Calling," *Harvard Civil Rights-Civil Liberties Law Review* 17(1982): 133–81 (proposing a tort cause of action against racial hate speech); Charles R. Lawrence, "If He Hollers Let Him Go: Regulating Racist Speech on Campus," *Duke Law Journal*, 1990, 431–83; Mari J. Matsuda, "Public Response to Racist Speech: Considering the Victim's Story," *Michigan Law Review* 87 (1989): 2320–81; Williams, *The Alchemy of Race and Rights*. Selections from these and other works are collected in *Words That Wound*, ed. Mari J. Matsuda, Charles R. Lawrence, III, Richard Delgado, and Kimberle Williams Crenshaw (Boulder: Westview Press, 1992).

32. Cf. "Note, A Communitarian Defense of Group Libel Laws," *Harvard Law Review* (1988): 682–701, at 687.

33. Gates, "Let Them Talk," 44.

34. Matsuda narrows the type of speech to be regulated to those with messages directed against a historically oppressed group. This narrows the range of speech at issue, but it does not narrow the range of harms. Mari J. Matsuda, "Public Response to Racist Speech: Considering the Victim's Perspective," *Michigan Law Review* 87 (1989): 2320–81.

Chapter 15

First Amendment Liberalism and Hate Speech: After R.A.V. v. St. Paul

David M. Adams

I

Among current social and legal disputes, perhaps none so powerfully illustrates the clash between "traditional" and "radical" jurisprudential perspectives as that over how institutions of higher learning ought to respond to the much-publicized rise in incidents of racial and sexual hate speech on college and university campuses.[1]

Traditional liberal legal theory supposes that government must remain neutral as between competing conceptions of the good and insists that this neutrality requirement is the backbone of First Amendment jurisprudence: government cannot be permitted to regulate or suppress speech based upon its "content," for to do so necessarily requires that it endorse some particular view about what is worth saying or doing, thinking, or believing, and this violates the neutrality constraint. That some speech is "hateful" is a claim plainly rooted in a specific moral judgment, one that government is neither entitled to make nor use as a predicate for action.

The liberal understanding of First Amendment doctrine has been challenged by critical race and feminist theorists,[2] who urge that the liberalism animating traditional First Amendment doctrine systematically excludes the voices or narratives of women and people of color, persons for whom victimization by hate speech marks a serious injury. For some of these theorists, the wrong done by racist and sexist hate speech warrants the complete exclusion of such speech from First Amendment protection, based on an open abandonment of the neutrality constraint.[3] For others, the evils of at least the most vicious forms of hate speech can be dealt with while continuing to operate within the confines of the neutrality requirement.[4]

Proposals for a radical constitutional and jurisprudential revision of existing free speech doctrine have met with several responses in the recent literature.[5] The rejoinder of traditional legal liberalism insists that hate speech must be condemned, not suppressed. Liberal analyses of the scope of free speech doctrine rely on the underlying presumption that expression may be abridged or suppressed consistent with the strictures of the First Amendment only where the harm sought to be avoided by a given regulation could not be averted through "more speech," that is, through continued dialogue and discussion.[6] While it is sometimes supposed, for example, that racial slurs and epithets, because they invite no response, fall outside the protective perimeter of the free speech guarantee, it is not necessarily the case that further discourse or dialogue would alter the attitudes and beliefs of the speaker in a direction many might deem positive. It is conceivable, according to legal liberalism, that even the crudest sort of hate speech might indeed bring about rational discussion, just as more "sophisticated" hate speech might leave little room for dialogue.[7] Because a fuller airing and examination of these attitudes, through reasoned exchange, is a necessary condition of moral instruction, the liberal rejoinder concludes, even if hate speech is harmful to members of protected classes, it does not follow that it is properly subject to regulation: "The crude hate speech incident could serve as an opportunity to open dialogue over abusive speech."[8] From these assumptions, it follows that hate speech regulations, of the sort chronicled throughout the literature, disserve their own underlying point or purpose: to combat subjugation and racism on college and university campuses.

Those among the revisionists who defend the implementation of campus hate speech codes generally fall into two classes. Some (what Simon has called the "strong regulators") seek to suppress the broadest range of hate speech, from the lowliest of gutter epithets and slurs to more disguised, veiled, or sophisticated expression of racial hatred and contempt; others (the"weak regulators") aim to isolate and suppress only the crudest forms of racial insults and epithets, those directed at specific persons with the intent to vilify and degrade their target.[9] It is, of course, clear that if the weakly regulationist or "accommodationist"[10] position turns out to be insupportable, so, a fortiori, will the stronger radical views. But even weak regulationism faces serious conceptual and doctrinal difficulties, as becomes clear from an examination of both the theories of First Amendment liberals and the recent Supreme Court ruling in the St. Paul hate crimes case (discussed below).[11] Weak regulationism is now commonly assailed on two

312 David M. Adams

fronts: first, that crude hate speech cannot be distinguished from the sophisticated kind that weak regulationists feel constrained to protect, nor, second, is it even proscribable in its own right consistent with constitutional requirements. In response to these claims, I will argue that although it is correct to think that weakly regulationists' restrictions on hate speech cannot reasonably be expected to rid campuses of racism, sexism, and other invidiously discriminatory attitudes and beliefs, it does not follow that they serve no useful purpose and constitute nothing more than a detour or diversion away from the genuine issue. Specifically, I will contend that the liberalism of traditional First Amendment jurisprudence gives insufficient weight to the specific kind of harm or injury flowing from racially and sexually assaultive slurs and epithets and that a weakly regulationist scheme properly should seek to address. In so doing I suggest a modest revision of free speech law, urging that explicit recognition be given to a new subdoctrine, excluding targeted vilification from First Amendment protection.

II

In a recent ruling, the Supreme Court, by a unanimous vote, struck down St. Paul's Bias-Motivated Crime Ordinance on the grounds that it was facially invalid under the First Amendment. The ordinance provided that "whoever places on public or private property a symbol, object, appellation, characterization or graffiti, including, but not limited to, a burning cross or Nazi swastika, which one knows or has reasonable grounds to know arouses anger, alarm or resentment in others on the basis of race, color, creed, religion, or gender commits disorderly conduct and shall be guilty of a misdemeanor."[12] The city had brought charges based on the ordinance against a youth who had burned a cross inside the fenced yard of a black family. The Minnesota Supreme Court had upheld the ordinance, attempting to confine its reach by bringing it within the realm of "fighting words," a category excluded from First Amendment protection under the U.S. Supreme Court's *Chaplinsky* doctrine: First Amendment protection does not include "insulting or 'fighting' words—those which by their very utterance inflict injury or tend to incite an immediate breach of the peace."[13] The Court reversed the Minnesota court and remanded the case on the ground that the ordinance was facially invalid under the First Amendment. Though it did not directly involve a campus hate speech code, the breadth and grounds for the Court's holding may well have implications for a number of existing campus codes, particularly those of the weak type, relying as many of them do on the continued vitality of the *Chaplinsky* doctrine.[14] Indeed, several campuses have recently set aside their regulations governing hate speech in apparent reaction to the Court's decision.[15]

Justice Scalia, writing for the majority of the Court in *R.A.V.*, argued as follows. The St. Paul ordinance is facially unconstitutional because it is impermissibly viewpoint-based. St. Paul does not prohibit fighting words on the ground of their being fighting words, and this because it does not prohibit all fighting words but only some: those relating to race, color, creed, religion, or gender. The ordinance thus applies selectively by aiming at those fighting words directed at victims on the basis of their membership in a protected class and expressing derogatory or bigoted attitudes. As Justice Scalia wrote:

> Displays containing some words—odious racial epithets, for example—would be prohibited to proponents of all views. But "fighting words" that do not themselves invoke race, color, creed, religion, or gender—aspersions upon a person's mother, for example—would seemingly be usable ad libitum in the placards of those arguing *in favor* of racial, color, etc., tolerance and equality, but could not be used by those speakers' opponents. One could hold up a sign saying, for example, that all "anti-Catholic bigots" are misbegotten; but not that all "papists" are, for that would insult and provoke violence "on the basis of religion." St. Paul has no such authority to license one side of a debate to fight freestyle, while requiring the other to follow Marquis of Queensbury Rules.[16]

St. Paul's ordinance seems to be nonneutral, both on its face and "as applied" to particular cases, disfavoring the ideology of the Klan or the gang of skinheads, while privileging the ideology of tolerance, respect, and equality. The city's basic error consists in permitting some to use fighting words while others cannot. St. Paul makes the further mistake, the Court adds, of proceeding as if fighting words constituted a content-based category outside First Amendment protection. This, says Scalia, is a mistake. Fighting words are merely vehicles for communicative expression, and are presumptively protected but proscribable on the same ground as other modes of communication subject to legitimate time, place, and manner restrictions—that is, on the basis of their "nonspeech" element. Though within the protective perimeter of the Constitution, fighting words are proscribable because their content embodies a particularly intolerable and socially unnecessary mode of expressing whatever idea the speaker wishes to convey. Fighting words are thus precisely analogous to the noisy sound truck. St. Paul, however, does not proscribe fighting words on the basis of this nonspeech element, and its ordinance is therefore ideologically skewed, aiming to suppress one viewpoint and endorse another. Such favoritism, the majority insists, violates the fundamental requirement of government neutrality. Slurs and epithets, if they are to be proscribed as fighting words, must, in order to comply with the demands of the Constitution, be suppressed without reference to their content.

The foregoing argument is, I believe, unpersuasive on the merits and sends a misleading signal to municipalities and campus communities concerned about racist speech. Exposing the flaws in the Court's reasoning is a task to which I now turn.

To begin, it is important to note, as does Justice White in his concurrence, that the majority's analysis proceeds first by rejecting outright a frequently cited feature of First Amendment doctrine: the view that certain categories of expression are completely excluded from free speech protection. The majority insists that fighting words are not *de minimis* but within the protective perimeter of the amendment because they are "quite expressive indeed,"[17] that is, they contain at least some minimal propositional content. That mere "expressiveness" in this sense is obviously insufficient to explain or support free speech protection is clear from the example of the bigot who, instead of screaming slurs and epithets at his target, simply spits in the person's face—this may well communicate a "message" statable in propositional form and do so even more effectively than a verbal barrage, but it is certainly not protected "speech" for that reason.

Fundamentally, the Court simply cannot be correct in its threshold assumption: it cannot be that fighting words fail to receive First Amendment protection because they are used in an improper manner, or at an inopportune time or place, like the noise of the truck at 3 A.M. The injury or harm caused by the truck has no necessary connection with the message conveyed, and hence the harm can be averted by a regulation crafted to make no reference to the words used or ideas disseminated. But it is obvious that this is not the case with racial slurs and epithets. It is just because of the words used and the messages they convey that injury results. If loud noise can be a nuisance and the messages conveyed by means of that noise may be restricted because of their volume, Scalia's analogy requires that assaultive epithets give rise to a kind of harm or injury having nothing to do with the content of the message conveyed and on the basis of which they too may be proscribed. But it is hard to see what that nonspeech element could be. A slur is a slur because of what it says, not for any other reason. If we say with Scalia that free speech protection does not extend to the nonspeech element of communicative activity—that aspect of a speech-act causing harm—then in the case of fighting words it is clear that the Court has not fixed on a nonspeech element: with the sound truck the "proscribable element" is the noise; with racial slurs the proscribable element can only be the injurious words themselves, as St. Paul recognized. The Court is therefore mistaken in assuming that a municipality or campus community can, if it chooses to do so, prohibit injurious racial slurs and epithets in a way that makes no reference to the "content" of what they express, and that failure to do so must result in the facial invalidity of its efforts. An analogous claim for the areas of obscenity or defamation would make equally little sense: any attempt to delimit or describe a category of obscene or defamatory speech must by its very nature do so by reference to the content of such speech. Similarly, there is no way to address the harm posed by racial slurs independent of the words used. Because slurs and epithets cannot be defined or specified in a content-neutral way, it is pointless to insist that municipalities or campus communities so define and specify them.[18]

First Amendment liberals may well accept the foregoing argument but insist that it makes their point: because no instance of crude hate speech can be picked out in a content-neutral way, the claim that it must be suppressed entails the further proposition that the government should enact legislation that privileges one viewpoint and stifles another. The Court's opinion in *R.A.V.* elaborates this point by insisting that categorically excluded speech is still speech and therefore cannot be proscribed on just any basis. For example, it would not be permissible, Scalia observes, for a community to ban only obscene speech that includes offensive political messages; whereas an ordinance prohibiting only obscene speech that is especially lascivious or offensive would pass constitutional muster.[19] The explanation for the difference here, Scalia declares, is that the reasons for picking out the subset of proscribed speech acts must go to the very reason for excluding from First Amendment protection the entire category of speech in the first place. That rationale explains the latter case, but it cannot justify the former. St. Paul's hate crimes ordinance, and by implication campus hate speech regulations of even the narrowest scope, pick from among the general domain of *Chaplinsky* speech on the grounds of criteria that refer to race, gender, and other traits entirely unrelated to the dangers posed by fighting words. "Selectivity of this sort," the Court concludes, "creates the possibility that the city is seeking to handicap the expression of particular ideas."[20] Thus, seemingly all efforts to suppress racist or sexist hate speech will suffer from the same basic constitutional infirmity: endorsement of a favored viewpoint.

Powerful as it appears, the force of the liberal argument here largely dissipates upon closer inspection. As I will try to show, it is not the case that a content-based exclusion for the most vicious and abusive forms of hate speech is either inconsistent with existing doctrine (at least when read expansively and with an eye to other areas) or violative of the fundamental liberal requirement of neutrality.

The core of the nonneutrality charge is succinctly put by Tom Grey: Even the narrowest of regulations, exempting from constitutional protection only targeted vilification on the basis of specified traits,

> may seem biased against the disfavored ideologies of racism, sexism, and homophobia, openly favoring "politically correct" egalitarians against their adversaries in the campus marketplace of opinion. It arguably takes from the bigots emotively powerful rhetorical weapons—the traditional hate epithets—without imposing comparable restrictions on the other side. It is as if terms like "commie" and "pinko" were barred from political debate, while "imperialist lackey" and "capitalist running dog" were allowed.[21]

But what is the actual bias or viewpoint discrimination here? Just how is it that bigots and antibigots are being treated asymmetrically? For liberal opponents of hate speech regulations, all such regulatory schemes yield the result that, for example, white skinheads may not use abusive or assaultive epithets directed at black civil rights advocates in order to promote the skinhead ideology of hatred and intolerance, but that civil rights proponents may use abusive epithets directed at skinheads so long as they do so in a way designed to promote the "favored" ideology of tolerance, respect, and equality. But to make the case for the asymmetry explicit in this way reveals that it is illusory. Civil rights advocates have no actual advantage here because the case liberals think they are imagining is actually one impossible to construct: it is simply incoherent to suggest that civil rights advocates could both (a) communicate or convey an ideology of racial tolerance and equality, and (b) do so by means of assaultive epithets or gutter insults directed at another person on the basis of his race that are calculated to humiliate or degrade. Hence, there is no bias or favoritism in a regulation prohibiting crude racist or sexist hate speech; both skinheads and civil rights advocates are precluded from resort to assaultive epithets commonly understood to convey contempt for another's race, sex, or religion in a way calculated to degrade, and both may communicate their respective ideologies in ways that do not involve using hate speech. Moreover, both groups may use epithets and slurs not touching on race or religion. This last point reveals that the only "group" in fact burdened here is one not definable in terms of ideology, namely, the group of people who wish verbally to assault and injure others. Their exclusion from First Amendment protection is thus not ideologically based, and such an exclusion is therefore not facially viewpoint discriminatory.

It is of course true that as an empirical matter, a regulation prohibiting hate speech will be asymmetrical in application, reflecting the cultural fact that those racial and sexual slurs and epithets commonly understood to express contempt and to humiliate their victim are connected in our culture to a history of discrimination against and vilification of women and people of color, not of whites.[22] It is this contingent feature of our history, and not the political bias or partiality of St. Paul or similar communities, that both defines the class of persons victimized by crude hate speech and explains why such hate speech injures.

A more abstractly stated effort to expose the viewpoint-based nature of hate speech regulations is developed by Post.

> The very reason that racist speech harms individual persons is because it so violently ruptures the forms of social respect that are necessary for the maintenance of individual personality. These forms of respect, when taken together, constitute a collective, community identity. Hence the state can prevent the individual harm caused by racist speech only by enforcing pertinent standards of community identity. The interdependence of individual and collective identity is thus presupposed in the very concept of individual harm.[23]

Post uses the interdependence alleged here as a premise for two distinct arguments. The first and more extreme argument states that

> questions of personal identity are in fact always at stake in discussion of collective self-definition. For this reason effective political dialogue requires that participants be constantly willing to be transformed. . . . As our collective aspirations change, so will our respective personal identities. Thus restrictions on public discourse designed to protect those identities from harm will necessarily also restrict self-determination as to our collective life. If group harm is an inevitable price of the political constitution of group identity, individual injury is an unavoidable cost of the political constitution of community identity.[24]

The argument is that because individual personal identity is constituted by values, roles, and understandings simultaneously constitutive of our "collective identity," aiming to affect the constitutive factors shaping the individual must also shape and thereby limit the collective. Aside from the problem of what precise meaning to assign to "collective" or "community identity" here,[25] the argument threatens to undermine itself, for if we grant that the community has an "identity" and is able to engage in acts of collective self-determination, nothing Post has said explains why the prevention of the individuated harm produced by targeted racist and sexist hate speech cannot be part of the community's collective aspirations.

Post's second tack argues, in the alternative, that the interdependence of individual and collective identity "lies behind well-established constitutional prohibitions on restricting public discourse because it is 'offensive' or 'outrageous,' or because it affronts 'dignity' or is 'insulting' or causes 'public odium' or 'public disrepute.' Such speech causes intense individual suffering because it violates community norms, yet the Court has required its toleration in order to prevent the state from using the authority of law to enforce particular conceptions of collective life."[26] This argument seems to strike at the very idea of having a collective identity, inasmuch as no endorsement of a particular conception of the collective good, Post assumes, should be tolerated. The suppression of hate speech must be animated by some substantive view of the overall good. Hence, any effort to suppress hate speech is freighted with specific normative bias.

But *any* suppression of speech acts that have potential to harm individuals will be grounded on *some* substantive norm or other, whether it be because the speech poses a "clear and present danger," constitutes incitement, or amounts to obscenity, defamation, or fighting words. Unless all such suppressions are unjustified, Post's second argument does not cut against hate speech regulation.

If I am right, then, the suppression of targeted vilification involves no de facto bias or ideological favoritism. But are weak regulationists not still confronted with the facial or de jure bias of an ordinance identifying the proscribable speech by reference to membership in certain protected classes? On the Court's view, no hate speech ordinance can stand unless the reasons for selecting among speech acts within an excluded domain of expression are the very ones that justify exempting the entire domain from First Amendment protection. Though the Court may have been right to find that this excludability requirement was not satisfied by St. Paul's "fighting words" ordinance, a more careful examination of First Amendment doctrine suggests that weakly regulationist hate speech ordinances arguably do meet the Court's test. To establish this requires a fresh analysis of two aspects of free speech law.

St. Paul's hate ordinance, as read by the Minnesota court, was bottomed on the Court's familiar *Chaplinsky* decision, upholding the prohibition of "insulting or fighting words," understood as "those which by their very utterance inflict injury or tend to incite a breach of the peace."[27] Though sometimes regarded with suspicion,[28] *Chaplinsky* has never been set aside, and in *R.A.V.* the Court pointedly refused an invitation to modify or overrule it. *Chaplinsky* formally excludes from First Amendment protection two kinds of speech acts: (1) those which "by their very utterance inflict injury," and (2) those inherently likely to provoke their hearer to violence. (2) is now often cited as the entire holding of *Chaplinsky*, (1) having dropped out.[29] Although it does appear that none of the Court's holdings has rested on the first prong of *Chaplinsky*, it has not been directly overruled, and attention to at least one developing area of tort doctrine suggests that it should be retained, for the kind of injury to which the first prong of the *Chaplinsky* test refers closely fits that caused by targeted vilification of protected groups.

The constitutional implications of tort actions for intentional infliction of emotional distress were recently addressed by the Court in *Hustler Magazine v. Falwell*.[30] There the Court held that states may afford remedies for intentional infliction of emotional distress consistent with First Amendment values, subject to the restriction that "public figure" plaintiffs must meet the *New York Times* "actual malice" standard as part of their prima facie case.[31] The Court explicitly linked its holding to "public debate about public figures," and expressed concern that a contrary result would hamper *political* speech.[32] Thus, *Hustler* apparently leaves constitutionally intact actions for intentional infliction of emotional distress for non-public-figure plaintiffs engaged in nonpolitical speech. At least one state appellate court reaching this issue has sustained the tort action in the face of a First Amendment challenge, holding that the actual malice standard does not apply to private-figure plaintiffs.[33]

It is not unreasonable to assume that if remedies for intentional infliction of emotional distress for non-public-figure plaintiffs are not constitutionally infirm, then speech acts that are in this way tortious—that is, are extreme and outrageous, intentionally produced, and the proximate cause of severe emotional distress—must fall outside the domain of protected expression. It would be difficult to identify speech acts more closely matching Justice Murphy's description of words "which by their very utterance inflict injury" than those actionable under this tort. The best explanation for continuing to permit suits for intentional infliction of emotional distress may well be that they are among those excluded under the first prong of *Chaplinsky*.[34]

Assuming it is correct, the foregoing argument is significant for the weaker form of hate speech regulation upon which I have been focusing, for the injury borne by those victimized by what I have called targeted vilification looks very much like the extreme emotional distress resulting from those tortious speech acts excluded from constitutional protection under the expanded reading of *Chaplinsky* offered above. To make out this case requires that we look to the harm caused by targeted vilification.

First Amendment liberalism generally assumes that counterspeech is the only proper and allowable remedy for offensive, hateful, or otherwise objectionable speech. But this may too hastily assume that slurs and epithets do not really give rise to a genuinely serious personal harm or injury. The opponent of the regulationists is likely to insist that victimization by hate speech can be avoided if one "toughens up," inuring oneself to the use of "bad words."[35] It is here, however, that one must listen to the voices or the narratives of women and people of color, as the revisionist jurisprudes have done. It is precisely where members of historically oppressed groups are victimized that the nature and effect of vilifying speech may be experienced quite differently from what members of nonprotected groups might think anyone could or should simply shrug off. Vilification through the use of racist and sexist slurs, the revisionists argue, cannot be classed along with routine forms of bullying, jeering, or name calling, and this because of the way in which racial and sexist slurs work and the effects that exposure to them can have.

Racial insults work by focusing on and intensifying an ideology of racial (sexual) supremacy and the correlative stigma of inferiority, and directing them at a particular person or group of persons with the result that the victim experiences humiliation and degradation. As Richard Delgado and Mari Matsuda have argued, for example, such attacks may have a wide range of harmful effects for those victimized by them.[36] Emotionally, victims experience a loss of self-esteem and sense of security; they may feel isolation and self-hatred. Physically, their mobility may be restricted for fear of future attacks. Victims of racially or sexually assaultive speech may also suffer pecuniary loss by, for example, being handicapped in the pursuit of a job or career.

Viewed in this way, understanding how those victimized by hate speech can be harmed does not require a privileging of group identity or a theory of the "social self"—criticisms leveled by Simon against communitarian defenses of hate speech regulation (chapter 14, this volume). Abusive hate speech injures individuals in direct and recognizable ways. Simon is concerned, however, that the characterization given by Delgado, Matsuda, and other critical race theorists of the harm allegedly involved here necessitates the fashioning of a new type of offense, or of a new kind of "sensitivity harm," defined as a harm "relative to the hearer's attitude." It is not clear just what this last means. Surely, though, there is nothing new in the recognition that certain forms of expression—defamation or verbal harassment, for example—can injure others deeply, or in excluding such expression from free speech protection. Nor, finally, is it novel to subject those who inflict such injury to civil or criminal sanction.

Assaultive racist and sexist epithets and slurs appear to be among the paradigmatic instances of the speech acts that "by their very utterance inflict injury" and are thus excluded from First Amendment protection. And this means that the test articulated in *R.A.V.* can be satisfied by regulatory schemes barring these forms of hate speech. Selecting from among the words whose very utterance inflicts injury those dealing particularly with vilification on the basis of race, sex, or religion *is* selection based squarely on the reason for which all such words are unprotected: because such assaultive words are just the sort most likely to injure simply by virtue of being said. Narrow or weak hate speech regulations, then, are both sustainable under *R.A.V.'s* rationale and consistent with the larger contours of First Amendment doctrine.

III

Traditional First Amendment liberalism resists restrictions on freedom of expression on a number of grounds, all related in one or another fashion to the risks thought to be posed by suppression: attempts to curtail expression will be overbroad, trampling into protected areas and chilling speech beyond the ordinance's perimeter;[37] speech-restrictive regulations will be unadministratable, or at least easily subject to administrative abuse; efforts to limit speech will place one foot on a very slippery and steeply inclined slope. These worries are not insignificant. But the risks mentioned can be substantially decreased, I believe, by a properly confined, weakly regula-tionist hate speech ordinance, one targeting only the uses of words com-monly thought to express contempt and calculated to degrade or humiliate by reference to traits or characteristics that group persons into suspect classes (e.g., race, religion, gender) and where such injury is likely to occur, as in a face-to-face confrontation or in front of a captive audience.[38] So framed, such an ordinance borrows from both the first and second prongs of *Chaplinsky* and is animated, as discussed above, by an interest in pro-tecting persons from extreme emotional or physical abuse and harm.

Weinstein is unconvinced that even such a narrow regulation could rest on the interest in preventing purely emotional harm:

> Forbidding speech to prevent emotional distress would be unacceptable. For such a prohibition would nonetheless be based on a *principle* that would allow the gov-ernment to proscribe speech that should not be forbidden in a democracy. . . . I have no doubt that many parents whose sons were killed by the Vietcong suffered extreme emotional pain when confronted with antiwar protesters carrying signs say-ing "Support the Vietcong." Similarly, a jury found that Jerry Falwell suffered extreme emotional distress as a result of a parody in a Campari advertisement declaring that Falwell's "first time" was with his mother in an outhouse. If psychic harm to someone who reads a racist pamphlet is sufficient to outlaw the pamphlet, why should psychic harm of a grieving parent or to Jerry Falwell be insufficient to prohibit the antiwar slogan or the Campari advertisement parody?[39]

Weinstein here states the liberal risk-of-suppression argument in its strongest possible form: no principle can be articulated sufficient to entail the proposition that targeted vilification resulting in severe psychic distress must be suppressed that would not also entail the proposition that at least some protected expression must also be suppressed.

Put strictly, this claim is not supported by the cases Weinstein cites because neither involves targeted vilification of a person on the basis of traits that group him or her into a protected class. Hence, the principle endorsed by the weak regulation I proposed does not entail the further claim that the expression in Weinstein's cases should be prohibited. More-over, Weinstein's cases are not on a par but come apart in an important way. Unlike the Campari ad, the placards of the war protesters were not directed at the parents of the dead soldiers and were not intended to degrade or humiliate them. The parents were neither "targeted" nor "vilified" by the speech in question. The Falwell case is different, for there the jury seems to have agreed that the foreseeable consequence, if not the intended aim, of the parody was to shock and demean the plaintiff and that this did in fact occur. Nonetheless, it is clear, I think, that a weakly regulationist scheme of the aforementioned sort would not reach the ad in this case because it involved neither a face-to-face confrontation nor vilification on the basis of race, sex, or religion.

Weinstein's larger point, of course, is simply that nothing significant seems to separate the emotional distress experienced by Falwell and that experienced by the victims of hate speech. This may be correct. But then, Weinstein asks, should ad parodies producing such a level of distress not be suppressed? And wouldn't such suppression be impermissible? To the first question, the correct answer, it seems to me, is that if such parodies are sufficiently outrageous and the distress sufficiently great, a form of de facto suppression will indeed occur through the operation of the tort system and the impact of large damage awards for plaintiffs like Falwell. Nor would this state of affairs be either morally objectionable or inconsistent with free speech values, any more so than would a similar de facto prohibition of defamatory or obscene utterances in the employ of commercial speech. So viewed, Falwell-type cases are not the counterexamples Weinstein takes them to be.[40]

It has further been claimed by First Amendment liberals[41] that the sorts of campus racial incidents that have spawned hate speech regulations are in fact ones that can be adequately handled without resort to restrictions on speech, and this because such incidents can be brought within the scope of other, existing prohibitions. For example, a group of white students trails a female student of color across the campus, taunting, "I've never tried a nigger before"; the words "die nigger" are scrawled across the door of a black dorm resident with a knife embedded in the woodwork. The first case seems plainly to amount to sexual harassment and to be prohibitable on that ground; the second is arguably close to an assault. But not all cases can be handled in these ways. Suppose two students, one white, the other black, are involved in a heated classroom discussion of affirmative action. At one point, the white student angrily points a finger at the black student and says: "You just want a handout because you're a nigger, a lazy goddamn nigger." Without more, this is not conduct rising to the level of an assault. Nor does it suffice to display a pattern of discriminatory behavior. It is, rather, direct vilification based on an immutable characteristic. It is difficult to see how such language can be eliminated from the classroom without a university regulation prohibiting targeted vilification.

In a recent essay, Simon has argued that any adequate hate speech regulation must be able to distinguish crude, assaultive hate speech from more sophisticated forms. As examples of the latter, Simon cites the following:[42]

1. "Black children in the United States have a mean intelligence quotient (IQ) score of about 85, as compared with one hundred for the white population, on which the test was standardized."
2. "I'd had too much experience that women were only tricky, deceitful, untrustworthy flesh." —Malcolm X

Other expressions of "sophisticated" hate speech might include[43]

3. "African Americans are better athletes than whites."
4. "AIDS is a product of reckless gay male sexual practices."

Though they exhibit significant differences, each of the foregoing statements, either by virtue of the words alone or when coupled with the implied contexts of utterance, could be taken to convey contempt or even hatred of blacks, women, or gays. Some, like 1 and 3, convey this message in a disguised form or by indirection; others like 2 and 4, are more straightforward. Whatever else may be said of such remarks, however, it is reasonably clear that none of them would be suppressible under a weakly regulationist scheme directed only at targeted vilification.

But weak regulationism, Simon insists, cannot deal with all forms of sophisticated hate speech so readily. The weak regulationist effort to distinguish unprotected from protected hate speech is scuttled, Simon believes, by consequences easily derivable from the familiar use-mention distinction. Simon discusses the case of a woman who was among the audience at a reading of Simon's paper on hate speech. In the course of explaining and developing his position, Simon mentioned various terms and words frequently used as epithets. Simon relates that the woman was "offended by my *use* of hate speech."[44] A more recent example of speech mentioning hate epithets occurred in Oregon, as an outgrowth of the controversy surrounding an anti-gay-rights ballot measure. During the 1992 campaign season, the state asked local television stations to air antibigotry public service announcements that flashed the epithets "honky," "nigger," "faggot," and "bitch" on the screen while background voices repeated jokes that needed slurs for their punch line. The ads ended with the message "Hatred thrives when bigotry is tolerated." [45] The larger objection posed to weak regulationism by these examples is potentially quite serious because it threatens to collapse altogether the "crude"/"sophisticated" distinction by insisting that mentioning (crude) hate speech is always an instance of its (sophisticated) use.

Given the analysis of injurious hate speech offered above, however, I do not believe it can be made out that a speaker actually *uses* hate speech in cases such as the above, or that mentioning slurs and epithets inevitably shades into their use. Complicating the picture here may be an equivocation on "use." The weak regulationist wants to draw a distinction between (what might be called) the use$_1$ of hateful words in a way calculated to inflict injury with the use$_2$ of words to express ideas of hatefulness. The distinction here turns on the speaker's intent, on the "use" to which the use of words is put: (roughly) to injure or to inform. This is not an entirely unfamiliar distinction: think again of the contrast between the use$_1$ of false words or statements to inflict injury (actionable defamation) and the use$_2$ of words to convey false ideas (nonactionable speech). It is a necessary condition for some use of words to count as what I am here calling "use$_1$," both that it be intentional and that it be likely to inflict injury. Regardless of what one wants to say on the admittedly thorny question of when "extreme offense" is transformed into "harm," it is reasonably clear that on no defensible theory of harm did either Professor Simon or the State of Oregon intend to inflict injury. Thus they did not use$_1$ hate speech.[46]

IV

Regarding the very narrowly drawn weakly regulationist scheme I have sought to defend in this chapter, First Amendment liberals object that so few of the recent campus racial incidents would be prohibited under it that as a practical matter, the "gain isn't worth the pain," that the exercise effectively does become a detour, an inefficient utilization of energy and effort.[47] On the other hand, the symbolic effects of such a policy can be positive, demonstrating to the members of a university its commitment to principles of respect and equality. It is true that much nastiness would be protected by the weak regulationist. But expressions of bigotry and hatred are so pervasively a part of our culture that attempts to reach all instances of them would require great intrusions into liberty, which few could tolerate. Implicit in the rejection of weak regulatory schemes in the face of this reality is a suspiciously "throw the baby out with the bath water" rationale. A more measured response would retain the baby while bailing out as much bath water as possible.

First Amendment liberalism, as I have tried to make clear, assumes that the only appropriate response to ugly, offensive, or hateful speech is more speech. And, indeed, most speech acts are ones for which counterspeech is both the preferred and perhaps the only remedy, and where, if counterspeech is to be encouraged and promoted, hateful speech must receive the fullest measure of constitutional protection. Equally, however, there are some circumstances under which counterspeech is not an adequate remedy for the harm done or threatened, and where hate speech regulations, narrowly drawn in the ways suggested above, are permissible. Yet such a code should not be construed to have as its aim the eradication of campus racism and sexism; for that purpose, as Simon correctly contends, no speech code will suffice. If the harm sought to be averted is the existence of invidiously discriminatory attitudes and beliefs, then counterspeech (including, and most especially, educational fora of various kinds) would indeed be the only feasible remedy and hate speech regulation would be both inappropriate and likely ineffective. But it is important to see that more speech is the answer only if challenging and changing the speaker's bigoted attitudes is the sole dimension of the problem. Plainly, the existence of such attitudes and the effort to limit their spread is not the only evil that a college or university campus might wish to avert; the actual injury brought about through the channeling of bigoted and racist attitudes into vicious slurs and epithets must also be recognized. Here again, an analogy to defamation law is instructive. On one of the traditional rationales supporting a strongly speech-protective constitutional doctrine, the "marketplace of ideas" must be allowed freely to function so that truth will emerge from the fray of competing ideologies. Hence, our interest in promoting truth and combating falsity is almost always best secured through the furtherance of counterspeech. But consistent with this realization, the law also seeks to suppress (with some restrictions)[48] speech that takes the form of disseminating defamatory falsehoods, and this stems from a recognition of the very real harm or injury they can cause.[49] There is no reason that the law should respond differently in the face of claims that other forms of speech also cause harm. This shows that the inability of hate speech regulations to combat racism and sexism by shifting attitudes and working structural ideological changes is not, as liberals like Simon charge, a fatal strike against them.

Though it is true that rational discussion may arise out of the use of racist slurs and epithets, this is beside the point. Even if the racist attitudes and beliefs of the speaker might be modified or eliminated through engaging in further speech, the kinds of harm thereby produced can be averted only if the expressive or communicative activity out of which it arose is itself suppressed, and suppressed just so far as is necessary to prevent the harm. It is to this end that I have tried to show that efforts to prohibit abusive and intentional forms of direct racial or sexual vilification are consistent with First Amendment jurisprudence even after *R.A.V. v. St. Paul* and that the case for such weak hate speech regulations can withstand the objections raised by the legal liberalism of First Amendment law.

Notes

1. See, for example, Katherine T. Bartlett and Jean O'Barr, "The Chilly Climate on College Campuses: An Expression of the 'Hate Speech' Debate," *Duke Law Journal*, 1990, 574–86; Alan E. Brownstein, "Hate Speech at Public Universities: The Search for an Enforcement Model," *Wayne Law Review* 37 (1991): 1451–68; "Regulating Hate Speech at Public Universities: Are First Amendment Values Functionally Incompatible with Equal Protection Principles?" *Buffalo Law Review* 39 (1991): 1–52; J. Peter Byrne, "Racial Insults and Free Speech within the University," *Georgetown Law Journal* 79 (1991): 399–443; Kent Greenawalt, "Insults and Epithets: Are they Protected Speech?" *Rutgers Law Review* 43 (1990): 287–307; Patricia Hodluik, "Racist Speech on Campus," *Wayne Law Review* 37 (1991): 1433–50; Charles H. Jones, "Equality, Dignity and Harm: The Constitutionality of Regulating American Campus Ethnoviolence," *Wayne Law Review* 37 (1991): 1383–1432; Elena Kagan, "Regulation of Hate Speech and Pornography After *R.A.V.*" *University of Chicago Law Review* 60 (1993): 873–902; David Kretzmer, "Freedom of Speech and Racism," *Cardozo Law Review* 8 (1987): 445–513; Ellen E. Lange, "Racist Speech on Campus: A Title VII Solution to a First Amendment Problem," *Southern California Law Review* 64 (1990): 105–34; Jeffrey Laurence, "Minnesota Burning: *R.A.V. v. City of St. Paul* and First Amendment Precedent," *Hastings Constitutional Law Quarterly* 21 (1994): 1117–47; Robert C. Post, "Racist Speech, Democracy, and the First Amendment, " *William and Mary Law Review* 32 (1991): 267–327; Thomas W. Simon, "Fighting Racism: Hate Speech Detours," *Indiana Law Review* 26 (1993): 411–32; James Weinstein, "A Constitutional Roadmap to the Regulation of Campus Hate Speech," *Wayne Law Review* 38 (1991): 163–247.

2. See, for example, Richard Delgado, "Campus AntiRacism Rules: Constitutional Narratives in Collision," *Northwestern University Law Review* 85 (1991): 343–87; Richard Delgado and Jean Stefanic, "Images of the Outsider in American Law and Culture: Can Free Expression Remedy Systemic Social Ills?" *Cornell Law Review* 77 (1992):

1258–97; Richard Delgado and David H. Yun, "Pressure Valves and Bloodied Chickens: An Analysis of Paternalistic Objections to Hate Speech Regulation," *California Law Review* 82 (1994): 871–92; Charles R. Lawrence, "If He Hollers Let Him Go: Regulating Racist Speech on Campus," *Duke Law Journal*, 1990, 431–83; Mari Matsuda, "Public Response to Racist Speech: Considering the Victim's Story," *Michigan Law Review* 87 (1989): 2320–81.

3. See, for example, Matsuda, "Public Response to Racist Speech;" Alon Harel, "Bigotry, Pornography, and the First Amendment: A Theory of Unprotected Speech," *Southern California Law Review* 65 (1992): 1887–1931.

4. See, for example, Alan Brownstein, "Hate Speech and Harassment: The Constitutionality of Campus Codes that Prohibit Racial Insults," *William and Mary Bill of Rights Journal* 3 (1994): 179–217; Thomas C. Grey, "Civil Rights vs. Civil Liberties: The Case of Discriminatory Verbal Harassment," *Social Philosophy and Policy* 8 (1991): 81–107; Toni Massaro, "Equality and Freedom of Expression: The Hate Speech Dilemma," *William and Mary Law Review* 32 (1991): 211–65; John T. Nockleby, "Hate Speech in Context: The Case of Verbal Threats," *Buffalo Law Review* 42 (1994): 653–713; Steven H. Shiffrin, "Racist Speech, Outsider Jurisprudence, and the Meaning of America," *Cornell Law Review* 80 (1994): 43–103; Rodney Smolla, "Academic Freedom, Hate Speech, and the Idea of a University," *Law and Contemporary Problems* 53 (1990): 195–225; Cass Sunstein, *Democracy and the Problem of Free Speech* (New York: Free Press, 1995), 167–208.

5. See, e.g., Gerald Gunther, "Good Speech, Bad Speech," *Stanford Lawyer* 42 (1990): 7, 9, 41; Nadine Strossen, "Regulating Racist Speech on Campus: A Modest Proposal?" *Duke Law Journal*, 1990, 484–573; Suzanna Sherry, "Speaking of Virtue: A Republican Approach to University Regulations of Hate Speech," *Minnesota Law Review* 75 (1991): 933–44; Simon, "Fighting Racism."

6. Cf. Justice Brandeis's well-known claim that "no danger flowing from speech can be deemed clear and present, unless the incidence of the evil apprehended is so imminent that it may befall before there is opportunity for full discussion. If there be time to expose through discussion the falsehood and fallacies, to avert the evil by the processes of education, the remedy to be applied is more speech, not enforced silence." *Whitney v. California* 274 U.S. 357 (1927). See also Justice Vinson's dictum in *Dennis v. United States* (341 U.S. 494 [1951]: "The basis of the First Amendment is the hypothesis that speech can rebut speech, propaganda will answer propaganda, free debate of ideas will result in the wisest governmental policies").

7. This point is made by Thomas W. Simon; see chapter 14, this volume.

8. Ibid.

9. See Simon, "Fighting Racism," 415–16. Strong regulators endorse what Tom Grey calls the full-blown "civil-rights" approach to the problem of hate speech; weak regulators defend a "moderate civil-liberties" view. See Grey, "Civil Rights vs. Civil Liberties: The Case of Discriminatory Verbal Harassment," *Social Philosophy and Policy* 8 (1991): 81–107.

10. The term is Massaro's, in "Equality and Freedom of Expression."

11. *R.A.V. v. City of St. Paul*, 505 U.S. 377 (1992).

12. Ibid., at 380.

13. *Chaplinsky v. New Hampshire*, 315 U.S. 568 (1942).

14. The Stanford University Code is one prominent example of this type of approach; for the relevant portion, see Grey, "Civil Rights vs. Civil Liberties," 106–7.

15. The University of Wisconsin Board of Regents repealed the university's revised, weak hate speech code in September 1992. A university spokesperson stated that the repeal was motivated by recent court opinions. *New York Times*, September 14, 1992, 10A. The University of Delaware set aside its code in October 1992 pending review by its Faculty Senate. *USA Today*, October 7, 1992, 10a.

16. *R.A.V. v. City of St. Paul*, at 391–92.

17. Ibid., at 385. As Laurence points out, this assertion by the Court seems inadequately supported by the precedents it cites. See Laurence, "Minnesota Burning," 1123ff.

18. This further suggests that even if Scalia were right and fighting words deserve at least presumptive free speech protection, a narrowly drawn hate speech regulation aimed at slurs and epithets in a face-to-face setting would likely survive heightened scrutiny under a "least intrusive means" test.

19. *R.A.V. v. City of St. Paul*, at 388.

20. Ibid., at 394.

21. Grey, "Civil Rights vs. Civil Liberties," 97. See also Charles Lawrence, ("If He Hollers Let Him Go"), who harbors similar concerns about the Stanford code. See, more generally, Strossen, "Regulating Racist Speech on Campus," 523.

22. See Grey's observation that "as best I can see, there are *no* epithets in this society at this time that are 'commonly understood' to convey hatred and contempt for whites *as such*." Grey, "Civil Rights and Civil Liberties," 95.

23. Post, "Racist Speech, Democracy, and the First Amendment," 300.

24. Ibid., 301.

25. This kind of talk is particularly problematic on the traditional liberal political theory of, for example, the Rawlsian variety, in which the state is precluded from endorsing any conception of the good robust enough to create or forge much of a "community." Indeed, the inability of liberal polities to erect themselves into such communities is frequently cited by critics of liberalism. See, for example, the well-known discussions by Alasdair MacIntyre, *After Virtue* (Notre Dame: University of Notre Dame Press, 1984); and Michael Sandel, *Liberalism and the Limits of Justice* (Cambridge: Cambridge University Press, 1982).

26. Post, "Racist Speech, Democracy, and the First Amendment," 300–301 (footnotes omitted).

27. *Chaplinsky v. New Hampshire*, 315 U.S. 568 (1942), at 572.

28. See, for example, Gard, "Fighting Words as Free Speech," *Washington University Law Quarterly* 58 (1980): 531–65; Weinstein, "A Constitutional Roadmap."

29. For a recent hate speech case taking just this view, see *UMW Post, Inc. v. Board of Regents of the University of Wisconsin System*, 774 F. Supp. 1163 (E.D. Wisconsin, 1991).

30. *Hustler Magazine v. Falwell*, 485 U.S. 46 (1988).

31. See *New York Times v. Sullivan*, 376 U.S. 254 (1964).

32. *Hustler Magazine v. Falwell*, at 53.

33. See *Van Duyn v. Smith*, 527 N.E. 2d 1005 (Ill. App. 3d Dist. 1988). For summaries of recent rulings upholding recovery for infliction of emotional distress where the plaintiff was subjected to racial, religious, or gender insults and epithets, see Jean C. Love, "Discriminatory Speech and the Tort of Intentional Infliction of Emotional Distress," *Washington and Lee Law Review* 47 (1990): 123–59; Shawna H. Yen, "Redressing the Victim of Racist Speech after *R.A.V. v. St. Paul*: A Proposal to Permit Recovery in Tort," *Columbia Journal of Law and Social Problems* 26 (1993): 589–632.

34. Even Weinstein, who argues at length against virtually any sort of hate speech regulation, concedes that some restrictions on racist and sexist epithets might be properly proscribable under the first *Chaplinsky* prong. See Weinstein, "A Constitutional Roadmap," 237.

35. That this may well be Scalia's view is supported by his vote to overturn the conviction in the Texas flag-burning case. See *Texas v. Johnson* 491 U.S. 397 (1989).

36. Richard Delgado, "Words That Wound: A Tort Action for Racial Insults, Epithets, and Name-Calling," *Harvard Civil Rights-Civil Liberties Law Review* 17 (1982): 133–81; Richard Delgado and David Yun, "The Neoconservative Case against Hate Speech Regulation," *Vanderbilt Law Review* 47 (1994): 1807–25; Matsuda, "Public Response to Racist Speech." The points made below are elaborated and defended in these essays.

37. The University of Michigan's hate speech code was struck down on just such grounds. See *Doe v. University of Michigan* 721 F. Supp. 852 (E.D. Mich. 1989). The code adopted by the University of Connecticut, later repealed, undoubtedly suffered from the same difficulty. See Post, "Racist Speech, Democracy, and the First Amendment," 269.

38. See Grey, "Civil Rights and Civil Liberties," for a defense of a similarly constructed proposal. Though, as Simon has observed, victims determine the social meaning of conduct in terms of whether it gives rise to actual injury ("Fighting Racism," 425), presumably some sort of "reasonableness" requirement will enter in here; that is, there must be reason to think it likely that the ordinary and reasonable members of the suspect class to whom the victim belongs would be injured by the verbal assault. Such a requirement is incorporated, e.g., into Delgado's tort proposal. See Delgado, "Campus AntiRacism Rules," 167; the Stanford regulation reaches the same through its use of the "commonly understood" requirement.

39. Weinstein, "A Constitutional Roadmap," 178.

40. It is worth noting that the only ground on which Weinstein is prepared to consider prohibitions on racist slurs and epithets is one equally subject to the risks of suppression of which First Amendment liberalism is so wary. Weinstein argues (ibid., 191ff.) that the use of racist or sexist epithets in the classroom might be proscribable on the

ground that the classroom, unlike many other areas of the university, is not a traditional public forum for the purposes of First Amendment analysis. It is difficult, however, to place much confidence in the discriminating capabilities of forum doctrine. Consider, for example, *Hague v. CIO*, 307 U.S. 496 (1939); *Lehman v. Shaker Heights*, 418 U.S. 298 (1974); *City Council v. Taxpayers for Vincent*, 466 U.S. 789 (1984); *Metromedia, Inc. v. San Diego*, 453 U.S. 490 (1981); *Heffron v. Int'l. Society for Krishna Consciousness*, 452 U.S. 640 (1981); *Southeastern Promotions, Ltd. v. Conrad*, 420 U.S. 546 (1975); *Marsh v. Alabama*, 326 U.S. 501 (1946); *Greer v. Spock*, 424 U.S. 828 (1976); *U.S. Postal Service v. Greenburgh Civic Assns.*, 453 U.S. 114 (1981); *U.S. v. Kokinda*, 497 U.S. 720 (1990). The thrust of these cases is that although streets and sidewalks are traditional public fora (*Hague*), a city-owned bus driving on the street is a nonforum (*Lehman*), as is a city-owned utility pole on the sidewalk (*Vincent*), but not a billboard next to the sidewalk (*Metromedia*). State-operated fairgrounds are limited public fora (*Heffron*), whereas city operated theaters are traditional public fora (*Southeastern*), as is a company-owned town (*Marsh*), but not a military base (*Greer*). Finally, although a mailbox is not a traditional public forum (*Greenburgh*), the sidewalk in front of the post office is, but the sidewalk leading from *that* sidewalk to the post office is not (*Kokinda*). In light of this record, it is difficult to see why anyone would think that forum analysis is either settled or any less subject to arbitrary manipulation, abuse, or slippery slopes than the determination of which are the words that "by their utterance inflict injury." As a tool for demarcating protected from excluded speech, forum analysis presents no fewer risks than the *Chaplinsky* test.

41. See, for example, Simon's discussion in "Fighting Racism," 423–24.

42. See ibid., 417 and 423, respectively.

43. See Massaro, "Equality and Freedom of Expression," 215.

44. Simon, "Fighting Racism," 424.

45. *Washington Times*, November 1, 1992, A2.

46. Nor, of course, was his mention of epithets "targeted" toward any particular person. The task of guarding against spurious claims of injury here could perhaps be handled by importing some of the requirements imposed in actions for intentional infliction of emotional distress, though, in the constitutional context, the reliance on "intent" to inflict injury may be restricted by *Hustler Magazine v. Falwell*.

47. See, e.g., Massaro, "Equality and Freedom of Expression," 253.

48. Stemming, for example, from *New York Times Co. v. Sullivan* (376 U.S. 254 [1964]) and its progeny. Justice O'Connor summed up the relevant thrust of those cases in this way: "When speech is of exclusively private concern and the plaintiff is a private figure . . . the constitutional requirements do not necessarily force any change in at least some of the features of the common-law landscape." *Philadelphia Newspapers, Inc. v. Hepps*, 475 U.S. 767 (1986).

49. Cf. Justice Brennan's remark in *Garrison v. Louisiana* (379 U.S. 64 [1964]) that "calculated falsehood falls into that class of utterances" excluded under *Chaplinsky*.

CONTRIBUTORS

David M. Adams is Associate Professor of Philosophy, California State Polytechnic.

Randall R. Curren is Professor of Philosophy, University of Rochester.

Natalie Dandekar is former Professor of Philosophy, University of Rhode Island.

Richard T. De George is University Professor of Philosophy, University of Kansas.

James F. Doyle is Professor of Philosophy, University of Missouri–St. Louis.

Joseph Ellin is Professor of Philosophy, Western Michigan University.

Norman Fischer is Associate Professor of Philosophy, Kent State University.

Emily R. Gill is Professor of Political Science, Bradley University.

Carol C. Gould is Professor of Philosophy, Stevens Institute of Technology.

Stephen M. Griffin is Professor of Law, Tulane University.

Suzanne Duvall Jacobitti is Professor of Political Science, Southern Illinois University at Edwardsville.

Bruce M. Landesman is Professor of Philosophy, University of Utah.

Douglas Lind is Assistant Professor of Philosophy, University of Idaho.

Larry May is Professor of Philosophy, Washington University (St. Louis).

Joan L. McGregor is Professor of Philosophy, Arizona State University.

Diana Tietjens Meyers is Professor of Philosophy, University of Connecticut, Storrs.

Robert C. L. Moffat is Professor of Law, University of Florida.

Richard Nunan is Professor of Philosophy, College of Charleston.

Wade L. Robison is Ezra A. Hale Professor in Applied Ethics, Rochester Institute of Technology.

Thomas W. Simon is Professor of Philosophy, Illinois State University.
Patricia Smith is Professor of Philosophy, University of Kentucky.
Lawrence B. Solum is Professor and William M. Rains Fellow, Loyola
    Law School (Los Angeles).

INDEX

335